Ethics and Humanity

Ethics and Humanity

Themes from the Philosophy
of Jonathan Glover

EDITED BY
N. Ann Davis, Richard Keshen,
and Jeff McMahan

OXFORD
UNIVERSITY PRESS

2010

OXFORD
UNIVERSITY PRESS

Oxford University Press, Inc., publishes works that further
Oxford University's objective of excellence
in research, scholarship, and education.

Oxford   New York
Auckland   Cape Town   Dar es Salaam   Hong Kong   Karachi
Kuala Lumpur   Madrid   Melbourne   Mexico City   Nairobi
New Delhi   Shanghai   Taipei   Toronto

With offices in
Argentina   Austria   Brazil   Chile   Czech Republic   France   Greece
Guatemala   Hungary   Italy   Japan   Poland   Portugal   Singapore
South Korea   Switzerland   Thailand   Turkey   Ukraine   Vietnam

Copyright © 2010 by Oxford University Press, Inc.

Published by Oxford University Press, Inc.
198 Madison Avenue, New York, New York 10016

www.oup.com

Oxford is a registered trademark of Oxford University Press.

Library of Congress Cataloging-in-Publication Data
Ethics and humanity: themes from the philosophy of Jonathan Glover/edited by N. Ann Davis,
Richard Keshen, and Jeff McMahan.
   p.   cm.
ISBN 978-0-19-532519-5
1. Ethics—History—20th century.   2. Ethics,
Modern—20th century.   3. Humanity.   4. Glover, Jonathan.
I. Davis, N. Ann.   II. Keshen, Richard,
III. McMahan, Jeff.
BJ21.E85 2009
170—dc22   2009018901

9 8 7 6 5 4 3 2 1

Printed in the United States of America
on acid-free paper

Contents

Contributors

Allen Buchanan is James B. Duke Professor of Philosophy and Investigator, Institute for Genome Sciences and Policy, Duke University. He is also a Distinguished Research Associate of the Oxford Uehiro Centre for Practical Ethics. He works mainly in Political Philosophy, Philosophy of International Law, and Bioethics. His most recent books are *Justice, Legitimacy, and Self-Determination: Moral Foundations for International Law* (Oxford, 2003) and *Beyond Humanity? The Ethics of Biomedical Enhancement* (Uehiro Lectures, Oxford University Press, forthcoming 2010).

Roger Crisp is Uehiro Fellow and Tutor in Philosophy at St Anne's College, Oxford, and Professor of Moral Philosophy at the University of Oxford. He is the author of *Mill on Utilitarianism* (Routledge, 1997) and *Reasons and the Good* (Clarendon Press, 2006), and has translated Aristotle's *Nicomachean Ethics* for Cambridge University Press. He is an Associate Editor of *Ethics* and of *Utilitas*, a member of the *Analysis* Committee, a Trustee of the Royal Institute of Philosophy, and a Delegate to Oxford University Press.

N. Ann Davis has been McConnell Professor of Human Relations and Professor of Philosophy at Pomona College in Claremont, California, since 1998, and is associated with the Environmental Analysis program there. Prior to that, she taught at the University of Pittsburgh, the University of California at Berkeley, and the University of Colorado at Boulder, where she was a member of the Center for Values and Social Policy. Her interests are primarily in the connections between theory and practice, and between science and values. Among her publications are papers on the abortion debate, disability, eugenics, moral dilemmas, and methodological issues in moral philosophy.

Jonathan Glover did his B.A. in Philosophy and Psychology and B. Phil. in Philosophy at Corpus Christi College, Oxford. He stayed in Oxford teaching Philosophy until 1997. He was a Fellow of New College, Oxford. He moved to King's College London, where he was Director of the Centre of Medical Law and Ethics from 1998 until 2008. His books include *Causing Death and Saving Lives; What Sort of People Should There Be?; Humanity: A Moral History of the Twentieth Century;* and *Choosing Children: Genes, Disability and Design.* Further information about his work can be found at www.jonathanglover.co.uk.

James Griffin is White's Professor of Moral Philosophy Emeritus at Oxford University, Visiting Professor at Rutgers University, and Adjunct Professor at the Centre for Applied Philosophy and Public Ethics, Canberra. His books include *Well-Being: Its Meaning, Measurement and Moral Importance, Value Judgement,* and *On Human Rights.* He is now writing a book on what philosophy can contribute to ethics.

John Harris, FMedSci, is Director of The Institute for Science, Ethics and Innovation and of the Wellcome Strategic Programme in The Human Body, its Scope Limits and Future, School of Law, University of Manchester, where is he is Lord Alliance Professor of Bioethics. He is joint Editor-in-Chief of *The Journal of Medical Ethics* and has been a member of The United Kingdom *Human Genetics Commission* since its foundation in 1999 and is a Member of the Medical Ethics Committee of the British Medical Association. Recent books include *Clones Genes and Immortality* (Oxford University Press, 1998). John Harris (ed.) *Bioethics Oxford Readings in Philosophy Series* (Oxford University Press, 2001); Justine C. Burley and John Harris (eds.) *A Companion to Genethics: Philosophy and the Genetic Revolution* (Basil Blackwell, Oxford. 2002); *Blackwell's Companions to Philosophy* series; and *On Cloning* (Routledge. London, 2004). *Enhancing Evolution* was published by Princeton University Press in 2007. In September 2006, *The Independent* included John Harris in "The Good List," purportedly a list of "the fifty men and women who make our world a better place." On the September 6, 2008 John Harris featured in *The Times* "Lifestyle 50—The top fifty people who influence the way we eat, exercise and think about ourselves." *The Times* citation noted "His book *Enhancing Evolution* is hugely influential." Harris has also appeared (as himself) as a minor character in novels by authors as diverse as Alexander McCall Smith (*The Careful Use Of Compliments,* Leslie Brown, 2007) and Dean Koontz (*One Door Away from Heaven,* Headline, London 2001), and is one of Nick Baker's 'Groovy Old Men' (Nick Baker, *Groovy Old Men,* Icon Books Ltd., London 2008).

Thomas Hurka is Chancellor Henry N. R. Jackman Distinguished Professor of Philosophical Studies at the University of Toronto, where he came in 2002 after many years at the University of Calgary. He works in moral and political philosophy and is the author of

Perfectionism (1993); *Principles: Short Essays on Ethics* (1993); *Virtue, Vice, and Value* (2001); and numerous journal articles, including several on the ethics of war. He is currently working on a project in the history of ethics: a book on British moral philosophy of the late-nineteenth and early-twentieth centuries called *British Moral Philosophers From Sidgwick to Ewing.*

Richard Keshen teaches Philosophy at Cape Breton University in Nova Scotia, Canada. He did his doctorate work at Oxford University, where he studied with Jonathan Glover. His publications include the book *Reasonable Self-Esteem* (McGill-Queen's University Press, 1996), as well as articles on desert, sexual ethics, aesthetics, media concentration in Canada, and on the way fossils were interpreted by the ancient Greeks and Medieval Christians on the island of Cyprus.

Jeff McMahan is Professor of Philosophy at Rutgers University. He is the author of *The Ethics of Killing: Problems at the Margins of Life* (Oxford University Press, 2002) and *Killing in War* (Oxford University Press, 2009).

Martha C. Nussbaum is the Ernst Freund Distinguished Service Professor of Law and Ethics in Law, Philosophy, and Divinity at The University of Chicago. Her most recent books are *Liberty of Conscience: In Defense of America's Tradition of Religious Equality* (Basic Books, 2008) and *From Disgust to Humanity: Sexual Orientation and Constitutional Law* (Oxford University Press, 2010).

Onora O'Neill is Professor of Philosophy at Cambridge University. She writes on ethics and political philosophy, including issues of international justice, the philosophy of Immanuel Kant and a range of questions in bioethics. Her books include *Faces of Hunger: An Essay on Poverty, Development and Justice* (HarperCollins, 1986), *Constructions of Reason: Exploration of Kant's Practical Philosophy* (Cambridge University Press, 1989), *Towards Justice and Virtue* (Cambridge University Press, 1996), *Bounds of Justice* (Cambridge University Press, 2000), *Autonomy and Trust in Bioethics* (Cambridge University Press, 2002), *A Question of Trust: The BBC Reith Lectures* (Cambridge University Press, 2002) and *Rethinking Informed Consent in Bioethics* (with Neil Manson, Cambridge University Press, 2007). Her current philosophical writing is mainly on conceptions or practical reason and practical judgment, questions of trust and accountability, and the ethics of communication. She was Principal of Newnham College, Cambridge, from 1992 to 2006 and President of the British Academy from 2005–09. She was created a Life Peer in 1999, sits as a crossbencher, and served on the House of Lords Select Committees on *Stem Cell Research, BBC Charter*

Review, Genomic Medicine, and *Nanotechnologies and Food.*

Alan Ryan was Fellow and Tutor in Politics at New College, Oxford, from 1969 to 1988; Professor of Politics at Princeton University between 1988 and 1996; and Warden of New College from 1996 to 2009.

Peter Singer was born in Melbourne, Australia, in 1946, and educated at the University of Melbourne and the University of Oxford. He has taught at the University of Oxford, La Trobe University, and Monash University. Since 1999 he has been Ira W. DeCamp Professor of Bioethics in the University Center for Human Values at Princeton University. From 2005, he has also held the part-time position of Laureate Professor at the University of Melbourne, in the Centre for Applied Philosophy and Public Ethics. He first became well-known internationally after the publication of *Animal Liberation* (Random House) in 1975. Since then he has written many other books, including *Practical Ethics* (Cambridge University Press, 1979), *The Expanding Circle* (Farrar, Straus, and Giroux, 1981, *How Are We to Live?* (Oxford University Press, 1997), *The Ethics of What We Eat* (with Jim Mason, Rodale, 2006) and most recently, *The Life You Can Save* (Random House, 2009).

Preface

This volume honors Jonathan Glover, whose writing and influence as a teacher have greatly contributed to the growth of applied ethics over the past forty years.

Even before Glover entered Oxford in 1960, he identified himself with the philosophical tradition that traces its origins to David Hume, J. S. Mill, and Bertrand Russell. A vital role of philosophy in this tradition is to understand ethics in purely secular terms. It is also characteristic of these philosophers that they wrote for, and successfully reached, a wide public.

The lectures of H. L. A. Hart supporting legal rights for gays, which Glover attended as an undergraduate, consolidated his commitment to the kind of philosophy he wanted to write. Later, "the stimulating and demanding standards" of A. J. Ayer, his graduate supervisor, were an important influence, not least on Glover's lucid philosophical prose: try to find a redundant word or a slack sentence in a Gloverian paragraph.

Glover's ideas on moral responsibility, abortion, euthanasia, war, genetic engineering, adoption policies for same-sex couples, and genocide have influenced both academic and public debate. Running through his work is the view that moral practices and beliefs are to be judged in terms of their consequences for human well-being. Glover has sought to undermine doctrines and intuitions, however sanctified by tradition or conventional wisdom, which obscure the way our actions cause harm. At the same time, he has emphasized the centrality to human life of values such as self-creation, autonomy, imagination, spontaneity, respect for human dignity, friendship, and love. In weighing and balancing these diverse values, Glover's writing achieves an exemplary richness and subtlety. These virtues are manifest in his recent book about the atrocities of the last century, *Humanity: A Moral History of the 20th Century*. The chapters that follow are connected in one way or another with the themes of that book, and many developed directly from reflections on it.

As Alan Ryan's essay testifies, Glover was a memorable undergraduate tutor at New College, Oxford. As a number of the other contributions testify, including those of the three editors, Glover has also influenced generations of graduate students. In the late 1960s and through the 1970s,

Glover offered, along with Jim Griffin and Derek Parfit, a legendary and pioneering seminar on applied ethics. The ideas that Glover worked through in that setting had an enormous impact on other philosophers in the field, a number of whom are represented in this volume. Over many years, Glover's friendship has meant a great deal to both his colleagues and his former students. This volume pays tribute to Jonathan Glover as a philosopher, teacher, and friend.

I

TORTURE

1

What Should We Do about Torture?

James Griffin

1.1 WHAT IS TORTURE? AN ANSWER FROM ETHICS

I want to write about only certain kinds of torture, not torture in general. We use the word 'torture' to denote the infliction of pain, either physical or mental, typically for certain purposes: to gain information, to elicit a confession, to bring about a conversion, or to intimidate a person into more acceptable behavior. Both the ends and the means are necessary to the kinds of torture I am interested in. The means need not be pain; it could, for instance, be the threat of pain. It need not be the pain of the immediate subject of the torture; it could be the pain, or threat of pain, to the subject's child or village. What is central to the sort of torture that concerns me is the subjection of the will of the victim to the will of the torturers. In the extreme, the means is to break the subject's will—to reduce the subject to a gibbering wreck, no longer capable of autonomous action. But threats usually work differently. One does not have to be reduced to a gibbering wreck to cave in when one's child is threatened with torture. It could be, rather, that the compulsion in this case is, for many of us, too great to withstand. The effect of a threat need not be that one's very capacity for autonomous action is temporarily suspended, though that can happen. It is enough if the compulsion is too strong for one to exercise the capacity. On the other hand, finding a way merely to circumvent the subject's will is not necessarily 'torture'. Suppose one could painlessly suspend the working of the subject's will with a truth drug. I think that we could not call this 'torture', though, as we shall see, the law does.

Those are the kinds of torture in which I am interested: torture that involves some sort of assault on its victim's will. There are other well-established senses of the word 'torture'. The word has been used for centuries for the infliction of severe pain as a punishment, though not all sorts of severe corporal punishment, I think, count as torture. If a medieval monarch ordered an offender to be punished with twenty-four hours on the rack, that would be torture, but if an eighteenth-century ship's captain, in enforcing naval regulations, ordered an offending sailor to be given twenty-four lashes, it would not be. A sadist may 'torture' a baby or a cat, though neither possesses a will in the sense I have in mind. Moreover, any particularly sharp or unbearable, or even exquisite pain may be called 'torture'—say, the torture of suspense. But none of these further, in some cases extended, uses of the word will concern me. Still, despite these exclusions, the torture in which I am interested covers more ground than the 'interrogational torture' on which recent writers have focused.

There are two things morally wrong with the kind of torture in which I am interested: first, and obviously, the infliction of great pain; second, that it constitutes an assault on perhaps our most valuable quality, our rational agency. It is in virtue of our rational agency that we were said in *Genesis* to be 'made in God's image'. Our rational agency constitutes what has been called—for example, in the title of Pico della Mirandola's famous tract—'the dignity of man.' The United Nations, in its *Universal Declaration* (1948), asserts that the source of all human rights is 'the dignity of the human person',[1] and to my mind, the best way to interpret the vague word 'dignity' here is as the value of rational agency. In this sense, torture destroys the very dignity of our human standing.

1.2 WHAT IS TORTURE? AN ANSWER FROM LAW

The legal answer to our question must be given jurisdiction by jurisdiction. I shall consider the US jurisdiction, because I write this chapter during the presidency of George W. Bush, and the behavior of his administration so invites question. In any case, since the United Nations' Convention Against Torture came into force in 1987 (now ratified by 130 countries, including the United States), there is a high degree of harmony between the laws on torture of the signatory countries.

The Convention defines torture like this (Art. 1):

> he term 'torture' means any act by which severe pain or suffering, whether physical or mental, is intentionally inflicted on a person for such purposes as obtaining from him or a third person information or a confession, punishing him for an act he or a third person has committed or is suspected of having committed, or intimidating or coercing him or a third person, or for any reason based on discrimination of any kind, when such pain or suffering is inflicted by or at the instigation of or with the consent or acquiescence of a public official or other person acting in an official capacity. It does not include pain or suffering arising from, inherent in or incidental to lawful sanctions.

This definition explicitly includes, as it should, mental as well as physical pain. It differs from the definition from ethics that I just gave by including wholesale extra-legal punishment and by limiting torture to acts of public officials. The law will specify its own scope, and there are obvious reasons why its scope might differ from the scope of ethics—for example, the understandable restriction in the Convention to the behavior of public officials. But one does not have to be a public official to be subject to ethical restrictions on torture.

Now, what exceptions does the Convention allow? Absolutely none (Art. 2.2):

> No exceptional circumstances whatsoever, whether a state of war or a threat of war, internal political instability or any other public emergency, may be invoked as a justification of torture.

This leaves no loophole.

Still, at the time of ratification, a nation is allowed to enter reservations to or interpretations of the Convention, which then qualify that nation's obligations under the Convention, a privilege that the United States availed itself of. The key phrase needing interpretation is 'severe pain or suffering'. It is especially unclear what 'severe *mental* pain or suffering' includes. The United States adopted this interpretation:[2]

> the *prolonged* mental harm caused by or resulting from (A) the intentional infliction of severe pain or suffering; (B) the administration or application, or threatened administration or application, of mind-altering substances or other procedures calculated to disrupt profoundly the senses or the personality; (C) the threat of imminent death; or (D) the threat that another person will imminently be subjected to death...[and so on].

The main clarification added here by the United States is that the mental pain or suffering must be 'prolonged', a term that needs no small amount of interpretation itself. Because the United States had ratified the Convention well before the present administration took office, President Bush found himself subject to an exceptionless prohibition of torture. He was forced to say, as he often did, that the United States does not torture. Given what his administration wished to do in interrogating suspected terrorists, the only option left to it was to change the definition of 'torture', which it promptly did.[3] On August 1, 2002, the Office of the Assistant Attorney General dispatched a memorandum (the Bybee Memorandum) to Alberto Gonzales, then Counsel to the President, on standards of conduct for interrogations. The phrase 'severe physical pain or suffering' is to be understood, the memorandum said [Sect. 1B; my italics]:

> as an indicator of ailments that are likely to result in *permanent and serious physical damage* in the absence of immediate medical treatment. Such damage must rise to the level of *death, organ failure, or the permanent impairment of a significant body function.*

And, as we saw, the phrase 'severe mental pain or suffering' was taken by the US government at the time of ratification to have to be 'prolonged', which the authors of the memorandum proceed, without any serious attempt at justification, to interpret as [1.C.1; my italics]:

lasting, though not necessarily permanent.... For example, the mental strain experienced by an individual during a lengthy or intense interrogation— such as one that state or local police might conduct on a criminal suspect— would not [be a violation]. On the other hand, *the development of a mental disorder such as post-traumatic stress disorder which can last months or even years, or chronic depression, which also can last for a considerable period of time if untreated,* might satisfy the prolonged harm requirement.

But a US administration, for all its power, does not have the power to suspend natural language. The ordinary meaning of the word 'torture' is the most important single piece of evidence for what the 130 ratifying nations had in mind in the Convention. The Bush administration's abandonment of the ordinary meaning of 'torture' shows up most glaringly in the contradictions between its own definition of 'torture' and its examples of it. It gives this list of examples [Sect. III]:

(1) severe beatings using instruments such as iron barks, truncheons, and clubs; (2) threats of imminent death, such as mock executions; (3) threats of removing extremities; (4) burning, especially burning with cigarettes; (5) electric shocks to genitals or threats to do so; (6) rape or sexual assault, or injury to an individual's sexual organs, or threatening to do any of these sorts of acts; and (7) forcing the prisoner to watch the torture of others.

There is no reason why these acts must be, as the memorandum requires them to be, 'likely to result in permanent and serious physical damage in the absence of immediate medical treatment' or in 'a mental disorder...which can last months or even years'. A prisoner may be stretched on the rack until he can stand it no longer, yet not suffer pain that results, or even be likely to result, in permanent and serious physical damage. Yet, he has clearly been tortured. And the memorandum seems to admit, as indeed it must, because the Convention is so explicit about it, that even a *threat* of the rack can break, or otherwise assault, a person's will and constitute torture. Threats would fall into the category of mental pain, but to count as 'torture' they need not, though admittedly they often do, cause damage that lasts for months or years. The requirement that torture be 'prolonged' applies to both physical and mental pain. But if a person's will finally breaks on the rack, we may not know whether the damage will last for months or years. We may not even know whether it is likely to. But we certainly know that the person has been tortured.[4]

Another useful exercise is to consider what count as paradigm cases of torture. There is the exquisite Chinese water torture: one is pinned underneath a receptacle of water, which drips on one's forehead until one can stand it no longer. Again, there does not have to be 'prolonged' damage, on the memorandum's interpretation of it, to be the Chinese water torture. Then there is the long-practiced, not at all exquisite, water torture, which Brian Simpson describes as 'a practice of pouring large quantities of water into a person's mouth, presumably with some sort of funnel, to produce fear of drowning'.[5] Once more, there need not be 'prolonged' damage. Indeed, water-boarding (in which a captive is strapped to a board and then, with wet rags or immersion in water or in some other way, made to feel as if he is drowning), our modern 'professional interrogation technique' which the Central Intelligence Agency (CIA) does not regard as torture, is just a version of the ancient water torture.[6]

1.3 AN ABSOLUTE PROHIBITION IN THEORY?

Many writers think that there is an absolute prohibition on torture to be found in such abstract moral considerations as human harms or as moral principles (e.g., respect for persons or never treating a person merely as a means). This sort of absolute ban in theory is to be distinguished from an absolute ban in practice—one that is based not on moral considerations alone, but also on facts about human nature (e.g., the limits of human understanding and motivation) and about how societies work (e.g., slippery slopes). One may wonder how sharp a distinction, especially in ethics, can be drawn between theory and practice, and I shall return to that question later.

What are these theoretical moral considerations? Let me just note some clearly inadequate answers. It is undeniable that to assault a person's will is to wrong a person. It is to assault what we regard as the dignity of the human person, which is always, and in itself, a wrong. But to do to a person what is always and in itself a wrong is not necessarily to do what is wrong, if that term is used, as it often is, to mean what, all things considered, it is wrong to do. Nor can one infer from one's doing what is always and inherently a wrong that one is doing what is absolutely prohibited. One cannot simply rule out that one may sometimes have to do the lesser of two wrongs.

These moral considerations, then, fail to justify an absolute ban: their premise is not strong enough to support that conclusion. What considerations might be strong enough? A morally repellent, perhaps the most repellent, feature the sort of torture I am considering is that it is an assault on a person's will, a person's dignity. Torture is yet more repellent if it not just assaults a person's will, but completely (though possibly temporarily) takes it away—reduces a person, as it can, to a gibbering wreck. It is useful to think of a rational agent as someone with autonomy and liberty, autonomy being a feature of thought and decision (one decides for oneself), and liberty being a feature of action (one may, within limits, pursue one's conception of a worthwhile life). Not all denials of liberty are torture. If one detains suspected terrorists without trial, one probably detains innocent persons as well as guilty.[7] A guilty terrorist's liberty does not extend to indiscriminate murder, but preventing one from going about one's perfectly innocent business does violate a person's liberty. But an innocent detainee whose liberty is violated is not, thereby, tortured. But if, in contrast, one is faced with an extremely powerful threat—say, one's child's being tortured—one has one's liberty assaulted, and one is, in my sense, tortured. Jeremy Waldron describes torture as inherently 'brutal' and 'savage',[8] 'a retrogression into barbarism'.[9] 'The aim of torture', he writes in a highly colored passage, is 'a sort of savage breaking of the will'.[10] But this, I think, carries the thought I am developing too far. Torture is not necessarily either savage or a breaking of the will; nor is it necessarily barbaric. Think of the case of a kidnapping in which the police have the kidnapper in custody and fear that the kidnapped child, the whereabouts of whom the kidnapper will not reveal, may be buried in a box and rapidly running out of oxygen. (I have in mind here a real case.[11]) If a senior police officer, after wide consultation and earnest deliberation, and in desperate hope of saving the child, threatens torture, and thereupon the kidnapper caves in, it is hard to think of the police officer's act either as 'savage' or as destroying the prisoner's will, even temporarily. Yet, the act is torture. (This is what happened in the case I have in mind.)

Let us, nonetheless, turn to the most extreme forms of torture: cases of reducing the subject to a gibbering wreck. They may most clearly reveal why torture is absolutely prohibited. Here we must turn for a moment to the idea of forfeiting a right.[12] It is a common view that an offender forfeits the human right to liberty, and possibly even, in the case of murder or treason, the human right to life. Perhaps the right not to be tortured can also be forfeited, thereby undermining the absoluteness of the ban on torture. The most common reply to this suggestion is that, although many human rights can be forfeited, the right not to be tortured never can be, though this reply leaves us wanting to understand why that is so. The better reply, it seems to me, is that the doctrine of forfeit is, in the case of human rights, bogus.

We all agree that a human right is a right that we have simply in virtue of being human—not a law-abiding or deserving human being, but simply a human being. And a transgressing human being remains a human being in the exact sense relevant here. The doctrine of forfeit is a factitious device, thought up to make susceptibility to punishment, in the form of loss of life or liberty or property, compatible with possession of human rights to life, liberty, and property. The doctrine was never deeply worked out. What exactly, according to the doctrine, does a murderer or a thief forfeit? Rights generally? The rights to life, liberty, property, or security of person (e.g., the right not to have one's hand cut off, as it might be under Shariah Law)? Forfeited entirely or just in part? And if in part, how large a part? The appropriate way to answer those questions is by appeal to desert: what punishment would fit the crime? Punishment typically involves taking away something valuable to human beings. What, and how much, is to be taken is determined by the offender's desert. What the offender should be thought to forfeit is not a right simpliciter; the 'forfeit' is whatever punishment turns out to be fair. There are cases in which different punishments are equally fair: the guilty party, let us say, might appropriately be given either six months in jail, or a £20,000 fine, or three years' community service. So, if one wants to use the language of forfeits, one could say that the offender forfeits either the right to liberty to the extent of six months (though this formula is still not precise enough: an offender might lose freedom of movement, but to take away further freedoms might be too harsh), or the right to property to the extent of £20,000, or occasional liberty to the extent of three years. However, what is important here are the judgments about desert, from which one can then derive, if for some reason one wants to, judgments about what is forfeited. But why should one want to? To speak of 'forfeit' suggests that the rights in some way disappear from the scene. But they do not disappear. On the contrary, we have just seen that the idea of a human right leaves no space for forfeits. An offender is still a human being, so still a bearer of all human rights. That is why an offender retains, among others, a right not to be tortured. In addition, an offender retains a right to kinds and amounts of liberty that justice does not demand. It is more perspicuous to say that the demands of justice can sometimes weigh against the entitlement of human rights. Justice and human rights can conflict, and, when they do, we should see whether we can discern weights to be attached to the conflicting demands.

So the doctrine of forfeits cannot be used to undermine the absoluteness of the ban on torture. But this excursion into forfeits prompts the question: is there any reason to think that the right not to be tortured cannot conflict with, and sometimes be outweighed by, other moral considerations? Can the guilt of the kidnapper, while not triggering a forfeit, still have weight in our decision about what to do? May the innocence of the kidnapped child also weigh with us? Does the fact that the damage the torture does is temporary (if that is so), and that the death of the child would be forever, also have weight? Can these weights be measured and compared?

It is universally accepted that I may act in self-defense against someone trying to kill me, even to the point of killing my attacker, if that should be necessary. My innocence and the attacker's guilt must be exerting weight here. May I defend myself against a poisoner who will not tell me the antidote I need? May I choke it out of him? If so, then the fact that my life is at stake and he will be subjected only to a choking seems to be exerting weight. If I may thus defend myself, why on earth may I not also defend the life of my helpless kidnapped child, to whom I owe duties of care, by choking out of the kidnapper where the child is buried?

I ask questions rather than make statements, because I am still searching for what is so especially evil about choking the information out of one's assailant, that it, unlike killing one's assailant, is *never* allowed.

I may have been unsuccessful in my search so far because I have been looking too exclusively at the phenomenology of torture: what it does to its victim. Perhaps what is morally important will be brought out by a more abstract characterization of the act, such as failing in respect for persons, or treating merely as a means and not as an end. Acting in either of those ways, one could say, is always forbidden. But it must be the case that killing my assailant because it is the only way to save my own life does not fail in respect for the assailant or treat the assailant merely as a means, because such self-defense is permitted morally. And one can see why that might be so. Treating a person merely as a means is always forbidden, it is plausible to think, because it does not treat the person as a center of interests, or more generally of value, of his or her own. But if I kill in self-defense, I can do it in full acceptance of my assailant's own interests and value. It is just that I give weight in my decision to my innocence and my assailant's guilt. How, then, does my choking the antidote out of my assailant differ from this case of self-defense? In this case too, I can in the same way grant weight—due weight—to my assailant's own value and interests; I just give weight also to innocence and guilt and also perhaps to the relative magnitude of the interests we have at stake in this case.

I do not deny that what may matter here is not just the consequences of torture, but also the nature of the act. The consequences of killing may be worse than the consequences of torturing, but we must also weigh the moral nature of the act of torture itself.[13] But that is what I am trying to do.

I do not advance my attempts as an answer to any of our questions about torture. The questions are extraordinarily difficult, and my remarks move quickly across the surface. All they really show is that I personally have trouble finding the justification, if there is one, for the ban's being absolute in theory. So I shall have to leave open the question of its absoluteness in theory.

1.4 AN ABSOLUTE PROHIBITION IN PRACTICE?

Even if there were no justification for an absolute ban on torture in theory, we would not have answered our question about torture. Our question is: what should we *do* about torture? And that question requires us to think about what we have so far not considered: such matters as the limits of human motivation and understanding, how moral infections travel through the body politic, and so on—that is, certain realities about human agents, individually and en masse. Perhaps when these realities are taken into account, we shall decide that the ban on torture at work in our society should, after all, be absolute.

This is why we should not put much weight here on a distinction between theory and practice. Ethics is about practice, and it has not performed its function fully until it issues in a judgment about what to do. And what I have meant by 'theory' is theory about what we ought to do, and it would be crazy to decide this in ignorance of the nature of the 'we' whose behavior is being regulated. There are various limits to our motivation and understanding that constrain what we can do—in a certain sense of 'can'. And *ought* implies *can*. Of course, we must establish the sense of 'can' in that principle. But, the limits on what we can do may use 'can' in the same sense. If so, facts about motivation are relevant to what we ought to do, in which case 'theory' cannot be sharply separated from practice.

What, then, should we as a society do about torture?

1. *More of what we do now.* Many would unhesitatingly answer: have laws that ban torture *absolutely*, teach in every school and preach from every pulpit that torture is *never* allowed, root out and severely punish all who torture, and, finally, hope that when there is a potentially catastrophic ticking bomb, someone will secretly resort to torture.

This is a tightening up of what we do now. The Convention bans torture absolutely. So do most of the 130 nations that have ratified the Convention. The law is pretty solid. No major political leader would think of publicly defending torture. But we are now considering how we might do all of this better. We could more energetically root out intelligence agents, police officers, and soldiers who torture. But how much of an improvement could we expect? The rooting out would have to depend to some extent on the cooperation of their superior officers, who themselves are often sympathetic to, complicit in, and beneficiaries of the torture. We can persuade academics and clerics to increase their condemnation of torture. We can improve the training of police et al. and probably thereby make the treatment of prisoners a good deal less brutal. But lectures and sermons and training are up against the raw native strength of the temptation to torture. The father would still be frantic to save his kidnapped child. Intelligence officers would still be determined to foil the terrorist plot.[14] Soldiers would still be desperate to keep deaths on their side as low as possible. We can do better, but I doubt that we can do very much better.

The power of the temptation to torture is too little acknowledged. Some writers are alarmed at our even discussing the morality of torture publicly, and certainly at our giving lectures that conclude that torture may sometimes be permitted. But their worry greatly overestimates the power of a philosophical lecture and underestimates the natural, unprompted strength of the temptation to torture. When confronted with the determinedly silent kidnapper of my child, I would not need to have heard any philosophical musings for the idea of torture to enter my head. Nations solemnly, some perhaps even sincerely, swear never to torture, but I know of no modern nation, faced with a serious threat of terrorism, that has not then tortured. It is chastening that the number of nations where torture is now practiced on a regular basis is 132,[15] while the number of nations that have ratified the Convention is 130. There must be a large overlap between these two classes. Oona Hathaway has done an empirical study of the practices of more than 160 nations over the course of forty years, one of the conclusions of which is that:[16]

not only does it appear that the Convention does not always have the intended effect of reducing torture in the countries that ratify, but, in some cases, the opposite might even be true.

2. *Torture warrants.* Alan Dershowitz proposes that we introduce torture warrants on analogy with search warrants.[17] One would appear before some legal authority and put one's case for torture. Dershowitz means this to apply to interrogational torture of suspected terrorists by government officials; he has Israel particularly in mind. He thinks that whether one likes it or not, torture in this sort of case will go on, and that a system of warrants will at least make things better than they would otherwise be.[18] Most of his critics object that, on the contrary, it would make things worse.[19] However, as a general response to torture, it would be ridiculous. Very many cases—most, I should think—in which a person is tempted to torture would not allow time to go through a warrant-granting procedure. And there would hardly be a legal official on a battlefield handy for a soldier who has just captured an enemy officer, or indeed handy to the site of every kidnapping or ticking bomb.

3. *Judicial review.* Richard Posner proposes that the constraint on torture should be that the torturer should have to appear in court, *post facto*, and convince a judge or jury that this particular act of torture was justified.[20] He would submit himself to the assessment of a court of law. But the law would have to have available to it some not too vague or vacuous account of when torture is justified (or at least excusable), and when not. Otherwise, the legal reasoning that is supposed to take place in the judicial review would be so jejune as to be a sham. The law is nowhere near having such a principle; nor is philosophy. Without it, Posner's proposed system of legal review would have negligible restraining effect. This objection applies equally to Dershowitz's proposal. Besides, the torturer on trial would usually be a member of one's own society who had acted in its defense. If the society is sufficiently rattled by, say, a terrorist threat to it, it is hardly likely to convict a protector—a jury almost never and a judge seldom. And how often would a case of torture even reach court? Senior officers in the police and army and intelligence service are noted for *not* reporting torture.

4. *Principled torture.* In each of the three previous attempts at an answer to what a society should do about torture, we ended up feeling the need for a principle that would help to distinguish justified torture from unjustified. It would, of course, be unreasonable to expect the principle to be easy to apply or pellucid or always to produce an answer. But, the principle would have to have a fair amount of ethical content, and to hold us back from the slippery slope. If we can find such a principle, it would give us *principled torture*—though, for some, that label will smack of oxymoron. But, as I have said, we are as yet nowhere near having such a principle. We should have to formulate it from scratch. But, one might think, what good are moral philosophers if they cannot help here?

Moral philosophers—indeed anybody—can at least list considerations that might justify the permission or prohibition of torture. There is the value of what the torturer seeks to protect (the lives of innocent civilians, the life of a kidnapped child); there is the pain suffered by, and the rational agency assaulted in, the victim of the torture; there is the evil of what the victim of the torture has done (plotted to blow up thousands of innocent people, kidnapped and buried the child); there is the evil act of torture itself—if this is a separate consideration; there is the good or evil done to society at large. In formulating the principle, we should have to decide which of these considerations count (all of them, I should say). We should then have to attach some sort of weights to these considerations, weights that would have to be comparable. And we should have to declare in the principle that torture is permitted/prohibited when such and such considerations outweigh thus and so considerations.

No small order. Can we attach nonsubjective weights to all the considerations that count? I do not think that the estimate of their weights is entirely subjective. I think, rather, that it is a matter of our trying to discern a weight that the item has independently of us. But if you and I should attach different weights to the same item, I do not know how to resolve our disagreement rationally. We may find that the more we talk to one another honestly and openly, and the more we refine our own assessments of the weights, the more our assessments converge. The convergence may happen in a way that suggests that there is something objective on which we have converged. But much of this is *terra incognita*, and at present not readily deployable in a court of law.

Can we attach *comparable* weights to the considerations that count? What comparable weights can be attached to the interests of the persons involved, the evil of the act of torture itself, and what the terrorist and the kidnapper may deserve as a result of their own acts? The simplest answer is the absolutist's: we can see that the evil of the act of torture itself outweighs all the other considerations. But that is the theoretical absolutism that earlier I found difficult to credit.

Can we even calculate the weight of all the relevant human interests reliably enough to take the calculation seriously? I shall come to that shortly.

The principle that is supposed to give us principled torture has so little content now, and such poor prospects for more content in the future, that this fourth proposed approach is likely to suffer much the same fate as Dershowitz's system of warrants and Posner's system of judicial review. Principled torture, if based on a principle very short on content, is likely soon to sink into unprincipled torture.

These four constitute just a sampler of options available to a society; there are many more. How is a society to assess them?

There is the obvious empirical test: what would their consequences be? As we have seen, Dershowitz says that a warrant scheme would at least reduce the amount of interrogational torture; his critics say that it would increase it. But neither side offers anything approaching serious evidence. For instance, Bob Brecher, in his book *Torture and the Ticking Bomb*, asks rhetorically:[21]

> Once torture were normalized in so called ticking bomb cases…what reasons are there to suppose its use would not spread to other sorts of circumstances?

Indeed. But what reasons are there to suppose that it would? Brecher replies: 'The *Economist*…certainly thinks it would.' But that others say what you say is hardly evidence for it. Jeremy Waldron claims that [22]

> were we to put up for acceptance as an integral part of the main body of human rights law the proposition that people may be tortured in times of emergency, I think that people would sense that the whole game was being given away, and that human rights law itself was entering a crisis.

These sound like disastrous consequences, but phrases like 'give the game away' and 'enter a crisis' have no clear meaning; in any case, Waldron does not give evidence for either claim. Brecher and Waldron are only two examples, but I think we may generalize. The arguments both *pro* and *con* torture that we have been given so far are largely on the level of rhetoric.

It is not that there is no hard evidence at all. How many terrorist disasters have been averted by information extracted by torture? In all the major struggles against terrorism—the French in Algeria, the Israelis in Palestine, the Americans in Vietnam, the British in Ulster, the Americans again in Iraq and Guantánamo—those close to the torture have leaked information. The trouble is that their leaks are inconsistent.[23] Here, to give just one example, are two experts on torture in Vietnam: 'So many American and Vietnamese interviewees testified to the effectiveness of torture that there can be no doubt that it extracted useful information in most cases';[24] 'torture did not provide any worthwhile intelligence and often yielded false information'.[25] It must be possible to get all the facts of the matter, but we have not got them yet.

The question in my title is not restricted to anything as narrow as Dershowitz's system of warrants, or even as interrogational torture as a whole. My question is: what should our society do about torture? To answer this question we need to know not just what disasters, if any, were averted by torture, which we might one day learn, but also how much torture was necessary to extract the information, how institutionalized or uninstitutionalized the torture was, if it was institutionalized, what other sorts of institutions might there be, what the effects of different possible social decisions about torture would be for society at large (for instance what the effects of institutionalizing the fourth scheme, principled torture, would be, assuming different formulations of the principle), what ways are there, other than torture, of getting the sort of information we need (e.g., the willing cooperation of a sympathetic public), whether torture impedes these other ways (e.g., the alienation of the Iraqi public by the brutality of the coalition forces), and so on and on.[26]

There are writers who think we can do such extraordinarily large-scale calculations, at least in principle. But we are now concerned with practice: how should our society actually conduct itself? To decide that, we need not be certain about the facts; much of our life is conducted on probabilities. But there are two points on which we are all likely to agree: first, *sometimes* we can adequately understand the consequences of the various actions open to us, adequately weigh their relative importance, adequately decide their probability, and rationally decide on that basis what to do; and, second, *sometimes* we cannot. Sometimes our identification of consequences and our calculation of their probabilities are so unreliable that we would not be willing to base our lives on them. The important question here is how many decisions fall into that second category, and how central to our life they are.

To my mind, the question that many rule utilitarians put at the heart of ethics falls into the second category: what set of rules and dispositions would, if they were the dominant ones in society, have best consequences throughout society as a whole and in the long run? We do not know, and more time is unlikely to remedy that. I have written about this more fully elsewhere.[27]

What about our present question: what policy on torture would, if adopted by our society, have best consequences throughout society as a whole and in the long run? Or, to take a more modest question and perhaps the only question that need exercise us: what change in our present policy on and attitude to torture would, if adopted by our society, have better consequences throughout society as a whole and in the long run? I suspect—I can put it no higher than that—that we cannot answer the first question to a reliable enough degree of probability for us to be willing to base our lives upon it. I suspect that we can sometimes answer the second, more modest question to a reliable enough degree of probability, but that sometimes—often—we cannot. For instance, would Dershowitz's warrant system be an improvement? No one knows.

Now, Dershowitz and others could use a *tu quoque* argument against me. I criticize Dershowitz and others for not having adequate evidence for their empirical claims. But I too make a strong claim: that we do not know sufficiently reliably whether it would have better consequences, and that this ignorance is not soon, or perhaps ever, going to be overcome. There are differences though: Dershowitz's claim is empirical; mine is epistemic. Both, however, are difficult to assess. In any case, mine is not a claim; it is only a suspicion. So let me proceed on that basis. Suppose my suspicion turns out to be right. What would that mean for ethical thought?

1.5 HOW SHOULD ETHICS ACCOMMODATE NEAR INVINCIBLE IGNORANCE?

Our thought about murder is a good example to start with. Most of us accept some such rule as, don't deliberately kill the innocent. However, we accept too that this particular rule is not the last word. Shipwrecked sailors in a lifeboat, in dire enough circumstances, may kill and eat one among themselves to give the rest a chance of survival. They may do so sometimes without having selected the victim by fair, random means; the victim may have had a poor chance of surviving anyway.[28]

As this extremely rare example shows, most of us—the law included—do not treat the ban on deliberately killing the innocent as absolute. But, what should a society do about killing? Most societies introduce an absolute ban on 'murder', defining 'murder' as unlawful killing. But what sorts of killing should be made unlawful? We do not ask: Which rule about deliberately killing the innocent would, if it were the dominant rule on killing in our society, have the best consequences in society as a whole and in the long run? This is, I think, a case of our being nearly invincibly ignorant of the consequences. It is not that we have sometime in the past realized that we cannot calculate the consequences to a reliable degree of probability and, as a result, have resorted to some other approach. Rather, it never occurred to us in the first place that we could do such calculations. From the start, we proceeded differently. Because of the great value we attach to human life, we prohibited deliberately killing the innocent, though not ruling out the possibility of exceptions. Again, because of the great value we attach to human life, we employ a highly conservative policy of requiring any exception to the rule to be especially clear in scope and to have an especially strong case made for it.

In some jurisdictions, a precedent was set some time ago for treating leniently sailors driven to killing in certain lifeboat cases. But the scope of the precedent in those cases is extraordinarily narrow, and all the relevant considerations fairly easy to see.

In some jurisdictions, legislators have only fairly recently made an exception for euthanasia. But they have done so extremely cautiously, with great concern to identify the boundaries of the exception. And the case for making an exception for euthanasia applies only to euthanasia. We are not remotely close to formulating universal conditions in which deliberately killing the innocent is either justified or, what is less demanding, excusable.

Probing philosophers ask: may a surgeon kill one of his patients on the sly to save five? Our immediate and strongly felt response is that such an act would be monstrous. The justification for such an act, if there were to be any, would lie in its consequences. But who knows the full consequences? Who can at all adequately estimate the ramifications throughout the society of surgeons' behaving like this? We do not, because we cannot, and never thought we could, use consequential reasoning here.

This, I believe, is the way that most societies in the modern world have behaved: they have adopted an absolute ban on deliberately killing the innocent and a highly conservative practice on exceptions. And because we have indeed been unable to formulate a universal rule on this matter, the way that most societies have behaved seems reasonable. What way would be better?

If torture too is in the second category, that might explain why most modern societies prohibit it absolutely. There are in this case even no socially agreed exceptions, comparable to the exception made for some kinds of euthanasia. And we have not come near adequately identifying universal conditions for justified torture. We do not reason consequentially. Instead, we accept that assaulting a person's will is a particularly terrible thing to do. We prohibit it—no exceptions.

But it is not quite as simple as that. Many persons think that in certain, perhaps rare and extreme circumstances, torture would be justified or excusable. They may not be able to provide any universal description of the kind of circumstances in which this is so, but they think that there are particular cases so extreme that we can identify *them*, at least, case by case, as exceptions.

But this position has a glaring problem. How do we tell when a particular case is truly exceptional? This is the problem that Robert Nozick faces over human rights.[29] They are near absolute, he says; they hold, unless one is faced with a 'catastrophe'. But this does not help us unless we know what is to count here as a 'catastrophe'. A 'catastrophe', Nozick explains, is something on the order of the nuclear holocaust. But why set the bar so extremely high? Would not a nuclear bomb's destroying a large part of Manhattan, while well short of the nuclear holocaust, still be a catastrophe? And do the numbers count? The father of the kidnapped child could not unreasonably regard the death of his young child as a catastrophe. The word 'catastrophe' will not save us from the slippery slope.

Perhaps we cannot do better than to work for what I earlier called an improved form of where we are now: an absolute prohibition of torture; much stricter training of police, military, and intelligence agents; much more energetic rooting out and more severe punishment of torturers and those who order or condone torture; and re-education of the public. We could then only hope that anyone who, despite all these changes, resorts to torture has correctly identified a particular exception. This will not, of course, prevent unjustifiable or inexcusable torture, but no permissible social arrangements will produce full compliance with any prohibition.

1.6 CAN WE NOT DO BETTER?

The weaknesses in that proposal are plain. Can we really not do better? The only approach that has prospects of being better is what I have called 'principled torture'. However, for the reasons I gave earlier, I doubt that we can come up with the principle we need.

I find the question in my title extraordinarily difficult, even by the standards of practical ethics. I do not offer my answer with confidence. An enormous amount is at stake.

Notes

1. *Universal Declaration of Human Rights* (1948), Preamble.
2. United States Code, title 18, sect. 2340 (2).
3. For a masterly critique of the Bush administration's attempts to reinterpret its legal obligations concerning torture, see the writings of David Luban collected in his book *Legal Ethics and Human Dignity*, Cambridge: Cambridge University Press, 2009.
4. The damage done by torture, even the forms of it that the Bush administration refuses to call torture, such as those used in Abu Ghraib, is very often "prolonged." See Allen S. Keller, "Torture in Abu Ghraib," *Perspectives in Biology and Medicine* 49 (2006) and Jonathan Glover, "Ethics and the Response to Terrorism" (unpublished manuscript on file with the author).
5. A. W. Brian Simpson, *Human Rights and the End of Empire: Britain and the Genesis of the European Convention*, Oxford: Oxford University Press, 2001, p. 1024.
6. Porter J. Goss, a former Director of the CIA, does not classify water-boarding, which the CIA admits to using, as "torture" but as "a professional interrogation technique," as if the latter could not also be the former. However, Mike McConnell, the Director of National Intelligence, the recently created agency to oversee most of US intelligence activities, in an interview with *The New Yorker*, said, "If I had water draining into my nose, oh God, I just can't imagine how painful. Whether its 'torture' by anybody else's definition, for me it would be torture." He went on implicitly to acknowledge why the Bush administration has been so anxious to keep it out of the class of "tortures." "If it ever is determined to be torture, there will be a huge penalty to be paid for anyone engaging in it." Lawrence Wright, "The Spymaster," *The New Yorker*, January 21, 2008, pp. 52–3.
7. The importance of the class of innocent detainees should not be underestimated. The Red Cross reports that "Certain CF [Coalition Force] intelligence officers told the ICRC [International Committee of the Red Cross] that in their estimate between 70 percent and 90 percent of the persons deprived of their liberty in Iraq had been arrested by mistake." *Report of the International Committee of the Red Cross on the Treatment by the Coalition Forces of Prisoners of War and Other Persons By the Geneva Conventions in Iraq during Arrest, Internment and Interrogation*, February 2004, Para. 7.
8. Jeremy Waldron, "Torture and Positive Law: Jurisprudence for the White House," *Columbia Law Review* 105 (2005), 1726.
9. Ibid., p. 1710.
10. Ibid., p. 1727.
11. "On September 28, 2002, 11-year-old Jakob van Metzler, a banker's son, was abducted on his way to his parents" house in Frankfurt. A sum of €1 million was demanded for his release. Three days after Jakob's disappearance, Magnus Gäfgen, a 32-year-old law student, collected the ransom from the arranged tram

stop in Frankfurt....Seventy-six hours after Jakob's disappearance, the police arrested Gäfgen...they found the missing ransom, but no sign of Jakob. "[The police followed up all leads and conducted a wide search.] None of these activities yielded any results." "And we knew," said one police officer, "that Jakob might be lying in a hole in the ground, dying a slow death." Wolfgang Daschner, the police president, ordered his men to threaten Gäfgen with violence to force a statement. Under duress, Gäfgen confessed immediately that Jakob was most probably dead and could be found in a lake near Schlüchtern. As a result, the police discovered a child's body, and death from suffocation or drowning was established. In July 2003, the kidnapper was found guilty of abduction and murder and sentenced to life imprisonment.

"The prohibition against duress or coercion is enshrined in German law based on the inviolable dignity of human beings." In February 2003, police president Daschner was charged with duress, and in December 2004, a law court ruled that Daschner had acted unlawfully. He was found guilty, and though he could have faced five years of imprisonment, no sentence was imposed.

"The case sparked a public debate of unexpected proportions...the threat of violence in the case of Magnus Gäfgen was supported by considerable parts of the population."

"According to Oskar Lafontaine, ex-Chancellor Kohl's most fervent left-wing challenger, Daschner obeyed elementary moral principles, as one cannot allow an innocent child to die in agony because of formal, constitutional articles....Likewise, but more unexpectedly, the then chairman of the German Judges' Association (*Deutscher Richterbund*), Geert Mackenroth, defended Daschner's decision. He stated in an interview that torture, or the threat thereof, might be allowed when a higher legal good is to be preserved." Doris Schroeder, "A Child's Life or a 'Little Bit of Torture?': State-Sanctioned Violence and Dignity," *Cambridge Quarterly of Healthcare Ethics* 15 (2006), 188–9.

12. I discuss the idea of forfeiting a right in *On Human Rights*, Oxford: Oxford University Press, 2008, pp. 65–6.

13. This is rightly stressed by Henry Shue, "Torture," *Philosophy and Public Affairs* 7 (1978), repr. Sanford Levinson (ed.), *Torture: A Collection*, New York: Oxford University Press, 2004, pp. 48–9.

14. Uncovering a terrorist plot is a more realistic, and far more common, example than defusing a ticking bomb. "Physical interrogation methods, like psychological methods, take time, time that interrogators do not have in emergencies. Real torture—not the stuff of television—takes days, if not weeks." Darius Rejali, *Torture and Democracy*, Princeton, NJ: Princeton University Press, 2007, p. 17. A kidnapper in police custody with nothing to gain by resistance (see note 11) may crack quickly under duress. An adherent to a cause is unlikely to.

15. Ariel Dorfman, "The Tyranny of Terror: Is Torture Inevitable in Our Century and Beyond?," in Sanford Levinson (ed.), *Torture*, p. 5.

16. Oona A. Hathaway, "The Promise and Limits of the International Law of Torture," in Sanford Levinson (ed.), *Torture*, p. 201.

17. Alan Dershowitz, "Tortured Reasoning," in Sanford Levinson (ed.), *Torture*.

18. Ibid., pp. 257, 266.

19. E.g., Jeremy Waldron, "Torture and Positive Law," pp. 1716ff.; Bob Brecher, *Torture and the Ticking Bomb*, Oxford: Blackwell, 2007, pp. 52–74.

20. Richard Posner, "Torture, Terrorism, and Interrogation," in Sanford Levinson (ed.), *Torture*.

21. Bob Brecher, *Torture and the Ticking Bomb*, p. 60.

22. Jeremy Waldron, "Torture and Positive Law," p. 1744.

23. Darius Rejali, *Torture and Democracy*, ch. 22.

24. Mark Moyar, *Phoenix and the Birds of Prey*, Annapolis MD: Naval Institute Press, 1997, p. 60, quoted in Rejali, *Torture and Democracy*, p. 515.

25. Darius Rejali, *Torture and Democracy*, p. 514.

26. Darius Rejali, *Torture and Democracy*, p. 24: "the key successes in gathering information in known cases come from other methods [than torture], most notably cultivating public cooperation and informants"; p. 458: "The best source of information bar none is public cooperation." Rejali cites the example of how the British police arrested five men for planting bombs on buses and trains in London on July 21, 2005: "Police captured the July 21 bombers using accurate public information, and they did this within ten days. Police identified Muktar Said-Ibrahim after his parents…contacted them; they turned in their son after seeing his picture on surveillance tapes," p. 459. "Torturing destroys bonds of loyalty that keep information flowing," p. 460.

27. *Value Judgement: Improving Our Ethical Beliefs*, Oxford: Clarendon Press, 1996, chs VI, VII.

28. For an actual case (there are several in maritime history), see A. W. Brian Simpson, *Cannibalism and the Common Law*, Chicago, IL: University of Chicago Press, 1984.

29. *Anarchy, State, and Utopia*, Oxford: Blackwell, 1974, pp. 28–33.

II

WAR

2

The Consequences of War

Thomas Hurka

A standing temptation for moral philosophers is to approach their subject in a primarily intellectual way. Many of us are initially drawn to it by the pressing human issues it raises, both about concrete moral problems and, more generally, about how we should live. But over time we can come to care more about making clever ethical arguments, formulating new theories, or detecting new subtleties. Our engagement with moral questions can become the more purely cerebral one found in, say, metaphysics or epistemology.

Jonathan Glover's writings are an antidote to this temptation. For alongside their philosophical acuity they always retain a profound interest in moral questions as moral, and a deep emotional engagement with them. He never subordinates ethical substance to intellectual flash. One reflection of this engagement is his willingness to explore the empirical issues relevant to a given moral issue, even though for many philosophers doing so is less prestigious than spinning abstract theories. Another is his strong focus on what must be central to any plausible morality, namely human well-being and how acts and policies affect people for good or ill. The result is an approach to moral questions that is broadly if not exclusively consequentialist, evaluating policies largely for their effects on human and other happiness.

This approach is evident in his writings about the morality of war, which he treats theoretically in *Causing Death and Saving Lives* and discusses from a more practical point of view, concerned to avert its horrors, in *Humanity: A Moral History of the Twentieth Century*.[1] Though the former discussion gives some weight to individual autonomy, its watchword is Bertrand Russell's insistence on a "vital realization of the consequences of acts," and it therefore sets aside such deontological distinctions as between doing and allowing harm, intending and foreseeing harm,[2] and even between soldiers and civilians. Throughout, its focus is on what war will do to people.

As Glover recognizes, this broadly consequentialist approach is revisionist. Both everyday thought about the morality of war and the international law governing it derive from the Catholic tradition of just war theory, which is avowedly deontological, attaching weight to just the moral distinctions that Glover ignores. But exactly how his view is revisionist depends on exactly what just war theory says, and that is the subject of this chapter. Operating within the just war model, or assuming *pro tem* that it is correct, I ask what general principles underlie the judgments it makes about particular cases of war. More specifically, I ask what general principles underlie its judgments about the consequences of war. Any credible theory makes the moral permissibility of war turn largely on its effects: both the suffering and destruction it will cause and the rights-violations it can, if justified, prevent. Consequentialism does this, of course, but so to a large extent does just war theory. It does so, however, in a distinctive way. Identifying the various features of the just war assessment of consequences will permit both a better understanding of what the theory says and a clearer contrast between it and consequentialism. How exactly do the two views differ when they assess war by its effects? Is one more likely to permit war than the other, and if so, why?

2.1 JUST WAR CONSEQUENCE CONDITIONS

A purely consequentialist approach identifies all the goods and evils that will result from a given war, whatever their type and however they will be produced, and weighs them equally against each other, so the war is justified only if it will produce more overall good than evil or, more strictly, if its balance of good over evil consequences is better than that of any alternative. This view is obviously difficult to apply in practice. Before a war, it must make probability estimates of the war's different possible outcomes, and even after the war it requires counterfactual judgments about the effects the alternatives to war would have had, to compare the war with those alternatives. But theoretically it is very simple, providing a single moral test that involves weighing all of a war's good and evil consequences equally against each other.

The just war assessment of the consequences of war is much more complex, first, because it involves a plurality of moral tests. The theory holds that to be morally permissible, a war must satisfy a number of conditions, of which some, such as that the war be initiated and declared by a competent authority and fought with a right intention, are purely deontological. But four other conditions concern the war's consequences. One says a morally permissible war must have a just cause. There is a small set of types of good effect that constitute just causes, such as resisting aggression and preventing genocide, and the war must be directed at one of them. More specifically, since all the just causes involve preventing or rectifying some wrong, there must be a relevant wrong committed or in prospect to which the war is a response. Second, the war must have a reasonable hope of success in achieving its just cause or, more generally, in producing relevant goods. Third, it must be a last resort, so there is no less-destructive way of achieving those goods; if there is, then the war is wrong. Finally, the damage that the war will cause must not be excessive, or disproportionate to the relevant good it will do. In short, a morally permissible war must satisfy just cause, hope of success, last resort, and proportionality conditions.[3]

This view faces the same practical difficulties as consequentialism, requiring both probability estimates before a war and counterfactual judgments after it. But it is theoretically more complex, because it imposes four different conditions about consequences rather than a single one. This plurality of conditions is by no means unique to just war theory, but is also found in the morality of self-defense and in constitutional provisions explaining when a state may legitimately infringe the rights of its citizens. Both allow only acts that have a specific type of good effect, such as thwarting an unjustified attack, and a reasonable hope of achieving it, while also being necessary, or the least harmful way of achieving that effect, and not disproportionate to the value of that effect. Therefore, the four-part assessment of consequences in just war theory instantiates a more widely accepted pattern.[4]

The multiplicity of these conditions can be reduced a little by subsuming the hope of success under the proportionality condition. If a war has no or only a negligible chance of producing relevant goods, the harm it will cause is excessive compared to any good it is likely to do, and the war is therefore disproportionate. In addition, the last resort condition, while distinct from the proportionality condition, is derivative from it conceptually. This may not be apparent if we consider only the artificial situation where war and some alternative will be equally effective at achieving relevant goods: then the last resort condition need only compare their levels of destructiveness. But often a war will achieve its just causes to a somewhat higher degree than an alternative like diplomacy, will achieve additional goods such as deterring future aggression, or has a higher probability of achieving some goods. Then the last resort condition must compare the extra benefits of war with its extra costs, which makes it in effect a comparative version of the proportionality condition. For each of war and its alternatives it does a proportionality assessment, weighing the relevant goods each will cause against its relevant evils to arrive at its net relevant outcome, and then permits the war only if its net outcome is better than that of any alternative. The last resort and proportionality conditions can still yield distinct verdicts: a war can be proportionate but not a last resort, because there is a less harmful way of achieving its goals, or the only way of achieving those goals but excessively destructive. Still, the last resort condition depends conceptually on the proportionality condition, since it is a comparative version of it.

Even with these reductions, the theory's plural conditions make it in one way more complex than consequentialism. But it is also more complex in how it identifies and weighs consequences. Whereas consequentialism counts all the goods and evils a war will produce, just war theory discriminates between types of good and evil effect, counting some more than others that are equally great, and also between the causal mechanisms that can produce effects, so some goods or evils count more or only when they have one kind of history rather than another. Finally, the theory does not always weigh good and evil effects equally, sometimes giving goods more weight than evils and sometimes doing the opposite. Let me turn to this second, less straightforward set of complexities.

2.2 RELEVANT GOODS

Just war theory discriminates between effects, first, in its just cause condition, which identifies certain types of good, such as resisting aggression, as pre-eminently morally important. If a war is not directed at one of these goods, then no matter what other benefits it produces, it is not permitted. By "directed" here the theory does not mean something about a person's intentions; it does not require an agent resorting to war to be motivated by desire for its just cause. If a political leader resists aggression against a distant nation only to boost his popularity with voters, he acts on a disreputable motive and thereby violates the right intention condition, but still has a just cause. But the just cause condition is also not satisfied merely by the existence of a relevant wrong. If one nation invades a province of a second nation, that does not permit the second to invade some third nation, or even to invade some province of the first. It only permits it to do things that are directed at the wrong in the sense that they are in principle capable of preventing it, such as trying to expel the invading forces from its own territory. The second nation's acts need not actually be able to prevent the wrong; that is a matter for the hope of success condition. But they must at least be of a type that can prevent it.

Some goods identified by the just cause condition have instances that are comparatively trivial. Thus, one nation can sponsor terrorist attacks that kill, not thousands of another's citizens, which would clearly provide a just cause, but only one or two, or its government can murder just a few members of a minority population. These wrongs seem insufficient to justify the full horror of war, but there are two possible explanations why: One is that the wrongs are too trivial to constitute just causes; the other is that they do constitute just causes but war to rectify them would be disproportionate. The second explanation may yield a more elegant version of just war theory, in which the just cause condition identifies only types of morally crucial good and leaves issues of their magnitude entirely to the proportionality condition.[5] But the first explanation seems more intuitive; surely most people would say the cases mentioned above do not involve a just cause. And I argue later that adopting this explanation saves the theory from some counterintuitive consequences. I therefore assume that the just cause condition not only identifies types of morally crucial good but also makes an initial assessment of their magnitude, so goods below a threshold of seriousness cannot constitute just causes.

The goods that do constitute just causes also clearly count toward the proportionality and last resort conditions: that a war will stop aggression or prevent genocide is obviously one thing that weighs against its destructiveness, both when we assess it in itself and when we compare it with alternatives. And a very restrictive version of just war theory says they are the only goods that count: on the negative side of a proportionality assessment is all the destruction a war will cause, on the positive side only the benefits in its initial just causes. But this version is too restrictive, for there are at least some other morally relevant goods.

The most important of these have been called "conditional just causes." Unlike "independent just causes" such as resisting aggression, they cannot on their own satisfy the just cause condition; if a war will achieve only conditional just causes, it is not morally justified. But once some other, independent just cause is present, they become legitimate aims of war and can contribute to its being proportionate and a last resort.[6]

One category of these causes contains lesser instances of the types of good that can, when greater, be independent just causes. Before their ouster, the Taliban oppressed the Afghan people, for example, by restricting the rights of Afghan women. But a war fought only to liberate Afghan women would on most views have been unjustified no matter how much other good it did, because it lacked an independent just cause. Once there was another just cause to remove the Taliban from power, however, based on their support for terrorism, the fact that war would benefit Afghan women became a factor that counted in its favor and helped to make it proportionate, so a good that could not justify the war on its own did help to justify it given other factors. It seems an essential feature of this case that the independent just cause already justified removing the Taliban. If they had merely invaded a neighboring nation, giving other nations a just cause to expel them but not to do more, it would not have been permissible to remove them in order to benefit Afghan women. But if the Taliban's support for terrorism already justified ending their regime, the fact that doing so would benefit Afghan women became a relevant good.

A second category of conditional causes contains goods that can never, whatever their magnitude, be independent just causes, but that also count in favor of war when an independent just cause is present. The central such goods are incapacitating an aggressor from further aggression by forcibly disarming him, and deterring both him and other would-be aggressors by showing that aggression does not pay. On most just war views, the mere fact that a nation has weapons it may use aggressively in the future is no justification for war against it now; *pace* the Bush doctrine, merely preventive war is wrong. But once a nation has committed aggression, eliminating its weaponry becomes a legitimate aim of war and can be pursued even after the war's initial just causes have been achieved. Thus, Iraq's possession of chemical and biological weapons before 1990 did not in itself justify war against it, but once Iraq invaded Kuwait, that permitted other nations not only to repel the invasion but also to partially disarm Iraq, either forcibly or by writing conditions about disarmament into the ceasefire agreement that ended the war. A similar point applies to deterrence of aggression. Even if invading a nonthreatening neighbor would decisively demonstrate our nation's military might and so deter potential aggressors against us, that does not make the invasion right. But if our neighbor itself commits aggression, the fact that resisting it will deter others can become an important factor favoring war and even the main one making it proportionate. The Argentinian invasion of the Falkland Islands in 1982 gave Britain an independent just cause for war, but given the islands' remoteness and sparse population, many would deny that considerations of sovereignty alone made a British military response proportionate. And British Prime Minister Margaret Thatcher's justification of the war did not appeal only to those considerations, citing also the need to maintain international security by resisting even minor aggressions. It may be that while the Argentinian invasion provided the independent just cause for the Falklands War, the main factor making it proportionate was its contribution to international deterrence.

It is of course hard to assess, and easy to exaggerate, the deterrent effects a given war will have. How many would-be aggressors today think consciously of the Falklands War? But in assessing this benefit we must consider not only a war's positive deterrent effect, but also the negative effect of not encouraging aggression. Once aggression has occurred, the status quo before the aggression is no longer an option. One can either resist the aggression, which will deter future aggression, or let it stand, which will encourage aggression by allowing a precedent of successful aggression. And a proportionality calculation must consider a war's avoiding the bad effect as well as its producing the good one, so the difference between the two is its total contribution to deterrence. A similar point applies to the last resort condition. In the lead-up to the 1991 Gulf War, the Soviet Union and France sought a negotiated Iraqi withdrawal from Kuwait. But it was evident that any such withdrawal would require diplomatic concessions to Iraq, for example about some disputed islands on the Iraq–Kuwait border. The United States and its closest allies vigorously opposed any such concessions, saying there must be "no rewards for aggression." In doing so, they recognized that the deterrent benefits of war include not only positively discouraging aggression, but also not making it more attractive.

The role of these conditional causes parallels that of similar goods in the morality of punishment. If a person has not yet committed a crime, the fact that he is likely to do so in future is on most views no justification for imprisoning him now, nor is the fact that imprisoning him may deter others. But once he has acted criminally, the facts that imprisoning him will incapacitate him for further criminal activity and deter others do become relevant benefits of punishment and can help fix the appropriate severity of his punishment. This parallel suggests a second, somewhat less restrictive version of just war theory, on which the only goods relevant to the proportionality and last resort conditions are those in a war's independent just causes and in conditional causes such as disarmament and deterrence.

This second version gains support from the fact that some goods seem entirely irrelevant to these conditions. Imagine that a war will give pleasure to soldiers who are eager for real combat or to citizens on the winning side, who will be elated by their nation's victory. Though certainly good, these pleasures do not, intuitively, count toward the war's justification. An otherwise disproportionate conflict cannot become proportionate because it has these effects. Or imagine that a war will stimulate more powerful art than would otherwise be created; that too cannot help justify it. It may be objected that these are such modest goods that even if relevant they would hardly ever make the difference between a war's being proportionate and not. But I think our intuitive understanding of just war theory goes further and says they are simply not relevant, and a similar point applies to more substantial goods. Imagine that the world's economy is now in a depression and that a war will end that depression, as World War II ended the depression of the 1930s. The economic benefits here may be significant, yet they surely cannot count toward the war's justification; an otherwise impermissible war cannot become permissible because it will boost global GDP.

One may conclude that all these goods—pleasure, art, and economic growth—are as types irrelevant to the justification of war, and then extend that conclusion to all goods not in the independent and conditional just causes. But this inference to the second view would be too hasty. While these goods are indeed, when brought about in one way, irrelevant to the proportionality and last resort conditions, when brought about in another way they seem relevant. This brings us to the second distinguishing feature of the just war view: its discriminating between the causal mechanisms that produce certain effects.

The point is best illustrated by the example of economic goods. I have said that when fighting a war will boost GDP, this is irrelevant to the war's justification. But imagine that in 1990 Saddam Hussein had annexed Saudi Arabia as well as Kuwait and then cut off all their oil exports, raising the world oil price and seriously damaging the world's economy. Imagine in particular that his action damaged the economies of African countries, which could not easily pay the higher price. In this case, preventing the economic harm would seem a relevant good of war. There is surely a stronger reason to reverse Saddam's aggression when it will cause significant economic hardship than when it will not, a reason that makes the war more probably proportional. Is there a moral difference between this case and one where war ends a depression?

Let me suggest a possibility. When war ends a depression, the economic benefits do not result from the achievement of the war's just causes, but instead derive entirely from the process of pursuing them. To reverse our enemy's aggression, we have to produce armaments; to do that we invest in military production and those investments boost our and the world's economy. So it is a means to achieving the war's goal rather than the goal itself that does the economic good. But in the Iraq case, the economic benefits do result from a just cause. The harm to the world's economy depends on Saddam's annexing Kuwait and Saudi Arabia, and we prevent the harm by preventing those annexations. Here the economic goods follow from our achieving a just cause; more specifically, they consist in our preventing harms that are causally downstream from the wrong that provides that cause, so the causal route to the goods runs through the just cause rather than coming directly from a means to it.

A similar point applies to diplomatic goods. In the mid-1990s, it looked as if the Gulf War was going to help resolve the Israeli–Palestinian conflict, by means of the Oslo Accords it helped make possible. That result did not in fact eventuate, but imagine that it had and that Israel and an independent Palestine were now at peace. It seems to me that, though substantial, the benefits of this peace would not count in favor of the Gulf War's proportionality. The reason again is that the benefits would result from a means to the war's just causes rather than from any such cause itself. In order to expel Iraq from Kuwait, the United States and its allies formed a coalition that united Arab states such as Syria and Saudi Arabia with Western ones and even had Israel as, if not a formal member, then an informal ally. And the contacts this coalition involved helped start the Oslo process. But the coalition was only a means to the Gulf War's just cause rather than any part of it, and the benefits it caused are therefore irrelevant to the war's justification. To confirm this, consider a contrasting case. One effect of the Iraq War in 2003 was to end Iraq's payments to the families of Palestinian suicide bombers. Stopping these payments has not had much effect, but imagine that it had: that suicide bombings ceased, leading to Israeli–Palestinian negotiations and a lasting peace. In this case the benefits of the peace would, I think, count in favor of the Iraq War, since eliminating support for terrorism is a just cause.

Or consider the other goods discussed earlier. The pleasure soldiers get from real action cannot help justify a war, because it results from a means to the just cause. But imagine that because of an oppressive regime's policies, its citizens enjoy much less pleasure than they otherwise would. Here the fact that removing the regime, assuming an independent just cause for doing so, would allow the citizens greater pleasure does seem a relevant good, and it likewise seems relevant if the regime suppresses great art that would otherwise be produced. There is a difficulty about the pleasure of citizens on the winning side, since it also results from the achievement of a just cause. But we can exclude this pleasure either by counting only those goods that result from the just cause, more specifically, by preventing harms causally downstream from its grounding wrong, as in the Kuwait–Saudi oil example, or by saying that some types of good, such as pleasure at winning, are irrelevant to proportionality and last resort however they come about. Either way, there will be some goods that do not count toward a war's justification if they result only from a means to the war's just cause, but can count if they result from the achievement of that cause itself.[7]

This distinction among causal processes is not important for the categories of good discussed earlier. An independent just cause such as preventing aggression is not excluded from contributing to the proportionality and last resort conditions by the fact that it will result from a means to itself, and something similar holds for conditional causes. Much of the disarming of an aggressor occurs during the war. In order to expel him from occupied territory, we use military force that destroys much of his military, leaving him in a weakened condition for future aggressions; this was a significant effect of the Gulf War on Iraq. But the fact that the disarming results from the process of pursuing the just cause in no way eliminates it as a relevant good. The same holds for deterrence: would-be aggressors will not be deterred much by knowing that aggressions they attempt will be reversed; that shows only that the attempts will leave them no better off. They will be much more affected by knowing that the process of reversing their aggression will degrade their military and leave them worse off. The benefit of deterrence can even count in favor of a war, it seems to me, when its independent just cause will not be achieved. Imagine that a powerful nation elsewhere in the world has invaded a neighbor and that military intervention by us will not be able to reverse that aggression. But the intervention will demonstrate our commitment to fighting aggression and will deter other, weaker nations from aggressions they might otherwise attempt. Here the deterrent effect seems to me a relevant benefit and can even make the war on balance justified, though its independent just cause will not be achieved.

That conditional just causes such as deterrence count no matter how they are caused is some justification for linking them terminologically with independent just causes and separating them from goods such as pleasure and art, which are not just causes at all. It also explains why the just cause condition must not only identify relevant types of good but also make an initial assessment of their magnitude. If it did not, a war could in principle be justified given only a terrorist or humanitarian threat to one or two people: that threat would constitute an independent just cause, and facts about disarmament and deterrence could then make the war proportionate. But if war, no matter how beneficial, is impermissible without any good of a relevant type, it is surely also impermissible given only a trivial good. And that is ensured if independent just causes must reach a threshold of seriousness.

It seems, then, that just war theory divides the goods resulting from war into three categories. There are independent just causes, which a war must be in principle capable of causing and which always count toward its being proportional and a last resort; conditional just causes, which cannot justify war apart from an independent just cause but, given one, count in war's favor no matter how they are caused; and further goods such as pleasure, art, and economic growth, which count only when they result from the achievement of a just cause rather than directly from a means to it. This three-part division makes just war theory in a further respect more complex than consequentialism, and there are related complexities on the side of evils.

2.3 RELEVANT EVILS

The just war assessment of evils does not involve the same divisions as among goods. The theory may hold that the disappointment citizens on an unjust side feel at their nation's defeat does not count against the war's justification, but most other bad effects, including the pain of soldiers, economic dislocation, and the stifling of art, do. Nor does it matter how these effects relate to the just causes. The vast majority of a war's destructiveness results from the means to its just causes. It is the process of, say, expelling an aggressor from occupied territory that causes people to be killed and buildings destroyed, yet that in no way reduces their weight against the war's benefits in a proportionality assessment. Nor do evils count less if, unusually, they result from a war's just cause. Imagine that winning a war against aggression will set a precedent of resolving disputes by violence and so lead to more unjust wars in the future. If so, the fact that the bad effect is downstream from a just cause does not make it count any less against the war now.

However, just war theory does make a different division among evils, which parallels one in its account of the morality of waging war. Central to the latter is a discrimination condition whose standard versions say that force may be directed only at combatants and not at civilians. Civilians may sometimes be permissibly harmed as an unintended side-effect of force directed at a military target, or as what is called "collateral damage," and only if the harm is unavoidable and not disproportionate to the target's importance. Civilians therefore have in two respects higher moral status than soldiers: they may not be the targets of military force, and even collateral harm to them must meet a stringent proportionality standard.

The theory seems to use the same division in its account of the morality of resorting to war, so in assessing the evils a war will cause, it weighs harms to enemy civilians much more heavily than harms to enemy soldiers. Thus, the deaths of a hundred civilians, even if merely collateral, can count more against the permissibility of a war than the intended deaths of a hundred soldiers. This is reflected in criticisms of the Gulf and Iraq Wars, which focus much more on the number of Iraqi civilians killed than on the number of Iraqi soldiers killed. (The latter are often barely mentioned.) Consequentialism makes no such division: since a civilian's death is in itself no worse than a soldier's, the view weighs the two exactly equally. And Glover takes a similar line in *Causing Death and Saving Lives*, saying he will treat killing in war as morally on a par with other killing.[8] But just war theory distinguishes sharply between military and civilian deaths, and not only on the enemy side but also on ours. Imagine that to prevent terrorist attacks that will kill a certain number of our civilians, we must fight a war in which a somewhat greater number of our soldiers will be killed. I think the theory will permit this war, again because it weighs civilian lives more heavily. As Paul Christopher says, the deaths of soldiers should always count less than those of civilians because "risking one's life is part of what it means to be a soldier."[9] Our government may have moral responsibilities to its own soldiers that it does not have to enemy soldiers, so the deaths of the former should have more weight in its deliberations. But on each side the interests of soldiers, because they are soldiers, count less than those of civilians.

Discussions of the discrimination condition have proposed several justifications for the lower moral status of enemy soldiers: that they are a threat to our soldiers, that they are morally guilty, or that even if morally innocent they are engaged in an objectively unjust proceeding.[10] But none of these justifications captures the full moral division in just war theory, because it does not apply to our soldiers. Since they are fighting on our side, these soldiers are not a threat to us, and if we have a just cause, they are neither morally guilty nor engaged in an unjust proceeding. A justification that does yield the desired results is most clearly available if there are volunteer militaries on both sides of the war. Then we can say that by voluntarily entering military service, soldiers on both sides freely took on the status of soldiers and thereby accepted that they may be killed in the course of war, or of formally declared hostilities between their nation and another. By volunteering, in other words, they freely waived their right not to be killed in war and so made their killing in war not unjust. Their status is like that of boxers who, in agreeing to a bout, permit each other to do in the ring what outside it would be forbidden as assault. And just as the boxers' interaction is governed by formalized rules, so is the soldiers': there are uniforms to distinguish those who have waived and gained rights from those who have not, and formal declarations of war and ceasefires to indicate when the permissibility of killing begins and ends. This waiver-of-rights justification of the soldier–civilian divide is not without its difficulties. It assumes that soldiers can alienate their right not to be killed, which some may deny. It also applies less clearly to conscript soldiers or ones who entered the military only because they had no other acceptable career options, and may therefore support a lesser reduction in moral status for them. But I will assume that these difficulties can be overcome and that their having freely entered military service gives the best explanation of the lesser weight soldiers' deaths have on both sides of a war.[11]

That soldiers' deaths in war are not unjust does not mean they have no moral weight, because there are duties other than ones of justice. In particular, a state has special duties of care to its own soldiers, which mean its soldiers' deaths have only somewhat less weight than its civilians'. But the state has no such duties to enemy soldiers, and their moral status is therefore much lower. Exactly how much lower, however, is harder to determine.

The morality of waging war seems to give enemy soldiers' lives almost no weight. The conventional view, expressed for example by Michael Walzer, is that once war has begun, enemy soldiers are essentially free targets that one's own soldiers may kill at virtually any time.[12] One's soldiers may not kill them wantonly or to no purpose; that would violate a necessity condition in the morality of waging war. But if killing a large number of enemy soldiers is necessary to achieve just a small benefit, say, to save just one of our solders, the killing is permitted. (In the movie *Saving Private Ryan*, there is surely no number n such that Tom Hanks and his men must be careful not to kill more than n German soldiers in the course of saving Ryan.[13]) Now, if a similar view were adopted in the morality of resorting to war, the fact that a war will kill large numbers of enemy soldiers would count only marginally against its permissibility. That is an extreme view, and there are surely versions of just war theory that weigh enemy soldiers' deaths more heavily than that. But there is one context, generated by the hope of success condition, where the extreme view does seem to be accepted.

This condition implies that when a war has no chance of achieving any relevant goods it is morally impermissible, and this implication is compelling for offensive wars. Imagine, as many would deny, that there are economic just causes, such as the unjust abrogation of a trade agreement. If war in response to an economic wrong will do nothing to redress it, the war is pointless and wrong. The same holds for humanitarian causes. If intervening against an oppressive regime will not remove it or change its policies, that too is wrong. But the implication is more problematic for wars of national self-defense, where hopeless resistance is not morally condemned but is often viewed as permissible and even heroic. The best-known example is Belgium's resistance to Germany in 1914, which had no hope of success but is nonetheless widely admired. In this case, the defense may have had significant benefits: by slowing the German advance into France, it prevented a quick German victory on the Western front and so may have altered the final outcome of the war. But those who applaud "plucky little Belgium" usually have no such consideration in mind; they approve the defense apart from any effects. And there seems to be a similar permission in the morality of individual self-defense. Imagine that Mike Tyson confronts me in an alley and starts beating me up. It may be that nothing I can do—no feeble punches I throw in his direction—will do anything to stop the beating or reduce its severity. Am I therefore forbidden to throw those punches? May I not give him, however fruitlessly, my best shot? Consequentialism says no, but that is surely not the intuitive view. May the parallel view about military defense not also be intuitive?

I think the answer depends on the type of harm the defense will cause. If a hopeless resistance to invasion will involve bombing targets inside the aggressor's borders, thereby killing, even if collaterally, some of its citizens, the defense seems morally wrong. (Likewise in self-defense: if giving Mike Tyson my best shot involves swinging a stick that will seriously hurt a bystander, I may not do so.) But when we think of cases like that of Belgium, we imagine the defense being mounted entirely within the defending nation's borders, so it will kill only enemy soldiers. And in these cases, many have held that the defense is permissible. Since the defense will not do any good, the harms it causes enemy soldiers must, as on the extreme view, have no moral weight at all.[14]

Whether it adopts this extreme view or not, just war theory makes one distinction among types of evil by counting soldiers' deaths considerably less than civilian deaths. It may also distinguish between the causal mechanisms that produce evils. This is, however, another difficult issue.

Often the good or bad effects of war result directly from our acts, as when bombs we drop kill enemy civilians, but sometimes they depend on later choices by other agents. The question is whether, when this is so, it diminishes our responsibility for the effects, so they count less in assessing the proportionality of our resort to war. In the case of good effects, the answer seems to be no. If resisting aggression now will deter future aggression, that is only because would-be future aggressors will decide not to launch invasions they otherwise would have launched, but the role of these right choices does not stop our war's deterrent effects from counting fully in its favor. The issue is more difficult for evil effects, however, since many hold that the intervention of another's wrongful choice does diminish one's responsibility for resulting harms, as in the legal principle *novus actus interveniens*. And this possibility can arise often in war. Imagine, to take the most compelling example, that if we fight and win a war with a just cause, resentful elements on the enemy side will with no moral excuse launch suicide attacks against our civilians. Setting aside the deaths of the civilians, does the fact that the war will lead to the deaths of the suicide bombers count morally against it? Surely one wants to say no. The bombers' deaths result from their wrong choices and are therefore their responsibility, not ours. But other cases are more difficult. Imagine that in a short war we bomb our enemy's infrastructure, damaging its electricity-generating plants. This damage would cause only limited harm to civilians if the enemy state repaired the plants immediately after the war, as it has a moral duty to do. But it does not do so, preferring to spend its limited resources on rebuilding its military, with the result that many more civilians die. In assessing the proportionality of our resort to war, do we count all the deaths that resulted from it given our enemy's immoral behavior, or only the smaller number that would have resulted had our enemy acted as it should?

A similar issue, though about others' earlier choices, arises in wars against insurgents who hide among a civilian population, as the Viet Cong

did during the Vietnam War, or who purposely locate military installations among civilians, as Hezbollah did when attacking Israel in 2006. If,
given these tactics, effective military action against the insurgents will
inevitably cause civilian deaths, do those deaths count fully against the
action's proportionality or are they discounted for the enemy's wrongful
contribution? The international law of war seems to say they are not discounted. Though it forbids placing military installations among civilians,
it holds that the violation by one side of its obligations in war does not
release the other side from any of its obligations.[15] But the US and Israeli
militaries seem to take the opposite view, saying that if an enemy hides
among a civilian population, that enemy brings the civilians into the line
of fire and so is responsible for their deaths. Early in the Iraq War, for
example, a fight outside Nasiriyah moved into the city when Iraqi forces
retreated there, with resulting civilian casualties. The commander of a US
artillery battalion firing on Nasiriyah "placed responsibility for any civilian deaths on the Iraqi soldiers who drew the marines into the populated
areas," saying "We will engage the enemy wherever he is."[16] Does just war
theory follow international law on this issue or discount evil consequences
that depend on others' wrong choices?

I find this a difficult issue, both in itself and as about what just war theory says. I suspect that if they consider the above cases intuitively, people
will have conflicting views about them. Some will say an enemy's failure
to repair power plants after a war does not affect the proportionality of
the original bombing of them while others will say it does, and there will
be similar disagreements about the deaths of civilians in attacks on insurgents. Nor do abstract principles clearly settle the issue. On one side, we
can say that we must make our moral judgments in the world as we find
it, and not ignore the predictable effects of a choice we can make because
we disapprove of some other causal factors that will help produce them.
On the other, we can say that agents should not be morally protected by
their bad characters; the fact that they will bomb civilians or let children
die if we take some otherwise justified action against them should not
make that action wrong. Because I cannot resolve this issue, I have to
leave undetermined what just war theory says about it. The issue is vitally
important for assessing particular wars: it will make a large difference to
our assessment of, for example, Israel's 2006 actions against Hezbollah if
the resulting deaths of Lebanese civilians count fully or only partly against
it. But I will leave this issue and move on to how just war theory weighs
goods and evils against each other.

2.4 WEIGHING GOODS AND EVILS

Consequentialism weighs goods and evils equally, holding that a war is
wrong if it will cause even slightly more evil than good or, on the stricter
criterion, if its net outcome is even slightly worse than some alternative's.

The just war "proportionality" requirement can also require equal weighing of goods and evils, but the term is sufficiently elastic to allow two contrary alternatives.

The first weighs good effects somewhat more heavily than bad ones, so a war can be proportionate even if it causes somewhat, though not a great deal, more evil than good. This alternative parallels the morality of individual self-defense, whose standard versions allow a defender to use somewhat more force than is threatened against her. Thus, on most views she may kill not only to prevent herself from being killed but also to prevent herself from being raped, forcibly confined for a long period, or caused serious injury. A similar view has been applied to war by Douglas Lackey. Though he joins consequentialism in counting all the good and bad effects of war, he considers a war proportionate "unless it produces a great deal more harm than good," thereby weighing goods somewhat or even significantly more heavily than evils.[17]

The contrary alternative counts evils more heavily, so a war is proportionate only if its good effects are considerably greater than its bad ones. This view parallels the central claim of moderate deontological moralities. They hold that an otherwise forbidden act such as killing an innocent person can sometimes be permitted, but only if it causes a great deal more good than harm, for example, if it allows not just one or two but a thousand extra people to be saved. And a parallel view says the resort to war is permitted only if it will cause a great deal more good than evil. Does just war theory employ this last view when judging proportionality, the contrary one that weighs goods more heavily, or the view that weighs values equally?

These questions only make sense given a common scale for measuring goods and evils, and that is not always available. Imagine that a war that will preserve our nation's sovereignty but collaterally kill 10,000 enemy citizens is morally permissible. We could say this is because the value of sovereignty equals that of 10,000 civilian lives and goods and evils weigh equally, or because the value of sovereignty equals that of 5,000 lives and goods count more. But there is no real difference between these explanations, because there is no independent scale for comparing sovereignty and lives. In cases like this, therefore, the issue of how values are weighed does not really arise. Sometimes, however, there is something like an independent scale. The goods and evils at stake in war are also the subjects of choice outside war, when the evils do not result from killing, and we can ask whether just war theory weighs either more heavily than would be appropriate in a nonwar context. The answer is that it sometimes does the one, sometimes does the other, and sometimes weighs the same as in peacetime.

For an example of the last possibility, imagine that to prevent terrorist attacks that will kill a certain number of our civilians, we must fight a war in which a certain other number of our civilians will be killed by enemy bombing. Here it seems the two sets of lives weigh equally. If the war will cost more civilian lives than it will save, it is surely morally wrong, but if it will save more lives, it may be right. The same holds for civilian lives in another nation. Imagine that to remove an oppressive regime that will murder a certain number of its citizens, we must fight a war in the aftermath of which an insurgency will kill another number of citizens. Setting aside issues of intervening agency, it again seems that the two sets of lives weigh equally: if the war will result in more civilian deaths overall, it is wrong.

In these examples, the deaths are all on the same side of the war, but the issue is more complicated when they are on different sides. This is because most who accept just war theory do not hold, as standard versions of consequentialism do, that governments must always be impartial between their own and foreign citizens. On the contrary, most accept the nationalist view that governments may and even should give more weight to their own citizens' interests, so in framing trade and immigration policy, for example, they should care most about effects on their current citizens. If just war theory applied this view unaltered in the context of war, it would give interests on one's own side considerably more weight than enemy interests. And since, especially in a defensive war, many of the relevant goods are on one's own side and of the evils on the other, this would mean giving good effects considerably more weight. But it seems to me that the theory does not apply the nationalist view unaltered: it makes two adjustments, one in each direction.

Imagine that to prevent terrorist attacks that will kill a certain number of our citizens, we must fight a war in which we will collaterally kill a certain number of enemy civilians. I think the just war view will give some extra weight to the enemy civilians' deaths because they will result from our acts, or because we will directly cause them. If a government has a choice between saving a few of its own citizens from a natural disaster and saving many more of another nation's citizens, it may prefer saving its own citizens. But it cannot do the same if saving a few of its own citizens from a disaster requires killing many of another nation's; then the saving is wrong. The degree of extra weight given enemy deaths here is not as great as when a moderate deontology allows deliberately killing an innocent person only if that is necessary to save some very large number of other lives. This is because the main deontological distinction in just war theory is not between causing harm and allowing it; it is between intending harm and merely foreseeing it, and when we kill enemy civilians collaterally we merely foresee their deaths. But the distinction between killing and allowing to die seems to retain some moral force; it is not simply ignored. And that means the theory gives some extra weight to enemy deaths we directly cause. It may be that, given the nationalist view, our nation may still show some preference on balance for its own citizens' good, so a war to protect them from terrorism may be permissible even if it collaterally kills a somewhat greater number of enemy civilians. Thus, the Afghanistan War may have been justified even if it collaterally killed somewhat more

Afghan civilians than it saved American civilians. But the degree of preference allowed here is far less than in trade, immigration, or other policies. Given a baseline of the normally allowed degree of nationalist preference, just war theory gives somewhat more weight here to evils than to goods, because the evils result from what we actively do.

But the theory makes the opposite adjustment for enemy soldiers' deaths. Outside war these soldiers have no special moral status. If our government has a choice between saving some of its own soldiers from dying in an accident and saving enemy soldiers, it may and even should, as before, prefer its own soldiers. But the degree of preference allowed here is no more nor less than for civilians, since outside war soldiers are in effect civilians. Within war, however, enemy soldiers have a drastically reduced status, and may be killed for almost any purpose. The best justification for this, I have argued, is that by freely entering military service they have waived their right not to be killed and so made their killing not unjust. If so, whereas the deaths of enemy civilians we kill in war have greater moral weight than they would in peacetime cases of saving, the deaths of enemy soldiers have much less. And this means that just war theory takes, in different contexts, all three possible views about the weighing of goods and evils. When comparing civilian lives on the same side of the war, it weighs goods and evils equally; when weighing the deaths of enemy civilians whom we will kill collaterally against the benefits of war, it gives the former more weight than it would outside war, or when the civilians would not be killed by us; and when weighing the deaths of enemy soldiers we kill against the benefits of war, it gives them drastically less weight.

2.5 JUST WAR VERSUS CONSEQUENTIALISM

These various points about the just war consequence conditions help explain how the theory reaches its conclusions about particular wars, but they also allow a clearer contrast between it and consequentialism, in particular as to which is more permissive. The answer turns out to be complex, going one way on some issues and the opposite way on others.

Let us begin with the issue of relevant goods. That just war theory requires a war to have a just cause makes it in an important respect less permissive than consequentialism. If a war will produce no goods of a type that constitute an independent just cause but will produce many goods of other kinds, consequentialism may approve the war while just war theory does not. Thus, consequentialism may approve an aggressive war that will significantly deter potential aggressors while just war theory does not. And this difference is accentuated by the theory's excluding certain goods from its proportionality assessment because they do not result from the achievement of a just cause. Thus, just war theory will not count even a significant boost to world GDP resulting from the process

of fighting a war as relevant to the war's justification, whereas consequentialism will. But the very same feature that makes just war theory less
permissive about the proportionality condition makes it more permissive
about the last resort condition. Some critics say that the Gulf and Iraq
Wars were wrong because the billions of dollars they cost would have
done more good if spent in other ways, say, on development aid to Africa.
This is a legitimate criticism by consequentialist lights, if these require a
war to have the best outcome possible. But it is not so according to just
war theory. If the goods relevant to the last resort condition are only those
in a war's independent and conditional just causes and in states causally
downstream from them, then the benefits of aid to Africa are not relevant to assessing the Gulf and Iraq Wars, and alternatives that produce
them need not be considered in determining whether those wars were
last resorts. The theory does not compare war with all possible alternatives, but only with ones that can achieve the same relevant goods, which
usually means only with diplomatic or other responses to the same initial
wrong. And requiring war to be the best of a small set of alternatives is less
demanding than requiring it to be the best of a large set. On the just war
view, the Gulf War was indeed wrong if there was a less destructive way
of expelling Iraq from Kuwait, but not merely if some policy unrelated to
Kuwait would have had better overall consequences.

When we turn to relevant evils, we again find a mixture of effects. Just
war theory's main distinction here is between harms to soldiers and to civilians, and the greater moral protection it gives civilians makes it in several
respects less permissive than consequentialism. During war, consequentialism can approve acts that intentionally kill civilians if those acts have sufficiently good effects. Thus, if Truman was right that bombing Hiroshima
and Nagasaki saved hundreds of thousands of soldiers from being killed
in an invasion of Japan, consequentialism can approve that bombing.
Glover himself condemns the bombing, but mainly on the consequentialist ground that there were less destructive alternatives that would have
ended the war as effectively. And he is not in principle opposed to targeting civilians, allowing that in other circumstances, such as those early in
the war against Nazi Germany, it can be morally permitted. But absolutist
versions of just war theory never allow the intentional killing of civilians,
and even moderate versions set a much higher threshold for such killing
than consequentialism does, requiring benefits that are not just slightly
but massively better·than any alternative, so the killing is needed to avert
disaster. Given the extra protection they give civilians, therefore, all versions of just war theory are less likely to permit the targeting of civilians
than consequentialism is, and this difference about the morality of waging
war extends to that of resorting to war. Just war theory holds that resorting
to war is permitted only if the war will be fought in accordance with all
the rules governing the waging of war. If there is a just cause that can be
achieved only by targeting enemy civilians, consequentialism may approve
a war in pursuit of it while just war theory does not.

Again, however, other features of just war theory have the opposite effect. If its adherents usually allow nations to prefer their own citizens' interests to those of foreigners, then even if the degree of preference allowed is reduced when enemy civilians will be killed rather than allowed to die, the theory may approve wars that standard consequentialism does not, for example, wars that will collaterally kill a somewhat greater number of enemy civilians while saving a smaller number of our civilians. An even more strongly permissive feature is the drastically reduced weight the theory gives to enemy soldiers' lives. Since consequentialism weighs these soldiers' lives equally against enemy and even our civilians' lives, it finds a major moral objection to war in the deaths it causes enemy soldiers, one as strong as any involving deaths on our side. But just war theory does not do the same, giving enemy soldiers' lives minimal weight in the morality of waging war and also, if not quite as clearly, in that of resorting to war. If a war in pursuit of a just cause will kill many enemy soldiers, this is a serious moral objection to it by consequentialist lights, but not on the just war view. In *Causing Death and Saving Lives*, Glover takes a broadly consequentialist line, but also gives weight to individual autonomy as a value competing with overall well-being. And I have argued that the best justification for giving reduced weight to soldiers' lives derives precisely from their having freely or autonomously waived their right not to be killed in war. The autonomy involved here is not quite like that Glover finds important in cases of suicide or voluntary euthanasia, since it does not involve a positive desire to die. But if he gives some moral weight to autonomy in general, should he not feel some sympathy for a feature of just war theory that likewise turns on the value of autonomy? In any case, that theory's strong discounting of enemy soldiers' deaths makes it much more permissive than consequentialism about wars in which many such soldiers will be killed. By consequentialist lights, a war in defense of national self-determination that will kill many enemy soldiers may not be justified, whereas by just war lights it is.

Just war theory will also be more permissive if, in assessing wars for proportionality, it discounts evils that depend in part on others' wrongful agency, such as their locating military installations among their civilians. Consequentialism ignores facts about others' agency, looking only at what will actually follow from a choice we can make. If just war theory does attend to such facts, which admittedly is not clear, it will in another way be more likely to find wars proportionate and therefore permissible.

So each of just war theory and consequentialism is in some respects less permissive than the other and in some respects more so. Just war theory is less permissive about the goods that can permissibly be sought by war and about the use of force against civilians, but more permissive when it compares war with alternatives, about the use of force against soldiers, and perhaps about intervening agency. But then a complex comparison between just war theory and a more consequentialist approach like Glover's is what we should expect if the theory has the complex elements that this chapter has tried to describe. Any credible theory of the morality of war will assess particular wars largely in light of their consequences, but there is more than one way to do this: not just the theoretically simple way of consequentialism, but the much more complex one of just war theory as well. Some, perhaps including Glover, may say the just war complexities are casuistical, their too fine distinctions diverting attention from the central question of how many people are harmed and how badly. And it is not the aim of this chapter to argue that this view is wrong. It is only to explain how there is a different approach, which assesses the consequences of war in a less straightforward way and has at least an intuitive integrity and some intuitive appeal.

Notes

1. Jonathan Glover, *Causing Death and Saving Lives* (Harmondsworth: Penguin, 1977), Ch. 19; *Humanity: A Moral History of the Twentieth Century* (London: Jonathan Cape, 1999).

2. In *Humanity*, Glover grants that the intention/foresight distinction has intuitive appeal (84), but defends the conclusions others draw from it mainly on different, more consequentialist grounds.

3. For accessible accounts of just war theory, see Joseph C. McKenna, "Ethics and War: A Catholic View," *American Political Science Review* 54 (1966): 647–58; and US Catholic Bishops, *The Challenge of Peace: God's Promise and Our Response*, reprinted in Jean Bethke Elshtain, ed., *Just War Theory* (New York: New York University Press, 1992), 77–168.

4. The Canadian Charter of Rights and Freedoms allows legislation that infringes citizens' rights only if it passes an "Oakes test" with four parts. The legislation must have a "pressing and substantial objective," or be aimed at a relevant type of good, as in the just cause condition; it must be "rationally connected" to that good, or have a reasonable hope of achieving it; it must pass a "minimal impairment" condition, or not infringe rights more than is necessary to achieve the good; and the cost of the infringement must not be disproportionate to the good achieved. For a discussion that notes the parallel with just war theory, see L. W. Sumner, *The Hateful and the Obscene* (Toronto: University of Toronto Press, 2004), 56, 63–69, 212n9, 214n31.

5. This version is defended in David Mellow, *A Critique of Just War Theory* (Ph.D. diss., University of Calgary, 2003); and Jeff McMahan, "Just Cause for War," *Ethics and International Affairs* 19 (2005): 1–21.

6. The conditional/independent terminology comes from McMahan, "Just Cause for War." The distinction was originally introduced, though using different language, in McMahan and Robert McKim, "The Just War and the Gulf War," *Canadian Journal of Philosophy* 23 (1993): 501–41, 502–06.

7. This causal distinction is similar to one used by F. M. Kamm to explain when deontological moralities do and do not allow acts that produce a lesser evil in the course of producing a greater good. Kamm applies the distinction to the production of evils, saying an act is forbidden if the lesser evil results from a means to the greater good, but not if it results from that good itself or from its non-causal flip side (F. M. Kamm, *Morality/Mortality, Vol. II: Rights, Duties, and Status*

(New York: Oxford University Press, 1996), Ch. 7). By contrast, I am applying the distinction to the production of goods.

8. Glover, *Causing Death and Saving Lives*, 252.

9. Paul Christopher, *The Ethics of War and Peace: An Introduction to Legal and Moral Issues*, 2nd ed. (Upper Saddle River, NJ: Prentice-Hall, 1999), 165.

10. For these justifications, see, for example, Thomas Nagel, "War and Massacre," *Philosophy and Public Affairs* 1 (1972): 123–44, 138–39, and Robert Fullinwider, "War and Innocence," *Philosophy and Public Affairs* 5 (1975): 90–97, 94; Jeff McMahan, "Innocence, Self-Defense, and Killing in War," *Journal of Political Philosophy* 2 (1994): 193–221; and G. E. M. Anscombe, "War and Murder," in her *Collected Philosophical Papers, Vol. III: Ethics, Religion, and Politics* (Minneapolis, MN: University of Minnesota Press, 1981), 53.

11. In his influential discussion, Michael Walzer says an enemy soldier is a legitimate target of force because "he has allowed himself to be made into a dangerous man" (*Just and Unjust Wars*, 2nd ed. (New York: Basic Books, 1992), 145). Sometimes Walzer emphasizes the "dangerous man" part of this phrase, as if it is just the threat the soldier poses that lowers his moral status. At other times he emphasizes the "allowed himself," which he thinks applies even when the soldier's options were few; this brings his justification closer to the waiver-of-rights one.

12. Walzer, *Just and Unjust Wars*, 138–51.

13. This example is not decisive, since in killing German soldiers Hanks also prevents them from killing later in the war. A clearer test-case is saving one of our soldiers at the very end of a war, when there is little chance the enemy soldiers will kill or engage in any military activity later. Perhaps some will say there is a relevant number *n* here, but I am confident the military will say there is not.

14. McKenna defends the Belgian defense by saying, "In extreme cases the moral value of national martyrdom may compensate for the destruction of unsuccessful war" ("Ethics and War: A Catholic View," 651). But this argument begs the question, since we do not call an act one of "martyrdom" unless we think it already on other grounds right. ("Martyrdom operation" is hardly a neutral description of the September 11, 2001 attacks.) On the other side, it may be objected that even defense within one's borders will harm enemy civilians, by causing pain to the families of dead soldiers, eliminating future productive workers, and so on. But a defender of the Belgian action can say there is a kind of estoppel: if the soldiers' deaths are not a relevant evil, any harms causally downstream from them are also not relevant.

15. *1977 Geneva Protocol I Additional to the Geneva Conventions of 12 August 1949, and Relating to the Protection of Victims of International Armed Conflicts*, Art. 51 (7–8), in *Documents on the Laws of War*, 3rd ed., ed. Adam Roberts and Richard Guelff (Oxford: Oxford University Press, 2000), 449.

16. "Marines Wade into Dreaded Urban Battle," *The Globe and Mail*, Mar. 25, 2003 (New York Times Service). For a similar view about the Vietnam War, see Paul Ramsey, *The Just War: Force and Political Responsibility* (New York: Scribner's, 1968), 47, and William V. O'Brien, *The Conduct of a Just and Limited War* (New York: Praeger, 1981), 100; and about Israel, see Asa Kasher and Amos Yadlin, "Military Ethics of Fighting Terror: An Israeli Perspective," *Journal of Military Ethics* 4 (2005): 3–32, 17–21.

17. Douglas Lackey, *The Ethics of War and Peace* (Englewood Cliffs, NJ: Prentice-Hall, 1989), 40–41.

3

Humanitarian Intervention, Consent, and Proportionality

Jeff McMahan

3.1 INTRODUCTION

However much one may wish for nonviolent solutions to the problems of unjust and unrestrained human violence that Glover explores in *Humanity*, some of those problems at present require violent responses. One cannot read his account of the Clinton administration's campaign to sabotage efforts to stop the massacre in Rwanda in 1994—a campaign motivated by fear that American involvement would cost American lives and therefore votes—without concluding that Glover himself believes that military intervention was morally required in that case.

Military intervention in another state that is intended to stop one group within that state from brutally persecuting or violating the human rights of members of another group is now known as "humanitarian intervention." Those against whom the intervention is directed are almost always the government and its supporters, though this is not a necessary feature of humanitarian intervention. It is, however, a conceptual condition of humanitarian intervention that it does not occur at the request or with the consent of the government. The use of force within another state with the consent of the government counts as assistance rather than intervention. The principal reason that humanitarian intervention is contentious is that it seems to violate the target state's sovereign right to control its own domestic affairs.

Because humanitarian intervention is a response to human rights violations within the target state, it is regarded as altogether different from wars of defense against aggression. Indeed, since aggression is normally understood to be war against a state that has not attacked another state, humanitarian intervention itself usually constitutes aggression. Yet, it can happen that a state will engage simultaneously in external aggression and internal oppression, so that a war against it could be intended to stop both the aggression and the domestic violation of human rights. Such a

44

war would not be aggression, but would be both a war of defense *and* an instance of humanitarian intervention. So not all instances of humanitarian intervention count as aggression.

There are two broad questions about the morality of humanitarian intervention. The first is whether humanitarian intervention can be *permissible* and if so what are the conditions of its permissibility. The second is whether it can be morally *required* and if so in what conditions, of whom, and at what cost. I will address both these questions.

In earlier debates, the question of permissibility was paramount. The reason why this was so is primarily historical. For a considerable period prior to the twentieth century, there were no legal constraints on the resort to war. According to a certain view of states that is traceable to the Treaty of Westphalia of 1648 and that thereafter achieved orthodox status within the theory of international relations, states are sovereign individuals that are not subject to any authority higher than themselves. By the nineteenth century, the notion of state sovereignty had become so inflated that it was generally accepted that states had the sovereign prerogative, both legally and morally, to go to war whenever it was in their interest to do so. There was therefore no special question about the permissibility of war for humanitarian reasons. Yet, it was also widely believed that war motivated by humanitarian concerns would simply never occur because states were thought to act only for reasons of national interest. Humanitarian intervention was thus not a significant issue.

During the twentieth century, however, conditions changed. In the aftermath of World War I, the importance of regulating not only the conduct of war but also the resort to war became widely recognized. States continued to be viewed as sovereign individuals, but the catalogue of their sovereign rights was revised: the right to make war was replaced by the right against intervention. Because states were regarded as individuals, it was natural to suppose that their relations must be governed by the same moral principles that govern relations among persons. Around the turn of the century, one such principle that had come to be widely accepted among liberal thinkers was J. S. Mill's "harm principle," which is

> that the sole end for which mankind are warranted, individually or collectively, in interfering with the liberty of action of any of their number, is self-protection. That the only purpose for which power can be rightfully exercised over any member of a civilized community, against his will, is to prevent harm to others. His own good, either physical or moral, is not sufficient warrant.[1]

Theorists of international relations embraced a collectivist analogue of this principle, according to which domestic violence was to be understood as analogous to a person's harming herself. Intervention to prevent a state from harming itself was therefore objectionably paternalistic. Michael Walzer, who has offered a qualified endorsement of this general mode of reasoning, puts the point this way: "As with individuals, so with sovereign

states: there are things we cannot do to them, even for their own ostensible good."[2]

After World War II, the UN Charter prohibited the resort to war except
in defense against aggression or with the authorization of the Security
Council. Humanitarian goals were ruled out as justifications for war
unless they were pursued either with the authorization of the Council
or as ancillary goals in a war of defense against aggression. During the
Cold War, the effective ban on humanitarian intervention seemed to be
vindicated by the way the United States and the Soviet Union carried out
their self-interested acts of aggression behind a veil of pretended altruism
that was usually transparent to all but their own citizens. Yet, near the
end of the twentieth century, conditions changed in important ways. The
Cold War ended and the United States was denied the pretext that its
predatory interventions were intended to protect people in other states
from subversion by domestic agents whose ultimate allegiance was to the
Soviet Union. A corollary of the end of the Cold War was the breakup
of the Soviet Union, which facilitated the emergence of nationalist and
secessionist movements in various regions, particularly in states where
they had hitherto been held in check by repressive communist governments that, with the collapse of Soviet communism, lost their grip on
power. At the close of the century, many governments throughout the
world were murdering and torturing their own citizens in great numbers,
often without the tangible benefits to the great powers that these activities had brought during the Cold War. Campaigns of genocide were being
carried out in such places as Rwanda, Yugoslavia, and Sudan, and the traditional obstacles to obtaining knowledge of such events and to address-
ing them effectively by military means were steadily diminishing. In these
altered conditions, many of which persist to the present, most observers
came to appreciate that the issue of humanitarian intervention urgently
required rethinking.

Yet, even in these conditions, the familiar objections to humanitarian intervention based on the notion of state sovereignty retain considerable force. The ultimate goal of most nationalist movements is to have
their own sovereign state. And particularly for smaller, weaker nations,
the doctrine of state sovereignty offers some protection for their ability to be collectively self-determining. Even when the process of collective self-determination within a state involves violent domestic conflict,
the doctrine of state sovereignty may still be right to prohibit external
intervention, for it is often vital to collective self-determination that the
outcome of a domestic conflict, even one that rises to the level of civil
war, should be determined by the internal balance of forces rather than
by external intervention. As Michael Walzer puts it, "The outcome of
civil wars should reflect not the relative strength of the intervening states,
but the local alignment of forces."[3] That this can be true even in a profoundly divided society is nicely illustrated in Graham Greene's novel,
The Comedians, in which a Haitian character who risks his life in opposing

the dictatorship of "Papa Doc" Duvalier nevertheless remarks that "I'm not sure I wouldn't fight for Papa Doc if the Marines came. At least he's Haitian. No, the job has to be done with our own hands."[4]

The Haitian rebel regards himself and his allies as sharing a collective identity and a collective fate with Papa Doc and his supporters. They all accept that they will live together in a common territory as a single nation. The issues in dispute concern the character of their association and the distribution of power among them, and these are matters to be properly decided among themselves, not by those outside their community.

Yet, as nationalist and secessionist conflicts in the 1990s vividly demonstrated, states sometimes comprise ethnic and political communities that are so estranged and antagonistic as not to constitute a single nation or community. These states cannot properly be called nation-states, but are instead multinational states. Particularly during the communist era, different nations were often yoked together with apparent success by a latent threat of force. Yet, in many instances, and most spectacularly of course in Yugoslavia and the Soviet Union itself, when the centralizing power disappeared, the decades of "nation building" within the borders of the state were exposed as failures. In Yugoslavia, for example, it turned out that the Serbs, Croats, and Bosnian Muslims did not, after all, constitute a single nation. At least after the initial conflicts had erupted, there was no single collective "self" whose self-determination was at issue within the borders of the state. There were, rather, various collective selves— various self-identified and exclusionary national groups—whose efforts at self-determination were mutually incompatible. External intervention in Yugoslavia, therefore, would not have violated the right of collective self-determination of a single people, but would instead have advanced the self-determination of one or more groups while thwarting the self-determination of others.

Thwarting a group's efforts at self-determination does not, moreover, necessarily involve violating the group's right to self-determination. If, for example, external agents had intervened militarily to prevent the Bosnian Serbs from massacring Bosnian Muslims in the mid-1990s, that would not have violated any right the Serbs might have had to collective self-determination, for the right to self-determination does not encompass a component right to persecute, expel, or massacre innocent members of another group. Such acts are not protected by any right.

In some states that contain more than one nation, the government is aligned with, and disproportionately representative of, one nation only. If the national group that controls the government begins to violate the human rights of the members of one or more other national groups, there are then two general reasons why external intervention against the government that *would* violate the state's legal sovereignty would *not* violate the right of collective self-determination of any group. When a society is divided and the government is representative of one group only rather than of the citizenry as a whole, intervention against it does not violate a right of collective self-determination of the citizenry, for the citizenry does not constitute a collective self. Nor does intervention against the government violate the right of collective self-determination of the group that the government does represent, provided that it is limited to action to which the government and its supporters have made themselves liable through the violation of the human rights of the members of other groups.[5]

Even in cases of this sort, however, it might be better, at least in current conditions, to have a legal or conventional rule that prohibits humanitarian intervention that is not approved by the Security Council. For powerful states continue to have various self-interested reasons for intervening militarily in weaker states, and a claim to be acting for humanitarian reasons can provide a convenient pretext for an essentially predatory intervention. Even so, there have been and will continue to be instances in which humanitarian intervention is morally justified even in the absence of authorization by the Security Council. The Security Council is not an impartial body and its ability to authorize a morally justified humanitarian intervention can be blocked by the veto of a single permanent member that is allied to the state that would be the target of the intervention. So even if humanitarian intervention ought to be prohibited by international law, the question remains in what conditions it might be morally permissible, or even morally necessary, to violate the law.

3.2 CONSENT

I suggest that it is in general a condition of the moral permissibility of humanitarian intervention that the ostensible beneficiaries should clearly welcome it.[6] The satisfaction of this condition provides some evidence that the intervening state can be trusted not to abuse the power it will acquire by intervening—or at least that the potential beneficiaries regard their situation as sufficiently desperate that they are willing to risk that abuse as the cost of being rescued. It also provides some evidence, though not much, that the intervention does not violate the right of collective self-determination of a single nation. For the willingness of the potential beneficiaries to risk the subordination both of themselves and of their oppressors to the intervening power in order to be rescued suggests that they may not identify themselves as members of the national and political community constituted by the government and its supporters. Yet a group's desire for external assistance in a struggle with a rival group certainly does not show that the two groups do not together constitute a single nation or political community. Even though the Haitian rebels in Greene's story are averse to American intervention on their behalf, dictators such as Papa Doc Duvalier have typically welcomed external military assistance in fighting their domestic foes, even when the conflict is clearly within a single national community rather than between different nations.

I will refer to the claim that it is in general a condition of justified humanitarian intervention that the beneficiaries should welcome it as the "requirement of consent"—though of course there is never any possibility that a persecuted community as a whole could explicitly give its actual consent to intervention on its behalf, and even if it could, the desire for intervention among the individual members of such a community is never universal. So the relevant requirement is much weaker and more nebulous than actual unanimous consent among the potential beneficiaries. It is something more like a widespread or general desire for intervention.

There is a parallel requirement of consent that governs third-party defense of individuals, or what is sometimes called "other-defense," though it is seldom discussed because there is a standing presumption that a person who is under unjust attack must welcome defensive assistance. But in the rare cases in which there is reason to doubt that presumption, and especially in cases in which the victim or potential victim of an attack explicitly forbids intervention on her behalf, the plausibility of the requirement of consent is intuitively obvious. Suppose, for example, that a woman is being lethally assaulted by her own child, who can be prevented from killing her only by being killed. If a third party could save her, but she pleads with this person not to kill her child, it seems intuitively plausible to suppose that it would be wrong to kill her child, assuming that he could afterward be rendered harmless, even if he is culpable for his action. The defensive killing of the child by a third party might not wrong the child, or violate his rights, but it would nevertheless be unjustified because it would wrong *the mother.*

In the individual case, the presumption is that the potential victim would welcome defensive assistance and thus that if self-defense is permissible, so is third-party defense. This presumption is seldom overturned unless the potential victim explicitly rejects the offer of assistance. But given that states have often sought to justify unjust interventions motivated by national self-interest by claiming that they were actually instances of humanitarian intervention, the presumption in the case of humanitarian intervention must be that the ostensible beneficiaries do *not* want a war fought by a foreign power allegedly for their benefit. This presumption is of course defeasible even in the absence of any overt indications of consent. In Rwanda in 1994, for example, when hundreds of thousands of ethnic Tutsi were being butchered with machetes by the Hutu majority, there could be no doubt that the Tutsi would have welcomed military intervention by the United States or any other major power. They had no reason to fear the loss of collective self-determination to an intervening power because Rwanda was too insignificant for any major power to have had an interest in dominating it—which of course explains why no major power could be bothered to intervene, even though the risks involved in intervening were very low.

The case of Rwanda, where there was no humanitarian intervention, can be instructively compared with the continuing war in Iraq, which the

Bush administration defended as an instance of humanitarian intervention, at least after the claims about weapons of mass destruction began to seem increasingly implausible. The situation in Iraq was a paradigm case in which the presumption was against intervention in the absence of clear and compelling evidence that the majority of domestic victims of the Baathist regime were receptive to such an intervention. The territory that is now Iraq has a long history of subjugation to and exploitation by Western powers, in part because of its extensive oilfields, on which Western economies depend. Although the Baathist regime had earlier committed large-scale massacres when it was an ally of the United States, and later did so again in response to a Shiite uprising encouraged but abandoned by the United States in the aftermath of the Gulf War, there were no massacres or large-scale expulsions in progress or in prospect at the time of the invasion. Despite the routine killing and torturing of political opponents characteristic of dictatorships in that region, the vast majority of Iraqis were able to live their daily lives in comparative security. Because of this, there were, prior to the U.S. invasion, no indications that a majority of Iraqis, or even a majority of non-Sunni Iraqis, welcomed a war to overthrow the government of Saddam Hussein. It may well be true that the great majority of non-Sunni Iraqis hated the Baathist regime—they certainly had reason to—but that is quite different from wanting the regime to be overthrown by means of war, especially a war fought by a foreign power, and especially if the foreign power is the United States. Although most Americans seemed to have difficulty remembering the recent history of American relations with Iraq, there can have been few Iraqis who were unaware that those who claimed to be their liberators were the same people who, a little over a decade earlier, had bombed their capital, destroyed the country's civilian infrastructure, and insisted on the continuing imposition of economic sanctions that caused the deaths of hundreds of thousands more Iraqis, and kept many others who had survived the war in deepest misery afterward. They even noticed that this second war fought in their country was led by the son of the man who had led the first, and that both were members of an American dynasty founded on oil wealth. They had little reason to trust the motives of the Bush administration in invading their country.

The most significant reason why the war in Iraq, considered as a putative instance of humanitarian intervention, illustrates the plausibility of the requirement of consent derives from the effects of the war so far. Although estimates vary considerably, virtually all observers accept that at least 100,000 Iraqi civilians have been killed in the course of the war since its inception in 2003. More than two million have fled the country and are living as refugees in neighboring countries, and nearly three million others have become refugees within the country, having sought safety in areas where the fighting has been less intense. Given that the prewar population of Iraq was fewer than 30 million, these figures mean that at least one in every 300 civilians has been killed while another seventeen percent of the population have fled their homes in an effort to avoid being killed. The number of seriously wounded and maimed of course significantly exceeds the number killed.

This is what happens when a modern war is fought in the cities and towns in which people live. Because wars of humanitarian intervention are directed against domestically repressive governments and their armed protectors, they are of necessity fought in the territory in which the potential beneficiaries live, and it is entirely predictable that such governments will seek to impose moral restraints on the intervening forces by forcing them to fight in the areas in which those whom they are trying to rescue are concentrated. So even if a war that is promoted as an instance of humanitarian intervention is genuinely motivated by humanitarian concerns, it can seldom promise rescue without also endangering its intended beneficiaries. In Iraq, the harms caused to the supposed beneficiaries have been vast and dreadful. It is wrong to expose people to the risk of such harm in the absence of compelling evidence that they are willing to accept that risk for the sake of the promised benefits. In Iraq, as I noted, there was no such evidence. Nor was any sought. The Bush administration simply arrogated to itself the right to decide the fate of the Iraqi people, and then predictably conducted both the invasion and the occupation with utter indifference to the security and well-being of those whose savior it proclaimed itself to be.

Some argue that the Bush administration may ultimately be vindicated, if Iraq does gradually evolve into a flourishing secular democracy. There are, however, two replies to this point. The first is: tell that to the dead, the mangled, the ruined, and those who love them. The second is that six years of failure constitute failure *simpliciter*. As the years pass, the counterfactual comparisons become increasingly difficult to make. If domestic security, prosperity, freedom, and democracy had been achieved within a year of the invasion, that would have constituted success, for they clearly could not have come about in that brief time by alternative means. Yet, if these goods come after ten years, it will no longer be plausible to claim that they could not have been achieved in that time by alternative and less destructive means. For no dictatorship lasts forever.

One might argue that the example of Iraq does nothing to support the requirement of consent. For the objection to the war that I have just presented is only that the war has proved to be objectively disproportionate, in that the harms it has caused have outweighed the good effects it has achieved. If instead the good effects had greatly outweighed the bad, it would be no objection to the war that there was no evidence that the majority of the victims of the savage and despotic Baathist regime wanted a war fought for their liberation. It has, indeed, been forcefully argued that if a war of humanitarian intervention would in fact be proportionate, and in particular if the harms from which the beneficiaries would be spared by the war would significantly outweigh those the war would cause them to suffer, opposition to the intervention even by a majority of the intended beneficiaries does not make intervention impermissible, for the majority have no right to prevent third parties from protecting the human rights of the minority.[7] This is particularly obvious if the opposition of the majority is based on factual beliefs, such as that the intervention would be disproportionate, or that the intervening state would exploit its position of dominance within the country to establish a puppet government, that are in fact false.

The claim that the familiar principles of *jus ad bellum*, and especially the proportionality condition, do all the substantive work that the requirement of consent is supposed to do is largely correct as an account of the conditions of *objectively* justified humanitarian intervention. Although the practice of humanitarian intervention is governed by a principle of respect for the collective self-determination of the beneficiaries, the constraints imposed by that principle are comparatively weak. In part this is because collective self-determination is quite different from individual autonomy in that the "will" or "desire" of a large political collective is never univocal in the way that the will or desire of an individual person can be. Suppose, for example, that within a certain state there is a minority nation that is being violently persecuted by the government and its supporters. Roughly eighty percent of the members of this nation, however, oppose external intervention on their behalf. The claim that in these conditions, respect for national self-determination requires nonintervention is only a remote analogue of the claim that respect for the autonomy of an individual requires that one not defend her when she expressly insists that she not be defended. For what we call the will of the nation is compounded out of the wills of the individuals who constitute the nation, and in this case their wills conflict on the issue of intervention. The claim that the national will is opposed to intervention is just a rhetorical overstatement of the true claim that eighty percent of the nation oppose intervention. It suggests unanimity where in fact there is none.

It might therefore be permissible to intervene in such a case, provided that the requirements of just cause, proportionality, and so on are objectively satisfied, even if the ground on which the eighty percent object is not unreasonable—for example, that they, those who constitute the majority, would prefer to achieve self-determination by themselves, even if it would take longer and involve greater suffering on their part, than to be rescued by a nation that once held their forebears in colonial subjection. This preference on the part of the majority, though reasonable, might nevertheless be overridden by the preference of the remaining twenty percent to be saved through external intervention rather than to continue to face the threat posed by their domestic persecutors.

Would intervention be permissible if *all* the intended beneficiaries object to it, though on the basis of beliefs that are in fact false?—for example, the belief that the intervening agents want only to steal their country's oil, a belief that the intervening agents themselves know with certainty to be false. The answer to this question is presumably the same as it is when a single individual, on the basis of mistaken factual beliefs, opposes an act that would spare her from harm and affect no one else. But we need not pursue this question about paternalism in these cases because there simply are no actual instances in which all the members of a nation or large political community oppose an intervention that would be intended to benefit them. For all such groups contain children and others who have no views about the matter of intervention and yet may have a vital interest in whether intervention is undertaken on their behalf. Those who oppose intervention for their own sakes may have no right to prohibit the protection that intervention would afford to those who do not oppose it, if only because they lack the ability to have a view.

I concede, therefore, that the consent of the beneficiaries is not a condition of permissible intervention that is imposed by a requirement to respect their collective self-determination. So why suppose it is relevant at all? The answer is that consent has a second-order role in the justification of humanitarian intervention. It has no role among the conditions of objective justification in ideal theory, but in practice, decisions about intervention are ultimately made by those with the power to intervene, and there must be principles that govern their action in conditions of uncertainty. It is at this level of justification that the requirement of consent has an important role. States contemplating what they can describe as humanitarian intervention often have interests that can be advanced by intervening. When they do, the temptation to engage in self-deception is strong even in well-meaning people. Potential interveners may also, as outsiders to the domestic conflict, have less reliable access to the facts than the intended beneficiaries of their action. A war fought in the towns and cities where people live exposes them to very grave risks. Both the risks and the benefits of a prospective intervention are speculative. But even if they could be assigned reliable probabilities in advance, there could still be reasonable disagreement about what constitutes an acceptable risk, or an acceptable trade-off between risks and benefits. While potential interveners may believe that the risks to which intervention would expose the intended beneficiaries are ones the latter should be willing to accept in exchange for the benefits, the beneficiaries themselves may disagree.

So, in realistic conditions in which the risks to the potential beneficiaries of intervention are very grave, the benefits uncertain, and differing attitudes to risk equally reasonable, it is usually wrong for a potential intervening power to be guided by its own judgment in deciding whether to impose great risks on innocent people, at least when there are ways of trying to determine whether those people would welcome military intervention on their behalf. To the greatest extent possible, the potential intervener must allow the people themselves to decide whether to accept the risks. Of course, in cases in which many or most of the members of a political community are in imminent danger of being killed or expelled from their homeland, and there is in consequence neither uncertainty about their preferences nor time to confirm them, the requirement of consent is obviously suspended. But, in less extreme conditions in which there is uncertainty about what the people want, the presumption must be against intervention. The onus is on the potential intervener to verify that its intervention would be welcomed by those for whose sake it would be done. And in cases in which the evidence suggests that the putative beneficiaries are hostile to the prospect of an intervention allegedly on their behalf, they have a *de jure* moral veto over the proposed intervention.

The reason that I call the requirement of consent a "second-order" principle of justification is that it is not so much a principle of right action as it is a principle about the allocation of rights to make decisions in conditions of uncertainty. According to some theorists, rights have this function quite generally. Michael Walzer, for example, claims that "rights are in an important sense distributive principles. They distribute decision-making authority."[8] Understood in this way, the requirement of consent is just the view that, for a combination of pragmatic reasons and reasons of fairness, decision-making authority with respect to humanitarian intervention, or at least a veto authority, must be vested in those identified as the potential beneficiaries.

Here, as elsewhere, rights are not absolute. As I have suggested, even if a majority of the beneficiaries are opposed to it, intervention may still be justified, particularly if the opposition is based on mistaken factual beliefs. Sometimes, for example, in countries in which the distribution of information is tightly controlled by the government, repression may be extensive but compartmentalized, so that each cluster of victims may think that their situation is unique. Still, whenever an external agent undertakes a humanitarian intervention in the absence of compelling evidence that it is welcomed by the intended beneficiaries, it takes a significant moral risk. If the intervention reveals that the beliefs that prevented the beneficiaries from welcoming it were false, and in particular if the beneficiaries are glad in retrospect that it occurred, this should vindicate the intervention as a justifiable infringement of the beneficiaries' right of veto. But if the intervention fails on balance to benefit those it was supposed to rescue, or proves to be unjustified for other reasons, its having been undertaken without the consent of the ostensible beneficiaries increases the culpability of the intervener.

It is perhaps worth noting that the requirement of consent as a constraint on humanitarian intervention has a parallel in wars involving aggression and defense. Suppose that one country initiates an unjust war of aggression against another. Especially if the fighting is occurring on the territory of the victim, third parties must not join the fighting on behalf of the victims without the consent of their government. Collective defense against aggression is generally permissible, but not if the state that is the immediate victim of aggression wishes to fight unassisted. It is, for example, generally accepted that if the government of a state that is the victim of aggression decides that having the forces of an ally join the fighting on its territory would cause a degree of destruction disproportionate to the advantages the assistance would provide, its judgment must be respected and its ally must not intervene. The reason that this constraint on third-party defense is less controversial than the requirement of consent is that states, as the presumed representatives or even embodiments of entire peoples, are accorded various sovereign rights, including the right to refuse unwanted assistance. The moral grounds for this veto power are really no different from those for the requirement of consent. The main differences between the two constraints are based on epistemic considerations: principally that the voice of the government, unlike the voices of the individual victims of domestic repression, is univocal and can be clearly heard. There is, however, no reason to suppose that the voice of a government is more representative of the views of the people it speaks for than the voices of a sample of the victims of repression are of the views of the victims in general.

3.3 OBLIGATION

The upshot of the foregoing discussion is that traditional objections to humanitarian intervention that appeal to principles of state sovereignty or collective self-determination by the citizenry of a state often lack force in conditions in which a state encompasses two or more self-identified national communities, at least one of which is engaged in extensively and egregiously violating the human rights of members of another, usually at the instigation and with the support of the government. Yet there remain significant moral restrictions on humanitarian intervention, particularly the *ad bellum* proportionality requirement and the largely pragmatic requirement of consent. In cases in which the conditions of permissibility are satisfied (or, as in the case of constraints such as the requirement of consent, justifiably overridden), the question may arise whether humanitarian intervention is also morally *required*. And if the plight of the victims is grave enough to make it seem that intervention *is* required, one must also ask, *of whom?*

The question of when one is morally required to go to war in defense of others is not specific to humanitarian intervention. It arises also in cases of unjust aggression by one state against another when third parties could join the war on behalf of the victim. Of course, circumstances are sometimes relevantly different in these latter cases because third-party states may be bound by treaty or other alliance commitments to provide military assistance to the victim, and all states have reasons to punish violations of the legal prohibition of aggressive war in order to deter further violations. But even after these considerations have been taken into account, the question remains whether and to what extent the people of one state are required to risk their own lives to save the lives of those who are not their fellow citizens.

One bold answer to the question of when humanitarian intervention is obligatory has been given by Kok-Chor Tan, who argues that whenever the violation of human rights within a state is sufficiently serious to override the sovereign right of the state against intervention, thereby making humanitarian intervention permissible, it must also be sufficiently serious to override the sovereign right of other states to neutrality. Thus, according to Tan, whenever humanitarian intervention is morally permissible it is also morally required—though the requirement is imperfect in the sense that it may apply only to states that are in a position to conduct the intervention successfully and without incurring prohibitive costs.[9]

There are, however, two problems with this argument. One is that a state's sovereign right against intervention is a different type of right from its right to neutrality. The right against intervention is a claim-right that constrains other agents, whereas the right to neutrality is primarily a liberty-right—in effect, a permission not to become embroiled in the conflicts of others, which derives not so much from the claims of sovereignty as from the assumption that people are not morally required to put their own lives at significant risk in order to save the lives of strangers for whose plight they bear no responsibility. The right to neutrality may also, though secondarily, be a claim-right, in that people generally have rights not to be forced or coerced to do what it is permissible for them not to do. This difference between the two rights could explain how one state's right against intervention could be overridden while other states' rights to neutrality would not be.

More importantly, however, when humanitarian intervention is permissible, this is generally not because the sovereign right against intervention of the target state is *overridden*; rather, it is because it has been *forfeited* through the wrongful action that the intervention promises to bring to an end. It is perhaps worth saying that, because I accept a reductionist account of the rights of collectives, I hold that the sovereign right against intervention is ultimately reducible to the rights of individuals against certain forms of interference in their relations with one another. On this view, when the perpetrators of human right violations have forfeited their right against intervention and their victims have waived theirs (which most have done when the requirement of consent is satisfied), no sovereign collective right against intervention remains to be violated. While intervention might infringe the rights of some innocent individuals who oppose it, there is no collective right against intervention that remains in place when the individuals who together constitute that collective are either eager for intervention or have made themselves liable to suffer its effects.

By contrast, people in other states have presumably done nothing to forfeit their right to neutrality. If they are morally required to intervene, it is not because their right to neutrality has been either forfeited or overridden. It is instead because they either have no right of neutrality in the circumstances or because their only right to neutrality in the circumstances is a claim-right. According to the first of these possibilities, the right to neutrality permits and protects neutrality only up to a certain point. Beyond that point, the consequences would be so terrible in the absence of intervention that nonintervention ceases to be a permissible option and states may, if possible, even be coerced to intervene. According to the second possibility, nonintervention ceases to be permissible at the same point, so that beyond that point there is no liberty-right to neutrality, but states nevertheless retain their claim-right to neutrality. In these conditions, the right of neutrality would become a "right to do wrong"— that is, a right not to be forced or coerced to do what one is required by morality to do.

These remarks do not directly challenge Tan's conclusion, but only the reasons he gives for that conclusion. Still, the conclusion that humanitarian intervention is morally required whenever it is morally permissible seems too strong. Among other things, while the question whether an act is permissible does not seem to depend on the cost to the agent of doing it, the question whether an act is morally required or obligatory does seem to depend on the costs. Suppose that you and I are strangers walking in opposite directions across a high bridge. You have just dropped a $1,000 bill that is about to be blown off the bridge into the river far below. I can prevent this simply by stepping on it. Since it would cost me nothing to prevent you from suffering a serious loss, it is reasonable to suppose that it is obligatory for me to step on the bill. But suppose that the only way I could prevent the money from being blown away would require me to go over the bridge and fall to my death. No one would say that I would still have the same obligation to save your money but that I am excused for not fulfilling it because of the prohibitive cost to me in this case of saving the money. Rather, what we believe is that in the second case I have no obligation to save your money because of what it would cost me to do so. What it would be obligatory for me to do in the absence of any cost is not obligatory if it would require of me a sufficiently significant sacrifice. So a permissible intervention that would be obligatory if it could be done without cost is not obligatory if the sacrifices it would require are very great. This is uncontroversial in cases in which the harms that the intervening agent would suffer would exceed the harms that the intervention would prevent. (One might object that this is not a counterexample to Tan's conclusion because such an intervention would be disproportionate and therefore impermissible, and if it would not be permissible it could not be obligatory. But proportionality does not prohibit people from *voluntarily* suffering a greater harm as a means or foreseen side effect of preventing someone else from suffering a lesser harm. So, such an intervention could be permissible and, if so, would also be obligatory on Tan's view.)

Although I think that Tan's argument is unsuccessful, it has the merit of avoiding any direct appeal to our intuitions about the morality of intervention. This is a merit because our intuitions about the sacrifices that we, both as individuals and in groups, may be required to make to save the lives of strangers are notoriously confused and inconsistent. Peter Singer, in his contribution to this collection, cogently challenges the consistency between common intuitions about the importance of preventing mass killing through humanitarian intervention and intuitions about the importance of saving people from natural threats. It will be instructive to explore this comparison further.

In various instances of mass slaughter during the past two decades—in East Timor, Liberia, Sierra Leone, Rwanda, Bosnia, Kosovo, Darfur, and elsewhere—many people have argued passionately for humanitarian intervention. But few voices have been raised with equal passion about the much larger numbers of people who have died over the same period from preventable disease and malnutrition in impoverished areas of the world. Is it really defensible to suppose that humanitarian intervention may be morally required in order to prevent people from being killed by their own government even when it is not a moral requirement to devote comparable resources to saving a comparable number of people from natural threats?

Like Singer, I suspect that common intuitions are distorted by a variety of factors. One is that the killings, tortures, and expulsions that provide the occasions for humanitarian intervention are dramatic and newsworthy, whereas the daily death tolls from disease and malnutrition are chronic and familiar, a constant background condition to which most people who are not among the victims have become inured. When, by contrast, natural calamities are sudden and violent, like the tsunami of 2004, people's intuitive reactions become more like those that prompt demands for humanitarian intervention, and external observers become more inclined to regard life-saving assistance as obligatory rather than merely permissible. But whether environmental conditions kill a large number of people suddenly and dramatically, over a course of days, or prematurely kill a comparable number of people insidiously over a longer period, seems in itself irrelevant to whether others have an obligation to prevent those deaths.

Another difference between humanitarian intervention and forms of aid that save people from natural threats such as disease and famine is that humanitarian intervention is *heroic*, or involves heroism on the part of those who carry it out, and forms of aid that require heroism are, in many cases, more likely to seem obligatory than ones that do not. This may seem paradoxical, yet it seems to be true of both individual and collective action. To test our intuitions about this, compare the following two hypothetical cases. In the first, a man is the sole bystander when a car that was traveling at a reasonable speed hits an invisible patch of black ice, skids off the road into a tree, and bursts into flame. There are five people trapped in the car. While there is no immediate danger that the car will explode, unless the man pulls them out, the five people will burn to death. In pulling them out, however, the man would predictably suffer third-degree burns to one of his arms. He notices that the car's license plate is from Mexico and, hearing cries in Spanish from within the car, correctly infers that the victims are foreigners. I conjecture that many people would say that he *ought* to intervene to save them, even at the cost of suffering third-degree burns on one arm. It is true that his saving them would involve a heroic sacrifice, but that does not entail that saving them is merely supererogatory. The fulfillment of duty can sometimes be heroic. It is also true that few would blame him if he refused to intervene, but that too is compatible with his having a duty to intervene. We frequently accept that people can be *excused* for failing to fulfill duties that require significant personal sacrifices.

Next, imagine another case involving this same bystander. Suppose that, entirely coincidentally, he has recently participated in some experiments performed by a team of psychologists and economists engaged in collaborative research on people's preferences about cost avoidance. Among the things that the team learned about this man is that he would be willing to pay $10,000 to avoid third-degree burns to an arm, but not $11,000. In other words, he regards the loss of $10,000 as less bad than the burns, but regards the loss of $11,000 as worse than the burns. Suppose that the same crash occurs but that in this version of the example he is temporarily confined to a wheelchair and is physically incapable of performing the rescue. Happily, a passerby shows up who declares his willingness to save the passengers in the car at the cost of suffering third-degree burns, but only if the man in the wheelchair pays him $10,000 to do it. The burning car is old and dilapidated and its occupants are clearly too poor ever to repay the cost of the rescue. Here I conjecture that most people would *not* say that the man in the wheelchair *ought* to pay $10,000 to save the five foreigners. That this is a reasonable conjecture is suggested by the fact that many people are aware that they could in fact save far more than five lives by donating $10,000 to an organization such as Oxfam, yet very few believe it is their duty to do it and even fewer actually do it.

If it is right that only a very small proportion of people would believe that the bystander has a duty to sacrifice $10,000 to save the five foreigners, while a significantly higher proportion would believe that he has a duty to pull them from the car at the cost of being burned, *even though* he regards the burn as worse than the loss of the money, this suggests that we sometimes demand heroic sacrifices in response to crises even when we do not demand more prosaic sacrifices. This, as I noted, seems true in the case of collective action as well. Many of us felt a certain disdain for the Clinton administration when it refused to intervene militarily in Rwanda. Its strenuous efforts to avoid going to the rescue of the 800,000 people who were slaughtered there in just a matter of months seemed contemptibly pusillanimous, even cowardly. But suppose there had been a country, such as Switzerland, that lacked the ability to conduct a large-scale overseas intervention but nevertheless had the opportunity to hire, at great cost, a large mercenary army that could have succeeded in stopping the massacres. Fewer people, I think, would have felt contempt for that country for failing to sponsor such a proxy intervention.

It seems, therefore, that whether an act of saving people requires heroism can make a difference to whether many people think of that act as
obligatory or merely permissible. So, the heroism involved in humanitarian intervention seems intuitively salient and makes many people more
disposed to find humanitarian intervention morally obligatory when they
would not find it obligatory to save a comparable number of lives by, for
example, increasing foreign aid to a country with a chronically high death
rate from malaria. Yet this seems to be an instance in which our intuitions
are unreliable. Heroic self-sacrifice may seem more admirable than merely
writing a check, and shrinking from a fight or from some other danger may
seem more contemptible than failing to write a check, but these reactions
provide no basis for supposing that there is a stronger moral reason to save
a life heroically than there is to save a life unheroically. So, if it is right that
our intuitions about the obligatoriness of humanitarian intervention are
responsive to the fact that it involves heroic self-sacrifice, that is a reason
to view them with skepticism.

The comparison between humanitarian intervention and foreign aid for
the prevention of cure of disease highlights a third factor that influences
our intuitions about humanitarian intervention—namely, that humanitarian intervention is intended not only to prevent serious *harms* but also to
prevent serious *wrongdoing*, or seriously immoral *action*. This is the fact on
which Singer's discussion rightly focuses: humanitarian intervention is a
response not just to misfortune, but to *evil*.

As Singer observes, many people feel that it is more important morally to prevent evil acts than it is to prevent natural events that would
have comparably bad effects. But on this matter I think Singer is largely
right. There are, of course, a number of reasons why it is often *contingently*
more important to prevent wrongdoing than to prevent an accident that
would cause comparable harm to the innocent. By preventing a person
from wrongfully harming another, particularly if it is necessary to harm
this person in order to do so, one may prevent or deter him from causing
further wrongful harms in the future. One may also deter others from
acting in the same way. One may prevent the person from morally defil-
ing himself through the completion of his immoral action. And, finally,
if immoral acts are impersonally bad events, one may prevent the occur-
rence of an impersonally bad event. Yet only the last two of these are
necessary or inevitable concomitants of the prevention of wrongdoing,
if indeed they are real effects. Suppose they are. Suppose that people do
defile themselves when they act in certain ways that are seriously wrong
and that this is a bad effect, and suppose also that in itself it is impersonally worse for wrongful acts to occur. Even so, these effects are easily
outweighed. Suppose that one can *either* prevent an innocent stranger
from being wrongfully pushed off a cliff *or* prevent an innocent stranger
from accidentally (and faultlessly) walking off a cliff *and* prevent another
stranger from losing (or even just breaking) a leg. And suppose that both
acts of rescue would be equally heroic. Provided that the murderer would

not commit any further murders and that his act would not weaken the general deterrence of murder, it would be perverse to prevent the murder rather than the accidental death together with the nonlethal injury.

Or consider again the first case of the burning car. Suppose we think that the number of people trapped in the car is just below the number that would make the heroic rescue obligatory. (If one thinks that the saving of more than six lives would be necessary to make it obligatory to suffer burns to one's arm, imagine that it is a bus rather than a car that is on fire.) Recall that in this case the accident was caused by a natural condition: an unforeseen patch of ice in the road. But suppose instead that the car had been forced off the road by another driver who was trying to kill all of the car's passengers. If one's reason to prevent harmful wrongdoing is stronger than one's reason to prevent the same harm from natural causes, the addition of this factor might be sufficient to make it obligatory for the bystander to carry out the rescue. That is, if the heroic rescue is just barely below the threshold of obligation if the crash is the result of natural conditions, it should be above that threshold if the crash is the result of serious wrongdoing. So, if the bystander has initially reached the reasonable conclusion that he is not morally required to save the passengers, he would have to revise that conclusion and accept that the rescue is obligatory after all, if he were then to discover that the crash had been caused by malicious human agency.

One might object that, at this point, saving the passengers would not involve the prevention of wrongdoing, since the wrongful act has already been done once the bystander has a chance to intervene. At that point, he would simply be preventing harms rather than wrongs. Yet, while it is not in the bystander's power to prevent *any* wrongdoing from being done, it is in his power to affect the nature of the wrongdoing that has been done, and in particular to make it less serious than it would otherwise be. If he saves the passengers, the wrong that will have been done will be a combination of attempted murder and the injury of innocent people, whereas if he does not save them, the wrong will be the murder of five people.[10] Much the same is true of humanitarian intervention. While it usually prevents some wrongdoing, many of its beneficial effects consist in preventing wrongful acts that have already been done from having their intended effects—that is, it also prevents attempts from becoming completed crimes, for example, by preventing orders from being carried out or polices from being implemented. And in any case, even those who think that the prevention of harmful wrongdoing is more important than the prevention of comparable harms from natural causes tend to accept that it makes no difference whether harmful wrongdoing is prevented by preventing the act from being done or by preventing its harmful effect. There is, for example, no more reason to prevent a murder by preventing the pulling of the trigger than by deflecting the bullet once the trigger has been pulled. If there were, and if one could attempt either of these means of preventing a murder, but not both, it might be morally preferable to try to prevent the pulling of the trigger when that would have a ninety-five percent probability of preventing the murder than to try to deflect the bullet when that would have a ninety-eight percent probability of preventing the murder. But to try to prevent the pulling of the trigger in these circumstances would clearly be the wrong choice.

It seems, therefore, that there are various explanations of our tendency to think of humanitarian intervention as obligatory that tend more to undermine than to support that intuition. Because the events that call for humanitarian intervention are dramatic rather than familiar, because humanitarian intervention is heroic rather than merely costly, and because it prevents not only harm but also evil, we tend to overestimate the strength of the moral reason to engage in humanitarian intervention *in relation to* the strength of the moral reason to save comparable numbers of unrelated foreigners from death from natural causes, such as disease and malnutrition.

Yet I believe—though I cannot argue for this here—that we *greatly underestimate* the strength of our moral reason to save foreigners who, through no fault of their own, will otherwise die prematurely of preventable disease or malnutrition. Hence, even though I suspect that Singer is right that the reason to save people from being wrongfully killed by their government is not significantly stronger than the reason to save people from an equally premature death from natural causes, and that when it is stronger, this is generally for contingent reasons connected with deterrence and other such extrinsic factors, I nevertheless think that *on balance* we tend to significantly *underestimate* the strength of the reasons to engage in humanitarian intervention. That is, when we estimate the strength of these reasons only in relation to reasons whose strength we greatly underestimate, we get a distorted estimate of the absolute strength of these reasons. I think, in short, that the reasons that favor humanitarian intervention actually rise to the level of obligation far more often than we intuitively recognize.

This is not, of course, a criterion for identifying situations in which humanitarian intervention is obligatory. The conditions in which the rescue of a people becomes obligatory are a matter that resists articulation in a simple formula, or indeed in a complex formula. The relevant variables are many: the number of potential victims and the severity of the harm they are otherwise likely to suffer, the probability of counterintervention on behalf of the government and the risks of uncontrolled escalation, the expected costs to the interveners, both in lives and resources, the risks involved in destroying structures of political authority if the repressive government must be removed, the harms caused to innocent people, including the intended beneficiaries, as a side effect of modern war, and so on. So, just as I cannot say exactly when humanitarian intervention is permissible, but only that it is permissible more often than people have hitherto supposed, so I cannot say exactly when it is obligatory, but only that it is more often obligatory than we are inclined to think, despite our bias in favor of humanitarian intervention in relation to our intuitive views about foreign aid.

3.4 PROPORTIONALITY

In cases in which humanitarian intervention is morally required, or even merely permissible and desirable, but not obligatory, the most significant obstacle to its actually being done is of course the cost to the potential interveners. One of the ironies of humanitarian intervention is that while many purely predatory interventions are cynically promoted as humanitarian by their perpetrators, these same states are wholly unwilling to intervene when there is genuinely an objective humanitarian justification but intervention would not serve their own interests. Many observers have suggested, for example, that it was the political unpopularity of the small losses that the United States suffered in Somalia that convinced the Clinton administration that it would be against its interests to intervene in Rwanda or Bosnia. Yet, as those genocides progressed unopposed, to the mounting horror of decent people everywhere, the Clinton administration became increasingly exposed to bitter criticism for its shameful efforts to *obstruct* intervention by others for fear that the United States would be dragged into the conflict and sustain unpopular losses as it had done in Somalia. This criticism probably helped to convince the administration that on balance it would be against its political interests to refuse yet again to intervene when the Serbs initiated a campaign to expel the ethnic Albanian population from the province of Kosovo. But Clinton discovered a way to reap the political benefits of intervention without incurring the costs. He decided to conduct a military intervention in which the United States would suffer no casualties.

The key to costless warfare in this case was to refuse to commit ground troops and to conduct the entire war from the air, always flying out of range of Serbian antiaircraft weapons. In this way the United States and its NATO allies succeeded in conducting the entire war without suffering a single casualty. Yet bombing from such great heights prevented the pilots from having more accurate information about exactly who or what they were bombing, and also, even with the precision-guided weaponry available to them, from being able to hit their intended targets with the degree of accuracy that flying at a lower altitude would have made possible. The net effect was that although the United States suffered no casualties, it killed significantly more Serbian civilians, and even more Albanian civilians whom it was supposed to be rescuing, than it would have if it had conducted the war in a different way—for example, by flying lower or committing ground forces, or both.

The Clinton administration again suffered some sharp criticism for this strategy, both from the left and the right wings of the political spectrum. On the left, Noam Chomsky cited the well-known dictum of Hippocrates:

"First, do no harm."[11] And on the right, Charles Krauthammer asked, "What kind of humanitarianism is it that makes its highest objective ensuring that not one of our soldiers is harmed while the very people we were supposed to be saving are suffering thousands of dead and perhaps a million homeless?"[12] These criticisms do not fit neatly into the framework for evaluating the conduct of war that has been provided by traditional just war theory. The objection is not exactly that the bombings violated the *in bello* requirement of proportionality. The proportionality test is usually understood to involve a comparison between an act of war, or a series of such acts, and engaging in no act of war at all. If the good effects of an act of war that are relevant to proportionality outweigh the bad, relative to what would have happened in the absence of any act of war, the act is proportionate. Since the effects of the bombings seem to have been better for the Albanian Kosovars than what would have happened to them in the absence of any intervention, it seems that the bombings were proportionate in the traditional sense. The objection to them is also not quite that they violated the *in bello* necessity requirement, usually referred to as the "requirement of minimal force." This is standardly interpreted to prohibit acts of war when their good effects could be equally well achieved by alternative means that would cause less harm. This is a perfectly straightforward requirement when the harms that would be caused by both alternative acts would all be suffered by people whose moral status in the war is the same. So, for example, if two possible means of achieving the same end would be equally effective, but one would kill more innocent civilians as a side effect, and all other things are equal, the option that would kill more civilians is clearly ruled out by the requirement of minimal force. What was at issue in Kosovo, however, was more complex. An alternative strategy involving more than high-altitude bombing alone would have caused fewer casualties among civilians, but would also have resulted in the deaths of NATO combatants, with the number of NATO casualties increasing in proportion to the seriousness of the effort to reduce the civilian casualties. So the issue raised by the bombings is not strictly an issue of either proportionality or necessity, but is instead an issue of the fair distribution of the risks and harms of intervention among the people involved in a conflict. The objection to the NATO strategy is that NATO forces ought to have been required (or even just permitted by their commanders) to expose themselves to greater risks in order to reduce the harm their acts of war unintentionally inflicted on civilians.

For convenience, I propose to consider this objection as an issue of proportionality, understood more broadly than it typically is in the just war tradition. Proportionality in war is already considerably more complicated than most people suppose. It is not just a relation between the harm caused and the harm averted. It is, for example, sensitive to whether those who are harmed are liable to be harmed, and among those who are liable, the proportionality restriction on harming them becomes weaker the greater the degree of their liability is. In common sense morality, proportionality is also sensitive to whether the harm caused is intended.[13] Perhaps we should also say that harm that is unintentionally inflicted on the innocent in war is disproportionate if it is excessive in relation to what they would suffer in a *fair* distribution of the harms between combatants and noncombatants. We might say that, in the Kosovo war, although the harms caused were not disproportionate overall, they disproportionately burdened the innocent.

It is generally agreed that even in a war of national defense, combatants are morally obligated "to accept some risk to minimize harm to noncombatants," as the *U.S. Army/Marines Counterinsurgency Field Manual* puts it. The *Manual* goes on to assert that

> Soldiers and Marines are not permitted to use force disproportionately or indiscriminately. Typically, more force reduces risk in the short term. But American military values obligate Soldiers and Marines to accomplish their missions while taking measures to limit the destruction caused during military operations, particularly in terms of collateral harm to noncombatants.[14]

But if combatants are obligated to accept certain avoidable risks to themselves in order to avoid harming noncombatants in the *enemy* population in a war of defense, it seems that they should be obligated to accept even *greater* risks to avoid harming the noncombatants whom it is precisely their mission to *save* in a war of humanitarian intervention. I will argue, however, that this view misses an important point and that there is something to be said on behalf of the Clinton administration's strategy, even if it was motivated by base calculations of political self-interest.

Most of the Albanian Kosovars whom the Serbs were attempting to drive out of the country were entirely innocent people going about the ordinary business of life. But the members of the NATO forces that were summoned to help them were equally innocent in the relevant sense— that is, they were in no way responsible for any of the wrongs being committed in the Balkans at that time. They were for the most part young people from distant lands who were ordered to leave the peaceful conditions of their own homelands to rescue strangers for whose plight they bore no responsibility. Why should they rather than the Kosovars bear the costs of the rescue?

Consider an analogous case of individual rescue. Suppose that a person is being swept along in turbulent waters toward a waterfall and that if he goes over the falls, he will be killed. A passerby can pull him from the water in either of two ways. One method of rescue would dislocate the rescuer's shoulder, but would not harm the victim. The other would break the victim's arm while he was being extracted from the water, but would leave the rescuer unharmed. A broken arm is a worse injury than a dislocated shoulder, but even if the victim is in no way responsible for being in the water, he should bear the costs of his own rescue. He would have no cause for complaint after being pulled from the water in a way that broke his arm.

Part of the explanation for this might be that it would be permissible not to save the person at all if saving him would require the passerby to sustain a dislocated shoulder. As I noted earlier in connection with the case of the burning car, our intuitions are not univocal in such cases. But if it would be permissible not to rescue the victim at all at the cost of suffering a dislocated shoulder, that would explain why the victim would have cause for nothing but gratitude if he were rescued in a way that foreseeably broke his arm; for one can have no justified complaint that another person failed to do what was supererogatory.

This case may, however, be different from the Kosovo intervention in one important respect. If the passerby chooses not to rescue the victim in the way that would be supererogatory, she would nevertheless seem to be morally required to rescue him in the way that would break his arm, since she could do that without any significant cost to herself. But the Kosovo intervention was costly in various ways, even though no American combatants were killed, and many people believe that those costs alone were sufficient to relieve the United States of an *obligation* to intervene. If that is right, then a permissible alternative to conducting the intervention in the way the United States did was not to intervene at all. If the intervention as it was carried out was better for the Albanian Kosovars than their situation would have been if the United States had not intervened, it is arguable that they had no justifiable complaint that the intervention was conducted as it was, and indeed had grounds for gratitude that it was done at all, even though many more of them died than would have if it had been conducted differently. On these assumptions, the intervention as it was conducted may have been unchivalrous, but it was neither disproportionate nor otherwise wrong.

We may even be driven to a stronger and indeed rather counterintuitive conclusion. Suppose that the Serbian civilians who were endangered by the intervention were wholly innocent in the same way that the United States and NATO combatants, as well as most of the Albanians, were: that is, they bore no responsibility for the conflict developing around them. That was in reality not true of many of them, who supported and collaborated in various ways in the unjust action taken against the Albanians. But suppose for the sake of argument that all those Serbian civilians who were put at risk by the intervention were entirely innocent in the same way that civilians in adjacent but neutral states were. It seems that the proportionality constraint on harming them as a side effect of military action should have been *even more restrictive* than that which governed the harming of the Albanian civilians.

To understand why, it may help to consider a variant of the individual rescue case. Suppose that the passerby has three options for rescuing the man who will otherwise go over the waterfall. In addition to the ones that would involve dislocating her shoulder or breaking the victim's arm, there is another that would shift the costs of the rescue to an innocent and uninvolved bystander, who would suffer harm comparable in severity to a dislocated shoulder, but less serious than a broken arm. It seems intuitively that it would be unjust for the rescuer to harm the bystander when the cost of the rescue could instead be borne by the victim himself. Indeed, shifting the harm to the bystander seems to be the least acceptable of the three options, at least without the bystander's consent. For given that the passerby has the option of imposing the costs on the victim, if she decides for whatever reason not to do that, it seems she must accept them herself unless she could accomplish the rescue by imposing costs on a third-party bystander that would be significantly less than those she would have to accept herself. For it was *her* decision not to adopt the best course, which is to channel the costs of the rescue to the victim himself.

We have moved from a discussion of humanitarian intervention to a case of individual rescue. Let us take a further step back to a case of individual self-defense. Suppose that one can defend oneself from an otherwise lethal attack by a culpable aggressor, but only by acting in a way that will also kill an innocent bystander as a side effect. Many people believe that this would impermissible. While there may be ways of shifting one's misfortune to another that are not unjust, one may not actively *harm or kill* another person to avoid an equivalent harm to oneself. There is, in particular, a moral presumption against killing, even unintended killing, that cannot be overcome unless the killing is necessary to avert a significantly greater evil. The saving of one life, even if it is one's own, is not sufficient to justify the killing of an innocent person, even if the killing is unintended. In general, the harms that one may permissibly inflict on other innocent people, even unintentionally in the course of individual self-defense, must be significantly *less* than those one would thereby avert.

This is true of third-party defense of others just as it is true of self-defense: one may not shift the costs of the defense to wholly innocent and uninvolved bystanders, even if one would harm them only foreseeably and not intentionally, unless doing so would substantially reduce the overall harm that innocent people would have to suffer. (And according to common sense morality, the reduction would have to be even greater still to make it permissible to harm or kill innocent people as an intended means of protecting others.) Yet, in cases of third-party defense, those who are beneficiaries of the defense have no such immunity to having the costs of the defense shifted to them. When it is those being defended rather than the defenders or others who stand to benefit from the action, the costs of the defense ought, in a manner of speaking, to be deducted from their benefits. If they would still derive a net benefit from the defensive action even after suffering the harms that are an unavoidable concomitant of a successful defense, they have no valid grounds for complaint that other innocent people were not made to take a share of those harms. This is why, if Serbian civilians were genuinely innocent bystanders, the proportionality constraint on harming them as a side effect of military action by NATO forces was more restrictive than the constraint on foreseeably harming Albanian civilians who were the intended beneficiaries of the rescue.

Many people will of course find this conclusion perverse. To the extent that they are right to do so, it is because they do not in fact accept that the Serbian civilians who were at risk of harm from the bombings intended for Serbian forces were genuinely innocent in the relevant sense. Suitably generalized, the conclusion is that the proportionality constraint on harming the intended beneficiaries of humanitarian intervention as a side effect of military action is weaker or less restrictive than that which governs the infliction of foreseeable but unintended harms on other civilians who are genuinely innocent bystanders to the conflict.

There is an obvious response to some of these claims about proportionality in humanitarian intervention. In my examples of individual rescue—the burning car and the man being swept toward a waterfall—the potential rescuer is a passerby who has made no antecedent commitment to save people in danger of being killed. But combatants in a national army occupy a professional role that gives them a duty to take risks or make sacrifices in the course of defending or rescuing others. A helpful analogy here might be with two cases in which a man is, through no fault of his own, trapped in a burning house. In one case, the only person who can rescue him is a passerby. In the other, that person is a firefighter. The risks involved in attempting the rescue may be such that the passerby is not morally required to intervene. And if he does intervene, he seems entitled to shift as much of the risk as possible away from himself and to the trapped man. If, for example, the passerby can lower the victim to the ground in either of two ways, one of which involves no risk for him but is moderately risky for the victim, and the other of which involves a small risk for him and no risk for the victim, he is permitted to choose the former, even though it involves a greater overall risk. The firefighter, by contrast, may be required to intervene and, if confronted with the same options for lowering the man to the ground, may also be required to adopt the method that is riskier for himself and less risky for the victim. And the difference is of course that it is part of the firefighter's *job* to take risks to save people from burning buildings. This is what he agreed to do when he voluntarily became a firefighter. And there are, of course, other jobs that require people to risk their lives for the sake of others: a lifeguard may be required to swim in dangerous waters to save a drowning person, and a police officer may be required to risk her life to capture a dangerous criminal. Similarly, combatants may be required to risk their lives to prevent innocent people from being killed by enemy combatants and may be required to shift some of the risks of combat away from those whom they are trying to save and toward themselves.

That it is part of the professional role of a combatant to take risks in the process of defending innocent people clearly supports the position taken by the critics of the Clinton administration's strategy in Kosovo. When United States and other NATO combatants bombed Serbian positions in ways that killed more of the people they were supposed to be defending, as well as more innocent bystanders, than they would have if they had exposed themselves to greater risks, they were arguably failing to do their job properly—though they were of course not the ones who made the decisions about how to carry out their missions, so none of the blame for their failure to take greater risks should be directed at them. This still leaves open the larger question of the appropriate distribution of risk between combatants and civilians in humanitarian intervention. What we can say, on the basis of the argument so far, is that the Clinton administration's assignment of nearly absolute priority to the safety of its own forces was wrong, in part because it treated its combatants as if they were passersby rather than professional warriors—and did so for cynical reasons of political advantage. Yet, it is also clearly true that combatants are not required to make literally *any* sacrifices that might be necessary to avoid harming noncombatants in the course of their military operations, whether in a war of national defense or in a war of humanitarian intervention.

Furthermore, nothing I have said about the professional role of combatants weakens the claim that in cases of humanitarian intervention, the proportionality constraint on causing unintended harm to the beneficiaries is less restrictive than the constraint that governs the infliction of unintended harms on other innocent civilians who are not among the beneficiaries of the intervention. This claim is, in fact, supported by the analogy with the case of the firefighter. If, in the course of rescuing a person from a burning building, a firefighter must act in a way that will harm either the endangered person or an innocent bystander, he should choose the course of action that will harm the endangered person, unless the other option would harm the innocent bystander to a significantly lesser degree (and unless the bystander has voluntarily assumed the risk or acted negligently or recklessly in exposing himself to risk). And it seems to be a corollary of this that a firefighter should accept greater risks to himself to avoid harming an innocent bystander in the course of a rescue than he is required to take to avoid harming the beneficiary of the rescue.

One might object to the claim that it is a combatant's professional duty to take risks in defense of others that, just as a firefighter has no special duty to save people from drowning, and a lifeguard no special duty to rescue people from burning buildings, so combatants have no special duty to rescue foreigners from their own government. Rather, the professional duty of a combatant is just to defend his or her fellow citizens. As soldiers often say, their duty is to serve *their country.*

The obvious response to this objection is that even if it were correct that a soldier's commitment is just to serve his or her own country, it is not the soldier's prerogative to judge or determine what constitutes serving the country. It is for the government to determine what is best or right for the country and it is the soldier's job to do what he or she is told (provided, I would add, that it is not morally impermissible). If the government judges that the country ought to go to war in aid of an ally that has been the victim of aggression, it is not the soldier's prerogative to judge whether participation in the collective defense of the ally is really in the national interest. And the same is true of humanitarian intervention.

Humanitarian intervention does, however, raise special issues that may not arise so acutely in the case of other forms of war. For example, if a proposed humanitarian intervention is morally optional for the state that is considering undertaking it, ought it also to be optional for individual soldiers? If, as I believe, there should be greater legal tolerance of a soldier's conscientious refusal to fight in a war that he or she believes is unjust, would not many soldiers seek to exploit more generous provisions for conscientious objection by mendaciously claiming to have moral objections to fighting in a war of humanitarian intervention when in fact their sole concern would be to avoid taking risks for the sake of people they do not care about?

Because of these and many other problems, we should ultimately aim to assign the task of humanitarian intervention to a special international force under the control, not of any national government, but of an impartial, democratically controlled, international body. Ideally, such a force should not be drawn from the forces of any national military organization, but should instead recruit its own soldiers from the world at large and train them itself. Their training should be specifically in the kinds of operation characteristic of humanitarian missions and they should be imbued with a sense of the nobility of their profession as defenders of the weak and oppressed. Humanitarian intervention should be the sole raison d'être of this force. Because the force would be under the control of an impartial, multilateral body that would itself have no stake in the domestic conflicts in which it might intervene, the members of the force could have greater confidence that its missions would be just than the members of national military forces are usually justified in having. This is, however, a topic for future discussion, when our international legal institutions have evolved beyond their current rather primitive conditions.[15]

POSTSCRIPT

I conclude on a personal note. When I went to Oxford in 1976, I had just completed a BA in English literature but wanted to study philosophy. As I was unqualified to begin a graduate degree in philosophy, I registered for two of the three years of Oxford's undergraduate program in Philosophy, Politics, and Economics. Although that was during a golden age of philosophy in Oxford, ordinary language philosophy was still clinging to life and I found much of what I was required to study almost unbearably tedious. I was seriously considering bailing out of philosophy altogether when, in 1978, I discovered Jonathan Glover's *Causing Death and Saving Lives*, which had been published the previous year. I knew then what I wanted to do, which was to write philosophy the way Jonathan Glover did. I decided to apply to do a D.Phil. at Oxford, and when I was accepted

I begged my tutor to intercede for me to see if Glover would be willing to supervise my dissertation work. It was a turning point in my life when he agreed to take me on. Not only did he prepare me to do the sort of work I have done ever since (so that, drawing on an idiom from the monster movies of my youth, I think of my book, *The Ethics of Killing*, as "Son of *Causing Death and Saving Lives*"), but he and his wife Vivette personally befriended me and my wife Sally, inviting us frequently to visit them for meals at their house in London and welcoming us into their wonderful family. As we felt at the time rather like abandoned waifs in a foreign land, the warm friendship that the Glovers offered us was more of a lifeline than perhaps they knew.

Not only was Jonathan my inspiration in philosophy, but he and Vivette were Sally's and my inspiration as parents as well. The Glover children—Daniel, David, and Ruth—always sat at the table with us and were encouraged to participate in the conversation, though no encouragement was ever needed by that point, as they were already accustomed to having their views on every conceivable subject elicited and received with interest and respect, and deservedly so, as they were remarkably bright and animated children. I recall my amazement on discovering that they called their parents by their first names—a practice that to me, a product of a South Carolina upbringing that required that parents be addressed as "sir" and "ma'am," was thoroughly unknown and even unimagined. (Because Sally and I referred to each other by our first names rather than by "mom" and "dad" when we later spoke to our own children, they too spontaneously called us by those names, which gave me a gratifying sense of continuity with the parental practices of Jonathan and Vivette.)

Jonathan is known as a utilitarian, though not as one who is altogether doctrinally orthodox. Although most of us who have studied philosophy were taught early on to beware of utilitarians, who would lie to us, break their promises, betray us, and even extract our vital organs for transplantation if by doing so they could promote the greatest good, it has been striking to me that the professed utilitarians of my acquaintance in general do far better by the standards of ordinary commonsense morality than their opponents in ethical theory who go on about human dignity, integrity, humanity, fidelity, honor, and so on. Here I can cite Jonathan Glover as Exhibit A: no one could hope for a kinder, more sympathetic, reliable, or generous friend and mentor than he.

Notes

1. John Stuart Mill, On Liberty, in Marshall Cohen, ed., *The Philosophy of John Stuart Mill: Ethical, Political, and Religious* (New York: Modern Library, 1961), p. 197.

2. Michael Walzer, *Just and Unjust Wars* (New York: Basic Books, 1977), p. 89.

3. Michael Walzer, "The Moral Standing of States," in *International Ethics*, Charles R. Beitz et al., eds. (Princeton, NJ: Princeton University Press, 1985): pp. 217–37, p. 101.

4. Graham Greene, *The Comedians* (New York: Viking Press, 1966), p. 222.

5. For a more detailed discussion, see Jeff McMahan, "Intervention and Collective Self-Determination," *Ethics and International Affairs* 10 (1996): 1–24.

6. For a defense of a similar constraint on violent political action by domestic rebels who claim to be acting on behalf of some community, see Christopher Finlay, "Legitimacy and Non-State Political Violence," *Journal of Political Philosophy* (forthcoming).

7. Andrew Altman and Christopher Heath Wellman, "From Humanitarian Intervention to Assassination: Human Rights and Political Violence," *Ethics* 118 (2008): 228–57.

8. Walzer, "The Moral Standing of States," P. 232.

9. Kok-Chor Tan, "The Duty to Protect," in Terry Nardin and Melissa S. Williams, eds., *Humanitarian Intervention: NOMOS XLVII* (New York: New York University Press, 2006), pp. 84–116.

10. Kantians reject the idea that luck can make a difference to the morality of action and thus think that attempts are as seriously wrong as completed crimes. But commonsense intuition and the law disagree. I cannot pursue this debate here.

11. Cited in David Luban, "Intervention and Civilization: Some Unhappy Lessons of the Kosovo War," in Pablo de Greiff and Ciaran Cronin, eds., *Global Justice and Transnational Politics: Essays on the Moral and Political Challenges of Globalization* (Cambridge, MA: MIT Press, 2002), pp. 79–115, 108.

12. Cited in ibid., p. 109.

13. On the relevance of intention to proportionality, see Jeff McMahan, *Killing in War* (Oxford: Clarendon Press, 2009), sections 1.3 and 5.3.

14. *The U.S. Army/Marine Corps Counterinsurgency Field Manual* (Chicago, IL: University of Chicago Press, 2007), pp. 244–45.

15. I am greatly indebted to Allen Buchanan for comments on an earlier draft of this chapter. I am also much indebted to the American Council of Learned Socites for its support of my work on this chapter.

III

ETHICS, TRUTH, AND BELIEF

4

Humanity and the Perils of Perniciously Politicized Science

N. Ann Davis

4.1 INTRODUCTION

In *Humanity*,[1] Jonathan Glover argues persuasively that our prospects of moral progress—and perhaps the prospects of our very survival—depend heavily on our being able to find effective ways to defuse the sort of tensions that can spark the kind of deeply destructive political and ideological conflicts that erupted around the globe during the twentieth century.[2] Glover makes it clear that we still have a lot more to learn about the social, economic, and psychological roots of such conflicts. Any optimism we might have that undergirding the arguments of moral philosophy with a deeper knowledge of the relevant history might enable us to make robust progress in figuring out how to forestall future tribal and global conflicts should thus be greeted with some skepticism, and tempered with a measure of humility.

Although those of us who live in western democracies may be confident that we will not be subjected to the brutality of a leader like Hitler, Stalin, or Pol Pot, we must take care not to underestimate the extent of our ongoing vulnerability to the tactics of master manipulators. After the events of 9/11/2001, even elected leaders of states that profess to be democratic have evinced authoritarian inclinations, and resorted to repressive tactics. In both the United States and the United Kingdom, both liberty-limiting secrecy measures and stunningly intrusive surveillance policies have been enacted by governments that issued only vague and insubstantial pronouncements to defend the wielding of such dramatically increased power over the citizenry: the draconian measures were enacted because it was 'necessary to protect national security.' Leaders have also been quite willing to exploit fear and xenophobia to rationalize both the sharp curtailment of civil liberties and the utter lack of transparency in the processes by which the decisions to curtail these liberties have been made. In the United States, those who have spoken up to criticize such policies have been subjected to harsh criticism, harassment, and overt intimidation and for being 'soft on terrorism.' Despite the fact that both social commentators and members of the citizenry have loudly condemned such harassment as intolerant, unconstitutional, and dangerous, and despite the alleged softening of policies reflected in some recent judicial decisions and in the passage of PATRIOT II, things seem to be getting worse, not better.[3] It is thus hard not to wonder where we are heading. One of the most important lessons to be learned from reading *Humanity* is that it is incumbent on us to ask.

The darkness of the Cold War years and McCarthy era was in some measure counterbalanced by the strength of the international resolve to institute safeguards against the reemergence of fascism, and the adoption of declarations and treaties that invoked the transcendent value of human dignity and the pivotal moral importance of respect for human rights. Sadly, however, the commitment to norms of international cooperation has proved to be fragile, and the will to honor international treaties has been too weak to withstand assault from imperial ambitions and parochial political interests.[4] Glover makes a compelling case for thinking that prospects of our attaining the deeper, more nuanced, and practically attuned understanding we need to resist the resurgence of tyranny in the twenty-first century turn on our acquiring a more robust understanding of human psychology, and of the ways in which people allow themselves to be silenced and distracted: Why it is that humans are so ready to descend into denial, self-deception, rationalization, and projection? Why have even the citizens of self-proclaimed democracies proved to be so vulnerable to manipulative tactics that erode democratic institutions and threaten to turn their state into something that is democratic in name only? *Humanity* makes it clear that we must make more of an effort to understand both the workings of our own psychology and the moral complexities of social contexts if we are to harbor reasonable hopes of being able to mount effective resistance to the techniques of political manipulation and control that are, once again, being actively deployed: the moral philosophy we draw upon to guide ourselves through the twenty-first century needs to be firmly grounded in the sort of critical self-reflection that is well informed by social science.[5]

However, if our improved social scientific understanding is in fact to yield more psychologically astute patterns of assessment and ground more mindful practice, it is not enough to for us to study social science along with history and moral philosophy, or to attend more carefully to the evidence adduced in support of proffered social scientific conjectures. Nor is it enough to conjoin these with more extensive teaching of critical thinking skills, even those that are enhanced by an understanding of scientific and social scientific methods and an awareness of the insights that can been achieved thereby. People must also be able to scrutinize reasons and values in contexts that are interactive, collaborative, and nonintimidating. And this, in turn, involves both learning more about the social institutions that frame our perceptions and choices, and taking steps to ensure that our society's systems of governance and regulation are relatively transparent and responsive. If democracies are to survive the latest series of authoritarian and ideological challenges to them, then more must be done to deepen our commitment to foster a culture of civic virtue that embraces open communication and access to education, and champions the creation of opportunities for people to apply their critical skills in a climate of tolerance. The cultivation of such a culture of civic virtue is, if not the foundation of democracy, the precondition of its continued survival in the twenty-first century.[6]

In what follows, I sketch the outlines of a strategy that both draws its inspiration from the argumentation in *Humanity* and is one that I hope will strengthen our determination to resist the erosion of foundational democratic institutions, practices, and habits of mind, and improve the efficacy of our efforts. Central to this strategy is the contention that our prospects of progress on these fronts may well turn on our finding a way to retreat from the full-bore commitment to neoliberal ideology that arose subsequent to World War II, and achieved ascendancy in the last quarter of the twentieth century.[7] More specifically, when we reflect on Glover's admonitions about the dangers that fact-twisting ideologies and politicized science pose to the survival of democratic governments and institutions, I believe that we will recognize that we must take more robust measures to counterbalance some of the most insidious and pernicious consequences of the embrace of neoliberal ideology: the corporatization of scientific research and higher education, and the privatization fervor that allowed for the creation of media monopolies that subordinate the public good of free and open communication to the pursuit of private profit.

Faced with the enormous challenge of rebuilding a shattered Europe while avoiding the recurrence of global economic crisis, the international participants at the Bretton Woods Conference in 1944 chose to jettison most of the remnants of the New Deal social safety net and retreat from Keynesian economic policies in favor of ones based on the neoclassical 'rational actor' models that had informed Operations Research (OR) in the later years of the war.[8] The resulting creation of global financial institutions and embrace of 'free trade' practices ceded enormous power and influence to those who were financially and politically well positioned.[9] Neoliberal policies quickly became both widely spread and deeply entrenched.[10] By the start of the 1980s, both Margaret Thatcher and Ronald Reagan were able to persuade voters that economists had 'proved' that state-owned industries and public services that were charged with providing public goods were 'inefficient': these services could be delivered much more cheaply if they were privatized, and the government's regulatory oversight was relaxed or removed altogether.[11] At roughly the same time, and for closely related reasons, intellectual property regimes acquired greater traction. According to neoliberal ideology, polices that impose the fewest restrictions on business and industry are the ones that are both morally superior, since they are most the most freedom-promoting, and most economically beneficial for the nation. Thus, as information technologies improved and potential scientific applications increased, neoliberal economists and politicians sought to enact policies that gave both the inventors and implementers of these technologies and the corporate investors that funded them the opportunity to attain a direct, robust financial return on their investment of capital and labor. The production of knowledge was subsumed under the industrial production model: since knowledge, too, was viewed as a commodity and a generator of wealth, it could and should be privatized.[12] The embrace of neoliberal policies thus embodied a radical departure from the Enlightenment-based views that placed great emphasis on the idea that knowledge is intrinsically valuable, and from the Progressive views of the state that saw it as properly charged with trying to improve the well-being of the populace by improving its knowledge base.

This embrace of 'market fundamentalism' and both the broad reverence for corporate autonomy and the toleration of corporate hegemony that have gone along with it have facilitated the use of science as a tool of the wealthy and powerful and magnified the untoward social consequences of its being thus used. Glover powerfully describes the scientific and human disasters that resulted from Hitler's and Stalin's subversion of science to the objectives of their political ideologies. Though Nazi eugenic policies and Lysenkoism are widely invoked as horrific instances of science steered wrong by the hands of madmen, they are often regarded principally as lurid tales from the past with little or no relevance to the present.[13] But in fact, in the twenty-first century, the opportunities for using science as a tool to advance dubious political objectives are more plentiful. And the risks of doing so have increased enormously in scope and now pose a greater threat of producing harms that are potentially dire and irremediable. As this century progresses, the course of human lives is likely to be affected even more profoundly by the use of genomic medicine and ever more sophisticated reproductive techniques, by reliance on powerful and potentially privacy-eroding nanotechnologies, by the application of chemical and biological weapons research to expand both the lethality and the scope of human weaponry, and by the proliferation of nuclear technologies. If things continue as they are, and corporate norms—rather than more disinterested or welfare-protecting ones—continue to be dominant in framing our cultural understanding of the nature and value of science and the proper implementation of knowledge and technology, the potential risks will increase in number, scope, and gravity. As a number of scientists and social commentators have recently argued, our experiences with some of the excesses and failures of corporate science should enable us to see the problems with corporate representations of science and with the science policies that have been fostered by neoliberal ideology. Both have been marred by bias, oversimplification, and the provision of incomplete, distorted, and sometimes overtly inaccurate information.[14]

Because the need for corporate owners to 'protect their investments' has been accorded the greatest primacy, there has been increased secrecy and expanded corporate control over research design and the publication of results. Scientists who have sought to abide by the norms that accord value to publicity, transparency, and the protection of the public—rather than prioritizing the corporation's pursuit of maximum profit—have been subjected to intimidation, research suppression, character assassination, and calculated career destruction.[15] And the private property quagmire of patents, trademarks, and enforced secrecy that restricts the free flow of information places all of humanity in a potentially perilous situation: There are far fewer people who now have unfettered access to the relevant (unmassaged) data, and far fewer public agencies that are staffed by informed and disinterested individuals who are committed to serving the public good, rather than to pleasing their corporate masters. We thus have good grounds to question whether our government will be able to be effective in foreseeing harm, or in enacting effective proactive preventative policies to forestall the premature implementation of powerful and potentially dangerous new technologies.[16] Continuing to allow neoliberal ideology to frame scientific research agendas and marketing paradigms to govern the dissemination of information and the implementation of technology poses serious risks, not only to the individuals or nations that seek to profit economically from the implementation of the technologies, but also to much broader swaths of humanity, if not to continued life itself. The ideologies that now threaten to undermine democratic institutions and weaken the commitment to promote citizens' well-being are different in salient respects from those that threatened such things in the early twentieth century, as are the postures of the politicians and technocrats who embrace the ideologies. But they are no less pernicious. We must heed Glover's warnings about the dangers of allowing ideological Belief to dictate Truth by politicizing science, and thus take steps to implement institutions that enable us to oversee and mitigate the effects of the unscrutinized, unregulated deployment of technologies by individuals and nations whose primary concern is with profit, and with securing their own advantage.[17]

I wish to focus attention here on two families of concerns that increase both the likelihood that science will continue to be politicized, and the likelihood that the consequences of such politicization will be more dire because of the globalization of technology, which stands to amplify the untoward consequences that ensue when there is an 'accident' and harm results from the implementation of a technology. In Section 4.2, I further develop the argument that the rise of neoliberal ideology has played a fulcral role in perniciously politicizing science. But it should be borne in mind that the market fundamentalism that emerged at the end of World War II and achieved dominance during the 1980s did not merely drive economic and fiscal policy. Because it also changed our understanding both of what knowledge is and of why we should regard it as valuable, it has also effected important changes in our conceptual and normative frameworks, and thus ultimately in our attitudes toward each other. The embrace of neoliberal ideology has allowed the state and its leaders to have a stronger commitment to enhancing the financial interests of the powerful corporate few than to trying to affect the Good of the many by means of the pursuit of the True. In Glover's parlance: our commitment to pursue 'truth-directed science' has been undercut by the neoliberal embrace of profit-driven science. It is pernicious to politicize science in this way, not just because it stands to magnify risks, but also because it erodes both our society's epistemic base and its moral core.

In Section 4.3, I briefly explain how the embrace of neoliberal ideology has also fostered dramatic changes in the ethos of the media and in the communications field more generally. As the neoliberal mandate has allowed dedication to the pursuit of an informed citizenry to be eclipsed by the embrace of the pursuit of profit for the well positioned, the interest in securing the knowledge base needed to produce an educated citizenry and retain a robust democracy has taken a back seat to the desire to distract and amuse consumers. It is the latter that is more quickly and more reliably financially lucrative, after all: it is easier to sell than to inform or instruct, and certainly more profitable. In the United States, ownership of the mainstream media (MSM) is now consolidated in the hands of six major corporations. Nor do the corporations that own the newspapers and television stations merely own other media outlets like film and music production and distribution studios. More worryingly, they also have extensive holdings in other domains—including 'defense,' weapons, energy, pharmaceutical, and agribusiness industries—in which corporate profits are augmented by the government's embrace of bullying and belligerent stances toward other countries rather than more cooperative ones.[18] The owners of the MSM have been able to exercise enormous political influence in shaping policy, and the policies that are financially beneficial to them have been ones that augment conflict rather than try to resolve it. By shaping what information gets communicated to the citizenry, they have been able to market war, violence, and political unrest. They have also fostered the medicalization of our view of social ills, which has resulted in a shift of focus to questions of 'individual responsibility and away from the examination of social institutions.'[19] There has thus been a wholesale retreat from the early twentieth-century commitment to pursue preventative and environmental strategies to promote public health in favor of a focus on treating ill individuals, which is surely more profitable for the insurance and pharmaceutical industries.[20]

The corporatization and privatization of the media are not bad just because they applaud selfishness and greed, or because they move the focus of the MSM away from informing people and toward marketing to them, and thus toward trying to buy our attention any way they can, including appeal to base human motives rather than to high-minded ones. They are also bad because they actively promote bias, censorship, shading, and artful concealment. Because corporations have a fiduciary obligation to maximize the profits to a small and select portion of the populace—to wit, their current shareholders—the CEOs who run them are effectively legally precluded from thinking about the long term or more global consequences of corporate policies. They are thus likely to assess the Good in a way that is both short-sighted and parochial. In addition, the mandated narrowness of corporate concern about the fortunes of only some beneficiaries (shareholders rather than stakeholders) gives CEOs of the corporate-owned media a powerful incentive to conceal or distort information that is presented to the public. If honest and accurate dissemination of information would be prejudicial to their shareholders' interests, CEOs have an incentive to discourage it, even in cases in which the dissemination of accurate information would be potentially vital to the long-term protection of public health or the environment. This is clearly dangerous, not merely undemocratic. But even this does not constitute a complete catalogue of either the evils or the dangers. Because there has been a precipitous rise in (what I shall call) 'public relations speak,' the corporatization of the media has not simply allowed for some restriction of the content of what gets communicated, and encouraged the practice of 'infotaining' people rather than informing them. It has also encouraged the use of more vigorous and underhanded forms of misrepresentation and manipulation. Since the objective is not to inform people but to sell things (and ideas) to them, the infotainment strategies that are deployed are not merely prurient, incomplete, biased, and misleading, but often also more actively manipulative. After all, it is not the education of the public or the provision of accurate and useful information that generates profit for advertisers or augments the gains of shareholders. Corporations have thus chosen to use public relations firms and to implement marketing strategies that employ overtly deceptive styles of communication, and—because pandering to people's most primitive emotions (fear, hate, prurience, and anxiety) is a more effective way of getting people to purchase things than appealing to reasoned argument—PR firms have helped corporations do what they can to grease the skids to get us to the ethical bottom.[21] I discuss some of the (other) implications of the rise of PR speak further in Section 4.3.

Questions about what we can and should do to loosen the vise of neoliberal corporate-centered ideology and to rescue public discourse from the stranglehold of PR speak are pointed, complex, and achingly difficult. The same can be said of more focused practical questions about what steps we can take to undercut the pernicious politicization of science: the erosion of the commitment to engage in 'truth-directed science' in favor of the embrace of privatizing policies that encourage the reckless pursuit of corporate profit, and attach greater importance to fattening corporate coffers than to protecting public health, the environment, and future people. The good news (insofar as there is any) is that a number of powerful critiques have emerged within the past few years. Faced with mounting evidence that espousing neoliberal ideology has led to the implementation of policies that have dramatically increased inequality by enhancing the wealth of those in the top one-tenth of the populace at the expense of the welfare of those in the bottom quartile; epidemiological data that suggest that inequality is detrimental to a society's overall public health, including the health of the rich; reports about the growth in inhumane labor practices and human trafficking, and increasingly powerful models that show that the continued reckless consumption of energy stands to increase pollution and accelerate global climate change in ways that may have dire consequences for all life on the planet, more and more commentators people have sought to deploy the abundant empirical evidence of significant social harm to bolster their contention that we must retreat from neoliberalism.[22] Applying these thoughts more specifically to matters concerning governments' use and abuse of science, there is reason to think that the replacement of the commitment to 'truth-directed science' with a paradigm that exalts commodified and corporate-controlled information is not merely short-sighted and inimical to democracy, but potentially catastrophic: Neoliberal ideology must be radically modified or rejected. *Humanity* reminds us that the stakes are enormous.

4.2 THE NEOLIBERAL NEXUS

The official emergence of neoliberal policies can be viewed as starting with the ratification of the agreements that were formulated during the UN Monetary and Financial Conference at Bretton Woods.[23] Sometimes also described as the 'Washington Consensus' or as 'market fundamentalism,' neoliberal views hold that personal freedom is best realized through the operation of the 'free market,' and that (more broadly) governments best promote freedom by refraining from imposing regulations on business, industry, or the financial sector.

Those who embrace neoliberal ideology construe freedom in narrow and contrastive terms, roughly as the libertarian notion of 'negative freedom' articulated by Isiah Berlin.[24] They assign more importance to refraining from encroaching on the negative freedom of entrepreneurs than they do to protecting the general public or to equitably distributing the goods that individuals need to exercise meaningful freedom in the twenty-first century world, most notably equal access and equal protection, security, and public health. However, it is not the question of the soundness of libertarian views of freedom that is my focus here, as much as the social and scientific consequences of embracing neoliberal ideology. As I noted in Section 4.1, neoliberals view science as valuable, less because they regard it as a truth-directed activity than because they regard it as a knowledge-generating one. The difference in emphasis is significant. Though access to knowledge can be restricted by trademark, patent, and copyright protections, one cannot meaningfully be said to own truth, and one cannot

sell it. But if—as the neoliberals would have it—knowledge can properly be viewed as just another commodity, then it is unproblematical to
assert that it can be privatized, and thus owned, as well as bought, sold,
traded, optioned, and so forth.[25] The adoption of neoliberal ideology has
thus had a profound impact on how people conceptualize the notions
of information and knowledge, and on how they weigh and balance the
values of private property and ownership, increased scientific knowledge
and understanding, and well-being. The adoption of a neoliberal perspective thus also potentially colors both our understanding of governments'
proper interest in encouraging scientific research, and our views about
how much weight should be attached to a government's obligation to
promote the dissemination of comprehensive and accurate scientific
information to its citizens. If the exchange of goods on the free market
is taken to be paradigmatic of free action—if not the ultimate expression
of freedom—and any government's or regulatory body's impedance of
free enterprise is treated as presumptively unjustified, then knowledge is
bound to be valued primarily because it is (and insofar as it is) regarded
because of its possession of commercial value. And scientific research is
likely to be seen as valuable because and insofar as it is thought to generate valuable products, namely ones that are marketable and that net
profits to their producers. As a corollary, the people who possess scientific
knowledge are likely to be urged to see themselves less as seekers of the
True and the Good than as entrepreneurs who own and manage property
that is valuable. Neoliberal views thus value good science not merely as
something that is good for business or the economy: for neoliberals, good
science is good because and insofar as it is good business. In a context in
which commodification is viewed as the embodiment of the structure and
logic of value rather than as just a metric for the calibration of one sort of
value, science is thus not merely politicized, but perniciously politicized:
the clear danger is that it will become yet another handmaiden of the
politicians and the powerful, another tool they can use to secure, extend,
and expand their power and influence.

The embrace of neoliberal ideology also spurred significant regulatory
and legal changes, particularly in the United States. The year 1980 can be
viewed as a watershed for the implementation of neoliberally influenced
public policies and legislation. As we have seen, the neoliberal vision of the
Good is, in fundamental respects, a commercial vision. By allowing Ananda
Chakrabarty, a microbiologist employed at General Electric, to patent the
oil-dissolving *Pseudomonas* bacterium that he had engineered through the
use of recombinant DNA technology, the Supreme Court's decision in
Diamond v. Chakrabarty paved the way for the extensive and largely unregulated commercialization of biomedical research.[26] Because they framed
the case as being principally about the need to interpret patent law in a way
that encouraged capital investment in scientific research, the five Justices
who upheld Chakrabarty's right to patent the life-form he 'invented' were
able to sidestep the ethical issues generated by the fact that the product

being patented was in fact a form of *life*, not simply an artifact, and hence to ignore questions about what it would mean to us to allow life to be thus completely commodified. They therefore bypassed substantive metaphysical and scientific concerns about the implications of treating a living organism as an artifact, as well as concerns about the potential ecological effects of introducing new, non-evolved forms of life into previously balanced ecosystems. No less significantly, they bypassed substantive normative questions about whether tolerating the patenting of forms of life constituted a retreat from the assignment of significance to the normative appraisals of human conduct that could not be reduced to economic calculations, something that might be thought to be a first step down a path that leads ineluctably to the trivialization or abandonment of conversations about the value of dignity. Though the Justices' determination to construe the issue as narrowly as possible jurisprudentially certainly played a role in their decision, so did their reflexive embrace of a neoliberal view of government and policy: it was the latter more than the former that allowed them to think that the fundamental ethical anxieties could simply be ignored or treated as clearly less important than the promotion of investment to generate more commodities. But it is hard to see how such a stance is defensible: by no stretch of the imagination can ecological or ethical concerns be viewed as peripheral to the issues being addressed in *Chakrabarty*.

The decision has also had significant institutional reach and powerful policy implications. By arrogating to itself the right to make a determination in Chakrabarty's case, the Court both bypassed Congress and effectively disenfranchised the people, thereby precluding wider social debate about how the value of respect for life and the value of promoting private profit should be balanced.[27] This was profoundly undemocratic, to say the least. In addition, some critics—including Justice Brennan, who filed a dissent—thought that the Court's understanding of patents was at odds with views embraced by the framers of the Constitution and articulated in previous judicial decisions.[28] Other critics questioned whether encouraging privatization of the fruits of discovery was the best way to support the quest for technological progress. In the end, because the Justices thought either that it was obvious that the ethical issues raised by *Chakrabarty* were less important than the policy issues the Court faced—to which it adopted a neoliberal approach—or viewed them as ones that lay beyond the Court's proper purview, we have been left in circumstances that are decidedly nonoptimal in both ethical and epistemological terms. The ethical and epistemological inadequacies of *Chakrabarty* have, in fact, cast long shadows in biology and medicine. The fact that *Chakrabarty* allowed portions of the human genome to be patented has both slowed collaborative research and increased both the costs of undertaking research and the costs of providing medical treatment. Both the True and the Good have been sacrificed to expand the domain of the profitable.

On the legislative front, the passage of the Bayh–Dole Act in 1980 and the subsequent passage of the Stevenson–Wydler Act enabled scientists working in government-funded laboratories to patent their discoveries, and obtain a great deal of money from doing so.[29] As the Cold War rhetoric that had enjoined American scientists to regard themselves as engaged in a struggle to the death with the Soviet Union waned, there was a retreat from belief in the importance of providing government-funded support for Big Science.[30] In this shifting political climate, neoliberals were able to be effective in lobbying the government to reduce its 'subsidies' to universities and other public institutions to encourage them to compete for funding in the 'free market.'[31] Faced with a myriad of problems in the wake of government funding cuts, universities were only too eager to try to make up their budget shortfalls and increase their competitiveness by forming partnerships with corporations. These partnerships proved to be enormously lucrative to many scientific researchers by enabling university-employed scientists to augment their faculty salaries—in some cases exponentially—both by forming their own corporations, and by enabling them to profit financially from the patenting of the results of their research. The number of partnerships between universities and corporations has thus continued to grow at an enormous rate.[32]

These changes have been problematical in a number of ways that have a direct bearing on the assessment of the consequences of politicizing science, and on the dangers that this sort of politicizing science poses to the health of a democracy. First of all, it is important to recognize that the claim that the creation of these partnerships has been financially beneficial to universities has been plausibly contested.[33] The introduction of patents and licensing agreements necessitated academies' addition of many bureaucrats and administrators, as well as vast legal departments. Significant portions of the academies' resources have gone into defending and initiating lawsuits and other forms of legal wrangling. While this has been beneficial to lawyers—intellectual property law became a growth industry almost overnight—it is hard to see how it has furthered universities' pursuit of their educational objectives, or enhanced their financial bottom line. Second, the institutional changes that were ushered in by *Chakrabarty*, Bayh–Dole, and Stevenson–Wydler and reinforced by subsequent legislation and judicial decisions have had profound intellectual and policy implications.

Together, these legislative policies and the *Chakabarty* decision effectively undermined societal commitment to public interest science, and profoundly affected people's view of the nature and value of science education. These policies greatly expanded the scope of what can be understood to be intellectual property, and both extended and strengthened the normative force attached to private ownership. Because within the neoliberal scheme of things, one's ability to accumulate capital is viewed both as a moral virtue and as the undisputed measure of one's success, scientists who ventured into the world of corporate-financed research and generated commercially viable products augmented their status, power, and funding opportunities. Those who were engaged principally in science education rather than in scientific research lost ground on many fronts, as did their colleagues in the humanities and in other fields perceived to yield little that was of immediate commercial value. The embrace of neoliberalism has thus had a profound impact on educational policy and practice: on how people view the function of higher education, and on the university as a social institution. And this has far-reaching implications for the broader society. When the value of acquiring knowledge is assessed by reference to people's perceptions of the immediate commercial value of its applications, people question the value of studying 'useless' things like literature, philosophy, history and cultural studies: humanities and social science are both revalued and devalued.[34] Coming to view education as valuable because and insofar as it directly enriches the coffers of those who are educated is something that threatens to diminish the scope and depth of human comprehension, and to erode the sort of imagination that (as Glover argues) is necessary for the operation of human compassion. Commerce may flourish thereby, but it is hard to be confident that our humanity will.

This recalibration of the basis of assigning value to scientific knowledge both reflected neoliberal beliefs about the presumed normative importance of acting to protect property rights, and contributed to the further normative strengthening of the notion of private property itself. The upshot is that property rights are now generally regarded as the bearers of great value (if not *the* bearers of value) in their own right. Their normative hegemony is largely unchallenged, and their normative force cannot easily be counterbalanced by appeals to the moral, social, or political importance of disseminating knowledge throughout the community, or easily contravened by those who seek to challenge the greed, consumerism, or untoward environmental consequences of embracing such a narrowly material interpretation of value.

What emerged in the wake of *Chakrabarty* and Bayh–Dole (et al.) has been a policy ambience that is harsh, crass, and profoundly undemocratic. It is one that lends silent legitimacy to the decision to attach more and more weight to the promotion of one kind of freedom, namely market freedom (itself a term of art), which only individuals and institutions that possess significant 'technology capital' can exercise effectively, and less and less weight to policies that seek to protect people who stand to be adversely affected by well-capitalized agents' unfettered pursuit of (short-term) profit. By actively encouraging scientists to embrace the role of scientist–entrepreneurs, neoliberals in the United States have not only sanctioned the creation of a new cadre of the scientific elite who amass power and status on the basis of their economic successes; they have also tacitly encouraged scientists themselves to embrace the terms of neoliberalism's assignment of greater entitlement, and greater distinction, to economically successful scientists. The 'democratic republic of science' has thus taken a direct hit, at least in the United States: It is less the noble embrace of wisdom, judiciousness or truth, or the desire to stem the tide of human misery that confers status and respect on scientists or constitutes the basis for praising them; it is, rather, their canniness and entrepreneurial skill. The politicization of science sparked by the embrace of neoliberal policies thus does not merely skew perceptions of what intellectual pursuits are worthy ones. In encouraging scientists to see themselves as entrepreneurs and to view scientific knowledge as just another marketable commodity, it also threatens to undermine scientists' integrity, and to degrade their character. Clearly, there is also a risk that the continued embrace of neoliberalism will erode both the foundations of people's respect for scientists and their trust in science. (I explore this further in Section 4.3.)

The proportion of scientists engaged in research in red biotechnology (biomedicine and public health) or green biotechnology (agriculture and food production and distribution) who do not have some corporate connections began to decline precipitously in the 1980s, and has now dwindled to the thinnest trickle. In consequence, there are now very few scientists who can be relied upon to dispense disinterested information to policy-makers. Virtually none of the scientists who serve on government regulatory commissions are free of conflicts of interest; indeed, individuals who sit on these commissions often have vested interests in the outcomes of the very policy deliberations in which they are participating.[35] The regulators have often had previous jobs in industry, and their prospects of returning to work for those industries at the end of their tenure on government commissions or advisory boards depend heavily on their advancing policies that are industry-friendly. (So common is this that the relationship between individuals in government and industry has been characterized as a 'revolving door.') Such an arrangement clearly does not conduce to the dispassionate assessment of evidence or to disinterested policy-formation.

The practice of allowing people with industry connections to sit on regulatory committees threatens not only to undermine the probity of the conclusions of the regulatory bodies on which these scientists serve, but also to erode people's trust in both science and government in more pervasive ways. If people come to believe that the scientists who appointed to serve on regulatory committees are shills for industry or puppets of politicians, then the pronouncements of such regulators are likely to be greeted not only with the sort of skepticism that generally attaches to the remarks of politicians and salespeople, but also with hostility. No one really expects politicians or salespeople to tell the truth, or to do so without putting a self-serving spin on it. But it is part of the legacy of our Enlightenment tradition that we take the norms of scientific assessment to be different from the norms that govern the conduct of salespeople and politicians. The norms of scientific research exalt such things as disinterestedness, publicity, and collaboration; arguably, if people do not think that researchers embrace these norms in the right way and to the right extent, then there is a risk that they will think that what these researchers are doing is not something we think of as science, but something else quite different.[36] The neoliberal norms that provide such zealous encouragement to scientists to become entrepreneurs and self-promoters, and politicians run the risk both of undermining science and upending the grounds of our attribution of value to its pursuit. There is thus a moral and intellectual crisis here, as well as an institutional one.

Instead of accepting the need for them to take steps to defuse conflicts of interest or engaging in frank discussion of how to mitigate the problems posed by pervasive conflict of interest, the response of both scientists and politicians—and certainly of the for-profit corporations that fund them—has generally been to evade the issues, or to deny the implications of the creation and exacerbation of deep, pervasive conflicts of interest. If everyone has such conflicts of interest, how serious can the problems really be?

Here Glover's plea that we do more to acquaint ourselves with empirical social scientific research has particular force. As studies from a number of fields show, norms of reciprocity are universal in human societies, and they are norms whose force people cannot easily surmount.[37] Even when we are not aware of being consciously swayed to repay a kindness with a kindness, the receipt of benefits from someone generally biases us in that person's favor.[38] Moreover, when we are confronted with evidence of our having been swayed by the norms of reciprocity, we are often inclined to deny that we have been unduly influenced.[39] This is research that has received considerable attention, but it seems to have had virtually no impact on the behavior of policy makers, and surprisingly small effect on practices within academic science. Yet, conflicts of interest are a serious problem, and both the acknowledgment of that fact and the attempt to identify and sequester the impact that previously unacknowledged conflicts of interest have on social policy formation may be crucial to the survival of democracy.

Nor is it only painfully naïve individuals or ones who are desperate for funding who engage in special pleading and evasion, or succumb to the need to engage in painful and strained self-justification. When critics suggested that the probity of the opinion of the former Surgeon General C. Everett Koop might have been undermined by his conflicts of interest—his views about the propriety of extending patent protection on a drug just might have been colored by the fact that his foundation had just received a $1,000,000 contribution from the manufacturer of the drug that Koop was charged with assessing—Koop was clearly both surprised and offended. He said:

> I have never been bought, I cannot be bought. I am an icon, and I have a reputation for honesty and integrity, let the chips fall where they may...It is true that there are people who could not receive a million-dollar grant and stay objective. But I do.[40]

As Koop's remarks remind us, people do not like to think of themselves as liars or apologists, or to believe that they can be bribed; still less do they like to admit that that they *have* been bribed. Thus, unless we are well informed, psychologically sophisticated and vigilantly self-critical—something we cannot realistically hope to be unless others know what we are doing and know that they can question our decisions without fear of reprisal—cognitive dissonance is likely to be the engine of massive and blatant self-deception: It is easier for us to *believe* that the truth is just as our benefactors wish it to be, than for us to regard ourselves as shills or liars.[41]

What this suggests is that even when there are not other more overt conflicts of interest and appointed regulators do not have glaring defects of character, scientists who have been appointed to regulatory positions by government officials whose policy predilections they know fully well, are under internal psychological pressure to toe the line as well as under external pressure. When we know someone has a vested personal or financial interest in the outcome, it is even more reasonable for us to doubt the soundness of his or her estimations and inferences. It would thus seem to be reasonable for us to be wary of the deliverances of regulators who are scientist–entrepreneurs; indeed, it may well be more sensible and prudent for us to doubt them than to trust them. Here, then, is the crux of the problem: if people have grounds for not trusting the scientists who advise government officials about matters of policy or have reason to question whether they are reliable, honest brokers, these are things that have the potential to erode the peoples' confidence in their government. Moreover, because they have the potential to lead people more generally to be skeptical about the assertions of scientists and to question when (and whether) a piece of scientific evidence that has been adduced should in fact be accorded credibility and used as a ground of public policy, they have the potential to undermine both people's interest in trying to be critical thinkers, and their capacity actually to be to be effective critical thinkers. And, as Glover points out, the erosion of the belief in the importance of critical thinking or in citizens' capacity to engage in it is something that has implications regarding their ability to be responsible citizens in a sustainable democracy.

Koop's response is likely to seem implausible to people who possess either social scientific knowledge or common sense. But being aware of Koop's self-deception does not render us immune to committing equally egregious errors. Even those of us who are less vulnerable to self-deception than Koop appears to be are sometimes prone to closely related conflations of intellectual acuity and moral probity, and thus liable to commit what I call 'the fallacy of the generalization of expertise,' which is clearly a version of the well-known 'halo effect.' We tacitly view our approbation of someone's scientific acumen as providing prima facie grounds for forming a favorable judgment of the person's character and general reliability, even in areas in which his or her competence has not been demonstrated.

Both social and psychological aspects of the way we live in the early twenty-first century facilitate the making of such patently fallacious inferences. In a large and highly technologized society, we often cannot undertake our own detective work to analyze our options. We are thus compelled to rely on the testimony of other people, particularly in complex and specialized areas, in which the stakes are high and the time is short. In addition, we must sometimes make relatively uninformed decisions about who is reliable, and about which experts we ought to trust. (As we see in Section 4.3, these are things that render us especially vulnerable to exploitation by the advertisers and public relations people.) And people who wish to influence the outcome of our choice can induce us to do things that we would not otherwise be so eager to do by ratcheting up the psychic and material costs of our abandoning belief in the reliability of avowed experts. It is thus not only ardent self-congratulators like Koop, televised actor–doctors, and conspicuously corrupt regulators whose deliverances we should question. Under the current neoliberal scheme which both exacerbates scientists' conflicts of interest and ignores the epistemic and ethical problems that such conflicts of interest pose, even thoroughly decent people may find themselves headed for the rocks.[42]

Here both Glover's discussion of human psychological failings and of the specific ways that the failure to possess adequate psychological knowledge and insight can lead us to accede to morally terrible things are very much to the point. Under a neoliberal regulatory regime, even regulators who were not antecedently corrupt are regularly put into positions in which they are more vulnerable to corruption, and more likely to deny that their judgment has been corrupted. Because it attaches primacy to the private pursuit of profit, neoliberal ideology is incapable of taking seriously the problems posed by the existence of conflicts of interest faced by scientists, entrepreneurs, and regulators with corporate or industry ties. The embrace of neoliberal ideology thus both increases the likelihood that science will be perniciously politicized, and our vulnerability to the consequences of its being thus politicized.

Though I am certainly not among those who are likely to be counted a friend of neoliberalism, it should be recognized that the criticisms raised here do not stem simply from my antagonism to neoliberal ideology or my dismay at the terrible inequalities and miseries that have resulted from its ascendancy. My argument here has been rather that turning scientists into entrepreneurs and allowing corporations to dominate the structural and normative framework of policy decisions contributes to the pernicious politicization of science by exacerbating the very psychological vulnerabilities that Glover persuasively argued had such dire consequences for our twentieth-century counterparts.

4.3 THE RISE OF PUBLIC RELATIONS AND THE EROSION OF TRUTH-DIRECTED SCIENCE

Glover makes it painfully clear that understanding how dangerous it is for us to live in a society in which the politically motivated subversion of truth is rife involves appreciating that manipulators of truth are likely to act in subtle and devious ways that may be difficult for ordinary people to detect and document.

We may lose sight of this if we treat Nazi eugenics and Soviet biology as our icons of perniciously politicized science. Both the Nazis and the Soviets enacted policies that were anything but subtle (at least in retrospect): the Nazis overtly persecuted intellectuals, especially those they deemed to be sympathetic to 'Jewish science' (*Juden Wissenschaft*), and Stalin arrested, tortured, exiled, and executed biologists who embraced 'bourgeois scientific theories' that did not comport with Marxist–Leninist ideology; famously, Stalin supported the abandonment of Mendelian genetics of in favor of the Lamarckian view embraced by Lysenko. But—as Glover reminds us—both the Nazis' and the Soviets' political domination of the bulk of the populace, including the nonscientists, was effected not only through sheer might and intimidation, but also 'through Belief' (253). The orthodoxies of the Nazis and the Soviets were not merely dictated to people, but *inculcated* in them as well.

Overt coercion can achieve only so much in a populace: a government that wants control over its citizenry must seek to dominate people through Belief as well as force. As Glover points out, the articulation of lofty, utopian visions of the Good can mesmerize, even as it inspires (311). When leaders present their vision of the Good in such a lofty manner, this eases the acceptance of their proposals and decisions; the artful use of propaganda and disinformation techniques can then have even more powerful effects. In both Nazi Germany and the Stalinist USSR, the governments did not merely exclude, banish, and persecute scientists whose beliefs did not comport with state ideology. Nor did they exercise control over the public's perception of what it was that scientific research revealed merely by the use of propaganda and the deliberate dissemination of disinformation. Importantly, they also distorted, filtered, and suppressed evidence in order to craft a version of the truth that was politically acceptable, and deployed these tactics of 'selective science' to manipulate people's views about what it was (and what it was not) to be a 'scientific expert.' Though the selective science tactics of twenty-first century governments may be different in detail from those of twentieth-century governments, many of the differences may be more superficial than substantive.[43]

It is not merely overtly authoritarian governments that seek to manipulate their citizens. Importantly, as things now stand in the early twenty-first century, even governments we regard as democratic both direct and craft the flow of information to their citizens. Increasingly, some of these avowedly democratic governments have come to severely regiment and restrict the flow of information. Though totalitarian governments can more easily impose political litmus tests on scientists and sanctify as experts those whose conclusions help further their political agendas than governments that profess to be democratic (and hence less secretive), even governments that are ostensibly democratic may abuse their power, suppress and distort information, and rely upon extra-scientific criteria to decide who is to be deemed a scientific expert (or a practitioner of 'sound science').

As commentators in a variety of fields have pointed out, politicians' and governments' reliance on public relations personnel and other individuals who are charged with 'shaping public opinion' has increased greatly. The techniques of those engaged in public relations and other forms of 'integrated communications' have become much sophisticated, manipulative and—at times—downright underhanded.[44] All but the most naïve of us know that salespeople, celebrities, and political campaign managers employ media specialists and public relations experts to craft people's perceptions in order to make sales, advance careers, and render clients more attractive. But most people are not aware of the tactics that public relations people use to effect these results: "People often equate public relations with the advertising industry…[but] PR firms carry out activities that are often considerably more secretive and sinister than designing clever slogans and video imagery"; these activities involve the use of a "strategic blend of paid media, free media, 'crisis management,' industrial espionage, organized censorship, and the infiltration of civic and political groups."[45]

The use of public relations techniques and other communication management strategies has become increasingly widespread; it is certainly not restricted to product promotion or celebrity image management. Public relations methods are now "used almost reflexively to promote and protect ideas, policies, candidates, ideologies, tyrants and hazardous products."[46] Indeed, politicians may have even more incentive to try to achieve their objectives by spinning information to ensure that citizens receive the message the politicians wish to transmit, since it is not merely money, celebrity, or market dominance that is at stake in politics, but power, which confers all three. Disconcertingly, there are reasons to worry that politicians' use of public relations techniques is likely to be more pervasive, not less, in a democracy than in an overtly totalitarian society:

> Governments that murder and jail their critics don't particularly need to worry about maintaining an attractive image among their own people.…Contrary to common assumptions, propaganda plays an important role—and certainly a more covert and sophisticated role in technologically advanced democratic societies, where the maintenance of the existing power and privileges are vulnerable to popular opinion.[47]

Those who currently occupy positions of power clearly have both the means and the incentive to represent their proposed policies in ways that accord with the beliefs and desires of the portion of the citizenry they deem to be most critical to the acceptance of those policies, and thus to the perpetuation of their power. Government officials may thus be moved to present complex issues in ways that are designed explicitly to forestall or undercut objections, and reduce dissent. Because people in government have easy access to the media and the ready attention of the public, they can easily find vehicles to publicize their reframed representations. They can thus use the media quite deliberately to shape people's perceptions of government proposals. The simplest and most effective 'information management' technique may be the creative use of redefinition or reframing to ensure that the issues are represented in ways that are palatable (and nonthreatening) to the populace.

In the United States, Republican legislators used such techniques in 2006 to help win passage of legislation to reduce estate taxes when they couched their position as opposition to the continuation of 'the death tax.' This was a very effective reframing, and one that was widely disseminated in the media. Everyone dies, of course; the Republicans' characterization of opposition to the repeal of the estate tax as expressing support for the (continued) taxation of death effectively defused public objections. Opposition to the repeal of the estate tax was made to seem both cruel and stupid. The Republicans' reframing also involved the artful concealment of the huge fiscal implications of repealing the estate tax, and diverted people's attention away from the recognition that cutting to taxes on estates worth in excess of several million dollars involved the conferral of an additional windfall on people who were already enormously wealthy—and people whose children had presumably already received great benefits of this wealth—as well as the loss of a huge amount of projected revenue to the state. (Death is the great leveler, but the elimination of estate taxes certainly is not.) The Republican administration chose to abide by the rules of the 'politics of perception,' and deployed the media very skillfully. It did what it could to forestall informed and intelligent public discussion of a controversial proposal—one that would further exacerbate inequality, decrease government revenue, undercut the motivation for the very rich to donate to charity to get the benefit of tax benefits on their inheritance, and provide an 'economic boost' to that segment of the population that least needed it by shifting a heavier burden onto those who were much less able to bear it.

The revelation that democratically elected governments spend enormous amounts of money on public relations, media management and 'opinion-shaping' should occasion profound unease, since the public relations worldview is both inherently secretive and antidemocratic, as well as uninterested in presenting a balanced view of the facts. And it should be noted that the citizenry subsidizes its own deception through the payment of tax dollars. Although technically proscribed from using funds to pay for PR, sitting administrations in the United States have found and forged technical loopholes that enable them to deploy PR strategies of belief manipulation, and to use billions of taxpayers' dollars to do it.

To understand better how underhanded and antidemocratic the public relations world is, it may be instructive to consider some of the intuitive differences between advertising and PR techniques. No adult expects advertisers to present an audience with an open or unbiased view of their

products. Both by statute and contention, advertisers are under no obligation to provide us with a full list of pros and cons about their products.
People of even moderate sophistication know that the thing being adver-
tised in the most glowing terms is not likely to work as flawlessly, look as
good, or achieve the range of wonderful results that the advertisements
suggest it will. This connects with other two other important differences
between advertising and PR that are relevant to understanding how science is currently being perniciously politicized.

People often suppose that they can tell when something is an adver-
tisement and when it is not. They also think that their ability to detect
when something is advertising insulates them from the influence of the
advertising; more generally, people tend to underestimate the degree to
which their own behavior is influenced by advertisements and exaggerate the vulnerability of others, and to think that they are less vulnerable
to the effects of advertising than 'most other people' are.[48] Advertisers
know that people overestimate their ability to withstand advertising techniques; indeed, this recognition forms the core of many advertising campaigns' success. But the use of PR techniques rather than just advertising
to shape public perception is often motivated by the desire to use techniques that do not rouse suspicion, ones that are persuasive, manipulative,
and underhanded, and thus may involve profoundly misleading concealment or misrepresentation. Video news releases (VNRs), for example, are
a popular PR technique that involves marketing a product by presenting a
'story' on the news that is, in fact, not a news story at all, nor even a piece
of accurate reportage, but a promotional piece produced to market the
products or services of a station's advertiser, complete with actors playing
the role of doctors or 'expert' scientists.[49]

Not all PR techniques are this patently deceptive. However, since people who resort to the use of PR techniques operate with the presumption that it is both legitimate and appropriate for some people to set the
agenda for others, and even to use the others' funds to implement that
agenda, the decision to use PR techniques bespeaks the embrace of a
stance that is both inegalitarian and frankly manipulative. Our continued
tolerance of the use of PR techniques by large corporations and the government thus involves our tacit assent to the view that it is unproblematical for those who are rich and powerful to use their wealth and power to
exert control over the beliefs, actions, and purses of the rest of us. This is
repugnant, and deeply undemocratic.

Traditionally, defenders of the use of public relations appeal to the
presumed ignorance of the common people: "The public is irrational and
poorly educated; in the minds of some, this makes democracy itself too
dangerous."[50] Philip Lesly, one of the most influential PR people of the
1970s, frankly embraced the antidemocratic implications of PR: Lesly
thought that one of the express objectives of PR should be to "curtail
people's democratic expectations."[51] Paternalism is also clearly operating
here: since the people are irrational and poorly educated, they are not to

be trusted to formulate policies that will benefit them. "A class of behind-the-scenes manipulators is necessary to shape public opinion for the public's own good."[52]

Those of us who live in countries that purport to be democratic are not likely to look favorably on the revelation that information is being concealed and manipulated 'for our own good,' especially when furthering our good just happens to be coextensive with further advertisers' and politicians' own interests. Nor are we likely to endorse allegations that we are too irrational and poorly educated to have our voices and votes accorded weight in policy deliberations. A government that makes extensive use of PR techniques and other communications management strategies to market public policy proposals that promote corporate interests (rather than embrace ones that assign greater weight to protecting public health or the environment, for example) will thus need to conceal its motives, since it is otherwise likely to alienate or antagonize people, and thus undercut the prospects of the tactics' success. If people come to suspect that their government attaches a PR spin to the information it supplies, and that it markets the policies it seeks to promulgate rather than attempting to fairly represent these policies, then people will eventually cease to trust government's pronouncements. This is clearly something that again has the potential to generate a downward spiral: as people become increasingly suspicious of, and resistant to the pronouncements of their government, a government that employs PR techniques is liable to be tempted to become even more secretive and deceitful, or more overtly self-serving and manipulative, and less truth-directed. It is reasonable to worry that a government that focuses its energy on shaping how it is that things are to be perceived by the people and expends energies to secure favorable perception will be less interested in what it is that people actually know, or in telling them the truth, and more interested in covering its own tracks. As *Humanity* makes only too clear, this has proven to be a recipe for disaster.

Our current tolerance of government's use of public relations and communications management techniques increases the likelihood of a reprise of the kinds of human rights abuses that had such dire consequences in the early twentieth century. It increases the gap between the governors and the governed, validates the government's reliance on secrecy and deceit, and threatens to subsume the government's commitment to promoting the public good to its pursuit of policies that are good for some people, notably the politicians, the corporate magnates, and their well-heeled friends. More generally, it both rationalizes and exacerbates the cynical pursuit of political power at public expense, and increases the likelihood of profound self-deception on the part of those wield political power. The danger is thus that hypocrisy will receive an institutional imprimatur: those in power will subvert the promotion of the public good to the furtherance of their own and their friends' interests while they—like Koop—self-righteously persuade themselves of their own rectitude.

These concerns are especially pressing at this juncture in history. In both the domestic and the international arena, transnational corporations now possess unprecedented amounts of capital and wield enormous influence over democratically elected governments. It is thus reasonable for us to worry not only that those in power will rank *our* interests lower than they rank *their* well-being or political survival, but also that our government will accord more weight to the promotion of *some* citizens' interests than it does to *others*: the interests of rich corporate executives will be more heavily weighted than are those of less affluent or less well-connected private citizens, who, because they lack financial clout, will also be denied political consequence. It would be disconcerting for citizens to come to suspect that their own government has little interest in promoting the welfare of the bulk of the populace. It might well also be something that destabilizes a democracy.

These problems have been greatly magnified by what has sometimes been called 'the problem of the media' and by the huge increase in the number of individuals who are paid lobbyists for private industry and special interests. In the United States, the major media are in the hands of only five large and heavily diversified corporations. These corporations actively lobby politicians, and they have made enormous campaign contributions and benefited handsomely from their investment. The number of paid lobbyists at the start of 2006 was estimated to be close to 35,000, which is double the number that there were in 2000; lobbyist spending also increased by fifty percent.[53] Politicians receive handsome campaign contributions if they support policies that are friendly to corporate interests; the same is obviously not the case if they actively support policies that promote the public interest, especially in contexts in which the promotion of interest of the public is seen as antagonistic to the support of powerful corporations. Members of the general public obviously do not generally have the resources to make enormous contributions to politicians, nor do they have the resources to counterattack if they are fired, served with lawsuits, and so forth. Once again when "the circulation of ideas is governed by enormous concentrations of wealth that have, as their underlying purpose, the perpetuation of their own power" it is the health of the democracy that is compromised.[54] In the United States, money certainly talks loudly: In the 2000 elections for the House of Representatives, the better-funded candidate was elected ninety-five percent of the time.

The implications of the entrenchment of the public relations world-view are thus both far-reaching and profound for a self-professed democracy that subscribes to neoliberal ideology; they are ones that suggest that our prospects of resisting the pernicious politicization of science may not be bright. Governments' and corporations' heavy reliance on communications management techniques results in their being able to succeed in framing scientific evidence to minimize the significance of their policies' environmental and public health impacts on the quality of life of those who are at the bottom of the economic heap, and thus lack political clout.

But it is not just the use of spin or the heavy use of techniques of reframing and skilled de-emphasis that are involved here. If this were the case, then we might hope to be able to mitigate (if not curtail) the effects of communications management techniques by educating people about them, and circulating critiques of the government-sponsored representations of its proposed programs. However, though it is important to educate people about PR techniques, this alone would not be sufficient to check the erosion of the commitment to truth-directed science in our society.

Even if we were able to get a government to foreswear engaging in practices that involve what we can characterize as clear wrongs—keeping important results and experiments secret from the people, or lying about the results of these experiments, or their implications—we cannot hope thereby to effect a sufficiently robust commitment to the pursuit of truth-directed science, or forestall the sorts of abuses and manipulations that lead to the pernicious politicization of science, and can lead a society into serious moral trouble. Scientific evidence does not wear its soundness on its face, and it is, moreover, something that can be fetchingly concealed and spun: what masquerades as truth may thus be an imposter.[55] In a context in which money can buy influence and beget special treatment for those who provide it, and one in which the scientists who serve on government regulatory commissions have intractable conflicts of interest, the scientific research that the government sponsors and the reports that it validates may be seriously biased, and thus seriously flawed. The process whereby people are certified by the government as scientific experts in matters of health and safety is thus often hopelessly corrupt: these 'experts' are anything but disinterested, and the 'results' that they arrive at were preordained, not discovered though the exacting application of scientific procedure or the unbiased scrutiny of the data.[56]

Reflection on the increase in both the scope of scientific knowledge and the number and complexity of its potential applications, and on changes in the institutional contexts in which this technoscience is evolving suggests both that there may well be more ways in which people may be deceived and manipulated by the politicization of science in the twenty-first century than there were in the twentieth century, and that the current manipulations may have more serious and widespread consequences. If we hope to avoid the sorts of political abuses and deceptions that were perpetrated on the populations of Germany and the Soviet Union in the name of progress and science, we need to be considerably more scientifically sophisticated than our twentieth-century counterparts were. But—as Glover makes clear, an increase in our scientific knowledge base and understanding is not sufficient. We must not only have enough analytical and empirical training to be able to evaluate public policy proposals. We must also acquire the critical acumen and psychological sophistication we need to be able to recognize when our policy formation practices are not working (for example, when those who have been charged with formulating and assessing our public policies have extensive and insidious conflicts of interests that are intractable). We thus must foster the creation of institutions and the promotion of the sort of social ambiance that allow people to raise their questions and concerns publicly, and encourage people to engage in public colloquy about how the government uses science in formulating its social policies. Are government appointees representing the evidence in a way that is misleading, simplistic, and unduly monolithic or according credibility to only one set of marginal voices? Are they framing issues in ways that are designed to mask controversy or distort scientific consensus in order to minimize citizens' dissent to policies that promote corporate interests at their expense? Are they both exaggerating the amount of disagreement there is among experts, or engaging in intentional misrepresentation of what that disagreement means?

As reflections on the implications of the government's increasingly heavy use of communications management strategies make clear, citizens who wish to maintain an effective oversight of their government need to have knowledge that goes beyond the sphere of scientific subjects like biology, genetics, evolution, chemistry, and statistics. They need also to possess background in the social sciences, and to be familiar with research and methodology: it is only if we possess this sort of grounding in social science that can we reasonably expect to be able to have either an appreciation of the damage that can be done by a government's reliance on the use of persuasive techniques like propaganda, advertising, and public relations, or the focused motivation to ascertain whether the things our government has told us bear the stamp of misinformation, disinformation, or other intentional manipulations of intelligence. To avoid falling hard into some of deeper quagmires that beset our twentieth century counterparts, we must try to cultivate the sort of cultural and educational environment in which there is more widespread understanding of both natural and social sciences on the part of the populace.

Scientists like to believe that they are more objective or clear-sighted than the rest of us. But this is certainly not obviously the case. Indeed, as reflection on Dr. Koop's remarks suggests, scientists who are confident that they are morally superior or more rational than the rest of us just because they are scientists are especially worrying precisely because this sort of confidence may grease the skids of self-deception and special pleading. Since "[t]he success of science depends on an apparatus of democratic adjudication" that is "more or less explicitly designed to counter human self-deception," there must thus be a thoroughgoing commitment to engage in critical self-reflection on the part of both nonscientists and scientists themselves.[57] As studies of individuals with authoritarian personalities have made clear, people who are not encouraged to examine their own behavior or to question their own motivations along with the motivations of others are much more vulnerable to the predations of demagogues and amoral exploiters.[58] People who are not inclined to engage in the examination of their own motives, or committed to the exploration of the implications of their beliefs, are vulnerable to people and institutions that can and will exploit them.

In *Humanity*, Jonathan Glover reminds us that the development of critical skills and the cultivation of habits of self-reflection are not merely things that are good in themselves, or means to the achievement of moral ends that there are good reasons for us to embrace. They are also skills that both shape and ground the sort of strategies we need to pursue to avoid the sorts of morasses that made the moral history of the twentieth century so dark. This may be the deepest and most important lesson to be gleaned from reading Glover's fine book: our hopes of avoiding the repetition of the errors of our twentieth-century counterparts turn not only on our commitment to championing the pursuit of wider scientific and social scientific understanding, but also on our cultivation of a fierce determination to work to foster the habits of critical engagement and reflective self-scrutiny, things that are necessary if we are to avoid falling prey to those who perniciously politicize science. I have argued that our success on these fronts is closely tied to a rejection of neoliberal ideology. It is hard to see how the stakes could be much higher: Reflection on both the science and politics of the early twenty-first century makes it abundantly clear that encouragement of critical thinking and citizen involvement in the formation and assessment of social policy is even more acute now than it was when Glover published *Humanity*.

Postscript

When *Humanity* was first published, I gave copies of the book to friends, colleagues, and family members, most of whom were not philosophers, or even academics. From their reactions, I learned that the passion, compassion, sensitivity, and erudition that infused the writing of *Humanity* are abundantly evident both to readers who are not philosophers or academics, and to those who have never met the book's author.

For those of us who have had the great good fortune to have met and interacted with Jonathan Glover, *Humanity* is also the embodiment of other important virtues and values, and it provides us with both an important reminder and inspiration. As Jonathan Glover shows, it is possible for a moral philosopher to write seriously about dark and important things without becoming a dark or self-important person, and to write about them in a way that renders them accessible to a wide audience without ever dumbing down the subject or talking down to readers. *Humanity* is thus not simply an intellectual tour de force, but also an accomplishment of the highest moral order. It is as estimable as it is both powerful and accessible.

It is not always the case that the finest works of moral philosophy are written by philosophers who are the most morally splendid of people. But when, in fact, the measure of the book is also the moral measure of the man, as is the case here, we are offered both luminous intellectual illumination and a deep affirmation of the power of moral philosophy: *Humanity* and Jonathan Glover provide us with a rare inspiration and the motivation to continue teaching and writing moral philosophy. There is here thus both a stunning intellectual achievement and the strongest possible pedagogical and personal inspiration.

Notes

I wish to thank Richard Keshen and Jeff McMahan for their helpful comments and suggestions.

1. *Humanity: A Moral History of the Twentieth Century* (London: Jonathan Cape 1999). All references to Glover are to *Humanity*, and are given as page numbers in my text.

2. Those who regard this formulation as too steeped in Enlightenment language or modernist presuppositions should substitute "the prospect of avoiding serious and abiding harm" for "moral progress."

3. For a discussion of the civil liberties implications of PATRIOT II, see the ACLU's comments at www.aclu.org/safefree/general/17203leg20030214.html. See also the text of the (proposed) H.R. 1955, *The Violent Radicalization and Homegrown Terrorism Prevention Act of 2007*, which would curtail the exercise of free speech and academic freedom, at www.govtrack.us/congress/bill. xpd?bill=h100-1955&tab=summary

4. Michael Ignatieff's dark diagnosis is apposite: "America's entire war on terror is an exercise in imperialism. This may come as something of a shock to Americans, who don't like to think of their country as an empire." Quoted in David Harvey, *The New Imperialism* (Oxford: Oxford University Press, 2005), p. 3.

5. Glover argues that philosophers need to attend more to the empirical realm, and especially to the facts of psychology. But—as a number of commentators have persuasively argued—it is not just the failure to be more psychologically attuned that is the problem, but also the fact that the theoretical lenses through which we interpret psychologically relevant data may be distorted ones. The dominance of neoclassical economics, with its attribution of priority to the pursuit of self-interest by rational actors, is especially problematical. See especially Philip Mirowski, *The Effortless Economy of Science?* (Durham, NC: Duke University Press, 2004); Philip Mirowski and Esther-Mirjam Sent (eds.) *Science Bought and Sold* (Chicago, IL: University of Chicago Press, 2002); David Harvey, *A Brief History of Neoliberlism* (Oxford: Oxford University Press, 2005), and John Dupre, *Human Nature and the Limits of Science* (Oxford: Oxford University Press, 2003). See also Joseph Stiglitz, *Globalization and Its Discontents* (New York: Norton, 2003) and John Perkins, *Confessions of an Economic Hit Man* (New York: Plume, 2006). I mean my invocation of the need for a more "social scientific focus" to include attention not merely to history and psychology (which Glover emphasizes), but also to economics, anthropology, and sociology. I also mean to be agnostic about whether it is the dearth of informed critical observation of psychological and social phenomena or the failure to formulate a sound explanatory framework that is (most) problematical.

6. Though *Humanity* can be read as plea for us to do more to promote a culture of civic virtue, there is comparatively little discussion that is explicitly focused on this powerful and central point. The discussion of moral identity and of bystanders are, however, especially relevant.

7. Neoliberalism can be characterized as Robert McChesney characterizes it in *The Problem of the Media* as "The political philosophy that dogmatically equates generating profits with generating maximum human happiness" (12), or as "[T]he view that markets and profit making should be allowed to regulate every aspect of social life possible." (49) (New York: *Monthly Review Press*, 204). For a fuller and slightly less tendentious characterization, see the text below.

8. See Mirowsky, ibid., and Harvey, ibid.

9. It is clear from the writings of those who attended the inaugural meeting of Hayek's Mont Pelerin Society in 1947 that these consequences were neither unforeseen nor unintended. See the essays collected in S.A. Hayek (ed.) *Capitalism and the Historians* (Chicago, IL: University of Chicago, 1963).

10. For a very recent and very powerful discussion of the extent of the implementation of neoliberal policies and their effects, see Naomi Klein, *The Shock Doctrine* (New York: Metropolitan Books 2007), which appeared after this chapter had been written.

11. Questions about the equality of access to these resources and about the equality of the opportunity to obtain them were largely ignored. Whether the turning away from questions of distribution and equality is more properly viewed as a feature of neoliberal policies or as a consequence of them is a point on which critics of neoliberalism are not clear.

12. See Sheila Jasanoff, *Designs on Nature* (Princeton, NJ: Princeton University Press, 2007); Sheldon Krimsky, *Science in the Private Interest* (New York: Rowman and Littlefield, 2004) and Corynne McSherry, *Who Owns Academic Work?* (Cambridge, MA: Harvard University Press, 2001).

13. See especially the discussion of the consequences of Lysenkoism in Chapters 29 and 30 of *Humanity* (274–98). It should be noted, however, that there is significant disagreement about what lessons have been learned about the evils of Nazi eugenics. Compare, for example, Gregory Stock, *Redesigning Humans: Our Inevitable Genetic Future* (Boston, MA: Houghton Mifflin, 2002) and Nicholas Agar, *Liberal Eugenics* (Oxford: Blackwell, 2004) with Edwin Black, *War Against the Weak* (New York: Thunder's Mouth Press, 2003) and Harriet A. Washington, *Medical Apartheid* (New York: Doubleday, 2006).

14. See especially Sheldon Krimsky, ibid., Devra Davis, *When Smoke Ran Like Water* (New York: Basic Books, 2002); Seth Schulman, *Undermining Science* (Berkeley, CA: University of California, 2006); Sheldon Ramptron and John Stauber, *Trust Us, We're Experts* (New York: Putnam, 2002); Chris Mooney, *The Republican War on Science* (New York: Basic Books, 2005); Mike Davis and Daniel Bertrand Monk (eds.) Evil Paradises: *Dream Worlds of Neoliberalism* (New York: New Press, 2007).

15. See the discussion of the cases of Betty Dong, Manuel Chavela, and David Healy discussed in Krimsky, ibid.; Devra Davis, ibid.; Ramptron and Stauber, ibid.; and Mooney, ibid.

16. One can argue about how robust our commitment to embrace precautionary strategies should be. (See Sheila Jasanoff, *Designs on Nature*, for an extended discussion of the differences between the United States and other countries with respect to the interpretation and embrace of the Precautionary Principle.) But the point I am making here is simply that we cannot even intelligently discuss the virtues of adopting a preventative strategy in a context in which access to full, unbiased information is in serious doubt.

17. Here Glover's concluding admonition seems especially significant, especially if we take the motives of greed and rapacious to be ones that can be counted

as part of the "destructive side of human psychology": "We have experienced the results of technology in the service of the destructive side of human psychology....It is too late to stop the technology. It is to the psychology we should now turn," 414.

18. See Jeremy Scahill, *Blackwater: The Rise of the World's Most Powerful Mercenary Army* (New York: Nation Books, 2007) and Naomi Klein, *The Shock Doctrine*.

19. See Peter Conrad, *The Medicalization of Society* (Baltimore, MD: The Johns Hopkins Press, 2007. See also Alan Horowitz and Jerome Wakefield, *The Loss of Sadness: How Psychiatry Transformed Normal Sorrow into Depression* (Oxford: Oxford University Press, 2007); and Lawrence H. Diller, *The Last Normal Child: Essays on the Intersection of Kids, Culture and Psychiatric Drugs* (London: Praeger, 2006).

20. It is important to point out that there is a strong connection between rising inequality and decreasing public health. "[T]here are diminishing returns to rising income....[T]he income/life expectancy curve is steep in the regions of absolute income deprivation; but it levels off beyond a certain standard of living....An important consequence of the shape of the income/life expectancy curve is that the *distribution* of income must influence the average life expectancy of a society....[T]he size of the gap between the rich and the poor—as distinct from the absolute standard of living enjoyed by the poor—matters in its own right for population health." Ichiro Kawachi, "Income Inequality and Health" in Lisa F. Berkman and Ichiro Kawwachi (eds.), *Social Epidemiology* (Oxford University Press: Oxford) 2000, 76–94, 77. Whether one wants to claim that health is central to welfare or that other forms of welfare may exhibit the same logic, the implications are clear, especially in the United States, which is "one of the richest countries in the world, yet...also one of the most unequal in terms of how that wealth is shared." Ibid. 76.

21. For a fascinating discussion of the use of tactics designed to appeal to people's fear, anxiety, insecurity, and narcissism to market SUVs, see Keith Bradsher, *High and Mighty* (New York: Perseus Books, 2003).

22. See, for example, David Harvey, *A Brief History of Neoliberalism*; Adam Phillips, *Wealth and Democracy* (New York: Broadway, 2003); Antonia Juhasz, *The Bush Agenda* (New York: Harper Collins), 2006; Amy Chua, *World on Fire* (New York: Anchor, 2004); Mike Davis, *Planet of Slums* (New York: Verso, 2007); Berkman and Ichiro Kawwachi (eds.), *Social Epidemiology*.

23. David Harvey, *A Brief History of Neoliberalism*. The official birth of the ideology can be traced to the first meeting of the Mount Pelerin Society in 1947, and to the ideas of Frederich von Hayek.

24. See "Two Concepts of Liberty" in Isiah Berlin (ed.) *Four Essays on Liberty* (Oxford: Oxford University Press, 1969), 118–72.

25. Here I skate superficially over interesting and dense terrain. See Lawrence Lessig, *The Future of Ideas: The Fate of the Commons in a Connected World* (New York: Vintage, 2002), and Kembrew McLeod and Lawrence Lessig, *Freedom of Expression: Resistance and Repression in the Age of Intellectual Property* (Minneapolis, MN: University of Minnesota Press, 2007). For a discussion of intellectual property in the context of the academy, see Corynne McSherry, *Who Owns Academic Work?*

26. 447 U.S. 303 (1980).

27. This constitutes a vivid reminder that the charge of "judicial activism," is one that can be made by those on the political left as well as those on the right.

28. 447 U.S. 303 (1980).

29. See Lori Andrews and Dorothy Nelkin, *Body Bazaar* (New York: Crown) 2001; Sheldon Krimsky, *Science in the Private Interest*; Derek A. Bok, *Universities in the Marketplace* (Princeton: Princeton University Press, 2003); Daniel S. Goldberg, *Science Money and Politics* (Chicago: University of Chicago Press, 2001); Chris Mooney, *The Republican War on Science*; and Marion Nestle, *Food Politics* (Berkeley, CA: University of California, 2002).

30. For a helpful discussion of the relevant historical background, see Daniel S. Greenberg, *The Politics of Pure Science*, new edition (Chicago, IL: University of Chicago Press, 1999).

31. Mirowski and Sent, *Science Bought and Sold*.

32. See Jennifer Washburn, *University, Inc: The Corporate Corruption of American Higher Education* (New York: Basic Books, 2005); Corynne McSherry, ibid.; Derek A. Bok, ibid.; and Sheldon Krimsky, ibid.

33. See, Jennifer Washburn, ibid.

34. Academic administrators and boards of regents have proposed to make universities "more efficient" by cutting back liberal arts programs. Nor it is only bureaucrats who have made such suggestion. Even intellectuals have signed on to such a program. For example, Richard A. Posner has suggested that courses in things like culture and gender studies be replaced by science and math courses. Unlike the bureaucrats, Posner's view does not seem to be that the worth of a course should be determined by the financial benefits that the faculty member teaching the course provides the university. The calculations are far cruder, and they have much more blatantly anti-intellectual and antidemocratic implications. It is worth quoting him at some length: "[T]he emphasis [in education] ought to fall on increasing the scientific literacy not of the population as a whole but of an elite consisting of the very bright students who go on to become officials and other policy makers and opinion leaders. Bright students have little to lose by sub-stituting math and science for courses in post-modern literary criticism and cul-tural studies, sociology, women's studies, black studies, [and] journalism....Society would not be worse off even if by concentrating on technical fields the bright stu-dents failed to become cultured persons." *Catastrophe: Risk and Response* (Oxford: Oxford University Press, 2004), 95. I imagine that Glover and most readers of *Humanity* would disagree.

35. See especially Philip Mirowski, ibid., and Sheldon Krimsky, ibid.

36. What we would take people to be doing when their "scientific research" appears not to be governed by the familiar norms good scientific methodology is not clear. Following what I take to be Glover's lead, I would maintain that they are allowing ideological Belief to dictate Truth. But, in fact, we need not explore that issue in any depth to recognize that people regard the norms of scientific research as fundamentally different from, and possibly in conflict with the norms of the marketplace.

37. See, for example, Robert Levine, *The Power of Persuasion* (Hoboken, NJ: John Wiley, 2003) and Robert B. Cialdini, *Influence: The Psychology of Persuasion* (New York: Collins, 2006).

38. It is often pointed out that the smaller the gift, the more likely we are to be influenced by it, in part because we do not think we are being influenced. See, e.g., Levine, ibid.

39. See, for example, Carol Tarvis and Elliot Aronson, *Mistakes Were Made (But Not by Me)* (New York: Harcourt, 2007).

40. Koop is quoted in Richard A. Deyo and Donald L. Patrick, *Hope or Hype* (New York: Amacon, 2005), 87.

41. Tarvis and Aronson, ibid.

42. See Sheldon Rampton and John Stauber, *Trust Us, We're Experts*.

43. See, for example, Donald T. Hornstein, "The Data Wars, Adaptive Management, and the Irony of 'Sound Science'" in Wendy Wagner and Rena Steinzor (eds.), *Rescuing Science from Politics* (Cambridge: Cambridge University Press, 2006), 103—s19.

44. See Stuart Ewen, *PR!: A Social History of Spin* (New York: Basic Books, 1996); Stauber and Rampton, *Trust Us, We're Experts*; and John Stauber and Sheldon Rampton, *Toxic Sludge is Good for You! Lies, Damn Lies and the Public Relations Industry* (Monroe, ME: Common Courage Press, 1995).

45. John Stauber and Sheldon Rampton, *Toxic Sludge is Good for You!*, 3.

46. Ibid., 4.

47. Ibid., 148 (quote from Alex Carey).

48. This is might be thought to be one of the pivotal recognitions that drives advertising, marketing, and PR. See, for example, Robert Levine, *The Power of Persuasion*.

49. See Sheldon Rampton and John Stauber, *Trust Us, We're Experts*.

50. Ibid., 111.

51. Ibid., 57.

52. John Dean, *Conservatives Without Conscience* (New York: Viking, 2006), 137.

53. Ewen, *PR! A Social History of Spin*, 410.

54. Robert W. McChesney, *The Problem of the Media*, 130.

55. The history of the machinations of the tobacco lobby is instructive here. See Devra Davis, *When Smoke Ran Like Water*, and The *Secret History of the War on Cancer* (New York: Perseus, 2007).

56. In addition, changes in the way the courts select scientific experts and in how much probative weight they give to their testimony threaten to amplify the effects of politicizing expertise. [See *Daubert v. Merrell Dow Pharmaceuticals* 509 U.S. 579 (1993), which changed the standard for admitting expert testimony in federal courts.]

57. Mooney, *The Republican War on Science*, 1, quoting Steven Pinker.

58. John Dean, *Conservatives Without Conscience*.

5

Social Moral Epistemology and the Tasks of Ethics

Allen Buchanan

5.1 GLOVER'S APPROACH TO ETHICS IN *HUMANITY*

Jonathan Glover is one of a handful of philosophers who helped create the field of 'Applied Ethics' during the 1970s. The term 'Applied Ethics' is unfortunate because it suggests that there is such a thing as an Ethics that lacks engagement with the question of what we ought to do. It would be more accurate, therefore, to say that Glover has played a major role in restoring Ethics as it traditionally has been conceived.

This last characterization underestimates the distinctiveness of Glover's approach in *Humanity*. His focus there is on the question "How can we avoid the worst behavior?" rather than the traditional moral philosopher's question "How ought we to live?", because he thinks that answering the former question should take priority, given the evils of the twentieth century *and their basis in human psychology*—our psychology. He is noncommittal on whether the circumstances that require us to focus on avoiding evil are permanent features of the human condition. Ironically, Glover believes that to achieve this relatively modest aim, a new and in some ways more ambitious conception of Ethics is needed.

Humanity is a long and rich book. I cannot pretend to do justice to it here. Instead, I will state what I take to be its distinctive virtues and then simply list its main theses in order to explore the new conception of Ethics it advances.

First, as I have already indicated, the book focuses squarely on one of the most important moral issues facing us at the beginning of the twenty-first century, whether or not, as Glover seems to think, it is *the* most important issue: Given the horrors perpetrated in the last century, what can we do to avoid large-scale evil in the future? Glover unflinchingly describes those horrors.

He makes it clear that his subject is not evil in *some* human beings, for example, the Nazis. He is describing the "the monsters inside *us* . . . [all of us] as part of the project of caging and taming them."[1] Given the proliferation of highly specific and sometimes arcane issues in contemporary Ethics, it is disturbing that this crucial issue has generally been neglected by philosophers. Instead of coming to grips with the twentieth century in order to prepare us for the twenty-first, 'applied' moral philosophers have often chosen to speculate about possible (and in some cases highly improbable) future problems concerning new technologies, largely proceeding as if we can hope to prepare ourselves for dealing with them without coming to grips with the moral failures of the recent past.

Second, Glover recognizes that if Ethics is to help us understand the past in a way that gives us guidance it will have to change its methodology. It will have to draw much more on both history and empirical psychology than has hitherto been the case. This is the sense in which Glover's conception of Ethics is ambitious when compared to the dominant contemporary conception, which largely regards the enterprise as a matter of conceptual analysis and the construction of arguments and principles by eliciting "our intuitions" about hypothetical cases.

Third, Glover avoids a pervasive error in contemporary Ethics: the assumption that the chief, if not the exclusive aim of Ethics, so far as it has anything to do with improving behavior, is to critique defective moral principles and arguments, and articulate sound ones. Glover believes that the main subject matter of Ethics is not arguments and principles, considered as abstract objects to be scrutinized by the moral philosopher, but rather the complex phenomena of moral good and evil.

There are two ways to look at the dubious but widely held assumption that the exclusive subject matter of Ethics is arguments and principles. It might betray a naively rationalistic view of what changes human behavior: the unsupported, *a priori* assumption that a thorough critique of defective principles and arguments will be sufficient to avoid bad conduct. Alternatively, one might admit that there is more to combating bad conduct than identifying sound principles and arguments, but assume that the only proper task *for the moral philosopher* is to evaluate principles and arguments and that all else is the domain of social science.

That Glover rejects the naive rationalist assumption is not surprising; it is after all extremely implausible, given the imperfect rationality of human beings. His rejection of the assumption that the proper role of the moral philosopher is restricted to evaluating moral arguments and principles is more interesting and raises an important question for which, in my judgment, his book does not provide a clear and convincing answer: what exactly is the proper role for the moral philosopher and how does it differ from that of the social scientist who offers causal explanations of bad conduct? Later I will propose an answer to this question. My answer will be grounded in my assessment of the incompleteness of Glover's project in *Humanity*, so I will first attempt to summarize what I take to be the core ideas of the book, in the form of eight theses.

1. To help us avoid large-scale evil, Ethics must *not* rely on the assumption that belief in "the moral law" can serve as an effective constraint on evildoing. Appeals to "the moral law" cannot achieve the needed constraint either because it is doubtful that there is an objective morality or because there is no accepted method of resolving disagreements among those who hold opposing views on what the moral law is. Glover is unsatisfyingly brief in his explication of what would count as "the moral law", saying only that it is a conception of morality as lying "outside" of human beings.

2. Given that we cannot rely on the "moral law," the chief resources for avoiding large-scale evil are self-interest, sympathy and respect, and moral identity.

3. Self-interest does not provide an adequate protection against large-scale evil, because, in a sufficiently corrupt society, social pressures can make it in the individual's interest to act immorally.[2]

4. Whether sympathy, respect, and moral identity can be effective in avoiding large-scale evil is a highly contingent matter, because sympathy and respect can be extinguished and moral identity can be corrupted.

5. Ethics should investigate the contingent conditions under which sympathy, respect, and moral identity can or cannot serve as effective constraints on large-scale evil.

6. To achieve its practical goal of helping us avoid large-scale evil, Ethics needs to be more empirical in two respects: it needs to take social psychology into account and it must be grounded in knowledge of history. History provides examples of what is to be avoided and data for psychology to explain; psychology explains the role of belief and feeling in the causation of evil.

7. Limited sympathy and respect—failures to extend sympathy and respect to all human beings—play a central role in the etiology of large-scale evil; so a main focus of the new Ethics should be understanding the psychology of limited sympathy and respect.

8. Although we cannot rely on respect for "the moral law" to motivate the project of avoiding large-scale evil, we can rely on the widespread moral conviction that we must avoid repetitions of the atrocities that stained the twentieth century; here Auschwitz is the paradigm. ("The thought at Auschwitz and other places, 'never again' is more compelling than any abstract ethical principle," p. 406.)

The connection between the last two theses warrants elaboration because it is the key to understanding the nature of Ethics as Glover reconceives it. Glover has described the Ethics he explores in *Humanity* as a kind of *consequentialist virtue ethics*.[3] The basic idea is simple: as virtue eth-ics teaches us, we should focus more on character traits, understood as including dispositions not only to make moral judgments and to act in certain ways, but also to have sentiments such as sympathy, thereby avoiding the almost exclusive preoccupation with principles and arguments that has characterized much contemporary moral philosophy, *and* we should recognize that the consequences of having various character traits are central to their being virtues or vices. In brief, Glover's proposal is that we start with what he takes to be a solid and virtually universal intuition, namely, that large-scale violence of the sort that stained the twentieth century must be avoided, develop an account of the virtues and vices that predispose us to avoid or to perpetrate such atrocities, and then try to cultivate the virtues and extirpate the vices.

I shall argue that Glover's rethinking of Ethics, though extremely valuable, does not go far enough—that it is insufficiently empirical and also lacks a conceptual framework capable of identifying the full range of topics for empirically informed research in Ethics. I will also show that this conceptual deficiency limits the practical payoff of Glover's approach. With a more adequate conceptual framework we can achieve not only a more complete account of the etiology of evil but also more effective strategies for avoiding it.

In Section 5.2, I argue that the needed conceptual framework must incorporate what I have elsewhere called *social moral epistemology* and sketch what this would look like. I make the case that we need a conceptual framework for Ethics that focuses on the interaction of the moral–epistemic virtues and vices of individuals with the moral–epistemic quality of institutions. By the moral–epistemic virtues of individuals I mean the character traits that play a central role in our getting and sustaining justified morally relevant beliefs, that is, beliefs that are important for determining how we ought to act. Impartiality, clarity of thought and judgment, the willingness to question assumptions, the ability to make valid practical inferences, and moral imagination are some of the more obvious moral–epistemic virtues of individuals. These are *moral*–epistemic virtues in a double sense: first, they enable us to have moral knowledge or at least justified moral belief. Second, they are epistemic virtues that are themselves morally commendable.

Morally relevant beliefs are of two kinds: factual beliefs needed for the application of moral principles and beliefs about which moral principles are valid. By the moral–epistemic quality of institutions I mean the characteristics of institutions that affect morally relevant beliefs of both kinds. The characteristics of institutions can affect morally relevant beliefs in either of two ways. First, institutions can foster morally relevant beliefs, chiefly through inculcating norms of epistemic deference, according to which certain individuals or groups are identified as reliable or authoritative sources of true beliefs. Second, institutions can affect an individual's morally relevant beliefs by creating incentives that either support or undermine his moral–epistemic virtues. Social moral epistemology places the ethics of believing at center stage, while understanding believing in a thoroughly social, anti-Cartesian way,

emphasizing that our ability to form and sustain justified morally relevant beliefs, as with beliefs generally, is sensitive to the character of
the institutional context in which we operate. 'Institutions' here is to be
construed broadly to include formal institutions like the state and the
church, but also informal ones such as the family, and political as well
as nonpolitical institutions. (Thus in this broad sense we may speak of
the institutions of science and the contribution they make to justified
factual belief. The latter institutions are the subject matter of the social
epistemology of science.)

This approach will confirm Glover's insight that a practical understanding of large-scale evil is not chiefly a matter either of refuting the
egoist or of showing that people who do evil or are cooperate with evil-
doers embrace defective moral principles or arguments. Part of the value
of social moral epistemology, as I shall demonstrate, is that it reveals how
people who are morally motivated, who embrace largely unexceptionable
moral principles, and whose ethical reasoning does not exhibit gross errors
of inference can nonetheless engage in profoundly immoral behavior. This
can happen if individuals' moral–epistemic virtues are undermined and if
they come to hold false factual beliefs that disable the proper functioning
of their moral powers.

In Section 5.3, I will show that as it stands Glover's attempt to develop
a more empirical approach to ethics is also *normatively* inadequate
because it puts too much weight on the assumption that we all can agree
that we must avoid a repetition of the large-scale evils of the twentieth
century. The problem is that at the beginning of the twenty-first century
we already have evidence that many people can agree in the abstract that
there must never be another Auschwitz and yet allow, condone, or even
perpetrate massive evils. One partial explanation of why this is so focuses
on the capacity of human beings to believe that their own actions or those
of their government fall outside the scope of moral prohibitions that they
may sincerely believe are valid. For example, a Turk who denies that the
Armenian genocide of 1915 occurred may sincerely avow that there must
never be another Auschwitz, but deny that the mass killing of Armenians
was, morally speaking, like Auschwitz. He may insist—and may sincerely
believe—that the number of dead is exaggerated and that the killing that
did occur was justified as a matter of national self-defense measure in a
war in which the Armenians were the aggressors and in which the survival
of Turkey was at risk. Similarly, at a time when the Executive branch of a
long-established democracy authorizes torture and when many on both
sides of the 'war against terror' apparently believe it is justifiable to kill
innocent people (whether deliberately or not deliberately but knowingly,
as with "collateral damage"), Glover's key motivational assumption of a
widespread conviction that we must at all cost avoid twentieth-century-
style atrocities appears to be somewhat shaky.

What these and other examples suggest is that we must pay more attention to the ethics of believing and to the role that institutions, broadly

conceived, play in the formation of systems of belief. We must take seriously the possibility that our own belief systems are distorted and that if there are distortions they may be due in part to the influence of our institutional environment. Doing this requires something more complicated than simply agreeing that we must avoid evils on the scale of twentieth-century atrocities and then trying to cultivate the virtues of *individuals* that provide protection against repeating them. It involves empirically and morally informed thinking about institutional design.

In Section 5.4, I explore the normative basis of the social moral epistemology approach I outline in Section 5.3 and ask whether it can avoid reliance on "the moral law." I argue that there are two distinct and compatible practical arguments for why it is important to develop a social moral epistemology and to use it to help ensure that our institutions facilitate the formation and preservation of justified morally relevant beliefs. The first argument is based on the rationality of avoiding the moral risks and the risks to our welfare that are involved in our profound epistemic independence on institutions. The appeal to avoiding moral risks here does not rely on there being a widespread belief in "the moral law" in the sense of a single objective set of substantive moral principles; it only assumes that people have moral commitments, not that they do or should have the same moral commitments. The second argument is based on the assumption that sympathy and respect are virtues and hence valuable to cultivate and on the assumption that false beliefs can undermine the proper functioning of the virtues or even transform them into vices. The simple idea here is that if we care about having these virtues then we should to that extent care about the moral–epistemic environment in which we try to cultivate and exercise them. I then conclude that these arguments provide a substantial normative basis for collective action to supply significant constraints on large-scale evil—a normative basis that neither reduces to rational self-interest nor relies on a consensus that there is a "moral law," at least if the latter is understood as a set of substantive, universally valid, substantive rules of action.

5.2 THE CONCEPTUAL INCOMPLETENESS OF GLOVER'S APPROACH: THE NEED FOR SOCIAL MORAL EPISTEMOLOGY

In *Humanity* Glover frequently stresses the importance of *beliefs*. For example, with potent economy he says: "Beliefs cause wars." He also shows an awareness of the role of *institutions* in the etiology of large-scale evil, emphasizing political institutions and the media. Further, by focusing on sympathy and respect as resources for constraining evil, and by his commitment to developing strategies for avoiding evil without relying on "the moral law," he focuses much more on *moral virtues* than on moral principles, implicitly favoring a Virtue Ethics approach, as I have already noted. What is lacking, however, is a developed conceptual framework that connects belief, institutions, moral–epistemic virtues, and conduct. The idea of social moral epistemology provides the main outlines of the needed conceptual framework.

The core idea can be clarified by beginning with something more general: social epistemology. This latter term has at present no single, universally accepted definition. For present purposes, however, it can be defined roughly as follows: social epistemology is the systematic comparative evaluation of alternative institutions as to their efficiency and efficacy in producing, preserving, and transmitting true (or on more modest accounts, justified) beliefs.[4] Social *moral* epistemology can then be defined as that department of social epistemology that focuses on the systematic comparative evaluation of alternative institutions as to their efficiency and efficacy in producing, preserving, and transmitting true (or justified) morally relevant beliefs, that is, beliefs that are of special importance for right conduct and for the proper functioning of the moral virtues, including the moral–epistemic virtues involved in sound moral reasoning and judgment.

The idea that social moral epistemology ought to play a central role in Ethics rests on five main propositions.

1. The types of human conduct that are liable to moral evaluation are causally heavily dependent upon the beliefs that human agents have.
2. The formation and maintenance of such morally relevant beliefs are in large part social processes in which institutions, broadly understood, play a central role. Human belief (and hence human conduct as far as it depends on belief) is characterized by strong social–epistemic dependence, though individuals tend to underestimate systematically their *own* social–epistemic dependence.
3. Some institutional arrangements are of better moral–epistemic quality than others—more reliable in helping us to form and preserve justified morally relevant beliefs and to avoid or correct unjustified morally relevant beliefs.
4. Sometimes we can determine which institutional arrangements are epistemically superior, and either support them if they already exist or create them if they do not.
5. Generally speaking, certain kinds of false beliefs (e.g., false beliefs about natural differences among various groups of human beings or about the history of nations) play an especially important role in the causation of morally wrong conduct.

An adequate conception of social moral epistemology links the moral–epistemic qualities of institutions, the morally relevant beliefs individuals have, the functioning of individuals' virtues, and their conduct. By focusing on how the institutional context in which the individual operates influences his beliefs and on the importance of beliefs for the proper functioning of the moral virtues, social moral epistemology enriches, rather than rejects the recent resurgence of Virtue Ethics. Social moral epistemology relies on social science, but it is an essentially normative enterprise, as epistemology generally is. (Epistemology attempts to understand what knowledge or justified belief is and knowledge and justification are normative concepts.)

Here is it useful to distinguish between *modest* and *ambitious* social moral epistemology. The latter considers only the role of institutions in the formation and preservation of the *factual* beliefs that play an important role in the moral virtues and moral conduct. For example, government-controlled media and public education can disseminate false beliefs about a nation's past—for example, narratives about its being victimized and betrayed by other nations—and these beliefs can be appealed to in order to mobilize ethno-national violence.

Ambitious social moral epistemology explores the role of institutions in the formation and preservation not just of factual beliefs that are relevant to moral beliefs but upon moral beliefs *per se*. In its more ambitious form, social moral epistemology would be concerned with questions such as this: under what sorts of social conditions is the belief that women have a moral right not to be forced to have sex or that nonhuman animals should not be made to suffer likely to emerge, become widespread, and be sustained?

It might be thought that ambitious social moral epistemology assumes ethical cognitivism while the modest form does not, but this is incorrect. Both assume that moral beliefs can be justified or unjustified. The point of investigating how institutions affect morally relevant factual beliefs is that whether moral beliefs are justified can depend upon their factual presuppositions and this presupposes that moral beliefs *can* be justified. The plausible assumption here is that if a moral belief relies on false factual beliefs, this can undercut its justification. For example, if the belief that Blacks ought not to be allowed to vote relies on the false factual belief that Blacks are not mentally capable of participating competently in politics, then to that extent it is unjustified.

On the face of it, it is implausible to think that the justification of any moral belief—at least any moral belief that is sufficiently contentful to play much of a role in our conduct—could be completely independent of factual beliefs. If this is the case, then it is a mistake to dismiss 'unambitious' social moral epistemology as an enterprise of minor significance.

The relationship between factual and moral beliefs is a central concern of social moral epistemology. This enterprise proceeds on the plausible assumption that factual beliefs are often relevant to the justification of moral beliefs while treating as an open question whether there is such a thing as a "pure" moral belief, one that has no factual presuppositions. To assume that what I have described as modest social epistemology is of very limited significance for Ethics is to assume not only that there are "pure" moral beliefs, but also that Ethics should be concerned exclusively or at least chiefly with them. Neither assumption is justified.

There is another way in which social moral epistemology may be modest or ambitious, one that does not depend on dubious distinctions between "pure" and factually dependent moral beliefs. Here the modest form would be restricted to an investigation of how institutions influence morally relevant factual beliefs and the ambitious form would do that but would also examine the effect of institutions on the moral–epistemic virtues individuals of individuals. In what follows I will focus mainly on the effects of institutions on morally relevant factual beliefs and say less about how institutions affect the moral–epistemic virtues. This limitation carries a risk, however: it may give the mistaken impression that the approach to Ethics I am exploring assumes that individuals' morally relevant beliefs are determined by institutions and gives short shrift to the role of individuals' moral–epistemic vices in morally bad conduct. This is certainly not my view of social moral epistemology; it is the interaction between institutions, morally relevant beliefs, and individual moral–epistemic virtues that matters. I mean my claim that Ethics should take the ethics of believing more seriously literally. An individual can be morally culpable for being uncritical about adopting or sustaining beliefs and he can be morally culpable for not taking an appropriately critical attitude toward the institutions that shape his beliefs.

Nevertheless, I think it is worth pointing out that institutions can create incentives that undermine the moral–epistemic virtues of individuals and that the processes by which they do this are likely to include the propagation of false factual beliefs. For example, if a repressive government, working through the media and educational institutions, fosters a cult of personality that inculcates false beliefs about the intelligence, wisdom, and rectitude of "the Dear Leader" (or Il Duce or the Great Chairman), this may contribute to a kind of atrophy of the moral–epistemic virtues of individuals, to the extent that they come to believe themselves incapable of exercising judgment on important issues. To that extent it is misleading to draw a bright line between a social moral epistemology that is concerned only with the role of institutions in the formation of morally relevant factual beliefs and one that also investigates the role of institutions in the ability of individuals to exercise the moral–epistemic virtues.

5.2.1 How a Web of False Factual Beliefs Can Subvert an Unexceptionable Moral Principle

In her valuable book, *The Nazi Conscience*, historian Claudia Koontz notes that teachers in the Third Reich were instructed to instill in their students the importance of following the Golden Rule—but with the proviso that it only applies to "racial comrades."[5] The identification of some people as racial comrades and others as not depended upon a web of false factual beliefs, about natural differences between so-called Aryans and non-Aryans, about the history of "the German people," and about the role that non-Aryans, and especially Jews, supposedly played in the social, political, and economic calamities that befell Germany after World War I. The systematically distorted, morally relevant factual beliefs conveyed by teachers in the Third Reich were disseminated by other authority-figures as well, including state officials, medical doctors, clergymen, and parents.

What is striking about the Nazi Golden Rule example is that it shows how the propagation of false factual beliefs can facilitate grossly immoral behavior, not by causing the abandonment of ordinary moral principles, but by subverting their application. The dark genius of this instance of Nazi propaganda, and I would argue, was that it encouraged morally motivated people—people who were not sociopaths but who instead had traversed the usual path of 'moral development'—to act immorally without requiring a wholesale abandonment of ordinary moral principles.

Glover rightly emphasizes the various techniques that are used to place members of some groups beyond the reach of our sympathy and respect. For example, concentration camp inmates were stripped of the outward signs of individuality, made to live in filth, and pitted against one another in daily struggle for survival—all of which made it easier for camp guards to regard them as subhuman. Here the technique is to create a kind of experience of the other that extinguishes the capacity to respond to him with respect and sympathy. Unless one believes, implausibly, that the moral sentiments of respect and sympathy are uninformed by factual beliefs about their objects, this technique also counts as an instance of the role that false factual beliefs can play in the etiology of immoral behavior. In other words, the blunting of the moral responses that this kind of manipulated experience of the other produces involves the creation of false beliefs about the other, including the belief that he is nasty, uncaring toward his own kind, etc. But whether or not such manipulated experiences of the other involve the fostering of false factual beliefs, examples like that of the Nazi Golden Rule patently do. These are cases of the explicit inculcation of systems of false factual beliefs that play a significant role in limiting sympathy and respect.

Under some circumstance or other, virtually any factual belief can be morally relevant. Social moral epistemology recognizes this point, but focuses on the ways in which social institutions influence certain types of factual beliefs that tend to be especially important for the proper functioning of the moral virtues. Conspicuous among these are factual beliefs that are thought to be relevant to determinations of moral status and to the determination of guilt and innocence. False beliefs about natural differences between Blacks and Whites, or Aryans and non-Aryans can play a role in assigning whole classes of people to an inferior moral status. Beliefs that exaggerate differences between the consciousness of human beings and that of nonhuman primates can similarly contribute to erroneous judgments concerning moral status. False beliefs about history can facilitate judgments about collective guilt that help rationalize wars and ethnic cleansings.

The process of constructing and transmitting false, morally relevant factual beliefs through explicit indoctrination, as in the Nazi teacher case, relies crucially on socially identified experts, people whose social roles confer epistemic deference, are critical. A key focus of social moral epistemology is therefore the processes by which experts are socially identified and empowered, as well as upon the interplay of individual vices, moral–epistemic and otherwise, and institutionally generated incentives that can result in experts becoming powerful resources for rationalizing immoral behavior. This complex phenomenon is perhaps nowhere more conspicuous than in the history of eugenics.

5.2.2 Eugenics: Biological Lifeboat Ethics

It is commonly said that the chief wrong of the most morally repugnant activities of the eugenics movements of the late-nineteenth and mid-twentieth Centuries was that the rights of the individual were sacrificed for the putative good of society—that the moral calamity of eugenics resulted from a repudiation of 'rights-based' morality in favor of kinds of consequentialism that took the good of the group (whether humanity or some particular 'nation' or 'race') to be the goal that was to be attained, no matter what. A social moral epistemology approach shows how dubious this widely held "ethical autopsy" on eugenics is.[6]

Some eugenicists, including some who endorsed the most repugnant policies, including compulsory sterilization and even medical murder of those thought to harbor "defective germplasm," might accurately be described as consequentialist in their ethical orientation. However, careful attention to the actual discourse of eugenicists indicates that the public justifications they gave for the worst eugenic policies generally did *not* repudiate 'rights-based' morality as such. Instead, part of what made certain strains of eugenic thinking so morally destructive was that it facilitated the rationalization of grossly immoral action without the abandonment of familiar moral principles and without a wholesale conversion to consequentialist morality. Perhaps the chief means by which this was achieved was the appeal to what I have called the "Emergency Exceptionalism" frame of eugenic thinking. In brief, the eugenicists who endorsed the most oppressive policies invariably justified them by appeal to the idea that humanity if poised on the brink of a disaster that can only be averted if we are willing to take measures that would in any less extreme circumstances be regarded as impermissible. The Emergency Exceptionalism Frame was based on two false factual beliefs that were pervasive among the more extreme eugenicists and which were publicly endorsed by alleged experts in the science of heredity: (1) the human gene pool is suffering a catastrophic decline, and (2) many of the most serious social problems (from crime and poverty, to drunkenness, 'promiscuity', and 'the breakdown of the family') are caused by behavioral traits of individuals that are determined in simple, Mendelian fashion by their genes.

Here is the key point: *if* one accepts these false factual assumptions, then one need not be a consequentialist to conclude that in this direst of emergencies ordinary moral constraints, including those imposed by individual rights, do not apply. To the extent that the public accepted these factual assumptions, there was no need to try to convince them to abandon the commonsense morality in which individual rights play a prominent role. After all, even the most ardent 'rights-based' theorists, including Robert Nozick, acknowledge that the most basic individual rights may be infringed to avert a "moral catastrophe."

The case of eugenics, perhaps even more clearly than that of the Nazi version of the Golden Rule, illustrates the role of socially identified objects of epistemic deference in the subversion of morality. In the case of eugenics, the false beliefs that constituted the Emergency Exception frame of thinking were presented and promulgated as scientific beliefs, not only by unqualified people posing as scientific experts, but also by scientists who possessed unexceptionable credentials according to the standards of the day. What is even more disturbing is that the falsity of the key factual beliefs upon which the Emergency Exceptionalist frame was constructed had already repeatedly been publicly exposed by a small but vocal contingent of scientists, at least from the 1920s onward. Two critical questions therefore arise: How did eugenic 'experts' come to have and sustain the false factual beliefs in question in spite of strong scientific evidence to the contrary and why did other people rely on these 'experts' (rather than on those who contradicted them)?

Some historians of eugenics have suggested that many people accepted the two factual assumptions of the Emergency Exceptionalism frame because it was in their interest to do so. The idea is that eugenics was largely a middle- and upper-class movement and that genetic determinist explanation for social ills was both exculpating and empowering from the standpoint of the bourgeoisie—exculpating because it diverted attention from the possibility that major social ills were caused by defective institutions from which they were benefiting quite handsomely, empowering because it implied that a wider domain of social control should be exercised by those who were already the most politically and economically powerful. If this is the case, then part of the explanation of the evils of eugenics must employ the idea of moral–epistemic vices, providing an account of the tendency toward a range of morally momentous cognitive errors, including motivated false belief, confirmation bias, and various forms of cognitive dissonance reduction that succeed only by repressing the truth in favor of falsehoods. What is needed, above all, is a conceptual framework that explains the interplay of moral–epistemic vices and flawed institutions, including institutions for the social construction of epistemic deference to supposed experts. Simply saying that eugenicists were willing to sacrifice individual rights for the sake of the supposed social good because it was in their interest to do so does not begin to touch the nature of eugenic evils and provides virtually no guidance as to how to avoid similar moral failures in the future.

The Nazi Golden Rule example and the case of eugenic biological lifeboat ethics share two features: in both cases false factual beliefs were used to justify grossly immoral behavior without requiring the explicit abandonment of widely held moral principles, and in both the false beliefs were propagated through mechanisms of epistemic deference grounded in existing social roles and institutions. In order to understand the epistemically based moral risks that these examples illustrate and to try to develop ways of reducing those risks, it is necessary to construct systematic, empirically supported explanations of the roles that institutions play in propagating and sustaining false factual beliefs that can undermine the proper functioning of the moral powers. The eugenics example also makes it clear that a social moral epistemology approach must include a systematic understanding of the ways in which epistemically defective institutions can increase the likelihood of immoral behavior by exacerbating the moral and moral–epistemic vices to which human beings are prone.

Suppose, for example, that in a particular society scientific expertise is valued, but that many members of the public are unable to distinguish reliably between genuine experts and those who falsely present themselves as such, either because public education is inadequate, or because the society has not developed reliable credentialing mechanisms for scientific experts, or both. Suppose also that some who are viewed as scientists of heredity but who lack genuine scientific expertise are racists who produce studies that purport to show that Blacks are genetically inferior in intelligence or have an unusually high genetic propensity to violent crime. Finally, suppose also that the society in question has a history of racism. Under such conditions some people may be too quick to believe the results of pseudoscientific studies when they seem to support the racist views that they already hold. The confirmation-bias that is a well-known feature of racist thinking may actually be exacerbated by defective educational and credentialing institutions that facilitate misplaced epistemic deference, thereby allowing people to sustain their racist beliefs and transmit them to others while appealing to scientific authority. A developed social moral epistemology, then, would not disregard individual moral psychology in favor of social determinist explanations; instead, it would explore the connections between the moral capacities of individuals and the effects that institutions have upon them. It would link a theory of the epistemic vices and virtues of individuals grounded in empirical moral psychology with an empirically based theory of the epistemic role of institutions. Instead of seeing institutions as only playing a role in the creation of morally competent individuals, as developmental psychology has done, this approach would evaluate institutional arrangements as to whether they support or impair the functioning of morally competent individuals.

5.2.3 Just War Theory as the Ethics of Imperfect Agents Operating in Imperfect Institutions

I will now briefly sketch one final area of moral concern explored by Glover where a social moral epistemology approach is fruitful: the decision-making of leaders regarding war. Glover offers a number of insights as to how leaders rationalize brutal, inhumane decisions, including the mass bombing of civilians. He suggests that if we have a greater awareness of the psychological mechanisms of cognitive dissonance–reduction that such rationalizations involve, this somehow will help protect us from such evils. My suggestion is that here, too, Glover's empiricism is admirable, but insufficient. Decisions concerning war do not take place in an institutional vacuum: they are made by people who occupy certain roles, operating within particular institutional processes, and who are thereby subject to distinctive incentives. Here, too, as in the preceding examples, what is needed is an integration of empirical individual psychology, institutional analysis, and Virtue Ethics. We need to understand the cognitive capacities of human individuals generally and their tendencies to commit cognitive errors that can have serious moral consequences. But we also need to understand how universal human cognitive capacities are channeled by various social roles and by the institutional setting in which people occupying the roles operate. For example, state leaders operate under role-specific incentives which can exacerbate the risks of cognitive errors as well as moral lapses in decision-making. To take a purely hypothetical example, the leader of a country that has just suffered a major terrorist attack may be under strong incentives to do everything to avoid another such attack. As a result, he may be tempted to justify a decision to go to war on the basis of the claim that the right of self-defense, under the allegedly unique conditions of the "war against terrorism," allows preventive war.

Efforts to justify going to war on preventive grounds carry exceptional risks of error and abuse, due to the inherently speculative character of the preventive war justification and the nature of the incentives to which state leaders are subject. Unless effective steps are taken to mitigate these special risks—say, by requiring that the preventive war decision only be made within a multilateral forum effectively designed to elicit good information about the putative harm to be prevented, to allow full consideration of less radical alternatives than war, and to hold decision-makers accountable *ex post*—the risk of relying upon this kind of justification for going to war are simply too great. Even if our intuitive responses to highly sanitized, philosophers' hypothetical examples convinces us that preventive war is in principle morally permissible, it is quite another thing to say that it is permissible for flesh and blood leaders, operating within seriously defective institutions, to engage in preventive war. Similarly, an ethical inquiry into the morality of torture must do more than describe an idealized "ticking time-bomb" hypothetical in which we assume perfect knowledge on the part of the decision-maker and then elicit the intuition that in these circumstances torture would be permissible. Instead, we must examine the issue of torture as it arises for cognitively and morally imperfect agents, whose imperfections may be exacerbated or ameliorated by the incentives created by the institutions within which they operate. Doing this requires not only what Glover urges—grounding Ethics in psychology—but it also requires integrating psychology with an understanding of the role of institutions in either enhancing or impairing the exercise of moral–epistemic virtues by individuals.

The chief difficulty with standard just war theory, as I have argued elsewhere, is that it is insufficiently empirical: It fails to appreciate that whether some 'causes' for war are just—and in particular, whether preventive self-defense is ever a just 'cause'—can be contingent upon both the psychological abilities and liabilities of decision-makers and the characteristics of the institutional setting within which they operate.[7] If state leaders had much greater knowledge of the intentions and capabilities of possible enemies than they do have and operated within institutions effectively designed to counter the risk of error and abuse, then preventive self-defense might be a 'just cause' for war. In the present circumstances, where neither of these conditions is fulfilled, it is not. This example shows that the value of a social moral epistemology approach to Ethics is not limited to providing practical guidance for avoiding the violation of valid ethical principles we already possess; it can also help us to determine which ethical principles are valid.

5.3 THE NORMATIVE INADEQUACY OF GLOVER'S VIEW

So far I have argued that Glover's understanding of the sense in which Ethics must be empirical focuses too exclusively on individual psychology and not enough upon the interplay between individual psychology and institutions. I now want to suggest that Glover's new empirical ethics is both motivationally and normatively inadequate: it provides a less than convincing account of the *motivation* for engaging in the process of cultivating the virtues of sympathy and respect in order to avoid evil; and it features an overly austere understanding of the *reasons* we have for engaging in this process.

Consider first the question of motivation. Glover believes—or at least hopes—that the conviction that "there must be no more Auschwitzs" will motivate people to work together to cultivate the virtues that protect us against evil. Earlier, using the case of the attitudes of some Turks toward the Armenian Genocide, I suggested that this answer to the motivational question does not take seriously enough the human capacity for rationalization and the complex dependence of moral beliefs on factual beliefs. More fundamentally, Glover's answer to the motivational question fails to articulate how difficult and complicated the task of cultivating the protective virtues is. If the proper functioning of these virtues depends significantly upon what sorts of institutions we have, then preventing evil may require significant institutional reforms. Further, it is one thing to say that people will agree that there must never be another Auschwitz, but quite another to say that this conviction will motivate significant institutional reform.

It seems clear enough that most people seriously underestimate their social–epistemic dependency and the moral vulnerability that this entails. If this is so, then translating the conviction that we must not repeat the horrors of the twentieth century into effective motivation for cultivation of the protective virtues may require a sea change in the way most people think, or fail to think, about how our morally relevant beliefs are formed and about their responsibility for the beliefs they hold. More precisely, it may require convincing people that *the ethics of believing* is more important than they have thought and more worthy of study than traditional Ethics has recognized. Perhaps prophylaxis against evil is more complex and indirect than Glover thinks. Perhaps the initial focus should be on the moral–epistemic virtues and the social conditions that support them, rather than on more direct efforts to strengthen the moral sentiments of sympathy and respect.

Glover focuses more on the motivation for cultivating the virtues than on our reasons for doing so. He seems skeptical that reasons can be given or at least he believes that no chain of reasoning in this regard could be as motivationally effective as the conviction that this must never happen again that we feel when we survey the wreckage of the twentieth century. My worry is that Glover's ambiguous remarks about the unreliability of "the moral law", along with his failure to consider any reason for cultivating the virtues other than the assumption that they protect against what we are convinced must never happen again, gives short shrift to the rational grounding of the virtues.

In the next Section 5.4, I focus on the rational grounding of the moral–epistemic virtues. I argue that we have two distinct, rather weighty reasons to try to ensure that we act on the basis of justified beliefs. Neither of these reasons neatly fits Glover's conception of the relationship between self-interest morality, and neither requires reliance on 'the moral law', if this means substantive moral rules of action. So, embracing them appears to be congenial to his project of developing constraints on evil that do not rely on "the moral law" and that do not depend unduly on congruence between self-interest and avoiding evil.

5.4 THE NORMATIVE FOUNDATIONS OF SOCIAL MORAL EPISTEMOLOGY

I have argued that the character of institutions can significantly influence the morally relevant factual beliefs that individuals have and their ability to cultivate and exercise moral–epistemic virtues. I now want to ask a simple but important question: Why should we work together to try to ensure the epistemic quality of the institutions within which we live— and why should we care about cultivating the moral–epistemic virtues in ourselves and others? There are at least two weighty reasons, neither of which relies on 'the moral law' in the sense of assuming that there are universally valid substantive moral rules of action or on a consensus that there are.

The first is that where adequate mechanisms for their correction are absent, practically relevant false beliefs tend to put at risk both our welfare and our ability to act morally *according to our conception of what is moral*. Both prudential action and attempts to comply with whatever conception of morality we take to be valid rely on beliefs about how the world is, at least to the extent that they both typically require means-ends reasoning and the ability to identify situations in which principles of action (whether moral or prudential) apply. If prudential and moral action generally require true factual beliefs and if the reliability of our access to true factual beliefs depends in significant part on the epistemic quality of the institutions within which we operate, then we should be concerned about whether our institutions are epistemically sound; and if they are not, then we should work together to improve them. For the same reasons, we should be concerned to cultivate moral–epistemic virtues in ourselves and, given our extreme epistemic dependence on others, we should encourage others to cultivate them as well.

Notice that this first argument does not presuppose the existence of universally valid substantive moral rules, much less a consensus on what they are.

The second argument appeals to the nature of virtues and the assumption that sympathy and respect are virtues. It can be outlined as follows. (1) Sympathy and respect are moral virtues and as such they are good: having them makes for a better life, at least under 'reasonably favorable circumstances' (i.e., circumstances in which being virtuous will not predictably result in severe costs to the individual, as may be the predicament of the person of conscience in a vicious society.) (2) Moral virtues (including sympathy and respect) can be seriously undermined by false beliefs. (3) Therefore, (at least under reasonably favorable circumstances), for the sake of cultivating the moral virtues, one ought to try to have true beliefs (at least of least of the sort that are critical for possessing the moral virtues). (4) Having true beliefs (of the relevant sort) depends in significant part upon the existence of epistemically sound institutions. (5) We have reason to do that which makes for a better life. (6) Therefore, we have reason to work together to try to develop epistemically sound institutions. For the same reasons we ought to try to cultivate the moral–epistemic virtues in ourselves and, given our epistemic dependence, encourage their cultivation in others.

As with the first argument, this second argument provides a normative basis for the social moral epistemology enterprise as a practical endeavor, not just a method of analysis, but it does so without assuming widespread agreement on substantive moral rules of action. That sympathy and respect are moral virtues, that moral virtues are valuable and ought to be cultivated (at least under reasonably favorable conditions), and that false factual beliefs can undermine the virtues, are all plausible assertions that are or can be the focus of a broad consensus, even for those who cannot agree that there is any one set of universally valid moral rules of action.

Notice that the fourth premise in the second argument does not say that having a moral virtue is incompatible with the falsity of any of the beliefs on the basis of which the virtue is exercised, which would be much too strong a claim. All it says is that falsehoods can undercut the virtues, by seriously impairing their exercise.

The second argument can be expanded in the following way. For some moral virtues—perhaps for all of them—the ability to form and sustain justified factual beliefs is a constituent of having the virtue. If this is true and if this ability can be undermined or supported by the institutions within which we operate, then, so far as the virtues are valuable, we have a reason to try to ensure that our institutions are epistemically sound.

Here it might be objected that the second argument does not meet the requirement of not relying on "the moral law," because it utilizes the claim that sympathy and respect are moral virtues and as such are good. In other words, the complaint is that even if the second argument does not assume that there is a "moral law" in the sense of some universally valid substantive moral rules of action, it does assume that having certain character traits is objectively good, indeed good for everyone (at least under what were referred to above as "reasonably favorable circumstances") or at least it assumes that there is a broad consensus that this is so.

My reply to this objection is twofold. First, even if the objection to the second argument is sound, the first stands and I believe it is a quite powerful argument, capable of grounding the enterprise of social epistemology and the attempt to apply its results to the reform of institutions so far as they affect belief. Second, I would be quite surprised if empirical research should yield the result that there are many people who deny that sympathy and respect are moral virtues or that, at least under reasonably favorable circumstances, they are good character traits to have. Further, it seems that the concept of a virtue that the second argument operates with is sufficiently abstract that it is accessible to and indeed most probably already understood in all cultures. Given this very general concept of a virtue, it seems unproblematic to say that the proper functioning of the virtues can be impaired by false factual beliefs. To deny this one would either have to deny that having a virtue includes, *inter alia*, a competence in the making of judgments of a certain sort or one would have to hold the equally implausible view that competent judgment cannot be undermined by false beliefs. Nevertheless, the second argument does require "thicker" normative assumptions than the first and to that extent one might argue that it violates the spirit, if not the letter of the requirement of avoiding reliance on "the moral law." For that reason, I will now focus only on the first argument.

If the first argument is sound, then we all have weighty reasons to support the development of a social moral epistemology and to use it to evaluate, and where necessary to reform, existing institutions. This argument is compatible with the recognition that self-interest alone does not provide a sufficient reason for supporting that project and it does not assume the existence of universally valid moral principles. Nor does it assume that there will always be a happy congruence between self-interests and compliance with universally valid moral rules of action, if there are any. To that extent, the integration of social moral epistemology with virtue ethics I am recommending here seems to fit the bill for Glover's new conception of Ethics.

Glover might respond as follows: "My concern was not so much with whether people have *reasons* for doing what is necessary to avoid large-scale evil, but with what sort of appeal can *motivate* (enough) people to do what is necessary. My point in *Humanity* was that the recognition that there must be no more Auschwitz's is likely to be more motivating, for most people, than any abstract ethical principle. I think the same is true for your appeal, in your first argument, to prudence, and to the desire to act well on one's own conception of morality as reasons for scrutinizing and reforming the institutions that shape our morally relevant beliefs: for most people, the conviction that there must be no more Auschwitz's is likely to be more motivating than your argument." At this point I think that Glover and I should both follow his good advice: we should look to empirical psychology to find out what most effectively motivates people to avoid evil; we can't determine that *a priori*. Nevertheless, I would surmise that, once we understand the basic message of social moral epistemology, some of us, at least, may be more effectively motivated by the thought that our own welfare and our ability to act well on our own moral convictions is imperiled by epistemically flawed institutions than by worries that we will be likely to participate in or condone another Holocaust.

I want to conclude by broaching a fundamental issue for social moral epistemology—one that I have evaded so far: By what standard are we to assess the moral–epistemic quality of institutions? Relying on historical examples, I have suggested that some institutional arrangements have in fact fostered unjustified, morally relevant factual beliefs and have encouraged moral–epistemic vices in individuals. In doing so, I have obviously appealed to 'moral intuitions'. For example, I have taken it for granted that Blacks, Jews, and women are entitled to equal sympathy and respect, and should not be exterminated or relegated to inferior positions in society and then suggested that when people fail to acknowledge that this is so the cause may in part be that they have ingested a web of false factual beliefs about natural differences among groups or false beliefs about who was responsible for this or that calamity. In effect, I have assumed that at least in some cases we know which moral beliefs are justified and then suggested that we should explore the role institutions play in our coming to have and to sustain those beliefs.

So far, this way of proceeding suggests that the relationship between valid moral beliefs and institutions is purely external and instrumental—that institutions should be regarded, *inter alia*, as instruments for producing valid morally relevant beliefs. A more ambitious social moral epistemology would challenge that assumption by arguing that, at least for some moral beliefs, if a belief would be fostered and sustained by epistemically sound institutions, this is itself a reason (not necessarily a conclusive reason) for thinking that the belief is justified. This latter view assumes that we can identify at least some of the epistemic virtues of institutions independently of knowing whether those institutions tend to foster particular moral beliefs that we have *other* reasons to believe are justified. The analogy here would be with a modest form of Virtue Ethics, according to which the fact that a virtuous agent would act according to a particular moral rule can count in favor of the conclusion that the rule is valid. If, as I have suggested, moral beliefs are much more dependent on factual beliefs than moral philosophers have usually appreciated, then it might turn out that institutions that are epistemically sound from the standpoint of the production of factual beliefs also tend to foster justified moral beliefs. Or, more likely, it might turn out that there are some basic characteristics of social institutions that both tend to foster justified factual beliefs and to make it more likely that individuals will come to have justified moral beliefs.[8] If that were so, then the fact that a moral belief tends to be fostered by epistemically sound institutional arrangements could provide a noncircular reason for believing that that moral belief is justified.

My aim here has not been to present a developed social moral epistemology, much less to show how such a theory could be fruitfully integrated with an appropriate theory of the virtues. Instead, I have only attempted to make a provisional case for attempting such a project and tried to show that this attempt would be very much in the spirit of Glover's new approach to Ethics in his valuable book *Humanity: A Moral History of the 20th Century*.

In a recent paper, Glover, still appreciative of the role of belief in evil and its prevention, urges philosophers concerned to lessen violent ideological conflict to focus on 'applied epistemology'.[9] If my analysis is sound, this advice is somewhat misleading. Philosophers interested in contributing to moral progress ought to recognize that Ethics is about belief as much as it is about conduct—or rather, that if it is about right conduct it must be about right belief—and that moral virtues depend on and partly consist of epistemic virtues, both of individuals and of institutions.

At the outset of this paper I suggested that Glover's emphasis on the empirical in Ethics raises a question about the role of the moral philosopher. Given Glover's view in *Humanity*, one might conclude that he is really endorsing the abandonment of the role of moral philosopher in favor of that of activist social scientist. What Glover seems to be endorsing—and doing—is using history to formulate empirical hypotheses about how sympathy and respect can be limited in their objects and urging us to learn more so that we can avoid their limitation and the evil that this facilitates. In contrast, the integration of a critical, evaluative inquiry into the epistemic quality of institutions with a Virtue Ethics that gives more prominence to the moral–epistemic virtues and their dependence on institutional context is an unambiguously normative, philosophical enterprise, even though it is one that relies heavily on social science. This is especially clear in the case of a social moral epistemology that explores the possibility that the fact that a moral belief is fostered by epistemically sound institutions can count as a reason for believing that the belief is justified.

Postscript

Reading Jonathan's work over the years has benefited me greatly. The benefits are all the more meaningful to me because of what I have learned in getting to know him personally. The sincerity, humility, and humaneness that his writing conveys are not simply a style of writing; they are features of his character.

Notes

I am grateful to Roger Crisp, Richard Keshen, Jonathan Glover, and Jeff McMahan for their excellent comments on earlier versions of this paper.

1. Jonathan Glover, *Humanity: A Moral History of the 20th Century* (London: Jonathan Cape, 1999, p. 7).

2. Ibid., p. 21.

3. Personal communication, January 9, 2007.

4. Alvin I. Goldiman, *Knowledge in a Social World*.

5. Claudia Koontz, *The Nazi Conscience* (Cambridge, MA: The Belknap Press of Harvard University Press, 2003, p. 119.

6. This and other examples are developed in much more detail in "Institutions, Beliefs, and Ethics: Eugenics as a Case Study," *The Journal of Political Philosophy*, 15(1): 22–45, 2007.

7. Allen Buchanan and Robert O. Keohane, "The Preventive Use of Force: A Cosmopolitan Institutionalist Proposal," *Ethics & International Affairs*, 18: 1–22, 2004. Allen Buchanan, "Institutionalizing the Just War," *Philosophy & Public Affairs*, 34(1): 2–38, 2006.

8. I have argued elsewhere in detail that some of the hallmarks of liberal societies fit this description. Allen Buchanan, "Political Liberalism and Social Epistemology," *Philosophy & Public Affairs*, 32(4): 95–130, 2004.

9. Jonathan Glover, "Conflict, Belief Systems and Philosophy," unpublished paper.

6

The Strains of Dialogue

Richard Keshen

Jonathan Glover's *Humanity*[1] is a disturbing book. It is also an inspiring and hopeful book. His analysis of twentieth century atrocities makes it terribly clear that "[d]eep in human psychology, there are urges to humiliate, torment, wound and kill people."[2] At the same time, he movingly conveys how humans are sometimes able to restrain and transcend the dark side of their nature. Auschwitz had its abhorrent torturers, but Le Chambon had its courageous citizens who defied the Nazis. A vital task of ethics, according to Glover, is to explore how it is that some of us but not others sustain our humanity in dire circumstances. To this end, ethics should be as much a psychological and historical investigation as a purely philosophical one, and "morality becomes tentative, exploratory and partly empirical."[3] I am sympathetic to this view of ethics, and hope to contribute to Glover's project by examining an important question he broaches but does not explore in depth. This is the role of dialogue in helping us transcend the forces in ourselves that lead to atrocity.

Humanity is replete with examples of the way rigid and murky systems of belief have contributed to atrocities. With disastrous results, ideological movements and autocrats are able to co-opt people whose minds have been made impervious to rational criticism. One of Glover's hopes therefore is that a culture that values holding reasonable beliefs (and all the epistemic virtues such an ideal entails) can help restrain the forces that lead to atrocity. In fostering this culture, philosophy has an important role to play, for the ideal of pursuing better beliefs through reasonable dialogue has partly defined philosophy since the time of Socrates. "The Socratic method," says Glover, "is even today, the best thing in philosophy" (27).[4] The assumption Glover makes is that dialogue helps to weaken barriers erected by tribalism and dogmatic belief. When this weakening occurs, sympathy and respect are more likely to break through and restrain the parts of our psychologies conducive to atrocity. Glover himself has recently written about the importance of dialogue "between those who are not Islamic and those who are,"[5] and has engaged in a number of public dialogues with Islamic leaders in London.

Glover's emphasis on fostering a culture of open-mindedness and reasonableness is surely important and correct. Yet there is an aspect of dialogue, between even the most reasonable people, which gives one pause. For it is undeniable that dialogue often has the effect of pushing people further apart intellectually (as Glover himself discovered in his London dialogues). Moreover, when dialogue is over differences that matter to the interlocutors, the result is often less, not more, mutual sympathy and respect. Here is an issue that calls for the "tentative, exploratory and partly empirical" approach to ethics that Glover recommends. In the main part of this essay, I explore the phenomenon of reasonable but intractable disagreement, or simply *reasonable disagreement*.[6] My discussion aims to uncover some of the structural tensions that often underlie dialogue, tensions which have the effect of pushing people further apart. In concluding the paper, I consider my rather pessimistic conclusions in the apparently more optimistic light of what Glover calls "a human moral identity."[7]

Reasonable disagreement, as I define it, has the following features:

1 The interlocutors in a disagreement are reasonable people (in a sense to be defined in a moment), and judge each other to be reasonable people.

2 They engage in sustained dialogue with the aim of resolving their differences.

3 But rather than finding themselves converging in their views, they continue to diverge.

4 The interlocutors conclude that their difference is irresolvable, or at least they see no reason to think it resolvable.

Now I understand a *reasonable person* in terms of four qualities. First, a reasonable person has well-developed capacities to weigh evidence, to detect inconsistencies and bad reasoning, and to draw logical inferences. Second, a reasonable person cares about exercising these capacities so as to transcend bias and wishful thinking. Third, a reasonable person sees herself as fallible. She understands that, however hard she tries, her beliefs may nevertheless be false or, even if true, be grounded in inadequate evidence or imperfect reasoning. These three features point to the third and defining quality of a reasonable person: That her mind is open to change for good reasons. Of course, we never think of our interlocutors or ourselves as perfectly reasonable: we know there are no such people. But I will assume that sufficiently reasonable people exist so as to investigate the phenomenon I am going to analyze. It is certainly part of our experience that we distinguish between reasonable and unreasonable interlocutors. We hold a certain respect for those we judge reasonable, whereas we distance ourselves from the unreasonable and, in the extreme, treat them as forces of nature to be controlled. It is the strains on interlocutors who not only are reasonable but who believe each other reasonable that interests me.

Here are two examples of reasonable disagreement. A reasonable atheist and a reasonable theist each regard each other as reasonable.[8] Their entire adult lives, they have argued over the existence of God. However, not only has there not been convergence in their views, but their views have also increasingly diverged. My second example, from which I will mostly draw in this essay, comes from a book-length debate over Israel between an American Jew, Hyman Bookbinder, and an American Palestinian, James Abourezk.[9] Both Bookbinder and Abourezk are intelligent, deeply informed, democratically spirited people of good will; and each recognizes the other as such. The dialogue starts with a mutual desire to reach agreement and shared understanding, but ends with the interlocutors further apart than when they began and exuding mutual dislike (to the point where they call each other names). What I want to emphasize is not so much the absence of convergence as the presence of continuing divergence. Bookbinder and Abourezk are like two people who have entered a maze from different directions with the intention of meeting at the center, but then with each fork in the path find they move further apart.

Recently, a number of philosophers have drawn attention to phenomena close to what I am calling reasonable disagreement (though often under different labels). These writers generally welcome reasonable disagreement as a reflection of a pluralistic and tolerant society, and even see it as a key to understanding modernity.[10] At the same time, most are adamant that giving reasonable disagreement its due should not undermine confidence in one's own beliefs. Thus Charles Larmore writes that we moderns must accept that reason is "as likely to push us apart [intellectually] as to bring us together."[11] "Nevertheless," he emphasizes, "we need not suspend judgment about the correctness of our own views."[12] And Rawls claims that "reasonable pluralism of comprehensive doctrines," a close cousin to my notion of reasonable disagreement, need not lead to skepticism or make us "hesitant and uncertain" about our own views.[13]

Contrary to Larmore and Rawls, I doubt that epistemic self-confidence and respect for the reasonableness of people with whom we disagree are so easily reconcilable, once we pay attention to the lived experience of interlocutors (as Larmore and Rawls do not). This is a key issue I explore in what follows, for it takes us to the heart of the structural tensions that frame reasonable disagreement. First, we need to understand why we should find reasonable disagreement perplexing, and so worth probing.

By hypothesis, my interlocutor in a reasonable disagreement is capable of understanding arguments and transcending blatant bias; and I too have these capacities. But now we have each examined the other's arguments, and rejected them. Moreover, we find ourselves increasingly diverging as the argument proceeds. This is *prima facie* problematic; for shouldn't reasonable people, each with the relevant capacities, mainly agree on what is a good argument? And even if they do not agree on every aspect of the argument, should they not at least show *some* convergence? Michael

Smith calls on this intuition in defending a brand of ethical realism when he writes:

> Since we are all in the same boat, so, it seems, we think that a conversation in which agents carefully muster and assess each other's reasons for and against their moral opinions is the best way to discover what the moral facts are. If the participants are open-minded and thinking clearly then we seem to think that such an argument should result in a *convergence* [Smith's emphasis] upon the truth.[14]

We need not deploy this intuition as uncompromisingly as Smith in order to recognize that continuing *divergence* in a dialogue between reasonable people calls for explanation. In pursuing possible explanations, we begin to uncover some of the structural tensions at the heart of reasonable disagreement, especially when seen from the point of view of a participant in such a disagreement.

One possible explanation of a reasonable disagreement is to say that at least one of the interlocutors is in fact not being reasonable. This would amount to saying that reasonable disagreements, as defined, do not exist (since, by definition, both interlocutors in a reasonable disagreement, are reasonable). One problem with this strategy is that it is ad hoc; it defines the problem without accounting for why we want to say that there are reasonable disagreements in the first place. If intractable disagreement implies that at least one of the interlocutors is being unreasonable, then surely this is a conclusion to draw after other possibilities have been explored. Another problem is that this strategy, if thought through consistently, must put strain upon a person's faith in her own reasonableness. Say I am an interlocutor who accepts this view of reasonable disagreements. Then whenever I believe I am in a sustained reasonable but intractable disagreement I must accept that either my interlocutor or I am not being reasonable. But then how does one determine which of us is being unreasonable, given that each of us is going to believe that the other is unreasonable? (I assume here that there is no privileged, impartial position from which to judge reasonable disagreements—a point to which I shall return). In this circumstance, it is impossible to justify that it is oneself who is the reasonable interlocutor without radically begging the question of one's own reasonableness. One is left simply with each side asserting her own reasonableness and the other's unreasonableness. But ironically when I am reduced to mere self-assertion in this way, I can easily fall into skepticism about my own beliefs. At a reflective level, I must realize that I have no more reason to trust the epistemic worth of my own self-vouchsafed reasonableness than I do that of my interlocutor's.

The article in this volume by Roger Crisp demonstrates the tension between epistemic self-confidence and maintaining belief in the reasonableness of those with whom we disagree.[15] Crisp describes an important ethical principle that he regards as true. He notes, however, that there is a long history of able philosophers who have rejected this principle. In light of this fact, Crisp believes it reasonable to reduce his confidence, indeed to suspend judgment, in the truth of the principle that appears to him true. Crisp's alternative, as he sees it, is to reject the reasonableness of all these able philosophers, which he does not believe it reasonable to do. Indeed, if the argument of the previous paragraph is valid, Crisp could not consistently reject the reasonableness of those with whom he disagrees without facing an even deeper skepticism about his beliefs than that which he countenances.

There is a further reason we need to believe in the reasonableness of at least some of our interlocutors in order to believe in our own reasonableness. A reasonable person understands that she is epistemically fallible, and therefore that she must be open to revising her beliefs. But one of the best ways to assess the epistemic worth of her beliefs is to test them against the views of others with whom she disagrees. This opportunity for epistemic self-improvement would be closed, however, if the reasonable person automatically rejected as unreasonable those with whom she disagrees. This is an instance of Mill's argument, made so powerfully in *On Liberty*, that to rationally hold our own beliefs we need to take seriously the reasonableness of those with whom we disagree, for "three-fourths of the arguments for every disputed opinion consist in dispelling the appearances which favor some opinion different from it."[16]

Another possible strategy to explain reasonable disagreement is to say that genuinely reasonable disagreements demonstrate that the problems at issue have no preponderance of good reasons on one side rather than the other; that there is, in this sense, no better answer. This way of dealing with reasonable disagreements, however, raises serious difficulties. In particular, it contradicts a key presupposition that frames most of our argument practices.[17] When we enter into a disagreement, we generally believe we have the better reasons on our side; if we did not, then we would not be trying to convince our interlocutor. But this in turn means we presuppose that there *is* a better answer, though, as reasonable people, we recognize that we may come to change our mind as to which side has the better answer. Call this the *Existence of a Better Answer Presupposition*. The strategy we are considering asks us to give up this presupposition.

Before considering this strategy, it is important to emphasize that we are examining the issue from the interlocutor's point of view. To be sure, one can think of several theoretical possibilities that would nullify or neutralize the Better Answer Presupposition in some circumstances.[18] But such possibilities are rarely invoked during a reasonable disagreement. It is theoretically possible, for example, that opposed interlocutors have exactly balanced arguments; or that there is no single best answer because any such answer is underdetermined by all possible set of reasons; or that relativism holds on moral questions such that there can be more than one right answer. These theoretical possibilities, however, do not negate the fact that interlocutors in a reasonable disagreement, as a general rule, presuppose that there is a better answer. Let us see, therefore, what light is shed on the structural tensions that frame reasonable disagreements if we try to abandon this presupposition.

One implication of this strategy would be that, as soon as a person recognizes he is in a reasonable disagreement, he should cease trying to change his interlocutor's mind (at least insofar as he is trying *rationally* to change the other's mind). But more than that, he should stop believing that his position has the preponderance of reasons on his side rather than the other side, for there does not exist a better side. Perhaps then an interlocutor can simply believe he has reasons for his own belief, and not worry about how these reasons weigh up against an opposing belief. The trouble with this is that most of the important beliefs we hold are held in contrastive form. Thus, Bookbinder could hardly believe that Israel's creation was legitimate without believing that the arguments against Israel's creation are illegitimate. And a person can hardly believe he has reasons for his atheism without at the same time believing these reasons outweigh the reasons for theism. On reflection, we see that giving up the Existence of A Better Answer Presupposition must often be destructive not only of continuing the argument (which one may be tired of anyway) but, more significantly, of one's ability to hold on to the idea that one's beliefs are grounded in any kind of justifiable reasons at all.

There are times when two interlocutors appear to recognize the reasonableness of the other's position, and yet continue to maintain preference for their own contrary and (in their view) equally reasonable position. Here we might refer to "agreeing to disagree," and think that these are cases in which reasonable disagreement does not presuppose the Better Answer Presupposition. But such cases are more rare, and difficult to sustain, than one might think, and are apt to be confused with other instances of agreeing to disagree. Consider the following instances of agreeing to disagree, neither of which entails giving up the Better Answer Presupposition: (1) A reasonable disagreement has practical implications, and the two interlocutors agree to disagree for pragmatic reasons (e.g., to get a law passed or to get on with their lives). Here the interlocutors do not give up the Better Answer Presupposition, but suppress or override it for practical purposes; (2) Two interlocutors discover that there is an irreducibly nonrational attitude, such as a question of taste or attitude to risk, at the root of their disagreement, and that what is reasonable is relative to this attitude. In this case, the interlocutors have discovered that they do not actually have a reasonable *disagreement*, and so the Better Answer Presupposition does not have relevance. Even once we take note of these cases, however, we still face instances in which we are convinced of the reasonableness of our own position, and are equally convinced of the sincerity and reasonableness of our opposing interlocutor. These are cases of genuine reasonable disagreement, and force us again to ask what to do about the Better Answer Presupposition.

It is at this point that one might be tempted to resort to the notion of an impartial reasonable spectator who could stand apart from any two interlocutors, and so come to an answer as to who has the better reasons. With this device, it could be argued, we can at least *formulate* the concept of there being a better answer, even if in a reasonable disagreement such an answer is, by hypothesis, never actually reached. This way of saving the Better Answer Presupposition does not explain why, if there is a better answer, reasonable people diverge in their views rather than converge, which is what we are trying to understand. There are other serious problems, moreover, with the resort to an impartial spectator, and I shall deal with this topic when I come to Rawls's analysis. Before turning to Rawls, I consider another way to understand reasonable disagreements that helps clarify our subject.

Robert Fogelin distinguishes between normal arguments and what I am calling reasonable disagreements (but which Fogelin calls *deep disagreements*).[19] Normal arguments, as he defines them, are resolvable because the interlocutors share a body of background beliefs and preferences that act as benchmarks for judging good and bad reasons. In this situation, Fogelin says the interlocutors share *framework propositions*.[20] We get deep disagreement, on the other hand, when interlocutors do not share framework propositions. In this case, Fogelin says, since the interlocutors have no common reference points by which to judge good or bad reasons, one simply gets clash—the clash of frameworks. Since reasonable people can, in Fogelin's view, hold opposing framework propositions, then there can be reasonable but intractable disagreement.[21] Fogelin's account does better than the other strategies; nevertheless, there are several serious problems with it.

One problem has to do with the concept of a framework proposition. Note first that Fogelin is not talking about people using different languages or incommensurable concepts. The underlying framework propositions can at least be formulated and understood by an opposing interlocutor.[22] (If the interlocutors were operating out of incommensurable frameworks, it is hard to see how they could understand each other, let alone judge their interlocutor to be reasonable. On the other hand, if they can understand each other, then it hardly makes sense to say they are operating out of incommensurable frameworks.[23]) But if the interlocutors are mutually understandable, then we must ask why they could not bring the underlying propositions to the surface and focus the argument on these, with the hope of moving the argument forward. However, if this could be done, then according to Fogelin's own definition these propositions could not have been framework propositions. Fogelin claims that the framework propositions are either so basic, or so tied to a whole web of other beliefs, that they cannot be reasonably debated. But his argument is not substantiated by the examples he chooses, nor is it easy to think of examples that could substantiate it. Fogelin's two examples of reasonable disagreement are abortion and affirmative action. He maintains that in the case of abortion, the clashing framework propositions are often over the personhood of the fetus. In the case of affirmative action, the clashing framework propositions typically involve the moral standing of social groups. But clearly propositions such as these *can* be made to surface in an argument and then be debated. Such propositions are neither so basic nor so tied to our other beliefs as to be immune to reasonable argument. As well, it is important to note that interlocutors can argue over propositions such as these by drawing out implications of their opposite's beliefs and then asking her to test the implications against her other beliefs. This kind of argument strategy can sometimes be successful, and does not require that interlocutors hold deep underlying propositions in common (what it requires is that they understand some basic forms of reasoning, such as *modus tollens*).[24]

But there is a more important weakness in Fogelin's strategy. This is that it misrepresents the phenomenology of reasonable disagreements. Fogelin would have us believe that the ultimate cause of reasonable disagreements lies in a number of clashing rock-bottom underlying propositions. But the reality is that the interlocutors in a reasonable disagreement generally come to their disagreement with their defining positions staked: (1) abortion is morally bad; abortion is not morally bad; (2) affirmative action is right; affirmative action is wrong; (3) Israel's existence as a Jewish state is morally legitimate; Israel's existence as a Jewish state is not legitimate. And it is these defining positions themselves which act as what I shall call a *weighting focus*, and which are often the main engine behind reasonable disagreements. They cause the interlocutors to give weight to different considerations, to notice different aspects of the evidence, or indeed to search for contrasting justificatory principles. To explain reasonable disagreement in terms of a clash of *underlying* propositions in fact gets the dynamic of reasonable disagreements exactly the wrong way around. The defining position we hold in a reasonable disagreement is usually more firmly held than any underlying proposition we might produce to defend our side of the argument (though given our definition of a reasonable person, the defining position cannot continue to be held in the light of good reasons to give it up).

Consider an example of one of the forks in the disagreement between Bookbinder and Abourezk. Bookbinder says that the Balfour Declaration of 1917, in which the British first announced the legitimacy of a Jewish homeland in Palestine, was significantly influenced by the moral claims of European Jews (especially as represented by the persuasive powers of Chaim Weitzman). Abourezk maintains, on the other hand, that the Agreement was motivated almost solely by the cynical self-interest of the British. The evidence is complex, and clearly what dictates each interpretation is not a clash of underlying frameworks, but the weighting focus each interlocutor brings to the debate. This same explanatory principle applies throughout the dialogue, as the two men move further apart, discovering new reasons for disagreement as the debate progresses; and this explanation applies equally to the way the two men marshal underlying moral principles. Hence we see how Fogelin's analysis misrepresents the nature of reasonable disagreements.

I turn now to Rawls's analysis, which is the most comprehensive attempt to explain reasonable disagreement of which I am aware. We shall see that here too structural features surface that deepen the psychological distance between interlocutors.

Rawls argues that reasonable disagreement is possible because people operate under what he calls "burdens of judgment."[25] In summary, these burdens of judgment are as follows: (1) The complexity of some empirical evidence relative to our intellectual capacities; (2) The indeterminacy, vagueness, and essential contestableness of some of our concepts; (3) The fact that the same consideration can legitimately be given different weight; (4) The fact that our life experiences, which can be so different in modern societies, lead us to look at evidence differently, weigh considerations differently, and focus on different values; (5) The fact that reasonable people can legitimately apply different moral approaches to the same issue; one person, for example, emphasizing deontological considerations, the other consequentialist; (6) The reality of value pluralism, that is, the fact that, in a given situation, noncomplementary values may each be legitimately pursued.

As a description of the factors that enter into reasonable disagreements, Rawls's burdens of judgment are richer and more accurate than Fogelin's. But there are serious problems that lurk.

First let us note that there is an important division in these six burdens of judgment, not noticed by Rawls (not noticed, I believe, because Rawls sees reasonable disagreement mainly from the spectator's rather than the participant's point of view). This is the distinction between #4 and the rest. Condition #4 says that our life experiences lead us to interpret evidence differently, weigh considerations differently, focus on different values, and so on. Let us call #4 the "Life Experience Condition." Rawls's analysis requires a distinction, I want to say, between (a) burdens of judgment internal to our reasons for belief, such as our citing various facts as evidence or, upon reflection, giving weight to a particular consideration, and (b) burdens of judgment external to our reasons for belief and which explain why in causal terms we focus on one set of internal considerations rather than another. In the first category we find all the burdens of judgment in Rawls's list except #4. In the second category we have only #4, though it is possible to think of other external factors not mentioned by Rawls such as various causal factors described by psychologists or sociologists of belief formation.[26] (That our experiences or other external factors can *sometimes* serve as reasons internal to our beliefs does not deflate the overall distinction.)

Let us now consider how we would regard our participation in reasonable disagreements, if we accept Rawls's analysis and have a view to the distinction I have drawn. We would then enter reasonable disagreements with the following set of beliefs:

1. Reasonable people can vary within some acceptable range in the way they interpret evidence, weigh considerations, focus on noncomplementary values, etc.

2. When reasonable people after prolonged debate do vary in these ways, then the variation is likely to be understood, at least in part, in terms of the Life Experience Condition. Let us now see how this analysis would apply to a genuine case of reasonable disagreement.

Bookbinder and Abourezk disagree over how to interpret the Balfour Declaration. They have each heard the other's reasons and, after careful examination, rejected them. It is also true that both Bookbinder and Abourezk have made clear to each other, and to the reader, the life experiences that have led them to care so deeply about the cause of their peoples. Following Rawls, then, it seems Bookbinder could say, "Abourezk's life experiences have led him to give a different interpretation to the evidence. But interpretations on this issue may differ between reasonable people; and so, even though I disagree with Abourezk, nevertheless I may still regard him a reasonable person." This *sounds* right; however, it doesn't bear up under closer analysis.

Recall that Bookbinder, by hypothesis, has examined Abourezk's reasons and rejected them as inadequate. Bookbinder does not *see* the good reasons which Abourezk sees, and moreover has reasons to believe the contradictory of what Abourezk believes. In a situation like this, Bookbinder must be disposed to think that Abourezk is being influenced by bias, prejudice, or some other distorting emotion. But these burdens of *mis*judgment can be as much rooted in our life experiences as can the burdens of judgment. Given this, Bookbinder can bring the Life Experience Condition to bear in either of two contrary ways: either to explain why, though Abourezk rejects the reasons Bookbinder sees, Abourezk is nevertheless a reasonable person; or as a way to explain why Abourezk fails to be reasonable in this particular case. However, given that Bookbinder rejects Abourezk's reasons, he must always be disposed to take the second option. It appears then that Rawls's analysis doesn't really help us understand how we can continue to regard our fellow interlocutor as a reasonable person.

Perhaps, however, this is too quick. We might think of using the Life Experience Condition in the following way. We could say that a certain act of faith is needed when we are involved in a reasonable disagreement, especially with someone whom we otherwise respect. What we must accept—and this is the act of faith—is that if we had had the experiences that our interlocutor has had, then we would become aware of legitimate reasons for holding beliefs, or giving weight to considerations, which we cannot now see or take to heart. This way of interpreting the Life Experience Condition no doubt points to an important, indeed essential truth. But what is its relevance to understanding reasonable disagreements from the participant's perspective?

One side-benefit of this option is that it helps us understand why the notion of an impartial spectator, who would adjudicate which side has the better reasons, is not useful in the present context. For if our experiences make us aware of reasons or cause us to give legitimate weight to reasons, then the spectator, by hypothesis, would not be aware of all the relevant reasons that weigh on both sides of a reasonable disagreement. Moreover, it would seem inevitable that any spectator would simply become another reasonable interlocutor who must enter into the discussion. But then the same underlying tensions we have been considering, would resurface in the new situation.[27] The Life Experience Condition helps us clarify this issue, but there is a problem that now arises when we try to apply it in the way Rawls wishes.

The problem is that the strategy leads to a train of thought that could undermine utterly a person's confidence in her own reasons. Take again Bookbinder and Abourezk's views of the Balfour Declaration. They hold contrary, and often contradictory, positions on how to interpret the evidence. Each believes that there exists a better answer. Each believes, moreover, that his position, subject to being shown otherwise, is the better answer. But now what if Bookbinder says to himself, "If I had been born a Palestinian like Abourezk whose people had had their home expropriated, etc., then this experience would lead me not only to interpret the evidence on Balfour differently but also actually to become aware of legitimate reasons to interpret the evidence differently, reasons which I cannot now fully perceive." This in turn means that Bookbinder believes that both he and Abourezk could be seen by a reasonable person to have the preponderance of good reasons on both their sides, if the reasonable person were able to experience what both Bookbinder and Abourezk had experienced. But to take this to heart is in effect to give up the idea that there *is* a better reason, and in particular that we have the better reason on our side, for having the better reason means better than the reason one is arguing against. But coming to hold this view must ultimately put pressure on our epistemic self-confidence. When an interlocutor, moreover, strongly identifies with the position he is defending, then the threat to epistemic self-confidence is easily felt as a threat to her identity. An intuitive grasp of the Life Experience Condition may explain why people in an intractable disagreement are often so reluctant to try to put themselves fully in the shoes of their adversary. Here then is a further underlying structural tension of reasonable disagreements that can push people apart to the point of deep distrust and rancor.

When deployed according to the above logic, the Life Experience Condition adds to the pessimistic view of dialogue that has emerged from my analysis. In concluding my chapter, I briefly examine a way to look at the Life Experience Condition that suggests a more optimistic possibility. Central to this understanding, I argue, is what Glover calls "a human moral identity."[28]

In understanding the causes of atrocity, Glover emphasizes the dangers of self-conceptions rooted in tribalism, dogmatic belief, and conformism. To counteract the way such self-conceptions often shut us off from others, Glover advances the notion that we strive to develop, collectively and individually, a human moral identity. This self-conception has at its core the moral responses of sympathy and revulsion against humiliation. When functioning properly, these responses act as "trumps" or "relevance prompts"[29] that override the cruelty or desire to humiliate to which our nature is prone. A human moral identity, moreover, discounts ethnicity, distance, and ideology in responding to the suffering or humiliation of a fellow human. (Glover is clear that he does not mean to exclude other species from some form of this concern, though it is not a topic he takes up in *Humanity*.)

A key question for Glover is how a human moral identity can be strengthened and made immune to subversion. Part of the answer must lie in the work of psychologists and sociologists. In this regard, Glover cites the suggestive studies of Milgram on obedience and of the Oliners on altruism. There is also the importance of "a shared moral culture"[30] which transmits the value of equal respect. But in terms of the immediate workings of the moral responses Glover places great emphasis on what he calls breakthroughs. Breakthroughs occur when sympathy or revulsion against humiliation break through our more circumscribed self-conceptions, and restrain us from participating in, or remaining indifferent to, an odious act. In *Humanity*, Glover gives many rich descriptions of such breakthroughs. Consider two examples: (1) An American pilot at My Lai thinks of his own children when he sees Vietnamese children being slaughtered. Sympathy goes out to the children, and he lands his helicopter to stop his fellow soldiers from continuing the massacre; (2) While fighting in the Spanish Civil War, George Orwell finds himself unable to shoot his Fascist adversary because the latter had his pants down, sitting on a readymade latrine. Orwell's implicit thought must have been something like, "Here is a person like me, performing a natural bodily function. It would be humiliating for him as it would be for me to be shot with his pants down, so I won't do it." Note that in these two breakthroughs, as in the others Glover describes, the moral response is triggered by an observation or a thought that causes a person to identify with a victim through some circumstance they share in common (being a parent who would grieve the loss of his children, being a soldier who would be humiliated if shot with his pants down). This recognition of common humanity, as we may call it, then triggers the breakthrough of sympathy or revulsion against humiliation, which in turn motivates action.

I want to say that breakthroughs may also occur in intractable disagreements, though perhaps they rarely do. Here the breakthrough is not between an agent and a victim, but between an interlocutor and a fellow interlocutor. There is an intimation of this point in a paper Glover wrote well before he started work on *Humanity*. In "Anna Karenina and Moral Philosophy,"[31] Glover describes a moral ideal he calls "seriousness,"[32] and writes how this complex ideal sometimes expresses itself in intractable disagreements. He describes a case of his own as follows:[33]

Seriousness may explain something I have often found puzzling in discussions between people on different sides of disagreements about values. It is

> something I have noticed sometimes when arguing for instance about abortion, a topic notorious for the hostility and vehemence it generates. I am broadly sympathetic to the case for seeing abortion as something which should be available to women if they choose it. I often discuss the issue with people who take the opposite view that even early abortion is murder. My view tells me that they are helping to maintain the unjustifiable coercion of women into having unwanted children, and creating massive unnecessary misery in doing so. Their view tells them that I am advocating treating babies as things, and contributing to a climate in which there is the mass murder of innocent and defenseless human beings on an unprecedented scale. But often I value the discussion and respect the things said by my pro-life opponent. And my impression is that often they have a similar view. At least, they talk to me in a much more friendly manner from what I would talk to some Nazi who was advocating mass murder.

In this case, the interlocutors have temporarily stopped trying to convince each other of the rightness of their own positions. Instead, moved by the seriousness of the other's commitment, they have found values to respect in the other's viewpoint. Here the moral response is not sympathy or revulsion against humiliation, but the restoration of mutual respect that transcends the deep differences between the interlocutors.

The Life Experience Condition, I want to say, could also be a source for breakthroughs in reasonable but intractable disagreements. The condition says that people with different life experiences are likely to find salience in, or even be aware of, different considerations. Taking this to heart, for example, Bookbinder could be forcefully struck by the following train of thought: "Abourezk and I are *alike* in that our positions are each shaped by our respective life experiences. It is unlikely therefore that I completely understand our differences. I can at least appreciate the sincerity of his commitment to the Palestinians, and even try to understand better the experiences that shaped his viewpoint." This train of thought does not imply the epistemic free fall I described earlier, because it need not suggest to Bookbinder that he does not have the better position. Rather, the breakthrough leads to a suspension of the disagreement on Bookbinder's part, as he comes to see Abourezk as a fellow human being subject to the same Life Experience Condition as himself. In Glover's terminology, Bookbinder's human moral identity overrides, at least for the moment, his self-conception rooted in ethnicity and religion. If now Abourezk were subject to the same train of thought, then perhaps the two men, in the space opened up by their common humanity, could begin to think about practical solutions.

Nevertheless, the fact is, Bookbinder and Abourezk do not undergo such a breakthrough. In spite of their goodwill and reasonableness, the dialogue drastically deteriorates. The fate of this dialogue leaves us, as does Glover's *Humanity*, with the following question: Is it plausible that a human moral identity could ever possess enough psychological richness, or broad enough appeal, to thwart the malevolent outbursts of our more circumscribed, deeply rooted identities?

PERSONAL POSTSCRIPT

I approached Jonathan to be my thesis supervisor in 1970 when I was 23. Jonathan (as it seemed) hesitated. But we fell into an intense discussion of Dostoevsky's *Crime and Punishment*, after which I found I had a supervisor.

The life of a graduate student can feel like being stuck on a high wire, unable to move forward or backward. Yet whenever I entered 13 Longwall St., and climbed the stairs to Jonathan's study (maneuvering around the bicycles in the hallway), I felt back on solid ground. Jonathan's focus was to explore my ideas incisively and critically, but always with understanding and in a spirit of equality. Looking back, I realize Jonathan never referred to his published work, even when we were discussing issues about which he had written extensively (such as free will and responsibility). He must have felt that to interpose his own published views would have curbed the egalitarian spirit of our conversations. When I left 13 Longwall into the busy Oxford traffic, I invariably felt buoyed about my work, student anxieties temporarily lifted.

There is a lot of pure fun in Jonathan. My wife and I have many happy memories of cycling with the Glovers to their favorite Soho café, watching old Ealing Studio comedies, and going for walks in London and Oxford. But to be Jonathan's friend is also to know that he is haunted by our species' cruelty, and by the maddening barriers we erect—conceptual, psychological, and political—that facilitate this cruelty. What unifies the diverse topics Jonathan has written about is his desire to help dismantle these barriers. I have come to see the depth of Jonathan's commitment to this goal, and I am moved with admiration.

I recently viewed a DVD of Jonathan conducting a seminar at King's College. There was his precise but considerate way of replying to criticism, the smile that comes as much from his eyes as his mouth, the exuberant laugh, the seriousness, the gentle humanity. I realized that my sense of what it is to be a teacher and a philosopher is bound up with my physical impressions of Jonathan from the time he and I first talked philosophy nearly 40 years ago. I don't think either of us could have predicted that those conversations would be the prelude to hundreds of further conversations, and a lifelong friendship that has encompassed our two families.

Notes

I would particularly like to thank Ann Davis, Mary Keshen, and Jeff McMahan for their insightful and encouraging comments. I was also helped by comments from Daylian Cain, Richmond Campbell, Jonathan Glover, Stan Godlovitch, Andrew Lugg, Rod Nicholls, Andrew Mason, Mike Targett, and Bruno Verbeek. Earlier versions of some of my ideas were tested before helpfully critical audiences at meetings of the Atlantic Philosophical Association, the Canadian Philosophical Association, the Inland Northwest Philosophical Association, and the UK Association for Legal and Social Philosophy.

1. *Humanity: A Moral History of the 20th Century*, Jonathan Cape, 1999.

2. Ibid., p. 33.

3. Ibid., p. 403.

4. Ibid., p. 27.

5. Jonathan Glover, "Dialogue is the Only Way to End this Cycle of Violence," *Guardian*, Wednesday July 27, 2005: p. 22.

6. I take the phrase "intractable disagreement" from Michele M. Moody-Adams, "On the Alleged Methodological Infirmity of Ethics," *American Philosophical Quarterly* 27 (July 1990): p. 225. See also Charles Larmore, *The Morals of Modernity*, Cambridge University Press 1996: chapter 7.

7. *Humanity: A Moral History of the 20th Century*, Jonathan Cape, 1999: p. 403.

8. For an example of an instructive debate in this regard see J.P. Moreland and Kai Nielsen, *Does God Exist?: The Debate between Theists and Atheists*, Prometheus, 1993. Also instructive is a recent article by Anthony Kenny in which he tries to show that both theism and atheism can be reasonably held: Anthony Kenny, "Knowledge, Belief, and Faith," *Philosophy* 82, 2007, 381–97. These sources are instructive not only for demonstrating how opposing positions can be reasonably propounded, but how reasonable disagreement can push people further apart.

9. *Through Different Eyes*, Hyman Bookbinder and James Abourezk, Adler and Adler, 1987; moderated by David K. Shipler.

10. John Rawls, *Political Liberalism*, Columbia University Press, 1993: pp. 47–66; Charles Larmore, *The Morals of Modernity*, Cambridge University Press, 1987: chapter 7; Thomas Nagel, "Moral Conflict and Political Legitimacy," *Philosophy and Public Affairs*, 17 (Summer 1987): pp. 227–40; and Thomas Nagel, *Partiality and Equality*, OUP, 1991: chapter 14.

11. Larmore, *Morals and Modernity*: p. 12.

12. Ibid., p. 171.

13. Rawls, *Political Liberalism*: p. 62. See also Nagel, "Moral Conflict and Political Legitimacy": pp. 229 and 235.

14. Michael Smith, "Realism" in *Ethics*, ed. Peter Singer, Oxford University Press, 1994: p. 170.

15. Roger Crisp, "The Foundations of Humanity," present volume, chapter 9: 180.

16. J.S. Mill *On Liberty*, Bobbs-Merrill, 1956: p. 45. I have discussed this issue in my book *Reasonable Self-Esteem*, McGill-Queen's: chapter 2. This passage from Mill was brought to my attention by Andrew Mason's *Understanding Political Disagreement*, Cambridge University Press 1996: p. 146. For further insight into this issue see David Christensen, "Epistemology of Disagreement: The Good News," *Philosophical Review*, 116(2), 2007: pp. 187–216. I found much to agree with in Christensen's paper. The paper appeared too close to my deadline to address specific arguments in Christensen's paper.

17. My thought in this paragraph has been influenced by Jurgen Habermas, *The Theory of Communicative Action, Volume 1*, Beacon Press, 1984. Andrew Mason has drawn my attention to a similar assumption employed by G.A. Cohen in chapter 1 of *If You're an Egalitarian How Come You're so Rich?*, Harvard University Press, 2000.

18. I owe my consideration of these possibilities to Jeff McMahan.

19. R. Fogelin, "Deep Disagreements," *Informal Logic*, 7 (Winter 1985): pp. 1–8. See also Andrew Lugg "Deep Disagreement and Informal Logic: No Cause for Alarm," *Informal Logic* 8 (Winter 1986): pp. 47–51.

20. Ibid., p. 5.

21. Ibid., p. 5.

22. This is clear from the whole tenor of Fogelin's discussion.

23. A point developed by Donald Davidson in "The Very Idea of a Conceptual Scheme," reprinted in *Inquires into Truth and Interpretation*, Oxford University Press, 1984: essay 13.

24. Further on this issue, see Karl Popper's essay "The Myth of the Framework" in Popper's collection of the same title, Routledge, 1994.

25. Rawls, *Political Liberalism*: pp. 54–66.

26. Thus, for example, Andrew Mason in *Understanding Political Disagreements*, gives a sociological–psychological account, based on the work of Nancy Chodorow and Carol Gilligan, as to why people are disposed to treat one kind of reason rather another as salient in their moral and political deliberations. For further external accounts, emphasizing sociological considerations, see Paul Seabright "Objectivity, Disagreement, and Projectability," *Inquiry*, 31, 1988: pp. 25–31.

27. Discussions with Andrew Mason and Bruno Verbeek helped me understand, even if that was not their intention, that the device of an ideally rational spectator, as opposed to a real-life spectator, is not relevant to my argument, however useful such a device might be for other purposes.

28. Glover, *Humanity*: p. 403.

29. Glover, "On Moral Nose"; essay to appear in Festschrift for John Harris, forthcoming.

30. *Humanity*, ibid., p. 387.

31. Though written much earlier, the paper was published around the same time as *Humanity*. See Jonathan Glover, "Anna Karenina and Moral Philosophy" in *Well-Being and Morality Essays in Honor of James Griffin*, edited Roger Crisp and Brad Hooker, Clarendon Press, Oxford, 2000: Essay #10; pp. 159–76.

32. Ibid., section 4.

33. Ibid., p. 173.

IV

BIOETHICS AND BEYOND

7

Humanity and Hyper-regulation: From Nuremberg to Helsinki

Onora O'Neill

In his thoughtful and sobering book on ghastly things that human beings did to one another during the twentieth century, Jonathan Glover repeatedly emphasizes the fragility of the psychological resources that stand between humanity and horror.[1] I think that he is wholly right about the fragility of human character and resolution, and about the many ways in which humanity toward others can fail. Good intentions falter, good behaviour is intermittent; commonly enough, bad intentions are not only entrenched but enacted. Glover's comment near the end of his book that "the ethics of preventing atrocities are an extension of the ethics of everyday life"[2] has an obvious point. However, reliance on our slender psychological resources is—fortunately—not the whole story. Much that happens in dark times is not an extension of everyday life, but rather a terrible distortion and collapse of everyday life that emerges when the institutional frameworks that help us to avoid cruelty and horror in much of daily life are destroyed or perverted. Reflecting on these realities, we have reasons to look not only to psychology, but also to politics and law; not only to the attitudes and capacities that individuals bring to the situations they encounter, but also to ways in which opportunities and temptations to harm others can be limited and regulated. Humanity to others depends on robust institutions as well as psychological strength.

In fact, many of the most significant responses to Nazi and other atrocities committed during the twentieth century have been institutional. The early post-World War II years saw the establishment of new institutions that still frame international life: the *United Nations* itself, which promulgated and subsequently elaborated the *Universal Declaration of Human Rights*, and established a range of specialist agencies, such as the *World Bank* and the *General Agreement on Tariffs and Trade*, precursor to the *World Trade Organization*. Many of these institutions are now much criticized (we do not, of course, know what might have happened without them), and there is widespread belief that some of them now urgently need major reforms.

However, at least one important institutional innovation introduced in the early postwar years, which was intended to prevent the repetition of horrendous inhumanity, is generally thought to have stood the test of time. The standards and codes adopted to prevent abusive treatment of human beings in medical experiments are widely thought to be in good shape, indeed better than they were in their original postwar version, partly because they have been continuously amended, codified and institutionalized. In this chapter I shall contrast the standards proposed in 1947 for the proper treatment of human subjects in medical research with subsequent revisions of those requirements. My focus will be on formulations of informed consent requirements for subjects of medical research, on their implications and on their practicality. My aim is to establish whether the post-World War II standards proposed for research on human subjects have been improved or damaged by subsequent revisions and reforms.

7.1 THE *NUREMBERG CODE* OF 1947

Human beings had been callously abused and murdered in the name of medical research, both in prewar Nazi Germany and subsequently in the concentration camps.[3] Some of the physicians who had undertaken this research were tried at Nuremberg in 1947 (the so-called Doctors' Trials). The defence lawyers claimed at these trials that the research on human subjects done by the defendants had not differed from medical research elsewhere.[4] In response to this claim, standards for the proper regulation of biomedical research on human subjects were set out in a document that has become known as *Nuremberg Code*.[5] Despite the fact that its legal status is unclear, the *Nuremberg Code* is still seen as setting the fundamental standards for research on human subjects.

The fundamental claim of the *Nuremberg Code* is that medical research on human subjects is ethically unacceptable unless the research subject consents:

The voluntary consent of the human subject is absolutely essential.

The phrase 'voluntary consent' is then explicated in these words:

This means that the person involved should have legal capacity to give consent; should be so situated as to be able to exercise free power of choice, without the intervention of any element of force, fraud, deceit, duress, overreaching, or other ulterior form of constraint or coercion; and should have sufficient knowledge and comprehension of the elements of the subject matter involved as to enable him to make an understanding and enlightened decision. This latter element requires that before the acceptance of an affirmative decision by the experimental subject there should be made known to him the nature, duration, and purpose of the experiment; the method and means by which it is to be conducted; all inconveniences and hazards reasonably to be expected; and the effects upon his health or person which may possibly come from his participation in the experiment.

These standards for the treatment of human subjects in biomedical research appear less demanding than those set out in more recent codes and regulations. Most obviously, the *Nuremberg Code* focuses on *capacities* to consent rather than on requirements for *actual* use of these capacities in consenting, let alone on (highly) *specific* or *explicit* consent. Research subjects must have "legal *capacity* to give consent"; they must be "*able* to exercise free power of choice"; they must be sufficiently aware of what is proposed to "*enable* [them] to make an understanding and enlightened decision" (my italics). Second, the Code makes no explicit reference to *information*, or to *informed consent*. It simply illustrates the cognitive *capacities* needed if research subjects are to have "sufficient knowledge and comprehension…to enable an understanding and enlightened decision" by offering a short list of points that must be "made known" to the research subject before an "affirmative decision." The Code can be read as accepting that ethical requirements will be met provided that the research subject *could have* made a free and enlightened decision, whether or not the consent he or she gave *actually* did so. The participation of research subjects who are able to exercise free power of choice seemingly counts as voluntary whether or not they actually exercise these capacities in deciding to become research subjects—or merely go along with whatever others propose.

This position has its appeal. By requiring that research subjects be so placed that they can exercise free power of choice "without the intervention of any element of force, fraud, deceit, duress, overreaching, or other ulterior form of constraint or coercion" the *Nuremberg Code* focuses on significant ethical standards that must be met if our most serious obligations are not to be flouted, and specifically on the standards that were violated by those who were convicted at Nuremberg. Medical research will not meet the Nuremberg criteria if it violates any of these fundamental obligations—even if the research subject had, but failed to exercise, a capacity to refuse consent. Yet in the sixty years since the *Nuremberg Code* was first promulgated, it has often been thought to set too low a standard, and supposedly stronger requirements have been proposed as improvements.

7.2 SINCE NUREMBERG: SPECIFIC CONSENT AND EXPLICIT CONSENTING

Despite the fact that the *Nuremberg Code* does not require research subjects to provide highly specific consent or to go through a highly explicit informed consent process, it evidently forms part of the long liberal tradition that views consent as legitimating, and more pertinently that views action that overrides lack of consent as lacking legitimacy. The legitimating potential of consent has dominated liberal and democratic thought for over three centuries, and has been reworked and reinvigorated in many areas during the last thirty years. It is most evident in the influential revivals of liberal contractualism in political philosophy and of market thinking in economics, but is also apparent in the constant emphasis on consent requirements in biomedicine, where informed consent has come to play a larger and larger part, not only in research but also in clinical ethics.[6]

Yet the extension of consent requirements from research to clinical ethics has proved highly problematic. Those who are incompetent to consent can be excluded from medical research, but cannot be denied medical treatment. So informed consent cannot be a universal or even a normal requirement in clinical ethics. Given that ill-health and injury often erode capacities to consent, this is not a marginal problem. Those who think informed consent necessary for clinical practice have tried to deal with this major difficulty by viewing the 'autonomous patient' as the standard case, and then trying to work out how to make consenting easier for those who are not 'autonomous patients', or at least for those with only marginal incapacity. Evidently this ameliorative approach cannot make consent possible for those whose cognitive competence is most impaired. Nor does it address the reality that descriptions of complex diagnoses and treatments may not be adequately grasped, even by those who are generally seen as 'autonomous patients'. Informed consent can be given only by those who can grasp *what* they are consenting to, and highly complex proposals are likely to overtax the capacities even of the cognitively competent. This mismatch between aspirations to make informed consent the lynchpin of clinical ethics is constantly discussed with reference to cognitively impaired patients. But the reality that consent is often overtaxing for competent patients as well is often neglected.

However, research ethics may face fewer challenges, since those whose cognitive capacities are marginal need not be accepted as research subjects. Such exclusion is not, however, ethically unproblematic, since it would mean that there could be no research on human subjects with conditions that impair competence, even when such research is needed to benefit those patients. And even if we were prepared to forgo research on conditions that impair competence, there would still be the problem that competent research subjects too often fail to grasp quite standard aspects of prospective research design, such as the use of randomization or placebos.[7] Should medical research that uses these very ordinary methods be prohibited?

The problem with setting more exacting standards for informed consent requirements is that this may make many sorts of research, hence many benefits to patients, impossible. At present it often looks as if clinical and research ethics are both being pulled in incompatible directions. On the one hand there are demands that consent procedures be made easier and more user-friendly so as to include the marginally competent.

On the other hand there are demands that they be made more elaborate, detailed, and rigorous in order to secure highly specific consent, and highly explicit consent procedures and protocols, and so improve the protection for patients and research subjects. One cost of pursuing both agendas has been a widespread tendency to draft and promulgate increasingly complex codes and requirements. Although this complexity is widely supposed to impose demands only on researchers (and on clinicians), it is in fact often experienced as imposing demands on research subjects (and patients).

This paradoxical agenda can be illustrated by the *Declaration of Helsinki*,[8] promoted by *World Medical Association*,[9] which sets out supposedly more exacting ethical requirements for research on human subjects. This Declaration is only one of many documents and codes[10] formulating standards for research on human subjects, that sets detailed, exacting and (I shall argue) implausible requirements.

The *Declaration of Helsinki* requires that

> 22. Participation by competent individuals as subjects in medical research must be voluntary.

This requirement is then glossed by setting out what research subjects must understand:

> 24. In medical research involving competent human subjects, each potential subject must be adequately informed of the aims, methods, sources of funding, any possible conflicts of interest, institutional affiliations of the researcher, the anticipated benefits and potential risks of the study and the discomfort it may entail, and any other relevant aspects of the study. The potential subject must be informed of the right to refuse to participate in the study or to withdraw consent to participate at any time without reprisal. Special attention should be given to the specific information needs of individual potential subjects as well as to the methods used to deliver the information. After ensuring that the potential subject has understood the information, the physician or another appropriately qualified individual must then seek the potential subject's freely-given informed consent, preferably in writing. If the consent cannot be expressed in writing, the non-written consent must be formally documented and witnessed.

In effect, *Helsinki 2008* requires researchers to ensure that research subjects understand *highly specific and complex information*, so that they can give *highly specific consent* to envisaged research projects. Research subjects are to grasp not only how the envisaged research might affect them individually—which the *Nuremberg Code* also requires them to understand—but also complex aspects of research design and funding, and other financial and institutional arrangements. And the consent that is sought and provided must not only be highly specific, but must also be given according to *highly explicit procedures*: consent forms will be long and consent will be signed off by both parties, recorded and if necessary witnessed. (These standards may be favoured as much because they protect against complaint and litigation as because they are thought to be ethically required). Whenever the cognitive capacities of research subjects do not enable them to meet these standards, then biomedical research ought not be done.

7.3 ETHICAL RIGOUR OR HYPOCRISY?

These demands for more specific consent, and for more explicit methods of consenting, are now widely prescribed and widely seen as more rigorous than the *Nuremberg Code*. Equally, they are widely flouted. There is ample evidence that research subjects do not grasp everything that the *Declaration of Helsinki* and similar contemporary codes require them to grasp, and that much research on human subjects consequently is done without the prescribed consent. If the standards set in these documents are convincing, then much consent to participate in research is invalid, and many sorts of research on human subjects ought to be abandoned. Alternatively, the defect may lie in the proposed standards, rather than in the research.

Fully explicit consenting, requiring longer and longer consent forms, signatures, witnesses, enduring records, cannot always be required, because it is not always possible. Implied consent can be replaced by explicit consent in some, but not in all cases. For example, it would be possible—if demanding—to replace implied with explicit consent for various aspects of research interventions now standardly done on the basis of implied consent, such as taking blood samples or recording temperatures. However, it would not be possible to do entirely without implied consent, because all explicit consenting presupposes and relies on implicit assumptions and agreements—and in particular on assumptions about methods and conventions for requesting, offering and refusing consent. The idea that because some consenting can be explicit, all consenting can be explicit is fallacious.

Fully specific consent also cannot always be required, because it too is impossible. Researchers can never communicate all details of a proposed piece of research to a research subject; indeed they cannot even include them all in a consent disclosure (which the prospective research subject might or might not understand): all descriptions are indeterminate, and there is always more that could be added. Nor can we assume that consent will travel from one (incomplete, indeterminate) description of a research proposal to others. Consent is a propositional attitude, and those who consent to one description of proposed research may not—and often do not—grasp either entailment relations or causal connections, with the result that their consent does not travel to other descriptions or implications of that to which they give consent. Indeed, on reflection, demands for specific consent make little sense. We can only demand specific consent if we can explain *how* specific it ought to be, and why it should be specific to that degree. Yet answering this question in any uniform or simple way is impossible in the same way that answering the pseudo-question 'How long is a piece of string?' is impossible.

Full or complete specificity is unobtainable, so cannot be necessary for valid consent; full explicitness can be achieved in some cases—but only on the basis of numerous assumptions to which no more than implicit consent is given. Attempts to improve or shore up standards for research ethics by striving for ever more specific consent and ever more explicit consenting not only ignore the real limitations of competence of those asked to consent, but founder in deep theoretical holes. Attempts to shortlist the types of content to which specific consent must be given are unlikely to be feasible if they require the research subject to grasp the "aims, methods, sources of funding, and any possible conflicts of interest, institutional affiliations of the researcher, the anticipated benefits and potential risks of the study."

7.4 HYPER-REGULATION OR HUMANITY?

Nuremberg and Helsinki are not only symbols but instances of real alternatives, between which any approach to research ethics must choose. If we persist with attempts to introduce 'Helsinki' approaches to informed consent, we are likely to end up pretending (hypocritically) that research subjects actually grasp and consent to far more than is likely, and to make excessive demands on them. In effect, we would be extending a culture of hyper-regulation into the relationship between researchers and research subjects. Many see this as the way to ensure that researchers are more accountable and research subjects better protected. Yet demands for greater specificity and explicitness are not always improvements for either party, and both may feel that they are colluding in a charade of informing and consenting. Hyper-regulation may lead not to better and better standards, but to more and more emphasis on a 'tick box' culture that demands unintelligent forms of accountability. Research ethics may not advance by insisting on more massive and detailed procedures, or specifically on more massive and detailed consent procedures.

If, on the other hand, we take a realistic view of the cognitive demands of informing and consenting, while persisting in setting 'Helsinki' standards for research ethics, then we must accept that many potential research subjects will simply lack an adequately specific and complex grasp of research proposals that are put to them. We would then have to view a great deal of medical research, including many studies that involve placebos and randomized trials, as ethically unacceptable. Biomedical research involving human subjects would have to be severely curtailed.

The only other possibility would be to take a more realistic view not only of the cognitive demands of informing and consenting, but also of the standards that should be required for informed consent, and to insist that researchers actually meet these more realistic standards. If we took this third route, the *Nuremberg Code* would offer a better model than the *Declaration of Helsinki*. The *Nuremberg Code* does not require highly specific consent or highly explicit consenting. It requires adherence to standards that are far more important for securing humanity and averting horror. The fundamental obligations of researchers under the *Nuremberg Code* are not to engage in "force, fraud, deceit, duress, overreaching, or other ulterior form of constraint or coercion." The *Nuremberg Code* sees the voluntariness of research participation as important not because consent is ethically fundamental, but because it provides evidence and assurance that a research subject has not been forced or duped or deceived, or abused in other fundamental ways, but rather acts voluntarily.

The Nuremberg approach to consent sees it as significant because it is a way by which research subjects can permit action that would *otherwise* flout fundamental obligations, so would *otherwise* violate fundamental rights or legitimate expectations. In consenting to a specific intervention we waive rights, entitlements, and expectations in specific ways, and may thereby permit action that would *otherwise* be gravely wrong, but which we have reason to permit in a particular case. Waivers are standard ways in which action that would *otherwise* be impermissible can be rendered acceptable. Once we see consent as a waiver, we can see that it presupposes and works against a background of more fundamental obligations, which individuals can waive in specific ways *when they have reason to do so*. Cutting someone open—as surgeons do—amounts to injury (and may involve coercion, constraint, deception, and the like) unless the patient has agreed to that specific operation. Giving someone a drug with unknown and possible adverse effects—as is done in clinical trials—may amount to poisoning (and may involve coercion, constraint, deception, and the like) *unless* the research subject taking a drug on an experimental basis has agreed to do so. Absent consent, such acts are likely to violate many of the fundamental obligations mentioned in the *Nuremberg Code*.

It is therefore an illusion to think that informed consent procedures must do all the heavy work in research ethics. The crimes that were tried at the Doctors' Trials in Nuremberg were wrong not because the perpetrators acted without informed consent—although they did—but because they used force, duress, constraint and coercion—and more specifically and horribly, torture and mutilation. The heavy work in research ethics, as in ethics for other domains of life, is done by these fundamental requirements. These are the requirements whose violation leads to inhumanity. Informed consent is only a secondary way of allowing some adjustment around these requirements by permitting selective waiver of fundamental obligations by those on the receiving end, when they have reason to make such adjustments. No doubt, observance of even the most elementary informed consent requirements would have been enough to ensure that the crimes tried at Nuremberg did not take place. However, what was wrong about those crimes is not captured—indeed it is trivialized—by pointing out that they were done without the consent of the research subjects. Even if (almost unimaginably) there had been consent, such acts would still have been gravely wrong: waivers are not ways of absolving others of their fundamental obligations wholesale, but of making specific adjustments on particular occasions. What is most important in a Nuremberg approach to research ethics is not informed consent itself, but the underlying obligations and corresponding rights that are held absent specific waivers.

If we rethink informed consent taking account of these issues, we are likely to end up with a view of informed consent that is closer to Nuremberg than to Helsinki. The emphasis shifts from aspirations—or, speaking more bluntly, pretences—that we can get patients and research subjects to grasp matters of great complexity in exorbitant detail, to a set of more traditional and fundamental ethical standards. If research subjects are "so situated as to be able to exercise free power of choice, without the intervention of any element of force, fraud, deceit, duress, overreaching, or other ulterior form of constraint or coercion," they can make or refuse to make specific adjustments to others' fundamental obligations. They can do this even if their cognitive capacities are fairly limited, and the consent they give is neither highly specific nor highly explicit. Equally, if researchers start from the assumption that "any element of force, fraud, deceit, duress, overreaching, or other ulterior form of constraint or coercion" is ruled out then they will be a long way toward humane research practice.

Notes

Many of the arguments in this article are discussed in the context of a wider consideration of ethical and epistemic norms in Neil C. Manson and Onora O'Neill, *Rethinking Informed Consent in Bioethics* (Cambridge: Cambridge University Press, 2007). In this article I focus more specifically on the themes of humanity and inhumanity, which have been so central to Jonathan Glover's work.

1. Jonathan Glover, *Humanity: A Moral History of the Twentieth Century* (London: Jonathan Cape, 1999).

2. Ibid., p. 408.

3. For discussion of Nazi abuses of medical research before and during World War II, see Michael Burleigh, *Death and Deliverance: "Euthanasia" in Germany, c.1900–45* (Cambridge University Press, 1994); *Ethics and Extermination: Reflections on Nazi Genocide* (Cambridge: Cambridge University Press, 1997).

4. For detailed discussion of some of the historical issues surrounding medical codes see Ulrich Tröhler and Stella Reiter-Theil (eds.), *Ethics Codes in Medicine— Foundations and Achievements of Codifications since 1947* (Aldershot, UK: Ashgate, 1998).

5. The Code was drafted by Andrew Ivy and Leo Alexander, doctors working with the prosecution during the trial. In April 1947, Dr. Alexander submitted a memorandum to the United States Counsel for War Crimes, outlining six points defining legitimate research. The verdict of the Nuremberg Tribunal reiterated these points and extended six into ten, which subsequently became known as the *Nuremberg Code*. For the text see http://www.ushmm.org/research/doctors/Nuremberg_Code.htm.

6. For a useful account of the increasing emphasis on informed consent in biomedicine see Ruth R. Faden and Tom L. Beauchamp, *A History and Theory of Informed Consent* (New York: Oxford University Press, 1986).

7. See Angus Dawson, "What Should We Do About It? Implications of the Empirical Evidence in Relation to Comprehension and Acceptability of Randomisation?," in S. Holm and M. Jonas (eds.) *Engaging the World: The Use of Empirical Research in Bioethics and the Regulation of Biotechnology* (Amsterdam: IOS Press, 2004).

8. *Declaration of Ethical Principles for Medical Research Involving Human Subjects*, 1964. For the text of the 2008 revision of the Declaration see http://www.wma.net/e/policy/b3.htm. For its history see http://www.wma.net/e/ethicsunit/pdf/chapter_4_decl_of_helsinki.pdf; For analysis see Robert V. Carlson, Kenneth M. Boyd, and David J. Webb, "The Revision of the Declaration of Helsinki: Past, Present and Future," *British Journal of Clinical Pharmacology* 57 (2004): 695–713.

9. The *World Medical Association* is an organization of medical associations and individual physicians that met for the first time in 1947—the year of the *Nuremberg Code*. Its aim is "to preserve...professional traditions from encroachment by.. hostile forces" and much of its work is on ethical standards for clinical and research practice. It claims that "by solid accomplishments in the field of medical ethics, the WMA has earned the right to call itself the international voice of organized medicine". Its best-known policy statement, the *Declaration of Helsinki* was first adopted in 1964, and has been repeatedly amended and clarified. The 2008 version is current.

10. See for example the *Belmont Report* on *Ethical Principles and Guidelines for the Protection of Human Subjects of Research* 1979 (US Department of Health, Education, and Welfare; http://ohsr.od.nih.gov/guidelines/belmont.html) and Article 16 of the *European Convention for the Protection of Human Rights and Dignity of the Human Being with Regard to the Application of Biology and Medicine: Convention on Human Rights and Biomedicine*, http://conventions.coe.int/treaty/en/Reports/Html/164.htm. The latter prohibits research on human subjects unless "the necessary consent as provided for under Article 5 has been given expressly, specifically and is documented."

8

Transhumanity: A Moral Vision of the Twenty-First Century

John Harris

In his book *Humanity: A Moral History of the Twentieth Century*, Jonathan Glover succeeds, as he puts it, in giving "ethics an empirical dimension," but he also reinforces his unparalleled success in making his own humanity central to his ethics. In an earlier book, Glover set out the ethical issues that face those who contemplate changing humanity in the descriptive sense. Glover's book *What Sort of People Should There Be?*, published, appropriately perhaps, in 1984, was one of the first, the first really excellent and serious, philosophical book in a field which now has been dubbed by some "transhumanism."

A deep question, implicit in *Humanity* and explicit in *What Sort of People Should There Be?*, is the question of what role "humanity," species membership, being a human being, in short the descriptive sense of being human, plays in our evaluative use of that term. When we identify humanity not simply with species membership, being a human being, but with being a moral being we may be claiming one of two very different things. The first is that we humans, the species *Homo sapiens sapiens*, is characterized by, among other qualities, moral agency and other important features like the capacities for sympathy, empathy and creativity. The second implies more: that the possession of these qualities is essentially human, possessed by us only because we are the species that we are. This second sense implies that our humanity in the moral sense is not simply species typical, but rather it requires being human in the biological or genetic sense. There is not only a danger, there is a long established and deeply ingrained habit, of identifying properties or qualities that are contingently possessed by human beings as necessarily possessed by our kind and, moreover, necessarily not possessed by other kinds.

When we ask questions like "what is it to be human?," or talk about a person's "humanity" or talk of the "human spirit" or "human values," we not only emphasize the properties that typically distinguish our species from species not capable of having values, we indulge in a sort form of chauvinism, celebrating our own kind as we do in a different sense when we talk of "British-ness," "European Culture," or "Western Civilization."

This human chauvinism is often given a pseudoscientific bent. We talk of species barriers as if, in so far as such things exist, they are laws of nature set up not simply to protect our supposed species purity, but to preserve those qualities we possess that may not only be currently particularly strongly represented in, or typical of, our species but may also be unique to this planet.

8.1 HUMANIMALS

The possibility of there existing part-human–part-animal creatures seems always to have fascinated human beings. Centaurs and mermaids are just two familiar examples. In our own times the possibility of creating such creatures has for the first time become a reality and the prospect fascinates and excites as well as causes horror and loathing. However, most importantly it offers immense promise for the treatment of disease and for the amelioration of the human condition.

While the prospect of mixing species exercises both popular and scientific imagination in different ways, the ethics and the permissibility of creating hybrids, chimeras, and other forms of novel combinations of cells, with some human and some animal elements, has become one of the most urgent problems facing contemporary science. This is because it has become obvious that not only can we learn much from the creation of such potentially ambiguous entities but the therapeutic prospects, the chance to use what we learn to treat and prevent disease, and to understand much more about ourselves and about animals, are also generally believed to be enormous.

In tribute to Jonathan Glover's interest both in the nature of humanity and in our own moral limitations, here I wish to explore the question of whether humanity as a species is surrounded by a moral, biological or social barrier, which there are or might be, powerful reasons not to cross. Is there a reason to suppose that a moral history of the twentieth century is necessarily, rather than contingently, a history of our species? In short, I shall explore the question of whether or not there exists a so-called species barrier, either in the sense of a line drawn by a moralist between his own kind and someone else's, or as a biological limit or indeed as a social or political divide.

In this discussion I use the term "humanimal" to cover any biological entities, whether individual creatures or cells, which have any mixture of animal and human elements, from cells to solid organs, from blood to tissue, wherever those elements are, and in whatsoever proportions they are combined.

As of now there is very little work in the field of the ethics of new technologies as they bear upon the creation of what we are calling "humanimals." Although humanimals have been created for many years, and hybrids have probably always existed naturally, the ethics of their creation and use may still be considered to be in its infancy. It is rare that a new technology raises important questions in so many areas of contemporary ethics; rarer still that such a technology has the potential to make a profound impact on the course of biomedical research and therapy, making it vital to consider carefully the possible regulatory approaches, their practical outcomes and the consequent impacts on humanity as it now is, including the possibilities of benefit, risk, and change.

8.2 THE MORAL REASONS TO BE TRANSGRESSIVE

I have suggested that there are important reasons to be transgressive of species barriers at least so far as humans and animals are concerned. Let's first remind ourselves of why this is so.

A recent report by the United Kingdom Academy of Medical Sciences [1] identifies many aspects of basic science that have been and continue to be studied in ways which involve the "mixing" of animal- and human-derived cells, in particular "understanding the nature and potential of stem cells" one of the most promising avenues of therapeutic and basic research that involves the study of the behaviour of these cells in animal models, including of course human as well as animal-derived stem cells. As the report notes: "there are thousands of examples of transgenic animals, mostly mice, containing human DNA, mainly used as models of human gene function and human disease."[2] The report notes that approaches "involving 'secondary' chimeras, that is the transfer of human cells into animals at a later stage of development, are already in widespread use in studies of human and mouse pluripotent and tissue-specific stem cells." It is also common practice to "investigate the potential of human neural stem cells to integrate appropriately into mouse or rat brain as a test of their potential safety and usefulness."[3] Such interspecies humanimal research is widespread and is required not only for basic science but to develop and prove applications designed to treat serious human disease. As with all research, long-term and established benefits are necessarily in the future. The ethical question is whether the sanctity of so-called species barriers, or other objections to interspecies constructs affords good or even plausible reasons to abandon such research and forgo or postpone whatever benefits it might yield. To answer this question the examination of the basis of objections to interspecies cells and creatures is both necessary and indeed urgent and important. It is not an exaggeration to suggest that the moral history of the rest of this and the next century may depend significantly on the answer.

8.3 THE MERMAID MYTH

It is important to distinguish between the creation of a human embryo incorporating animal material that will not be allowed to develop further, and the possibility of bringing such an embryo to term so that it will become a living independent creature. In the case of the embryo what will be created will simply be cells that will be maintained solely in vitro, and will never be permitted to become human–animal hybrid or chimeric creatures. If, on the other hand, we are talking about the creation of fully formed mature hybrid creatures, then such a situation is clearly more dramatic and may involve different moral issues.[4] However, here also we may be letting our expectations of what humanimal creatures would look like, and hence might be like, be conditioned by mythology, by what we might call the "mermaid myth," which involves the belief that if you mix the genes of a man and a fish you will necessarily make a creature with the recognizable features of both the progenitor creatures—you will make a mermaid, a creature which is half-fish and half-human.

8.4 CONTEXT IS KING

From diet to vaccines,[5] and from drugs to xenotransplantation in its various forms, as Guiseppe Testa has noted: "humans and animals have always been exchanging bits of their biological matter, intentionally or by chance, naturally or through artificial aids of various sorts."[6] It is worth noting that the majority of these encounters do not elicit particular fear or opposition. Diet is a good example, except for vegetarians for whom objections are usually rooted in moral issues concerning animal welfare rather than species mixing, there does not seem to be any preoccupation with the entry of animal genes, cells, tissue, muscle, and other bodily products into our daily metabolism. However, we know, and we learn more almost on a daily basis, that diet influences our body at both genetic and epigenetic levels. "The effect of certain classes of nutrients on the methylation level of our DNA (one of the most meaningful types of epigenetic modification) is just the best defined example of the enduring effect of diet on our genetic networks, an effect that might even be passed on to future generations."[7] In fact, if one were consistent in maximizing the purity of human matter, the only dietary choice would be cannibalism.

Vaccines and the various kinds of xenotransplantation are other, more visible, instances of animal–human mixing. Although whole organ xenotransplantations are still in very early experimental phases, porcine neural stem cells have been transplanted into a few patients, and millions of patients worldwide live with heart valves harvested from pigs or cows. In such cases, objections have tended to concentrate on specific dangers (e.g., the risk of transmitting animal viruses to the human population) rather than on a more general condemnation of human–animal mixing.

A typology of different modalities of human–animal mixing emerges:

1. The daily crossing of species boundaries through diet, largely unnoticed and completely normalized, in our culture.
2. The widespread use of animal products of various kinds as medical remedies, usually well accepted though with specific safety concerns, as in the various kinds of xenotransplantation.
3. The mixing of human and animal genes as proposed, albeit at a very limited level, in research.
4. Finally, there is the possibility of full-fledged hybrid or chimerical creatures mixing human and animal elements.

The difference is then at the level of the "fundamental units" that get mixed in the four modalities: animal cells broken down to simple metabolites through the diet; cells that become parts of host tissues through xenotransplantation; and genes that mix up within the host cell in research or in the creation of humanimal creatures.

However, is the sharp distinction between these different types of chimeras—and the equally sharp distinction in their moral evaluation—scientifically or ethically justified? The mixing of species is surely better understood as a continuum in which as Testa notes "the lines to be drawn between the acceptable and the non-acceptable do not align neatly with pre-existing biological categories (such as genes, cells, or metabolites) and the often inaccurate understandings that underlie them."[8]

We need to reframe the notion of animal or human genes starting from the very problem of defining what it means to say that something is an animal or a human gene. For, again as pointed out by Giuseppe Testa and others,[9] in the light of the evolutionary conservation of many signalling pathways, "human" or "animal" gene can refer only to the fact that these sequences are sourced from a human or an animal. However, from this it does not follow that an animal gene, once put into a human, behaves as an independent unit of "animal agency" or vice versa. In addition, a clear reminder of this point comes from some of the most spectacular results of molecular biology in the 1990s.

In the mid-1990s, scientists defined the genetic hierarchy underlying the development of the eye. The experiment was spectacular, and the very wording in which we still describe its outcome (genetic hierarchy) is a legacy of its seminal character. "A single gene, transplanted in tissues of the fly embryo such as the wings and the legs, was able to direct the formation of a whole eye, an ectopic eye. And yet, when the human homolog gene was transferred into a mouse to check for its ability to repair the *small eye* mutation, the result remained compelling: again, an eye was formed, testifying to the remarkable evolutionary conservation of genes and developmental pathways."[10] However, the eye formed from a human gene, when inserted into the mouse "forms" a mouse eye. Context, in other words, is just as essential as genes.[11] This shows that genes that had their origin in one species may when inserted in another species express themselves in ways adapted to their context. When we mix the genes of different species we do not necessarily mix the characteristics of those species.

Mythology has not prepared us well for the advent of humanimals. Adding fish genes to human embryos is unlikely to give us mermaids, creatures with a woman's upper body and the tail of a fish, adding human genes to horse embryos will probably not create centaurs.

When we turn from hybrid creatures to the cellular level the possibilities are multiplied and again there is a reasonably long (since the 1960s) and reasonably successful history of the safe creation of cell hybrids combining elements of different species. At the level of cells cultured in the laboratory, it is possible to create cells with genetic contributions from different species. Indeed, as we have noted, thousands of cell lines, involving such hybrid cells have been created worldwide.

Remarkably, plant hybrids are extremely common and extremely well accepted. There can be few formal gardens in Europe without an example of a Hybrid-T rose bush and many of our most cherished foods are hybrids. A pertinent question here is: Why is species purity in animals, and particularly in human animals prized, preserved, and defended in a way that it is not in plants? Of course even in animals arbitrary endpoints are constantly devised—thoroughbreds are simply thoroughly bred, not purely bred and so called crossbreeds are simply combinations of breeds that have not yet become a pure-bred type.

Serious science is at the moment concentrating on cells and embryos in which animal and human materials are combined, but in the future there may be therapeutic and indeed other sorts of moral reasons to consider the creation of hybrid or chimerical creatures that will develop to maturity.

One group of these moral reasons for creating humanimal creatures has been identified by Sarah Chan.[12] She notes that if we grant that the powers and capacities that are species-typical of humans and which confer advantages on us not possessed by animals it is probable (leaving aside the reaction of humans) that animals would be advantaged by the development of such powers and capacities. In so far as duties of beneficence and non-maleficence extend to animals we (other things being equal) might/ would have duties to confer such benefits on animals.

Duties of beneficence and nonmaleficence are normally regarded as "person-affecting," in Derek Parfit's sense. However, any duty to create animals with advantages rather than *different* animals without those advantages could not be person-affecting but would have to be impersonal, unless of course these changes had the effect of creating persons out of animals. Assuming the possible enhancements leave the animals short of personhood then, insofar as we have moral reasons to create bet-ter-off rather than less-well-off beings when all other things are equal, it seems that we would have a moral reason to create advantaged animals using human genetic materials.[13]

It is possible that many of the instinctive, as well as the reason-based, reactions against the creation of entities with animal and human ele-ments arise from the supposition that this will necessarily involve the creation of hybrid or chimerical creatures participating in the mermaid myth. The creation of creatures that will be born or grow to maturity, that may themselves suffer from the way they are, from how other crea-tures perceive them, that may pose unimagined or unimaginable dangers, that may be able themselves to mate with humans or with animals and indeed who/which may become our competitors on earth, pose intellec-tual, moral, and social challenges that do not arise from the creation of cells or even embryos that are not creatures that can "run about on the carpet" or "frighten the horses,"[14] but as we have noted the context into which cells from other species are introduced may mean that while the resulting creatures may indeed run around on the carpet they may fail to frighten the horses.

8.5 HUMANS ARE ALREADY HUMANIMALS

We know we are descended from apes, but we perhaps need to remind ourselves that this descent is seamless and means that our genetic constitu-tion contains a mixture of the genes of all the creatures, all the other spe-cies, that are part of the origin of our transient and transitional species.

In his essay "Gaps in the Mind,"[15] Richard Dawkins conducts a thought experiment. He asks us to imagine a contemporary woman, you or your sister, holding her mother's hand on the coast of Africa. She holds her mother's hand, her mother holds *her* mother's, and so on. Each daughter is as much like her mother as daughters usually are. Each person takes up about a meter, a yard, of space as they hold hands back into the past. In just 300 miles (a small distance into Africa), the imaginary human chain reaches our common ape ancestor. We then need to imagine our ape ancestor holding by her other hand her other daughter and she hers and so on back to the coast. Again each daughter looks as much like her mother as mothers and daughters usually do. By the time the chain reaches back to the coast two contemporary females are looking at one another each holding the hand of her mother stretching in seamless connection back to a common ape ancestor. The two—shall we call them women?—looking into each other's eyes are a modern human and a modern chimpanzee.

Dawkins's story is a salutary reminder of our ape ancestry and most importantly of the seamless transition between apes and humans. We need to bear in mind another lesson from evolution related to Dawkins's par-able and outlined in the same book. That lesson is that it is an accident of evolution that ape species with whom (which?) we humans might have been able, successfully, to breed have not survived. So while the chimpanzee who shares a common ancestor with humans probably cannot breed with human beings (at least without technological assistance), there were certainly once nonhuman apes that, had they survived, could have been procreational partners for us, using "normal" sexual reproduction. To this extent, our ability to define ourselves as a species distinct from the other great apes is, in one of the most commonly used definitions of a species, namely, that its members are able to breed successfully with one another but not with other types of animals, an accident of history, not an immutable law.

The lesson of Dawkins's example most significant for our present discussion is that *we humans* are humanimals. We are humans because we result from a process—evolution—that has allowed us to evolve from our ape ancestors not least by incorporating most of their genes and epigenetic features into our human constitution. In that we incorporate and retain these genes of animal origin, we are indeed humanimals. While there may be no obvious point in Dawkins's chain where the mother was an ape and the daughter a human, some mothers were apes whose daughters or grandchildren were more human than she was. For those who believe that humans are uniquely ensouled, some ape mother without a soul must have given birth to some daughter with a soul (unless souls also admit of degrees). For those who, like Francis Fukuyama, define "what it is to be human" in terms of a factor—factor X—that humans possess and nonhumans do not, there must have been a daughter with factor X that her mother or great grandmother lacked. But in all of these cases mothers and daughters must have been made of both human and animal elements (at least in the ways that those who object to the creation of humanimals find objectionable).

8.6 CONFUSION

One of the most frequently made appeals by objectors to crossing boundaries of all sorts is a triply problematic objection to "confusion"—three ways problematic in the sense that it suggests that confusion is to be avoided, that once confused it is impossible (or impossibly difficult) to become unconfused, and the paternalist suggestion that whereas those who appeal to the objection from confusion are not themselves confused and see clearly the way out of the fly bottle, ordinary people require to be protected from the necessity of thinking their way through the relevant issues.

8.7 CONFUSION IS TO BE AVOIDED

As a philosopher in the analytic tradition I am of course committed to clarity and as much precision as language permits. As a citizen in a liberal democracy

I am further committed to openness and even to transparency,[16] at least in the public dimensions of my life. However the confusion objected to is not of these kinds. This notion of confusion has many roots but in modern times a usual starting point is Mary Douglas's seminal work, *Purity and Danger*.[17] It is unnecessary to paraphrase all of Douglas's main conclusions here and I will not do so. She is, however, usually credited with pointing to and explaining rules and taboos, such as the abominations of *Leviticus*, which to some extent seem to be analyzable in terms of the desirability of clear identity and perhaps separateness of particular groups and with providing explanations of rules designed to protect from ambiguity of various sorts.

8.8 ROBERT AND BAYLIS

Jason Scott Robert and Françoise Baylis have argued vigorously against crossing species boundaries, mainly by appealing to the necessity of avoiding the kind of confusion that, according to Douglas's analysis, may undermine certain taboos.[18]

Before considering their arguments in detail we should note two questions that lie at the heart of this inquiry. The first is what appears to be an empirical question: What would subvert the species boundary between humans and animals? The second, more fundamental, question is whether this boundary is of any moral significance at all. For example, is this boundary in so far as it can coherently be maintained given our evolutionary past, any more important (or morally respectable) than the boundary that was alleged to obtain between human races, giving rise to racism and a particularly odious form of discrimination against individuals of mixed race? Without argument it is not obvious that the alleged human–animal species boundary is any more important, significant, or respectable than that between races. Many would argue that the subversion of this latter boundary has been liberating and wholly beneficial. In any event the value of the species boundary needs to be articulated and established before any fears about breaching it can be considered coherent.

Robert's and Baylis's main thesis is that we humans have "a strong desire to avoid introducing moral confusion, as regards the moral status of the novel being. In particular we explore the strong interest in avoiding any practice that would lead us to doubt the claim that humanness is a necessary (if not sufficient) condition for full moral standing."[19] I will refrain from saying that as humans with a vested interest in their status, "they would say that, wouldn't they."[20] They give some reasons of doubtful force for an interest in making humanness a necessary condition of full moral standing but no evidence nor indeed any arguments as to why we have a *moral* (rather than a selfish or prudential) interest in any such thing. It is worth examining further the arguments they do produce, not least because of course we share their vested interests in exclusive occupancy of the executive suite of the moral universe.

Robert and Baylis produce a number of suggestions as to why "human-ness is a necessary (if not sufficient) condition for full moral standing." Let's look at them all. The first two suggestions concern ambiguity.

"A plausible 'thin' explanation for the intuitive 'yuck' response is that the creation of interspecies creatures from human materials evokes the idea of bestiality—an act widely regarded as a moral abomination because of its degrading character."[21] Typically, as we shall see, no argument is offered in support of this view. However, wide the revulsion against bes-tiality on the grounds that it is a "moral abomination," thinking so does not make it so; we have to ask "why?" The reason we are invited to think of it as an abomination seems to be its alleged "degrading character," but whether it is degrading to the animals or to the humans who might be involved we are not told. It is difficult to see why having sex with animals is more degrading to either party than caging and butchering them for food. It would have been helpful to have been provided with a possible reason why bestiality is degrading other than the tendentious use of the terminology: "abomination" and "degradation." These are emotive terms but not helpfully descriptive terms. The lack of a powerful reason other than supposedly self-evident abomination, is further confirmed when we find the following illuminating gloss on the ideas of abomination and degradation. "[T]he revulsion is directed towards the shepherd who lusts after his flock and acts in a way that makes him seem (or actually be) less human." How sexual preferences affect species membership is not further elaborated. However in Robert's and Baylis's defence it can be said that they admit this is a "thin" explanation of the 'yuck' factor attached to interspeciesism.

The second argument is canvassed as being less "thin":

> A more robust explanation for the instinctive and intense revulsion at the creation of human-to-animal beings...can be drawn from Douglas's work on taboos. Douglas suggests that taboos stem from conceptual boundaries. Human beings attach considerable symbolic importance to classificatory systems and actively shun anomalous practices that threaten cherished con-ceptual boundaries. This explains the existence of well-entrenched taboos, in a number of domains.... Classic examples include the Western response to bi-sexuality or intersexuality.[22]

The alleged thickness of this explanation seems to derive from two sources. The first is the invocation of the distinguished work of Mary Douglas; the second is the addition of two extra adjectives namely "instinctive and intense" governing "revulsion." It must be these latter factors that do the thickening because Mary Douglas's wonderful explanations do not help the Robert and Baylis thesis. Douglas explains the existence of practices and the functions they perform in tribal societies. Douglas does not pro-vide justifications for the perseverance of such practices or the conceptual boundaries they establish or reinforce in the absence of the social and intellectual circumstances and beliefs that animate them. This can be seen from the fact that few intelligent people any longer feel (and have ceased to feel for good reason) "instinctive and intense revulsion" at the idea of bisexuality.[23]

Robert and Baylis sum up this part of their discussion in these terms: "All of this is to say that when faced with the prospect of not knowing whether a creature before us is human and therefore entitled to all the rights typically conferred on human beings, we are, as a people, baffled."[24] I accept that Robert and Baylis are baffled but I have more faith than they do in the capacity of people to think their way through dilemmas such as that posed by humanimals. True, we might need to think a bit and be reflective about the basis upon which we accord rights and respect interests but that is what moral philosophy and moral philosophers are for. In addition, if we, as ethicists, are doing our job in, among other things, clarifying the ethical issues, I doubt not but that citizens will be able to think their way through the issues.

In any case, bafflement is not a moral failing, although it may be indicative of a failure of moral reasoning. Instead, the prospect of humanimal or transhuman entities should lead us to consider the reasons for this bafflement and how our moral theory should incorporate these new beings and indeed the old beings from which they will have developed. It cannot be said that creating humanimals is morally wrong because they fall outside the scope of our (or at least, Robert's and Baylis's) moral theory. Rather we should say that the inability to cope with the prospect of new humanimals demonstrates an inadequacy in the theory itself, and perhaps use the perceived moral problems created by these creatures to grapple with and address this deficit.

Having surveyed these arguments with some approval Robert and Baylis set out their "beginnings of a plausible answer" to the question as to "why there should be any ethical debate over crossing species boundaries."

Here is the first of the remaining arguments they produce:

> All things considered, the engineering of creatures that are part human and part nonhuman animal is objectionable because the existence of such beings would introduce inexorable moral confusion in our existing relationships with nonhuman animals and in our future relationships with part-human hybrids and chimeras. The moral status of nonhuman animals, unlike that of human beings, invariably depends in part on features other than species membership...In the case of human beings, moral status is categorical insofar as humanness is generally considered a necessary condition for moral standing.[25]

Why, however, should the existence of humanimals introduce confusion if not for the fact that we possess an imperfect understanding of the basis of our moral obligations to other beings? It is simply too easy to say of a being that he is entitled to moral status because he is "human": that tells us nothing about the attributes of "humans" in respect of which moral status should obtain. It is precisely when the term "human" or the idea of "human-ness" is thrown into question that the weakness in this logic becomes evident. The so-called inexorable confusion that Roberts and Baylis perceive to arise from the creation of humanimals actually reveals an inexorable lacuna in the moral theory they attempt to apply.

Further, far from making the creation of humanimals morally unacceptable, the problems this might be seen to cause, and the consequent need for a refinement of our understanding of moral status, would seem to make it almost imperative that we pursue these lines of research and the ethical reflection to which they give rise. For if improving our understanding of our moral relationships with other creatures is beneficial, then perhaps we have a moral duty to create these circumstances of confusion in order to ultimately produce greater clarity in a different direction. The importance of an adequate evidence base is often underestimated in philosophy, particularly when extravagant empirical claims are made on the basis of...well nothing at all! The alleged harms and dangers of confusion and ambiguity are of course just empirical claims. If scientists made such claims without any experimental or observational data to back them up, they would not find themselves members of national academies let alone win Nobel prizes. Let us then rather treat Robert's and Baylis's fears as pleas for empirical research of an appropriate sort that could create the data that alone could test their hypotheses.[26]

Robert and Baylis then simply make species membership "categorical," stipulative of moral status. They conclude that "it follows that hybrids and chimeras made from human materials are threatening in so far as there is no clear way of understanding (or even imagining) our moral obligations to these beings."[27] And as a final flourish, they state the creation of humanimals "is sufficiently threatening to the social order that for many this is sufficient reason to prohibit any crossing of species boundaries involving human beings."[28]

We have seen that such creation may be no more threatening that is knowledge of our evolutionary heredity, which of course many still regard as threatening but most of us have managed to come to terms with.

While it is true that many, perhaps most, people simply assume that it is human beings as a natural kind that have full moral status it is false that this is necessarily categorical or required. I will not argue the point at length here but many moral theories including perhaps the two leading contemporary approaches, Kantian ethics and personhood theory, accord full moral status in terms of a combination of rationality and autonomy.[29] We would use the same methods of determining whether humanimals are persons or indeed are rational in the Kantian sense, as we do with members of the human species.[30]

Since it is in my view the best approach to moral status, I will concentrate for a moment on personhood approaches to the problem of moral status. We are familiar with the idea that there are nonhuman persons, and humans who are not, or may not be, persons or full persons. Nonhuman persons may include gods, ghosts, extraterrestrials, angels, and devils. They may also include animals, perhaps educated primates, like the apes Washoe and Sarah,[31] and might include some humanimals other than human beings depending on their powers and capacities. Human non-persons or humans who are not full-fledged persons, and who therefore lack legal personality, include zygotes, embryos, anencephalic infants, and human individuals who are "brain-dead"; they may also include individuals in a permanent vegetative state (PVS). The English courts have ruled repeatedly that individuals in PVS may have their lives ended deliberately when other humans may not. In the words of Lord Keith of Kinkel in the famous PVS case "It is, however, perhaps permissible to say that to an individual with no cognitive capacity whatever, and no prospect of ever recovering any such capacity in this world, it must be a matter of complete indifference whether he lives or dies." Here Lord Keith seems to appeal to something like the conception of personhood with which we are here concerned. For what he identifies as mattering from a moral, and indeed a legal, perspective is not life, nor yet human life, but a certain cognitive capacity.[32]

In addition, it is not only philosophers who are able to make the relevant determinations. Lawyers and even judges have proved capable of deciding whether human individuals have the moral status that accords them rights and protectable interests of various sorts. To give one further example, in most jurisdictions the developing human individual (possessing full species membership) does not achieve full moral status or "legal personality" until it is born alive.[33]

8.9 UNNATURAL PREJUDICE AND NATURAL KINDS

One final question needs to be addressed: Will our attitudes to humanimals weaken or strengthen our moral attitudes to other humans and the moral rights and obligations we usually feel or recognize towards other humans?

In advance of empirical evidence this is not a question that is currently susceptible of anything but an anecdotal or impressionistic response. However, if we think of other cases where individuals formerly regarded as subhuman or less than fully human have belatedly been included in the human community as full-fledged members, the evidence seems to be that our moral respect for the new inclusive class of humans has not been significantly compromised. Women suffered from such prejudice well into the last century and many would argue they still do.[34]

Humanimals who there is reason to suppose have attained relevant capacities are our equals, fellow persons if not fellow humans and their inclusion within the moral and political community is not only right and proper but also in every respect consistent with, indeed required by, our moral attitudes to other persons. Those humanimals who might attain the relevant capacities should, like present-day children, be regarded as full

members of the moral community if with a different political status justified only by a plausible need for paternalistic control and protection.

The Report on interspecies embryos cited above put the point in this way:

> On a more fundamental level, we judge it unlikely that "human dignity,"
> a phrase used to emphasise the special moral status and importance of
> human beings, derives simply from species membership. If the concept of
> "human dignity" has content, it is because there are factors of form, function
> or behaviour that confer such dignity or command respect. Either hybrid
> creatures would also possess these factors or they would not. If they do pos-
> sess these factors, they would also have a specific type of dignity analogous
> or identical to human dignity that other creatures lack; if not, they would
> not. Either way, the distinction between creatures that possess dignity and
> those that do not remains as it is now. The hypothetical possibility of allow-
> ing human embryos incorporating animal material to come to term might
> be thought to threaten dignity in two distinct ways: either the dignity of the
> hybrid creatures would suffer because they are not fully human, or human
> dignity would suffer because of the creation of creatures that are close to,
> but not quite, human. Regarding the first possibility, we again emphasise
> that dignity arises from the qualities possessed by a creature, rather than
> species membership per se. This focus on the possession of qualities also
> applies to the second possibility. Our dignity does not depend on our
> distance from all other creatures, but on the intrinsic nature of our
> endowments.[35]

It seems appropriate to end with a homage to the seminal work of Jonathan Glover.

> If instead of there being a clear gap between monkeys and ourselves, genetic
> mixing resulted in many individuals varying imperceptibly along the con-
> tinuum between the two species, this might undermine our present belief
> in the moral importance of the distinction. If it did, the effects might go
> either way. There might be a beneficial reform in our attitudes towards
> members of other species. Alternatively, there might be a weakening in the
> prohibitions that now protect weaker or less intelligent human beings from
> the treatment animals are subjected to. If the second possibility is a real
> danger, there is a strong case for resisting the blurring of this boundary.[36]

I would wish only to add that this strong case must be balanced against
two countervailing gains. The first is that if these prohibitions require the
acceptance of false assumptions about the relevance of species membership to moral significance, then this should be a spur to reconsider the
moral basis of respect for other creatures. The second is that the expected
benefits of the interventions that might have the effect of blurring this
boundary must also count. Currently these benefits can predominantly
be obtained by research on humanimal embryos, so that there is little
need to create humanimal creatures. The creation of humanimal creatures that would not simply contain an admixture of cells from other
species related to the mixture with which we have been endowed by

Darwinian evolution, but also would exhibit physical and mental attributes that might lead to a "a weakening in the prohibitions that now protect weaker or less intelligent human beings from the treatment animals are subjected to" awaits reliable justification in terms of the moral good or public interest that might thereby be served. When and if these justifications become clear the dangers of rival courses of action will require a more careful balance. Meanwhile we have strong intellectual reasons to found moral prohibitions on morally relevant considerations and we have strong moral reasons to base our morality on considerations that can be rationally justified. The alternative is to be bereft of a way of distinguishing principle from prejudice.

Jonathan Glover has created a body of work of a distinction and a personal example of a decency that few can or will rival. He has set an example of moral engagement, originality, and intellectual courage, which has influenced not only all of us privileged to know him but also all who have reflected on humanity and its moral history in our times.

Notes

I am grateful to the editors of this volume for many helpful comments and suggestions.

1. *Inter-species Embryos: A Report by The Academy of Medical Sciences*, June 2007. ISBN No; 1–903401–15–1.

2. Ibid., pp. 3 and 33.

3. Ibid., p. 34. See O. Lindvall and Z. Kokaia (2006) Stem cells for the treatment of neurological disorders. *Nature* 441: 1094–96.

4. I use here words also used in "Inter Species Embryos," A Report by *The Academy of Medical Sciences*. June 2007 ISBN No: 1–903401–15–1. of which I was a coauthor.

5. In this section I have, with his permission, borrowed extensively from the work of my friend and colleague Giuseppe Testa. We are working together on the ethics of humanimals but this section on context belongs to Giuseppe.

6. Insoo Hyun et al. (2007) Ethical standards for human-to-animal chimera experiments in stem cell research. *Cell Stem Cell* 1: 159–63, p. 159.

7. Ibid.

8. Ibid.

9. Ibid., p. 160.

10. Ibid.

11. G. Halder et al. (1995) Induction of ectopic eyes by targeted expression of the eyeless gene in drosophila. *Science* 267: 1788–92. G. Oliver and P. Gruss (1997) Current views of eye development. *Trends in Neuroscience* 20(9): 415–21. R. Quiring et al. (1994) Homology of the eyeless gene of Drosophila to the small eye gene in mice and Aniridia in humans" *Science* 265: 785–89.

12. Sarah Chan, personal communication, 2007.

13. I am grateful to Jeff McMahan for his suggestions here. For the sense in which I am using the term personhood see John Harris, *The Value of Life*, Routledge and Kegan Paul 1985. For Parfit's ideas on person affecting morality see Derek Parfit (1984) *Reasons and Persons* Clarendon Press, Oxford.

14. The focus on, and hence fear of, the creation of creatures may be a by-product of conceptualizing regulation of these practices as part of the regulation of IVF and other assisted reproductive technologies which are emblematically focused on the creation of new beings.

15. In Richard Dawkins (2004) *The Devil's Chaplain* (London: Phoenix): 23–31. I use the summary of Dawkins that appears in my *Enhancing Evolution*, Princeton University Press, Princeton, NJ and Oxford 2007.

16. Although not transparency in the sense in which Tom Wolfe famously described thin fashionable women as "X-Rays" in his *The Bonfire of the Vanities*, Farrar, Strauss and Giroux, 1987.

17. Mary Douglas, *Purity and Danger*, Routledge & Kegan Paul, London 1966.

18. Jason Scott Robert and Françoise Baylis (2003) Crossing Species Boundaries. *American Journal of Bioethics* 3(3): 1–13.

19. Ibid., p. 2.

20. Mandy Rice Davies notoriously used this phrase, which has passed into common usage. In this case Wikipedia gives an accurate account of the circumstances: "While giving evidence at the trial of Stephen Ward, Rice-Davies made the quip for which she is most remembered and which is frequently used by politicians in Britain. When the prosecuting counsel pointed out that Lord Astor denied having an affair or having even met her, she replied, "Well, he would, wouldn't he?." http://en.wikipedia.org/wiki/Mandy_Rice-Davies.

21. Jason Scott Robert and Françoise Baylis (2003) Crossing Species Boundaries. *American Journal of Bioethics* 3(3): 1–13, 7.

22. Ibid.

23. Lest I also be accused of asserting a conclusion without justifying it, I refer the reader to the good reasons I provide in my discussion of sexual morality in John Harris (1980) *The Value of Life*. Routledge, London, chapter 9.

24. Jason Scott Robert and Françoise Baylis (2003) Crossing Species Boundaries. *American Journal of Bioethics* 3(3): 1–13, 7.

25. Jason Scott Robert and Françoise Baylis (2003) Crossing Species Boundaries. *American Journal of Bioethics* 3(3): 1–13, 9.

26. Put another way, if the social order is morally blind, then threatening it might well be a good thing! Here again I am very much indebted to Sarah Chan.

27. Jason Scott Robert and Françoise Baylis (2003) Crossing Species Boundaries. *American Journal of Bioethics* 3(3): 1–13, 9.

28. Ibid.

29. See Mary Anne Warren (1997) *Moral Status*, Clarendon Press, Oxford.

30. See for example John Harris (1985) *The Value of Life*, Routledge, London; Mary Ann Warren (1997) *Moral Status* Clarendon Press, Oxford; Michael Tooley (1998) Personhood, in Helga Kuhse and Peter Singer (eds.) *A Companion to Bioethics*, Blackwell Publishers, Oxford, pp. 117–27.

31. R. A. Gardner and B. T. Gardner (1969) Teaching sign language to a chimpanzee. *Science*, 165(894), 664–72; Eugene Linden (1975) *Apes, Men and Language*, Penguin, Harmondsworth, UK.

32. See for example *Airedale NHS Trust v Bland* [1993] 1 All ER 821, 894 HL.

33. In: The European Court of Human Rights [*Case of VO v. France (Application no. 53924/00)* Strasbourg July 8, 2004]. And most recently in [*Evans v. The United Kingdom (Application no. 6339/05)* Judgment, Strasbourg, March 7, 2006].

34. Women who were householders and over the age of 30 were given the right to vote in the United Kingdom in 1918; however women between 21 and 30 did not get the right until 1928.

35. "Inter Species Embryos," A Report by *The Academy of Medical Sciences*. June 2007 ISBN No: 1–903401–15–1. p. 29. The present author declares his interest as one of the authors of this report. I worked on the passage quoted from our report with my friend the Cambridge philosopher Peter Lipton, also a member of the Academy's working group. Peter died tragically on the November 25, 2007 while I was writing this chapter. I miss him. He exhibited a humanity that would transcend any species barriers.

36. Jonathan Glover (1984) *What Sort of People Should There Be?* Penguin, Harmondsworth, UK, p. 41.

V

SOME SILENCES IN *HUMANITY*

9

The Foundations of Humanity

Roger Crisp

Jonathan Glover's important book *Humanity: A Moral History of the Twentieth Century* is primarily what its title implies—a history.[1] But the history rests on a philosophical analysis of our ethical circumstances, and is put to use in generating certain ethical conclusions. In this chapter I intend to tease out and examine some strands in Glover's philosophy. Although I am inclined to disagree with some of the main elements in his skeptical diagnosis, I am in some ways more pessimistic than him about how valuable a resource philosophical ethics can be.

Glover begins the book with the claim that the beginning of the twentieth century was marked by a widespread acceptance of 'the moral law', and the end by skepticism brought on by the decline of religion (1; see 222, 231, 405). The phrase 'the moral law' is of course Kantian, and Glover sometimes understands it as making 'absolute' commands to act in certain ways, regardless of the consequences (e.g., 221). But more often it is clear that he is speaking of the notion of any morality with 'external' authority. So, for example, he suggests that it is not worth seeking an 'external validation' of morality (41). I shall take it that a morality with external authority would be one which asserts that reasons for action are not dependent on the beliefs and desires of the agents within its scope—that is, roughly, what Bernard Williams calls 'external' reasons.[2] So, to adopt an example of Williams's, a man who is cruel to his spouse, and who has no desire (and would have no desire after deliberation and reflection) to stop, might be said on an external reasons account to have a reason to stop. That reason might be a brute fact, or it might have some basis in natural law, or other system. According to the view that all reasons for action are internal, this person has no reason to stop (though that does not mean we cannot continue to classify him as cruel, of course).

It would take some hard and detailed historical and sociological research, underpinned by a sound philosophical analysis, to test Glover's claim about the decline over the last century of belief in the moral law. Even in the United Kingdom some statistics on religious belief might be taken to suggest that the majority are still believers: only 15 percent of those polled in the 2001 UK Census, for example, said they had no religion.[3] And in the world at large there seems on the face of it to be a rise in religious fundamentalism. These views might well be seen as providing a platform for an external reasons account. But I am as far from being a sociologist as I am from being a historian; so I shall not enter into any further speculation.

Glover himself, however, seems to be skeptical about any external support for morality, suggesting that '[t]he prospects of reviving belief in a moral law are dim' (41). So there is room for philosophical debate here. There are two problems with his attempt to link ethical skepticism with atheism (to which I assume he is sympathetic), and with that skepticism itself. First, religion cannot ground ethics anyway, so theism would not help. Second, if there is no prospect for grounding ethics non-religiously, it is in trouble.

That theism cannot ground ethics was of course suggested long ago in Plato's *Euthyphro* dilemma.[4] Imagine that you are trying to persuade some tyrant to stop torturing his subjects for his own gratification, and appeal to the alleged fact that God forbids it. The tyrant may ask where the 'authority' of your claim resides. If (the first horn) you are claiming that torture is wrong just because God says so, the question remains why the tyrant should obey God, especially a god who is effectively a moral tyrant by requiring obedience to what amount merely to his whims. But if (the second horn) you are suggesting that God is merely in an especially good position to know what is right and what is wrong, then the foundations of ethics will be independent of his commands. So it is not clear why there should be any direct route from atheism to moral skepticism, unless we think that God was really our only hope of obtaining any ethical understanding. And that would be an odd position for someone attracted by the second horn of the *Euthyphro* dilemma, since the second horn seems to depend on our having some independent grasp of what morality requires. Without that independent grasp, why are we entitled to think that God has any special claim to ethical knowledge?

Glover's view is that, without an external grounding, we are faced with an ethical void to be filled by self-creation (17, 22, 41). That leaves few philosophical resources to answer the tyrant, though of course it need not prevent our seeking to encourage projects of self-creation that involve respect and sympathy for others (23–4). All we can do is, first, change the sociological and psychological conditions of humanity so that tyranny becomes much less likely, and then, if some tyrant does emerge, describe such conceptions of the self and hope that the tyrant will be inspired by them. But, surely, what many of us will want to say is not that such conceptions of the self are an *option* for the tyrant, but that he *should* act in the light of such a conception? In other words, the tyrant has external reasons to stop torturing, grounded in the suffering of his victims and independent of his own project of self-creation. And this point applies even if we manage (perhaps through genetic manipulation) to make tyranny impossible for human beings, since we can ask what we *would* want to say in a counterfactual situation in which a tyrant exists.

What might Glover have against the idea of external reasons, given that their source need not be, and indeed cannot even be plausibly be said to be, divine? One worry I suspect he might have is that the postulation of external reasons has implausible and extravagant metaphysical and epistemological implications.[5] It suggests that the world 'contains' reasons, and that we have some mysterious capacity to detect them.

At this point, we need to note two interpretations of Glover's position on moral reasons. On the strong interpretation, the notion of any kind of reason is so metaphysically and epistemologically outlandish that we should assume that there are none.[6] This would imply that, though of course we *can* fill the ethical void with self-creation, there is no reason to do so, and no reason to create any particular kind of self. It would imply also that there can be no epistemic reasons, so that Glover could not in good faith claim that we have, or indeed he has, any reason to believe his conclusions, or indeed anything at all. The implications of this kind of nihilism do not show it to be false, but it has costs that I suspect Glover would be unwilling to pay. On the weak interpretation of his position, there may be some reasons—such as to believe that this is a pen in my hand, or to engage in self-creation—but there are no external or moral reasons to act independently of self-creation, broadly construed along the lines of Bernard Williams's 'subjective motivational set' or S. If that is Glover's position, then any unqualified metaphysical or epistemological objection to reasons would seem to be out of place.

It might be thought that internalism about reasons provides a comfortable middle ground between possible metaphysical or epistemological extravagance on the one hand, and nihilism on the other. We do indeed have reasons for action, but those reasons are grounded in our desires, projects, and commitments. Desires, however, cannot ground reasons for action.[7] Desire is a mere psychological state, with no value in itself or in its fulfillment. If I desire something worth having, then in ordinary cases I shall desire that thing *as* worth having, that is, as being such that I have a reason to pursue it. My desire itself rests on the assumption that I have reasons to pursue its object independently of desire. This is to say not that we cannot have reasons to fulfill our desires, or to engage in projects of self-creation; merely that those reasons cannot be grounded in the mere fact of our having those desires or projects.

There is, then, a danger that Glover's antipathy to the notion of the moral law, alongside his general metaphysical and epistemological concerns, may lead him towards the strong interpretation. So at this point it is worth asking just what the philosophical cost of accepting external reasons or a moral law amounts to. Let us begin with the assumption that if a tyrant has an external reason to stop torturing people, then there is a moral law. Accepting this need not involve one in any kind of heavyweight platonist (with a lower-case 'p') metaphysics, according to which there is some special 'realm' of value or peculiar kind of property. It is certainly true that the world does not 'contain' reasons in the same way that it contains objects such as tables and chairs. But the claim (call it C) that the world—indeed any world—is such that no one should inflict severe suffering on others for the sake of their own trivial pleasure need not be taken to imply that reasons are objects. In just the same way, someone who claims that $7 + 5 = 12$ is not thereby committed to any heavyweight platonist account of numbers as a special kind of abstract entity.

That deals with metaphysics—or rather shows how to avoid dealing with it. But what about epistemology?[8] How can we be justified in our belief that C? How can we know it, and with which of our faculties? Two possible answers have often suggested themselves (and there are of course others): through our senses, or through reason. Glover himself suggests that ethics should be conceived of in a more empiricist way (6, 43), and it may be that he would be tempted by the Millian position that ethical knowledge is itself empirical.[9] But this position is unlikely to succeed unless it enriches the notion of experience to the point that the distinction between empiricism and rationalism in ethics largely disappears. If we take C, for example, there is no occasion on which C can plausibly be said to be part of the content of any experience of mine, even an experience in which I come across a tyrant torturing someone for his own gratification. Nor would it be plausible to claim that in such a case my experience tells me that this particular torturing is wrong, so that I might conclude something like C on the basis of induction after experiencing similar cases. Vision just does not work like that.[10]

That leaves reason, and here it is useful to return to the analogy with mathematics. Moral judgments seem to have several features in common with mathematical ones. Both are grasped by reason, and may plausibly be said to be a priori, in the sense that their justification is independent of experience and can rest purely on grasp of the concepts involved. (This is not to say that the having of, or the capacity for, certain experiences is not required in order to make moral judgments.) Both may plausibly be said to be necessary, in the following sense: they are true in all possible worlds. Just as in all possible worlds $7 + 5 = 12$, so in all possible worlds C is true.

This analogy suggests that the moral law is as secure, metaphysically and epistemologically, as certain basic mathematical statements. There is, however, a difficult question to be answered about our knowledge of mathematics, which would arise also for ethics understood in terms of the analogy. What are the objects of mathematical knowledge? The most immediate and natural view is platonism: they are abstract, non-physical, beyond space and time, independent of our minds. But this view runs into what has come to be known as 'Benacerraf's problem':[11] if mathematical objects are independent in this way, what plausible causal account can be given of *how* we gain epistemic access to them? In particular, as Hartry Field puts the challenge, the difficulty is to account for the *reliability* of our mathematical knowledge, given that we would want to avoid saying that our getting things right in mathematics, when we do, is a mere coincidence.[12]

One immediate point to make here is that, though it may be unclear exactly how we grasp mathematical or moral truths, that in itself does not give us a reason to doubt that there are such truths and that we can grasp them.[13] There is no consensus on the best explanation of consciousness or perception, but we do not doubt that we are conscious or that we can see. Further, as I have already suggested, for my present purposes there is no need to get heavily into metaphysics. The alleged objects of mathematical and ethical knowledge are propositions—'7 + 5 = 12', and C—and though the nature of propositions is an interesting philosophical question it is one extraneous to our present discussion. And in fact a plausible causal story can be told about how human beings have acquired the capacity to grasp a priori propositions, and why that capacity can function reliably. The story is evolutionary. Consider an animal with very limited cognition faced with a dangerous object such as a fire. Having burned itself, it may unthinkingly avoid fires in future. But faced with a new kind of danger, such as a tiger, it cannot act in a way which might be explained by any kind of grasp of the a priori principle that any being with a capacity for well-being has a reason to avoid threats to that well-being. A similar story could be told about our capacity for grasping mathematical truths. An animal stalked by three tigers who can grasp the fact that only two have run away is more likely to survive than an innumerate creature. Evolution, then, can explain our rational capacity to grasp a priori truths, and of course once a being has that capacity it can be employed in the acquisition of any such truths, even those whose grasp could play no plausible part in biological evolution. I am of course claiming not that this evolutionary account is correct, merely that such accounts are available and not implausible.

So it might seem that we are now in a position to confront the tyrant with an ethical principle grounded as securely as basic mathematics. Unfortunately, however, there remains a further, and this time insurmountable, problem, since there is one significant aspect of basic mathematical statements which does not carry across to much of ethics: consensus.

Consider C again. How might I assess it for its plausibility? Henry Sidgwick suggests four conditions that I might reasonably expect C to meet if it is to be established 'in the highest degree of certainty attainable'.[14] The terms of the proposition must be clear and precise, and acceptance of it must be grounded in careful reflection. Further, I must ensure that C does not conflict with any other proposition I am inclined to accept. These three conditions might often be met. The fourth, which one might call the *consensus condition*, moves from intrapersonal to interpersonal consistency, and is worth quoting:

> Since it is implied in the very notion of Truth that it is essentially the same for all minds, the denial by another of a proposition that I have affirmed has a tendency to impair my confidence in its validity... And it will easily be

seen that the absence of…disagreement must remain an indispensable negative condition of the certainty of our beliefs. For if I find any of my judgments…in direct conflict with a judgment of some other mind, there must
be error somewhere: and if I have no more reason to suspect error in the
other mind than in my own, reflective comparison between the two judgments necessarily reduces me temporarily to a state of neutrality. And
though the total result in my mind is not exactly suspense of judgment, but
an alternation and conflict between positive affirmation by one act of
thought and the neutrality that is the result of another, it is obviously something very different from scientific certitude.[15]

The problem with ethical statements, made within normative philosophical ethics itself, is that they are highly contested. My confidence need
not be dented merely by another's disagreeing with me. The tyrant, for
example, may be very poor at articulating his view, and clearly unable to
reflect upon it or to test it for consistency against his other beliefs. So my
suspicion of an error may itself be so well grounded that his view holds
almost no evidential weight. But philosophical ethics, since its earliest
days, has included among some of its most distinguished practitioners
normative egoists, who believe that each agent has strongest reason maxi-
mally to promote his or her own interests, regardless of any cost to others.
The interests of others, in themselves, count for nothing.[16]

As Glover points out (ch. 3), a plausible case can be made for the
claim that respecting certain moral constraints is often in a person's best
interests overall. But—as Plato's Thrasymachus recognizes[17]—that is why
the tyrant, and many of those who inflicted such serious harms on others
in the twentieth-century horrors described by Glover, pose such a serious
ethical problem. The self-interest argument, in its most common form,
relies on the notion that wrongdoing will be punished; but this point
will not touch a tyrant who is himself in charge of the judicial system.
An alternative line of argument, one developed especially in the ethics
of Socrates and others, is to claim that being moral is itself an important, perhaps an overridingly important, component of self-interest.[18] It
is hard to accept this view when one reflects upon the horrible suffering
often inflicted on the virtuous by tyrants and others. Further, like any view
about the components of well-being, it is itself highly contested, and so
is in the same insecure epistemic position as the original moral claim it is
being used to support.

What I must do, then, is suspend judgment on C. C will of course still
appear to me to be true, and what attitude one should take to such appearances I shall discuss shortly. But first note another depressing aspect of the
tyrant example. It might seem that the best case the tyrant can make in
defense of the rationality of what he is doing will depend on normative
egoism. Normative egoism is as contested as any other position in ethics,
so his defense appears to be no stronger than our attack on him. But in
fact the tyrant does not need full-blown egoism to defend his position,
but only something like the following principle:

The self-interest principle (SI): Any agent at time *t* who has (a) a life that can go better or worse for her and (b) a range of options available to her at *t* which will affect whether that life does go better or worse for her has a reason to act at *t* in any way that makes her life go better, the strength of such a reason varying directly in proportion to the degree of promotion of her well-being.

In other words, the tyrant requires only the claim that his own interest gives him a *pro tanto* reason to torture others, not the claim that his own interest provides him with overriding reasons or even his only reasons. SI seems well placed to command significantly greater convergence than C or other other-regarding ethical principles, and to that extent it is on much securer epistemic ground.[19]

So I have ended up being as doubtful as Glover about the status of ethics, though for different reasons. What are the implications of this for philosophical ethics? I believe there is sufficient consensus on the notion that we have *some* reasons for action to justify the project of philosophical ethics. Its tone, however, should perhaps be rather different. At present discussion consists in a debate between proponents of different ethical theories which appears somewhat dogmatic in the light of the consensus condition. But this is not to say that the suspension of judgment required by the consensus condition must result in some kind of dialectical paralysis. There is nothing to prevent those to whom some ethical position appears to be true from elucidating that position, as well as providing arguments for it and against others. But the result of this being carried on in awareness of the consensus condition is likely to be a greater willingness to seek enlightenment in the positions of others and to turn a critical eye on one's own view, as well as to inquire further into the sources of our beliefs and of disagreement itself.[20] A debate in that spirit seems more likely to advance ethical understanding, as well as to provide opportunities for possible convergence on other-regarding principles. It must be admitted, however, that the personal ethics of a thinker who suspends judgment on those ethics may well become less stable. If I come to think that some quite demanding ethical principle, which I was attempting to live up to, is no better grounded than some entirely undemanding principle, that provides me with a self-interested reason—itself well grounded—to engage in a strategy of self-reeducation. Philosophical ethics could proceed, then, only if enough of its participants were prepared to allow their own lives to include space for some degree of impartial comparison of different positions.

What, then, should we say to the tyrant? As we have seen, from the philosophical point of view there is nothing we can say except that, to us, his actions appear to have certain qualities which he is unable to detect. But perhaps the philosophical point of view is not that best suited for engagement with tyrants. Rather, if there is a chance that we can have some influence over him, we should say whatever is most likely to stop him torturing people. That may well involve us in deceit, but in these circumstances that seems a small price to pay.

At the level of ethical theory itself, I suspect that the way things appear to me is quite similar to the way they appear to Glover. But it does seem to me (and this is perhaps a largely empirical point) that the kind of ethics to which Glover subscribes may imply that the focus of many readers of his book should be different from that he proposes. According to Glover, we should create a morality designed to serve human interests (41; see 109, 231, 310, 406), and he places special stress on the creation of a moral identity and capacity to sympathize which would constrain one from participating in activities such as torture. He is no doubt right that such a morality, if we were to accept it and encourage its acceptance in others, would make some contribution to the furthering of human interests. But in so far as such a morality is largely in line with the morality we are already brought up to accept, it will fail to deal with two of the most serious defects of that morality: its implication that actions are more important than omissions, and that what matters in particular is what each of us does as opposed to what we together do.[21] From the point of view of human interests, my failure to prevent torture by others, or suffering from hunger or disease, by spending money on myself and my family rather than donating to Amnesty International, Sight Savers, or Oxfam, is as bad as torture itself. The so-called 'acts and omissions doctrine' is, and has been, significantly more damaging to human interests than the 'monsters inside us' (7). Further, from the point of view of human interests—both those of actual and of potential people— the primary concern of those in the developed world in the twenty-first century should be not the creation of conditions inhospitable to war and tyranny, but the preservation of an environment which will support human life.[22] There are several difficulties here. We again face the problem of the acts and omissions doctrine. Further, most of the individual activities which are causing climate change are, in themselves, relatively harmless. What is needed here is not so much an individual but a collective moral identity. The sanctions of common-sense morality—and in particular guilt, shame, and blame—must somehow be attached to actions which, though in themselves largely harmless, are part of a set of actions by a group with very bad expected consequences.[23] It will not be history that enables us to do that, since humanity has never before faced the possibility of self-inflicted global catastrophe with so little moral protection. The moral history of the twenty-first century, if it can ever be written, is likely to be quite different from that of the twentieth.[24]

Notes

1. J. Glover, *Humanity: A Moral History of the Twentieth Century* (London: Pimlico, 2001). References in the text are to this volume. Jonathan was a brilliant and supportive supervisor during my B.Phil. in Oxford, 1983–5, and since then he and his work have been continuing sources of inspiration.

2. B. Williams, "Internal and External Reasons", reprinted in *Moral Luck* (Cambridge: Cambridge University Press, 1981), 101–13.

3. http://www.statistics.gov.uk/cci/nugget.asp?id=395.

4. *Euthyphro*, 10a2–3.

5. See J.L. Mackie, *Ethics: Inventing Right and Wrong* (Harmondsworth: Penguin), 1977, ch. 1. Though he does not use the term 'invention', Glover speaks of morality as a 'human creation' (41).

6. It is significant that the term 'self-creation' is also used by Richard Rorty; see, e.g., *Contingency, Irony, and Solidarity* (Cambridge: Cambridge University Press), 1999, ch. 5 (on Proust, Nietzsche, and Heidegger, all authors on which Glover has himself written).

7. See, e.g., T.M. Scanlon, *What We Owe to Each Other* (Harvard: Belknap Press, 1998), 41–55; D. Parfit, "Rationality and Reasons", in D. Egonsson, J. Josefsson, B. Petersson, and T. Rønnow-Rasmussen (eds.), *Exploring Practical Philosophy: From Action to Values* (Aldershot: Ashgate, 2001), 17–39.

8. I have discussed these issues also in my *Reasons and the Good* (Oxford: Clarendon Press, 2006), ch. 3.

9. J.S. Mill, *Utilitarianism* (ed. R. Crisp, Oxford: Oxford University Press, 1998), ch. 1.

10. For a contrary view, see, e.g., John McDowell, "Values and Secondary Qualities", in Ted Honderich (ed.), *Morality and Objectivity* (London: Routledge & Kegan Paul, 1985), 110–29. But McDowell himself admits that evaluative properties *merit* a certain response, and this seems to imply that there is more to 'seeing' them than can be provided merely by a properly functioning visual system.

11. P. Benacerraf, "Mathematical Truth", reprinted in P. Benacerraf and H. Putnam (eds.), *Philosophy of Mathematics: Selected Readings* (Cambridge: Cambridge University Press, 2nd edn., 1983), 403–20.

12. H. Field, *Realism, Mathematics and Modality* (Oxford: Blackwell, 1989), 25–6.

13. Lawrence BonJour, "Replies", *Philosophy and Phenomenological Research* 63 (2001), 673–93.

14. H. Sidgwick, *The Methods of Ethics* (London: Macmillan, 1907), 338–42.

15. We might add: 'where it exists'. Sidgwick should be taken to be unaware of scientific disagreement.

16. See e.g. David Gauthier, *Morals by Agreement* (Oxford: Clarendon Press, 1986). It is not the views of tyrants that matter so much as the views of others who are at the very least one's 'epistemic peers' in philosophical ethics. See S. McGrath, "Moral Disagreement", *Oxford Studies in Metaethics* 3, ed. R. Shafer-Landau (Oxford: Oxford University Press, 2008): 87–107, sect. 3. McGrath refers to work by T. Kelly and R. Feldman, noting that Kelly attributes the term to G. Gutting.

17. Plato, *Republic*, 344a–c.

18. See Brad Hooker, "Does Moral Virtue Constitute a Benefit to the Agent?", in R. Crisp (ed.), *How Should One Live?* (Oxford: Clarendon Press, 1996), 141–55; R. Crisp, "Socrates and Aristotle on Happiness and Virtue", in R. Heinaman (ed.), *Plato and Aristotle's Ethics* (Aldershot: Ashgate), 55–78.

19. If we allow that *SI* ethical in a broad sense, this provides an answer to those who doubt, because of the fact of disagreement, my claim above that ethical judgments are a priori. I suspect that *most* philosophers (now) would accept something like C. But what seems significant here is that hardly *any* will deny *SI*.

20. See e.g. Allen Buchanan's essay in this volume.

21. Glover himself has played an important role in bringing out and criticizing these aspects of commonsense morality. See, e.g., *Causing Death and Saving Lives*

(Harmondsworth: Penguin), 1977, ch. 7; "It Makes No Difference Whether or Not I Do It", *Proceedings of the Aristotelian Society*, supp. 49 (1975), 171–90.

22. Of course, that is likely to include the creation of conditions inhospitable to war and tyranny.

23. See Parfit, *Reasons and Persons* (Oxford: Clarendon Press, 1984), ch. 3, esp. 86; "What We Together Do", this volume.

24. I am grateful to each of the three editors for helpful comments on an earlier draft of this chapter. That earlier draft was written during tenure of a Leverhulme Major Research Fellowship. I thank the Trustees for their support.

10

Bystanders to Poverty

Peter Singer

10.1 THE ACTS AND OMISSIONS DOCTRINE

My copy of Jonathan Glover's pioneering work in applied ethics, *Causing Death and Saving Lives*, has on its cover three lines of verse:.

Thou shalt not kill;
But needst not strive/
Officiously to keep alive

These lines are followed by an oversized red question mark. In the pages that follow, Glover devotes a chapter to discussing "the acts and omissions doctrine," that is, the view that in certain contexts, it is less bad, morally, to omit to do an act than it is to perform a different act, even though the act and the omission have identical consequences. "It will be argued here," Glover writes, "that we ought to reject the acts and omissions doctrine."[1]

Glover begins his discussion of the acts and omissions doctrine by acknowledging what can be said in its support. For a start, it is part of our common moral convictions. Glover refers to Philippa Foot's comment:

Most of us allow people to die of starvation in India and Africa, and there is surely something wrong with us that we do; it would be nonsense, however, to pretend that it is only in law that we make a distinction between allowing people in the underdeveloped countries to die of starvation and sending them poisoned food.[2]

Glover also notes the argument that abandoning the acts and omissions doctrine would be intolerably burdensome, because:

It is arguable that we would have to give money to fight starvation up to the point where we needed it more than those we were helping: perhaps to the point where we would die without it. For not to do so would be to allow more people to die, and this would be like murder.

A third ground for support for the acts and omissions doctrine, Glover says, comes from the way it is presupposed by our moral language, including the distinction we draw between doing our duty, and doing something that is supererogatory.

Nevertheless, Glovers thinks we should reject the doctrine. He argues that we mistakenly believe that there is an important distinction between acts and omissions, because we confuse different kinds of omissions, and wrongly consider as part of the distinction itself, factors that are only contingently associated with it. The doctrine also gains support from our failure to separate the standpoint of the agent from that of the moral critic or judge.

Later in the essay, I return to the question of whether Glover is right to reject the doctrine. For the present, it is enough to see how unflinchingly Glover draws the conclusions that follow from his rejection of the idea that there is an intrinsic moral difference between acts and omissions. After accepting that there are often significant differences in the side-effects of killing and allowing to die, Glover affirms that nevertheless, "deliberately failing to send money to Oxfam, without being able to justify our alternative spending as more important, is in the same league as murder."[3]

10.2 A GAP IN GLOVER'S MORAL HISTORY OF THE TWENTIETH CENTURY

I turn now to Glover's *Humanity*, a work that bears the ambitious subtitle *A Moral History of the Twentieth Century*. Perhaps we should not take that subtitle too seriously. (I am only too well aware of the pressure that publishers can put on authors regarding the title or subtitle of a book.) For, as a moral history of the previous century, the book is seriously incomplete. It contains, for example, no account of twentieth-century progress toward equality between men and women, or of the changes in sexual morality, both for heterosexuals and for homosexuals, during that period. The revolution in European thought regarding the treatment and moral status of animals that occurred late in the century also goes unremarked, as does the environmental movement and its attempt to find value in nature and ecological systems. Glover knows, of course, that the book does not really live up to its subtitle. He tells us, in its opening pages, that he has focused *Humanity* more narrowly in order to avoid the superficiality that would be inevitable if one really were to try to write a moral history of the twentieth century in a single volume.[4] Instead he offers an account of, and a reflection on, some of the most tragic moral failings of the twentieth century.

Even if we ignore its subtitle, however, there is a conspicuous gap in the chronicles of tragedy that *Humanity* contains—a gap that is particularly surprising, given its author's arguments in his earlier book on the acts and omissions doctrine. For much of the twentieth century, as for the initial years of the twenty-first century, more than a billion people have been living in absolute poverty—a level defined by the World Bank as living on the purchasing power equivalent—usually much less than the actual exchange value—of $1 per day. According to organizations like UNICEF and the Food and Agriculture Organization, each year approximately 18 million people die from causes related to poverty.[5] Some of these people starve to death. Many more, especially children, succumb to malnutrition, and the increased susceptibility to disease that an inadequate diet brings. Diarrhea is a major killer of children. Deaths from diarrhea could be dramatically reduced by providing safe drinking water, or less expensively, by making simple and inexpensive oral rehydration therapy more widely available. Most of the victims of malaria, tuberculosis, and HIV/AIDS are people living in poverty. By the beginning of 2006, AIDS had already killed 25 million people, since 1981, and left behind 14 million orphans. Another 2.9 million died from HIV/AIDS in 2006. Almost 40 million people are estimated to be living with HIV/AIDS now, nearly three-quarters of them in sub-Saharan Africa.[6] In developed countries, AIDS is now a treatable disease and effective health-education programs have greatly reduced its spread. But in developing countries, few people with HIV can afford even the cheaper generic drugs, so many of those infected will die.

Since *Humanity* deals only with events in the twentieth century, let us confine our focus to that century, and specifically to its last decade. This avoids some fuzziness about moral responsibility during the earlier decades of the century, when resources were more limited, and everything, including information, moved more slowly. By 1990, however, economic prosperity in the developed world, coupled with technological improvements in communication and transport, had given the rich nations the capacity to significantly reduce poverty-related deaths. The end of the Cold War made this easier, too, both because the developed nations reaped a substantial "peace dividend" from the reduced need for military expenditure, and because the hostility between communism and the liberal democracies no longer stood in the way of global cooperation in combating poverty. The Columbia University economist Jeffrey Sachs believes that it is now within our power to end absolute poverty, and thus prevent the overwhelming majority of the deaths that now occur from poverty-related causes. We could do it, he believes, with an additional $124 billion in annual aid—that is less than $0.60 in every $100 that the industrialized nations earn.[7] It is also only $8 billion more than the $116 billion that is spent on alcohol each year in the United States alone.

What happened during the last decade of the twentieth century, when the peace dividend became available? Instead of using the funds to substantially increase foreign aid, most nations, and in particular the United States, sharply reduced the percentage of their gross domestic product that they gave as foreign aid. It seems that, without Cold War politics to spur giving aid for geopolitical purposes, the motivation for giving aid was not strong enough to maintain the Cold War levels. This was not because aid had been shown to be ineffective. On the contrary, a study prepared for the United Nations Conference on Trade and Development noted the irony of the fact that official aid was "experiencing a steady decline even as conditions are improving for its greater effectiveness."[8]

During those ten years, when the industrialized nations were getting richer, but giving a smaller proportion of their wealth as foreign aid, approximately 180 million people died from poverty-related causes. If Sachs is right, the great majority of these deaths could have been prevented by a relatively modest increase in well-planned aid. But let us assume that Sachs is wrong, and only one-third of these deaths could have been prevented. Even so, we would then have been saving, every year, as many people as died in the entire period of the Holocaust. (If someone objects that the figure of 18 million poverty-related deaths each year is not reliable, and the correct figure is only 10 million, or even, implausibly, just 1 million, I will not argue. Even with the optimistically low figure of only 10 million poverty-related deaths over the entire decade, and the pessimistic claim that we could have saved only a third of these lives, there are still 3.3 million people dead who could have been alive, about twice as many as died in the killing fields of Cambodia under the Khmer Rouge, or four times as many as died in the 1994 massacres in Rwanda.)

Granting that Glover has chosen to keep the focus of his book narrow to avoid superficiality, it still seems odd that the failure to prevent such a large number of deaths does not rate a mention in *Humanity*. That puzzle is made more acute by a chapter that does appear in the book, to which I now turn.

10.3 BYSTANDERS TO GENOCIDE

Part VI of *Humanity* describes the crimes committed by the Nazis. One of its chapters, titled "Bystanders," discusses the moral responsibility of those who knew what the Nazis were doing to Jews. A few, like the villagers of Le Chambon, in France, took grave risks to hide Jews who would otherwise have been deported and murdered. Some who gave refuge to Jews paid with their lives for the moral stand they took. A larger number were less heroic, but still brave enough to make small gestures of solidarity, like giving food or cigarettes to "non-Aryans." But the great majority, of course, did nothing. Glover quotes from an account given by Inge Deutschkron, a Jewish girl hiding in Berlin. Deutschkron describes people peering out from behind curtained windows as their Jewish neighbors were taken away. They would whisper to each other in the streets, but they did not act.

Although some people in Berlin may not have known exactly what fate awaited the deported Jews, people who lived near the death camps and concentration camps did not have this excuse. Glover quotes the inappropriately named Sister Felicitas, who lived near the Austrian concentration camp at Mauthausen. She did protest to the authorities—about the dreadful stench coming from the burning bodies. She describes her father collapsing because "he had forgotten to seal up the windows completely tight." But her concern seems entirely for those who had to breathe in the smell, not for those whose bodies were being burned, or others who might suffer a similar fate.

Glover rightly says that it is difficult for those of us who have never been in such a situation to condemn those who did not protest, for had they protested in any serious way, they would have risked their lives. In a penetrating line he writes: "We all hope we would be like the villagers of Le Chambon, while fearing we might be like the people Inge Deutschkron saw peering out from behind curtained windows."[9] Nevertheless, Glover thinks that as long as we do not try to get too specific, the ethical position is "fairly unproblematic":

> When people's lives are at risk from persecution, there is a strong moral obligation to do what is reasonably possible to help. It is not enough to seal up the windows against the smell. The world would be a terrible place if the whole truth about this aspect of us was what Norman Geras has called "the contract of mutual indifference": we leave other people in peril unrescued and accept that others will do the same to us.[10]

The principle becomes more problematic, Glover then tells us, if we attempt to specify how much risk it is reasonable to require someone to take for others. He adds: "Particularly if rescuing a stranger means putting your family at risk, good people may divide about what morality requires."

But what if there is no risk to oneself at all? Glover describes the failures of government leaders and officials in countries not under Nazi rule to assist the Jews, for example by accepting more Jewish refugees. Not surprisingly, Glover finds it "harder to find things to say for the free bystanders who refused to help":

> What comes over most strongly is the contribution made to their failure by distance and by lack of moral imagination. People immersed in bureaucratic rules easily forget what is at stake. A code of ethics for officials should include having the imagination to look through the rules to the human reality.[11]

With all this, we can readily agree. But before we condemn the distant officials who did nothing to help those Jews attempting to flee Nazism, should we not consider our attitude to other cases in which people knowingly fail to come to the aid of innocent people who are likely to die without assistance?

10.4 PEERING OUT FROM BEHIND CURTAINED WINDOWS

The Nazis systematically murdered approximately 6 million people. That statistic has become so familiar that it no longer shocks, but when we read individual stories of one or two of those who lost their lives, and think of such a story multiplied six million times, we may be able to get some inkling of the enormity of suffering that the Holocaust involved.[12] As we saw earlier, it is reasonable to suppose that during the 1990s, at least the same number of people—6 million—died every year from avoidable, poverty-related causes. Even if that estimate is wrong, it is virtually certain that the total number of avoidable poverty-related deaths, over the decade, exceeded the total number of victims of the Nazi Holocaust.

As mentioned earlier, I have focused on the last decade of the twentieth century because Glover's book is a moral history of (at least some aspects of) that century, but, notwithstanding all the promises made at the United Nations Millennium Development Summit, poverty-related deaths did not end with the end of the century. To take just one cause of death as an example: at the current rate of deaths from AIDS, at present, approximately as many people die every two years from AIDS as died at the hands of the Nazi murderers. Poverty—both individual poverty and problems with rural infrastructure—prevents most AIDS victims in developing countries from obtaining the drugs that are available in developed countries, and could save their lives. Some will object that the victims of AIDS are less deserving of our concern than the victims of genocide, because they brought the disease on themselves by their own actions. Some add that they chose to engage in immoral forms of sexual behavior or drug use, while others may content themselves with the claim that many of them knew the risk they were taking, and nevertheless took that risk. For the point I am making, however, I don't need to consider the merits of these claims, because there is a sufficiently large number of HIV/AIDS victims who had no choice at all. Many infants have contracted the disease because their mothers had it. In addition, women now comprise 48 percent of all the people living with HIV/AIDS.[13] Many of these women were powerless to resist sex, or to insist on safe sex, with the men who infected them. So, even if we were to focus only on these "innocent" victims of AIDS, it is still highly probable that over a longer period, say a decade, the number will equal the number who died in the Holocaust.

During the last decade of the twentieth century, when governments in democratic countries cut foreign aid, citizens of those countries had various options by which they could have done something to decrease the toll of poverty-related deaths, and to protest against the failure to save more lives. They could have made the cuts in foreign aid an election issue, and voted out of office governments that reduced, or failed to increase, foreign-aid budgets. They could have written to their elected representatives, or protested in the streets against cuts in foreign aid. And, with the exception of a small proportion of people who were themselves so poor that they had no surplus at all, they could have given some of their own money to nongovernment agencies that, with additional funds, could have done more to reduce poverty, and could have saved more lives.

· For citizens of the rich democratic nations, these political activities and personal donations, were completely safe. In contrast to protests on behalf of the Jews from the people Inge Deutschkron saw peering out from behind Berlin's curtained windows, the antipoverty actions described would not have put any of the protesters or donors in danger of arrest or execution. The most they would have suffered is some loss of disposable income and of leisure time if they actively protested. Most middle-class citizens in the developed world—and, for that matter, the comfortably off middle classes of developing countries in Latin America and Asia—could give away a lot of disposable income before their lives ceased to be comfortable and secure. Yet, most of these people gave little or nothing, and did not protest the cuts in foreign aid.

Given these facts, it would seem that the condemnation Glover applies to the actions of the "free bystanders"—those who did not assist the victims of Nazi persecution to escape the Nazi threat, even though they were living beyond the reach of the Nazi regime and could safely have done so—can be applied equally well to virtually all the citizens of democratic nations during the 1990s, and at present. If it is true that, as Glover says, a world dominated by Norman Geras's "contract of mutual indifference" would be a terrible place, then it seems that the world we now live in *is* a terrible place. We have the chance to be at least a little bit like the villagers of Le Chambon—but at a far lesser risk—and we are failing.

10.5 IS STOPPING GENOCIDE A HIGHER PRIORITY THAN STOPPING POVERTY-RELATED DEATHS?

Nicholas Kristof, a *New York Times* columnist, writes frequently about the continuing genocide in the Darfur region of Sudan, and why it is morally imperative to end it. In a column headed "Why Genocide Matters" he wrote about being asked why he always harps on Darfur. He admits that it is a fair question because the number of people killed in Darfur "is modest in global terms"—he estimates that it is in the range of 200,000–500,000, compared to an annual death toll from malaria of 1 to 3 million. He then goes on to make an argument that would, if it were successful, not only answer the question he was asked, but also explain why the failure to prevent genocide should figure more prominently in a moral history of our times than the failure to prevent deaths from disease or poverty:

> So yes, you can make an argument that Darfur is simply one of many tragedies and that it would be more cost-effective to save lives by tackling diarrhea, measles and malaria.
> But I don't buy that argument at all. We have a moral compass within us, and its needle is moved not only by human suffering but also by human evil. That's what makes genocide special—not just the number of deaths but the government policy behind them. And that in turn is why stopping genocide should be an even higher priority than saving lives from AIDS or malaria.

Even the Holocaust amounted to only 10 percent of World War II casualties and cost far fewer lives than the AIDS epidemic. But the Holocaust
evokes special revulsion because it wasn't just tragic but also monstrous,
and that's why we read Anne Frank and Elie Wiesel. Teenage girls still die
all the time and little boys still starve and lose their parents—but when this
arises from genocide, the horror resonates with all humans.
Or so it should.[14]

Kristof then goes on to lament that in the case of Darfur, the genocide
there "has aroused mostly yawns around the globe."

In this passage, Kristof bases his claim that we should give priority to
stopping genocide, rather than, say, reducing the number of deaths caused
by malaria, on how we feel about genocide, the special way in which it
moves our moral compass. In discussing the acts and omissions doctrine
in *Causing Death and Saving Lives*, Glover considered something like this
argument when he acknowledged that the resentment we feel against
someone who does not care enough about others to do what is necessary
to keep them alive, is nowhere near as strong as the resentment we feel
against someone who wants people to die.[15] The fact that people do feel
this differential resentment is, he suggested, a side effect that we should
take into account, in weighing up the consequences of allowing to die, as
compared with killing. But in Glover's view, the existence of this feeling
of much greater resentment against those who actively kill, as compared
to those who allow to die, does not go any way toward justifying the view
that it is, *in itself*, worse to kill than to allow to die. Glover, in other words,
doesn't take the feelings as a pointer to what is morally right. Kristof,
in contrast, does seem to think that our "moral compass" provides some
accurate guidance as to what we ought to do.

I shall consider this argument about the accuracy of our moral compass, or our feelings of resentment, as a guide to action. But before I do,
I shall just note that reliance on the moral compass creates a problem for
Kristof with regard to Darfur, because he admits that, in that particular
case, the compass isn't working as he thinks it should. This is awkward
for him. He wants to assert that we ought to give priority to stopping the
genocide in Darfur because genocide evokes such horror in us, but he also
laments that most people greet news of the Darfur genocide with yawns.
That consideration would point toward selective discrimination in regard
to which genocides we try to stop, with Darfur rating at the bottom.
Presumably genocide directed against people more like us—white, educated, living in an industrialized nation—would evoke more horror and
therefore ought to receive priority. No regular reader of Kristof's columns
can believe that this is the conclusion he would wish to draw.

Putting the specific problem of our response to the genocide in Darfur
aside, let us grant that when we hear of, or think about, genocide, we are
moved by a strong sense of great evil, and perhaps other feelings of horror,
outrage, and resentment against the perpetrators, desire for retribution
and so on. And let us also grant that when we hear of, or think about,

people dying from malaria who could have been saved by timely donations from affluent people, we do not have such feelings, or do not have them to nearly as strong a degree. I take it that this is what Kristof means by our "moral compass" but I will avoid that term, since it presupposes that there is some magnetic north of morality, that is, something objective by which the compass is moved. Instead, I will refer to the attitudes that Kristof considers a compass as "moral intuitions." Following Jonathan Haidt, I use that term to refer to a system of rapid responses or reactions to particular situations. These rapid responses are not the outcome of reasoning processes and we do not have conscious control over them.[16]

Translated into this terminology, the judgments delivered by Kristof's "moral compass" fit well with a growing body of research in evolutionary psychology about our moral intuitions, including our intuitions of reciprocity and fairness. For example, we know that both humans and nonhuman primates reject offers that they consider unfair, even though this costs them something they would otherwise want. And we know that people will incur some cost, without any prospect of recouping the cost, in order to punish people who have acted unfairly. Consider, for example, the results of the psychology experiment known as the "ultimatum game," in which two players interact, anonymously and only once, so that reciprocity is irrelevant. The players are told that one of them—the proposer—will be given a sum of money, say $10, and must divide it with the second player—the responder—but can offer as much or as little as she wishes. If the responder rejects the offer, neither player will get anything, but if the responder accepts the offer, he will keep what was offered, and the proposer will keep the remainder. According to standard self-interest theory, the proposer should offer the smallest possible amount and the responder should nevertheless accept it, because after all, even a small amount is better than nothing at all. But in fact, in many different cultures, most proposers offer an equal split of the money, and if the proposer does offer less than 20 percent, the responder often rejects it. This suggests that many people, even when interacting with a complete stranger with whom they will never interact again, prefer to punish unfairness than to get some money.[17] Even monkeys reject a reward for a task if they see another monkey getting a better reward for performing the same task.[18] From this research, plausible accounts have emerged of how developing such a set of moral intuitions may have enhanced the reproductive fitness of those who had them.

It is, however, one thing to say that we evolved to have certain moral intuitions, and another to say that these intuitions are right, or should be followed. To equate the two commits the fallacy, noticed so long ago by David Hume, of deducing an "ought" from an "is," or in other words, of drawing value judgments out of purely factual statements.

Even if no logical fallacy were involved in moving from facts about our intuitions to judgments about what is right, we would need to be wary about assuming that the intuitions that enhanced our fitness over most of our evolutionary history are still the ones we should act upon today. As Joshua Greene has suggested, physical violence from another human being has been possible throughout our evolutionary history, and we have developed a strong moral intuition against it. Hence, most people say it would be wrong to push a heavy person in front of a runaway trolley, thus stopping the trolley and saving the lives of five people in a tunnel further down the track. On the other hand, since switches and train tracks are relatively recent inventions, we have no evolved negative response to throwing a switch that will divert the same trolley onto a sidetrack, saving the five people in the tunnel, but killing one who is working on the side track. So, most people say that would not be wrong. Yet, the outcomes are the same in both cases—one person dies but five are saved—and it is hard to find good reasons for differentiating between the two judgments.[19]

Perhaps our differing intuitions about genocide and the prevention of poverty-related deaths derive from this difference. Our strong visceral opposition to genocide draws on our negative responses to physical violence and killing, which in genocide happens on a large scale and in ways that make the innocence of the victims obvious. For most of our evolutionary history, however, we have not been able to do much to help others who are needy, but not nearby. We have often had difficulty in meeting our own needs, and those of our extended family, for food. Hence, although we do have a positive response to helping our kin and those immediately in front of us, we have not evolved any intuitive response to failing to help strangers who are far away. Now, however, we have the means to drastically reduce poverty anywhere in the world, and thereby to save millions of lives every year. In these changed circumstances, why should we rely upon our intuition that stopping genocide is a higher priority than saving a much larger number of people who will otherwise die from preventable diseases?

Putting aside intuitions that may mislead us, then, is there a reason to think that it is worse to do nothing about genocide than to do nothing about preventing a death by disease? Let us assume that, as Kristof accepts, we could save more lives by targeting our sizable, but still limited, resources against disease than we could by using them to stop genocide. Let us also assume that those who are killed in the genocide do not suffer any more than those who die from the disease. Whether this assumption holds in the real world will, of course, depend upon the circumstances. Many of the victims of the Nazi Holocaust suffered unspeakably. In addition to the fear about what was going to happen to them, they had to endure long journeys in crowded cattle trucks, in freezing cold, or stifling heat. Others had their children taken away from them, or killed before their eyes. Some were imprisoned in inhuman concentration camps, on semi-starvation rations, with endemic diseases, and ever-present threat of brutal beatings if they did not work hard enough. Such factors do, of course, provide additional reasons for stopping genocide. But poverty-related diseases may also cause terrible suffering, and parents living in desperate poverty may also see their children die in front of them, knowing that if only they had money, they could get treatment that would save their children's lives. Even if this suffering is generally less than that of the victims of genocides, our interest here is in whether stopping genocide as such should have higher priority than stopping deaths from poverty-related causes, and so we should put aside possible differences in the amount of suffering that accompanies the deaths in particular circumstances.

One argument for giving priority to stopping genocide might be that those committing genocide are doing something morally very wrong. When we stop them, therefore, we not only save the lives of innocents, but we also stop a moral evil. When we prevent deaths from poverty-related diseases, we "only" save the lives of innocents. Hence, we have an extra reason to stop the deaths from genocide that we do not have in the case of preventing deaths by disease.

Should we give independent weight to stopping a moral evil, beyond the harm that has been prevented by stopping the evil? Suppose that two people are suffering great pain by having parts of their body burned. One of them is the victim of a torturer, while the other is trapped in a building that is on fire. Should we give higher priority to saving the one who is being tortured? We might answer affirmatively because we have in mind that if we don't stop the torturer, he will move on to other victims. Or we might be influenced by the thought that the torturer may enjoy the plight of his victim, because many people think that it is bad that anyone should get pleasure from torture. So, let us assume that although the torturer has set in motion machinery that will, unless we intervene, continue to inflict pain on the victim, he then committed suicide, and so can neither torture anyone else, nor enjoy his victim's suffering. Then I think our priority should be to save the victim who is suffering more. As I have argued elsewhere, I know of no better way of deciding what we ought to do than to put ourselves in the position of all those affected by the actions open to us and do what we would prefer if we had to live all their lives.[20] In the situation we are not considering, if the victims could choose the decision procedure that would lead to one of them being rescued, and they did not know which one of them would be suffering more, nor which of them would be suffering because of an accident, and which would be suffering because of the torturer, it would be in their interests to choose that the one who is suffering more should be the first one to be rescued.

The same argument applies when lives are at stake, rather than suffering. Suppose that Sherlock Holmes has deduced that a cunning murderer plans to kill his next victim by rolling a boulder down a hill onto the victim, who is picnicking, all alone, in an alpine meadow. The plan will succeed, unless Holmes warns the intended victim, but to do so he must first run a short distance toward the victim in order to be in earshot. He is about to set off when he sees that a mountain goat has dislodged a different boulder that is beginning to roll down the opposite side of the ridge, where it will kill two unsuspecting picnickers. Holmes can save them if he runs a short distance down that side of the ridge to warn them. If he first saves the intended victim of the murderer, he will not have time to save the two picnickers who are in the path of the boulder dislodged by the goat. I think that Holmes should save the two victims, not just one. The fact that their deaths would be accidental and the other death would be intended is not of sufficient weight—if, indeed, it is of any weight at all—to overcome the difference in the number of lives saved. (We can assume that Holmes has alerted the local police to the presence of the murderer, and that despite their usual limited competence, they will apprehend him and he will be convicted of several other murders and locked away for life, whether or not his latest attempt succeeds.[21])

Against this view, one might attempt to employ an argument once put forward by Elizabeth Anscombe.[22] Anscombe argued that, if I have a choice between rowing my boat so as to save one person from drowning, or rowing it in a different direction to save a group of people, I have no obligation to save the group. If I save just the one, none of the others can make any justified accusation against me. I may have had an obligation to save someone, but I had no obligation to save any particular person. No one has been wronged. In *Causing Death and Saving Lives*, Glover has no difficulty in showing that this view leads to paradoxes, and should be rejected in favor of what he calls a maximizing policy: "other things being equal, we ought always to prefer to save a larger to a smaller number of people."[23] This is surely correct. It is question begging to assume, as Anscombe does, that the rights and wrongs of all actions depend on whether the action gives an individual a ground for complaint. Instead, we can again look at it as a choice under conditions of uncertainty. If three people know that they will need rescuing under the circumstances described by Anscombe, and know that they have an equal chance of being any of the people needing to be rescued, but do not know whether they will be the isolated individual or a member of the larger group, it would be rational for them to choose that the rescuer go to the larger group. For if the rescuer saves the isolated individual, they have only a one-in-three chance of being saved, whereas if the rescuer goes to the larger group, their chance of rescue is twice as high.

So the numbers do count, and stopping moral evil should not be allowed to outweigh the good of saving as many lives as possible. But there is a different distinction between genocide and poverty-related deaths that may also lead people to think it more important to stop genocide. When genocides succeed, they extinguish an entire people, along with their distinctive culture and way of life. This is an additional tragedy, on top of the tragedy of the individual lives lost, and arguably gives greater urgency to the case for preventing genocide.[24] But this consideration does not seem to weigh heavily with most of us. If it did, then the Armenian genocides and the Nazi Holocaust would be much worse than Stalin's mass purges, or the massacres committed by the Khmer Rouge in Cambodia. In thinking about these events, the cruel deaths of so many individuals outweigh the additional loss of the people and their culture. Conversely, when a people and their culture disappear because of their own choices—as when they marry into a larger community and their language falls into disuse—we may regret the loss, but we do not think of it in anything like the same moral terms as would have been the case if the people had been massacred. This suggests that if, given our available resources, we could save the lives of many more victims of poverty than we could save, if instead we attempted to save the lives of victims of genocide, we should save the victims of poverty.

There may be a good consequentialist reason for giving priority to saving lives and preventing suffering that occur as a result of genocide, rather than as a result of natural causes. Just as we resent unfairness and are prepared to punish it at some cost to ourselves, so perhaps those who know that they are the victims of injustice suffer more than those who know they have only natural causes to blame for their suffering.[25] This claim is plausible, but one can ask how much more the victims of injustice suffer, and whether, for example, it is enough to justify giving priority to ending the genocide in Darfur, with its 200,000–500,000 victims, rather than reducing the annual 1 to 3 million deaths caused by malaria. This seems doubtful. To the extent that victims of injustice do suffer more, this will be taken into account by a formulation that says that we should give priority to preventing the greatest amount of suffering. Then we need to add a warning that the degree of suffering may depend, not only on the physical harm done, but also on what caused it.

In *Causing Death and Saving Lives*, Glover considers a different reason for giving priority to stopping massacres rather than preventing harmful omissions. It is, he imagines someone arguing, more important to condemn people who show the kind of character that leads them to commit violent, hostile acts, than to discourage people whose omissions show a lack of concern or imagination. Therefore, blaming people for their acts rather than their omissions will have good consequences. But this is, Glover says, "not obviously true" because:

> It is arguable that indifference plays as large a part in causing the world's misery as positive hostility. The existence of wars, poverty and many of the other things that destroy or stunt people's lives may be as dependent on widespread unconcern as on any positively bad motives. It may well be because of tacit acceptance of the acts and omissions doctrine that we acquiesce in the worst evils in the world.[26]

This is a plausible claim. But it adds to the puzzle of why the only omissions Glover discusses in *Humanity* are the inadequacies of the bystanders to the Holocaust, while the "widespread unconcern" of most of the citizens of the affluent world about the avoidable poverty-related deaths of tens of millions of people are themselves omitted from the book. Other things being equal, I can see no adequate grounds for giving a higher priority to stopping genocide than to stopping poverty-related deaths. Recognizing the serious nature of our failure to aid those dying from poverty-related causes, by giving the topic at least one chapter in *Humanity*, would have been a good way of making this point, and would not have run the risk of superficiality.

There is also one speculative, but plausible, consideration that points in the opposite direction, for giving priority to preventing harmful omissions rather than to preventing massacres. It is reasonable to suppose that acts of helping strangers are more under our conscious control than are genocidal acts. This view is supported by much of the historical material about genocide that Glover so ably presents in *Humanity*. Genocidal behavior may be the result of specific historical circumstances in which political leaders are able to tap into strong emotional responses deep in human nature. In these particular, but fortunately rare circumstances, neither the power of example, nor reminders of high moral standards, may have any influence. On the other hand, good examples and high moral standards may be more likely to have an effect in the more normal conditions in which people help strangers in need. If this is right, then encouraging people to help strangers escape poverty may be more effective than trying to stop genocide.[27]

10.6 CONCLUSION

Although *Humanity* does not discuss our moral failure to take the steps needed for a drastic reduction in global poverty, Glover's own work offers two distinct lines of thought that should lead us to take this failure very seriously. One is his critique of the acts and omissions doctrine in *Causing Death and Saving Lives* and the other is his discussion of the moral culpability of bystanders to the Holocaust. The former leads us to review again the way in which we sharply distinguish letting someone die, when we could save them, from killing that person. The other leads us to ask what can justify our condemnation of those who fail to act to save the victims of genocide, when we ourselves are failing to save an even larger number of victims of poverty.

As I have argued elsewhere, whether or not we consider allowing to die as morally equivalent to killing, we cannot justify our inaction when we could be helping those living in desperate poverty.[28] What then should we do? In *Causing Death and Saving Lives*, Glover says that living up to the morality that is entailed by his own rejection of the acts and omissions doctrine is "a very unattractive prospect: it is the prospect of a huge reduction in income and the loss of a lot of our spare time." But, he continues, if we assume that the acts and omissions doctrine cannot be saved, then the only other approach is to accept "a huge discrepancy between professed beliefs and actual conduct" About this Glover candidly remarks: "This is not very admirable, either."

Indeed, it is not. But the choice is not either/or. We can give substantial amounts of money to organizations working to aid those who are desperately poor (and we can give some of our time to the same cause), without giving so much that we have no money or leisure left for indulging in our own desires. We might then be doing more to prevent death from poverty-related causes, in proportion to our income and our spare time, than 99 percent, or perhaps 99.9 percent, of those living in the rich nations. Even at that level, we will still be failing to do things that could save lives, without putting our own lives in danger. So, judged by the demanding standards that confront us when we reject the acts and omissions doctrine, we will still not be doing enough. Our behavior will be less admirable than that of the villagers of Le Chambon. Nevertheless, in one sense what we are doing *will* be admirable. We will be doing far more than most people, and we will be raising the standard of what morality requires in regard to the poor. This is a reason for not being too hard on ourselves. Moreover, a life lived in this way is not lacking in attractions. Making a substantial contribution toward what is, by any reasonable standards, a worthwhile goal, can give meaning and fulfillment to our lives.[29]

Postscript

I was a graduate student at Oxford from 1969–71. In 1970, I attended Glover's lectures on Free Will, Determinism, and Moral Responsibility. They were among the best lectures I attended, laying out the issues clearly and full of interesting examples. The most stimulating classes I attended during my time at Oxford, however, were seminars given by Derek Parfit, Jonathan Glover, and Jim Griffin on what we would now call applied ethics, although that term was not then in use. Each week, one of them would give a talk that initiated a lively discussion. Though it was difficult for either Jonathan or Jim—or anyone else, for that matter—to match Derek's originality and sheer philosophical brilliance, Glover's contributions always raised intriguing philosophical issues in serious practical problems. Some of them later appeared in *Causing Death and Saving Lives*. His work blazed a trail that I was to follow into applied ethics.

Indirectly, Glover was responsible for changing my life in a more fundamental way. After one of his lectures on moral responsibility in 1970, I fell into conversation with Richard Keshen, who was attending the same series of lectures and had asked a question I found interesting. He suggested we continue the conversation over lunch at his college, Balliol. That day there was a choice between spaghetti with some kind of reddish-brown sauce over it, or a salad plate. Richard asked if the sauce had meat in it, and when told that it did, took the salad plate. I took the spaghetti, and when our discussion of free will and determinism had run its course, I asked Richard why he avoided meat. I had met very few vegetarians up to that time, and those I had met thought meat was bad for their health, had religious grounds for avoiding it, or were pacifists, holding that killing is always wrong. I was neither religious nor a pacifist, and I didn't believe meat, in moderate quantities, was unhealthy. Richard's answer was more challenging. He told me that he did not think we had a right to treat animals in the way that the animals that had become the meat I was eating were treated. That made me ask about how the animals were treated, and started me thinking about how we ought to treat animals. The result was that I soon became a vegetarian myself, and a few years later, wrote *Animal Liberation*, which some have credited with helping to start the modern animal movement.

Notes

1. Jonathan Glover, *Causing Death and Saving Lives*, Penguin, Harmondsworth, Middlesex, 1977, p. 94.

2. Philippa Foot, "The Problem of Abortion and the Doctrine of the Double Effect," *The Oxford Review*, 1967, quoted by Glover, *Causing Death and Saving Lives*, p. 93.

3. *Causing Death and Saving Lives*, p. 109.

4. *Humanity* pp. 2–3.

5. See Food and Agriculture Organization of the United Nations, *The State of Food Insecurity in the World 1999*, www.fao.org/news/1999/img/sofi99-e.pdf and UNICEF (United Nations Children's Fund), *The State of the World's Children 2002*, www.unicef.org/sowc02/pdf/sowc2002-eng-full.pdf. I owe these references to Thomas Pogge, "Severe Poverty as a Human Rights Violation," in Thomas Pogge, ed., *Freedom from Poverty as a Human Right: Who Owes What to the Very Poor?* Oxford University Press, Oxford, 2007.

6. UNAIDS/WHO, *AIDS Epidemic Update, December 2006*, http://www.unaids.org/en/HIV_data/epi2006/default.asp; Avert, "Worldwide HIV and AIDS Statistics" http://www.avert.org/worldstats.htm.

7. Jeffrey Sachs, *The End of Poverty*, ch. 15.

8. Kwese Botchwey, "Financing for Development: Current Trends and Issues for the Future," a paper prepared for the UNCTAD High-level Round Table on Trade and Development: Directions for the Twenty-first Century, Bangkok, February 2000, p. 11, www.unctad.org/en/docs/ux_tdxrt1d11.en.pdf

9. *Humanity*, p. 392.

10. Page 393. The reference is to Norman Geras, *The Contract of Mutual Indifference: Political Philosophy after the Holocaust*, London, 1998.

11. Page 393.

12. I wrote *Pushing Time Away: My Grandfather and the Tragedy of Jewish Vienna* (Ecco, New York, 2003) in order to, at least in part, remember the life of one of those victims.

13. Global Health Reporting, http://www.globalhealthreporting.org/disease info.asp.

14. Nicholas Kristof, "Why Genocide Matters," *New York Times*, September 10, 2006, sec. 4, p. 13.

15. *Causing Death and Saving Lives*, p. 99.

16. Ref to Haidt—emotional dog and rational tail? Check his Web site.

17. There is a substantial literature on the ultimatum game. For a useful discussion, see Martin Nowak, Karen Page, and Karl Sigmund, "Fairness versus reason in the ultimatum game." Science, September 8, 2000, 289(5485), pp. 1773–75.

18. S. F. Brosnan and F. B. M. de Waal, "Monkeys reject unequal pay." *Nature*, September 18, 2003, 425, 297–99.

19. See J. D. Greene, R. B. Sommerville, L. E. Nystrom, J. M. Darley, and J. D. Cohen, "An fMRI investigation of emotional engagement in moral Judgment." *Science*, September 14, 2001, 293, 2105–08. See also J. D. Greene, "The secret joke of Kant's soul," in W. Sinnott-Armstrong, ed, *Moral Psychology, Vol. 3: The Neuroscience of Morality: Emotion, Disease, and Development*, MIT Press, Cambridge, MA, 2007.

20. See *Practical Ethics*, Cambridge University Press, Cambridge, 2nd ed. 1993, ch. 1; "Reasoning towards Utilitarianism," in D. Seanor and N. Fotion (eds.), *Hare and Critics*, Clarendon Press, Oxford, 1988, pp. 147–59; Ethics and Intuitions, *The Journal of Ethics*, October 2005, 9(3–4), 331–52.

21. This example derives from a similar one that Jeff McMahan outlined in conversation.

22. G. E. M. Anscombe, "Who is Wronged?" *The Oxford Review*, 1967, cited by Glover, *Causing Death and Saving Lives*, p. 207.

23. *Causing Death and Saving Lives*, pp. 207–09.

24. I am grateful to Jeff McMahan for pointing this out to me.

25. I owe this suggestion to Tony Coady.

26. *Causing Death and Saving Lives*, p. 112.

27. I owe this point to Agata Sagan.

28. See, for instance, my "Famine, Affluence and Morality," *Philosophy & Public Affairs*, 1972, 1, 229–43; *Practical Ethics*, 2nd edition, Cambridge University Press, Cambridge, 1993, ch. 8; *One World: Ethics and Globalization*, Yale University Press, New Haven, 2002, ch. 5; and *The Life You Can Save*, Random House, New York, 2009.

29. For comments on earlier drafts, I am grateful to the editors, Agata Sagan, Tony Coady, and participants in seminars at the Center for Human Values, Princeton University, the Centre for Applied Philosophy and Public Ethics at the University of Melbourne, and the University of Oxford.

11

Compassion: Human and Animal

Martha C. Nussbaum

I think I could turn and live with animals, they are so placid and
self-contain'd,
I stand and look at them long and long.
They do not sweat and whine about their condition,
They do not lie awake in the dark and weep for their sins,
They do not make me sick discussing their duty to God,
Not one is dissatisfied, not one is demented with the mania of
owning things,
Not one kneels to another, nor to his kind that lived thousands
of years ago,
Not one is respectable or unhappy over the whole earth.
So they show their relations to me and I accept them,
They bring me tokens of myself, they evince them plainly in their
possession.

Walt Whitman, *Song of Myself*

Frau von Briest had meanwhile sent in the coffee and was looking toward the round tower and the flower-bed. "Look, Briest.
Rollo is lying in front of the gravestone again. He is more deeply
affected than we are. He isn't even eating any more."

"Yes, Luise, animals. That's what I'm always telling you. We
aren't as wonderful as we think. We always talk about their
'instinct.' In the end that is, after all, the best." ...

[Frau von Briest now raises the question whether they, as Effi's
parents, are to blame for the disaster: was she simply too young
to be married?]

Rollo, who awoke at these words, wagged his head slowly back
and forth, and Briest said softly, "Let it go, Luise, let it go ... that
is *too* wide a field."

Theodor Fontane, *Effi Briest*

11.1

Human compassion is diseased. I do not speak primarily of its all-too-familiar failures of extent, the way we work up tremendous sympathy for thirteen people dead in Minnesota, but have no emotional response to hundreds of thousands of people dead in Darfur. Those failures are common ground between humans and other animals,[1] and we may plausibly see a tendency to focus on the near-at-hand as part of our animal heritage, tenacious and difficult to overcome. No, I am speaking about failures of compassion that we would *not* expect to find in any other animal, cases of the most close-up and horrible human suffering that evoke, from its witnesses (and, often, perpetrators) no compassionate response. History, it often seems, is full of little else. Let me, however, confine myself to three closely related examples, cases in which it is plain, not only that the emotional and moral failure in question is peculiarly human—an ape or elephant on the scene would do far better, or at least less badly—but also that the failure is at least partly explained by what primatologist Frans de Waal has called "anthropodenial," the implicit denial (on the part of humans) that we are really animals.[2] It is no accident that all three of my cases concern misogyny, so often a prominent aspect of anthropodenial.[3]

To put my thesis in a nutshell: anthropodenial, a uniquely human tendency, is not simply a pernicious intellectual position: it is a large cause of moral deformity.

My first case is the ending of Theodor Fontane's novel *Effi Briest*.[4] Effi is married by her parents, at the age of sixteen, to a much older man who neglects her. Loneliness and immaturity led her to have a brief affair, which she then breaks off, deciding that she did the wrong thing. She lives happily with her husband and child, until her husband, by sheer chance, discovers the long-ago indiscretion. At this point, husband, child, and parents all repudiate Effi, and she dies, miserable and alone. Only her dog Rollo feels compassion for her at the end of her life, attending to her supportively and seeming to understand her unhappiness; only he manifests deep sorrow after her death. The parents find themselves emotionally frozen: the shame at being known as the parents of a fallen woman quite overwhelms their parental feeling. Looking at Rollo's unalloyed sadness, Effi's father concludes that in some ways animals behave better than humans.

My second case is Tolstoy's famous novella, *The Kreutzer Sonata*.[5] Describing the events that led him to murder his wife, the leading character describes a long-lasting pattern: the pressure of sexual desire compels him to have intercourse with her, and afterward he feels revulsion. He sees her as bestial and himself as dragged unwillingly into the bestial by his bondage to desire. Only when he has finally killed her does she become, for him, an object of compassion: he tells his interlocutor, with evident sympathy for women's social situation, that women will never be treated as full human beings as long as sexual intercourse continues to exist. They will always be "humiliated and depraved slave[s]." The abuse he repeatedly inflicted on his wife by his repeated acts of sexual violence and nonconsensual intercourse caused her great pain, which he sympathetically describes. During her life, however, her pain never aroused compassion, because compassionate response was swamped by disgust at the bodily act to which her presence summoned him. Only when, being dead, she no longer arouses desire can she become an object of compassion. No nonhuman animal is mentioned, but it goes without saying that the twisted emotions of this man are all-too-human. Had the poor wife had a Rollo, he would have shown sadness at her suffering.

My third case is, sadly, reality rather than fiction. It concerns the massacre of 2,000 Muslims civilians by Hindu mobs in the state of Gujarat, India, in February 2002.[6] During the pogrom, many women were tortured, raped, and burned: by one estimate, about half of the dead were women. A common device was to rape the woman, then torture her to death by inserting a large metal rod into her, and then torch her body. The horrible suffering of these women, which was later the occasion for a tremendous outpouring of compassion and helping behavior in the nation as a whole (as scholars and activists went to Gujarat to take down the testimony of survivors, help them file police reports, and write a record of the horrors for posterity), occasioned jubilation on the part of the Hindu right-wing rioters, who produced pornographic hate literature celebrating their conquests. In one pamphlet circulated during the riots, written in verse, the Chief Minister of the state of Gujarat, Narendra Modi (who masterminded the pogrom) is imagined as raping to death a woman who is simply called "the mother of Muslims"; this iconic woman is imagined as dead because she is penetrated by an uncircumcised penis which becomes, somehow, a fatal weapon (remember those metal rods that were actually used to torture and kill women), and yet, in the fantasy, she enjoys it to the last. The "poem" ends with a picture of the land of India completely cleansed of Muslims. Presumably there can be no more of them, once the "mother of Muslims" is dead.

I don't even need to mention the fact that this orchestration of horror corresponds to nothing in the animal world.

Most discussions of the relationship between humans and animals, where empathy and compassion are concerned, focus on two things: *continuities* between human and animal emotion, and *good discontinuities*, meaning discontinuities in which we humans have something morally valuable that animals don't have. Thus, Frans de Waal has consistently emphasized the way in which human sympathy, while in some ways more comprehensive than animal sympathy, is yet continuous with animal sympathy. He uses the image of a Russian doll: the outside doll is bigger, but inside we will find a little doll (the animal origins of the human emotion) that is in most respects isomorphic to the outer. Most of the commentators on de Waal's recent Tanner Lectures[7] grant that these continuities obtain and are important, but they focus on *good discontinuities*, stressing the fact that humans possess a range of desirable traits that nonhuman animals don't appear to possess.[8] These include: the ability to choose not to act on some powerful desires; the ability to think about one's goals as a system and to rank and order them; the ability to think about the good of people (and animals) at a great distance from ourselves, the ability to test the principles of our conduct for impartiality and respectfulness to the claims of others.

In this way, many, if not most of the people who write on this topic evoke the image of a *scala naturae*, in which we humans are at the top, the largest Russian doll in the set of dolls, the only one who is capable of full moral agency. Few mention the other side, the corruptions of sympathy that are so ubiquitous in human experience. Christine Korsgaard does prominently, if very briefly, acknowledge these, writing, in response to de Waal, "that human beings seem psychologically damaged in ways that suggest some deep break with nature."[9] On the whole, though, the recent discussion of the human–animal relationship, where compassion is concerned, neglects this "break," which it is my plan to investigate here. I begin by mapping out an analysis of compassion that I have proposed for standard human cases.[10] I then use this to investigate differences between human and animal compassion. This investigation will give us a set of reference points as we pursue our investigation of the "break." The end result, I hope, will be a picture slightly different from de Waal's, though agreeing with many of his most important claims: a picture in which the Russian doll on the outside is malicious and contorted in ways that do not correspond to any deformation of the inside dolls.

In short, Walt Whitman's account of the animal kingdom (in my epigraph) is no doubt too rosy and a bit sentimental, but in its most essential aspects it is correct.[11] Animals do bring us "tokens of [ourselves]," and we should "accept them." As Whitman knows and emphasizes, however, acceptance of our animality involves an uphill battle against denial of animality and stigmatization of those whom a dominant group of humans views as quasi-animal (including prominently, in Whitman's universe, both women and African–Americans). Animals don't have to fight that battle. They don't need a poem like Whitman's "I Sing the Body Electric"—because they are that poem.

Jonathan Glover's *Humanity* is a major achievement.[12] Like no other book known to me in philosophy, it takes on the challenge of describing the moral horrors of the twentieth century and dissecting them perspicuously, so that we can understand a little better what human failings produced them, and how a program of moral education and culture-creation might begin to combat these failings. Richly detailed, informed by deep knowledge of history and psychology, the book goes further than any other I know, in any field, in presenting a rich and variegated understanding of inhumanity and its sources—in part because, being a philosophical book, it is so clear and compellingly argued, in part because, being a book by a reasonable and open-minded man, it refuses to plump for one of the monocausal explanations of atrocity so common in the literature about the Holocaust, where we find endless and sometimes fruitless debate about whether the Final Solution was caused by family structure, or culture, or ideology, or universal human tendencies to submit to authority and peer pressure. "All of the above," is the obviously reasonable answer, but those who seek fame often eschew complexity in order to create a distinctive identity for themselves in the marketplace of ideas. Glover lacks such vices, and thus his book is delightfully complicated and non-reductive.

Despite its rich texture, however, there are two important silences, and the purpose of this chapter is to continue and extend Glover's project by speaking about what he has chosen not to speak about. Much though Glover discusses human compassion,[13] he fails to include any discussion of the relationship between the human emotion and closely related emotions in the lives of nonhuman animals. Since I believe that I myself said too little about this question in *Upheavals of Thought*, this is an occasion to remedy that defect. Glover's second and related silence concerns the human denial of kinship with the animal, and the misogyny that is all too often a concomitant of that denial, since women have repeatedly been portrayed as somehow more bodily than men, more viscous, less hard, with their indissoluble links to birth and sexual receptivity. At one point, Glover does broach this topic, when he discusses Klaus Theweleit's *Male Fantasies*, with its analysis of the wish of the German males in question to become men of steel, hard and superhuman.[14] Here Glover appears to endorse Theweleit's view that hatred of mere humanity is an important motive in bad behavior, saying, "Those who think of themselves as men of steel have to subdue anything which threatens to return them to the old type of person with soft flesh and disorganized human feelings."[15] He does not carry this analysis further, however—perhaps because he is skeptical of Theweleit's psychoanalytical orientation.[16]

The two silences are mutually reinforcing: not asking how human emotional experience differs from that of animals, Glover fails to focus on the fear and hatred of mere animal existence that is so conspicuously absent in nonhuman animals and so ubiquitous in human animals. The failure to pursue this lead, in turn, means a failure to explore the topic of misogyny, such a prominent feature of males' hatred of their animal embodiment. And yet, it seems to me that the evidence for such emotional realities is as clear and compelling as the evidence for most of the other psychological responses that Glover does eloquently discuss. The emotions that I discuss have been studied by experimental psychology and by clinically and empirically oriented psychoanalysis, often in productive conversation with one another. Once one grants that emotions such as anger, disgust, and shame have an ideational content, one cannot avoid asking what that content is, and how it relates to the peculiar situation of the human being, as a highly intelligent being in a weak and mortal body. Experimental psychologists have not evaded these questions, and the hypotheses I shall advance are as testable as anything in a psychology that eschews narrow behaviorism and insists on interpreting the intentional content of living creatures' responses—which is to say, I believe, the only sort of psychology that could possibly illuminate human emotional life.

I offer this analysis in the spirit of extension, not replacement, since, like Glover, I mistrust all reductive monocausal accounts of human depravity. I do so with the greatest admiration for Glover's philosophical courage and insight, here and elsewhere, and also with deep gratitude to a philosophical friend.

11.2

In *Upheavals of Thought*, I argue for an analysis of the human emotion standardly called "compassion" that derives from a long Western philosophical tradition of analysis and debate.[17] According to my account (to some extent agreeing with this tradition, to some extent criticizing it), compassion has three thoughts as necessary parts.[18] (I call them "judgments," but I emphasize elsewhere that we need not think of these thoughts as linguistically formulated or formulable, although they do involve some type of predication or combination. Most animals can see items in their environment as good or bad, and this is all we are ascribing, in ascribing emotions to animals, defined as I define them.) First, there is a judgment of *seriousness*: in experiencing compassion, the person who feels the emotion thinks that someone else is suffering in some way that is important and nontrivial. I argue that this assessment is typically made, and ought to be made, from the point of view of an external "spectator" or evaluator, the person who experiences the emotion. If we think that the suffering person is moaning and groaning over something that is not really bad, we won't have compassion for that person. (For example, we don't feel compassion for rich people who suffer when they pay their taxes, if we think that it is just right that they should pay their taxes.) If we think, on the other hand, that a person is unaware of a predicament that is really bad (e.g., an accident that removes higher mental functioning), then we will have compassion for the person even if the person doesn't think his or her situation bad.

Second is the judgment of *non-fault*: we typically don't feel compassion if we think the person's predicament chosen or self-inflicted. This judgment, as we shall later see, is not a conceptual condition for all forms of compassion, since there are forms present in both the human and the animal cases that do not involve any assessment of responsibility. It is, however, a conceptual element in the most common forms of adult human compassion. In feeling compassion, we express the view that at least a good portion of the predicament was caused in a way for which the person is not to blame. Thus, Aristotle held that compassion for the hero of a tragedy views that hero as *anaitios*, not responsible for his downfall.[19] When we think that a person brought a bad situation on himself, this thought would appear to inhibit formation of the emotion. Thus, as Candace Clark has emphasized in her excellent sociological study of American compassion,[20] many Americans feel no compassion for the poor, because they believe that they bring poverty upon themselves through laziness and lack of effort.[21] Even when we do feel compassion for people whom we also blame, the compassion and the blame typically address different phases or aspects of the person's situation: thus we may blame a criminal for a criminal act while feeling compassion for him, if we think that the fact that he got to be the sort of person who commits criminal acts is in large part an outgrowth of social forces.

Blame comes in many types, corresponding to different categories of fault: deliberate malice, culpable negligence, and so forth. These will remove compassion to differing degrees. People's responsibility for their predicaments can also be more or less serious, as a causal element in the overall genesis of the event. In many such cases, compassion may still be present, but in a weakened form. To the extent that compassion remains, it would appear that it is directed, at least in part, at the elements of the disaster for which the person was not fully responsible.

The tradition then includes a third allegedly necessary element of compassion, namely, the judgment of *similar possibilities*. The person who has compassion often does think that the suffering person is similar to him or herself and has possibilities in life that are similar. This thought may do important work, removing barriers to compassion that have been created by artificial social divisions, as Rousseau valuably emphasizes in Book IV of *Emile*. For most humans, the thought of similar vulnerability probably is, as Rousseau argues, an important avenue to compassionate responding. I argue, however, that the thought of similarity is not absolutely necessary as a conceptual condition: we can in principle feel compassion for others without seeing their predicament as like one that we could experience.[22] Our compassion for the sufferings of animals is a fine example: we are indeed similar to animals in many ways, but we don't need that thought in order to see that what they suffer is bad, and in order to have compassion for them. For the purposes of the present argument, however, we shall see that the thought of similar possibilities has considerable importance in preventing or undoing anthropodenial; its absence is thus a sign of grave danger.

Finally, there is a further thought that is not mentioned in the tradition, which, according to me, must be mentioned: it is what I call the *eudaimonistic judgment*. This is a judgment or thought that places the suffering person or persons among the important parts of the life of the person who feels the emotion. It says, "They count for me: they are among my most important goals and projects." In my more general analysis of emotions, I argue that the major human emotions are always eudaimonistic, meaning focused on the agent's most important goals and projects, and seeing the world from the point of view of those goals, rather than from some impersonal vantage point. Thus we feel fear about damages that we see as significant for our own well-being and our other goals; we feel grief at the loss of someone who is already invested with a certain importance in our scheme of things.

Eudaimonism is not egoism. I am not claiming that emotions always view events and people as mere means to the agent's own satisfaction or happiness; indeed I strenuously deny this.[23] But the things that occasion a strong emotion in us are things that correspond to what we have invested with importance in our thoughts, implicit or explicit, about what is important in life. The thought of importance need not always antecede the compassionate response: the very vivid presentation of another person's plight may jump-start it, moving that person, temporarily, into the center of the things that matter. Thus, when people hear of an earthquake or some other comparable disaster, they often become intensely focused on the sufferings of the strangers involved, and these strangers really matter to them—for a time. As Adam Smith already observed, however, using the example of an earthquake in China, this focus is unstable, easily deflected back to oneself and one's immediate surroundings, unless more stable structures of concern are built upon it that ensure a continued concern with the people of that distant nation.[24]

What of empathy?[25] I define empathy as the ability to imagine the situation of the other. Empathy is not mere emotional contagion, for it requires entering into the predicament of *another*, and this, in turn, requires some type of distinction between self and other.[26] Empathy is not sufficient for compassion, for a sadist may have considerable empathy with the situation of another person, and use it to harm that person.[27] An actor may have consummate empathy with his or her character without any true compassion. (Indeed, an actor might play empathetically the part of a person to whom he or she deliberately refuses compassion, believing, for example, that the person brought all his suffering on himself, or that the person was upset about a predicament that is not really worth being upset about.)

Compassion is sometimes an outgrowth of empathy.[28] But it seems plain that we can have compassion for the suffering of creatures whose experience we cannot imagine well, or perhaps, even, at all. Of course we need some way of making sense to ourselves of the idea that they are suffering, that their predicament is really bad. But I believe that we can be convinced that animals of various sorts are suffering in the factory food industry, for example, without making much of an attempt to imagine what it is like to be a chicken or a pig. So I would say that empathy is not necessary for compassion. Often, however, it is extremely helpful. Given the imperfection of the human ability to assess predicaments, we should try as hard as we can to imagine the predicaments of others, and then see what we think about what we've imagined. I have also suggested that empathy involves something morally valuable in and of itself: namely, a recognition of the other as a center of experience. The empathetic torturer is very bad, but perhaps there is something worse still in the utter failure to recognize humanity.[29]

11.3

Now we are in a position to think about the continuities and discontinuities between human and animal compassion. The first thing to be said is that no nonhuman animal, so far as we know, has a robust conception of fault and non-fault; thus, the compassion of animals will potentially include many suffering people and animals to whom humans refuse compassion on grounds of fault. Animals notice suffering, and they notice it very keenly; they do not, however, form the idea, "This person is not a worthy object of compassion, because she brought her suffering upon herself." This difference is at work in my *Effi Briest* example: Effi's parents are blocked in their compassion for her suffering and her early death by the obsessive thought of her transgression against social norms. Although they are strongly inclined to have compassion when they see their child waste away, they nonetheless cannot in the end experience that emotion, because of the power of the thought that their daughter has done one of the worst things imaginable. Effi's father wonders whether Rollo is not to that extent wiser than they are, because his displacement of feeling toward Effi is not blocked.

We see here a defect of my account in *Upheavals*, which I have already acknowledged in responding to John Deigh's excellent critique of the book: I do not mention that there is a type of human compassion that is in that sense very similar to Rollo's, focusing on suffering without asking the question of fault. Young children typically have that sort of compassion, as Rousseau observes in *Emile*, saying of the boy's emotion: "Whether it is their fault is not now the question. Does he even know what fault is? Never violate the order of his knowledge..."[30] (Later on, *Emile* does learn about fault, and this is an important ingredient of his social maturity, since compassion must be regulated by the sense of justice.[31]) Even after the notion of fault takes root, humans remain capable of the simpler type of compassion. The idea of fault, however, will often block this simpler type, as it does in the case of Effi's parents.

Further research in this area may show that some animals have a rudimentary idea of fault. To the extent that they have an idea of rule-following, and of deviation from rule-following, as does seem likely for some species, they may well be able to form the idea that some creatures bring their predicaments upon themselves by violating rules.[32] To the extent that they lack the idea that one can choose to pursue some purposes rather than others, however, they would not be likely to go very far in the direction of distinguishing appropriate from inappropriate choices. To the extent that they lack that conception, the idea of bringing misery on oneself would remain in a rudimentary form.

The comparison between humans and animals, then, must focus on the idea of seriousness, the idea of similar possibilities, and what I have called the eudaimonistic judgment. To move further, let us consider three examples of animal compassion or proto-compassion.

Case A: In June 2006, a research team at McGill University.[33] gave a painful injection to some mice, which induced squealing and writhing. (It was a weak solution of acetic acid, so it had no long-term harmful effects.) Also in the cage at the time were other mice who were not injected. The experiment had many variants and complexities, but to cut to the chase, if the non-pained mice were paired with mice with whom they had previously lived, they showed signs of being upset. If the non-pained mice had not previously lived with the pained mice, they did not show the same signs of emotional distress. On this basis, the experimenters conclude that the lives of mice involve social complexity: familiarity with particular other mice prepares the way for a type of emotional contagion that is at least the precursor to empathy.

Case B. In Amboseli National Park in Africa, a young female elephant was shot by a poacher. Here is a description by Cynthia Moss of the reaction of other elephants in her group, a reaction typical in all three species of elephants:

> Teresia and Trista became frantic and knelt down and tried to lift her up. They worked their tusks under her back and under her head. At one point they succeeded in lifting her into a sitting position but her body flopped back down. Her family tried everything to rouse her, kicking and tusking her, and Tallulah even went off and collected a trunkful of grass and tried to stuff it into her mouth.

The elephants then sprinkled earth over the corpse, eventually covering it completely before moving off.[34]

Case C. George Pitcher and Ed Cone were watching TV one night in their Princeton home: a documentary about a little boy in England with a congenital heart ailment. After various medical reversals, the boy died. Pitcher, sitting on the floor, found his eyes filled with tears. Instantly their two dogs, Lupa and Remus, rushed to him, almost pushing him over, and licked his eyes and cheeks with plaintive whimpers.[35]

In the first case, we see something that we might call emotional contagion, that is, distress at the sight of another's distress, but we have no reason to ascribe to the mice any complex empathetic exercise of imagination, and no reason to ascribe any sophisticated thoughts, such as the thought of seriousness or the thought of similar possibilities. I would therefore not be inclined to call the response a genuine emotion. The experiment is certainly interesting, showing a natural response to the sight of the pain of another that is certainly among the precursors of compassion. (Rousseau made much of this natural response, observing that the sight of pain is more powerful in this respect than the sight of happiness: thus our weakness becomes a source of our connection to others.) The most interesting feature, obviously, is the fact that the mice are moved by the plight of mice they know, and not mice they don't know. This suggests a surprising degree of cognitive complexity, and something like an ancestor of my eudaimonistic judgment. The mice are not precisely *thinking*, "These are

my familiar pals, and their fate matters to me, whereas the fate of strangers doesn't matter"—but they have responses that are at least the basis
for forming that very standard human thought. (Moreover, in humans
the thought often influences action without being fully formulated, so
humans are in that sense not always so far from these mice.) They have
a personal point of view on the world that differentiates between some
mice and other mice.

The second and third cases are rather similar, though with significant
variations. In both, we see recognition of the seriousness of the other creature's plight. The elephants are obviously aware that something major
has happened to their friend: they recognize that her collapsed posture is
the sign of some serious problem, and their increasingly frantic attempts
to lift her up show their gradual awareness that the problem will not be
rectified. Pitcher's dogs know him well; like the elephants, they see that
something unusual is going on, something that looks serious. Notice that
the thought of seriousness tracks the actual suffering manifested by the
other party: there is not the same possibility as in the human case of
forming the thought, "This person is moaning and groaning, but the plight
is not really serious." Thus, if Pitcher were a rich person for whom the
thought of paying a just amount of tax brought tears of suffering to his
eyes, Lupa and Remus would behave in just the same way. On the other
side, if Pitcher were in a seriously bad way without being aware of it, and
thus without manifesting suffering, the dogs would not have compassion
for him.

Notice that, as in the case of Rollo and the Briests, there is a subtle difference between Pitcher's compassion for the little boy in the documentary and the compassion of the dogs for Pitcher: for the former is mediated
by the thought of non-fault in a way that the latter is not. Pitcher draws
attention to the fact that he was raised by a Christian Scientist mother
who thought that children (and others) were always to blame for their
illnesses, a very severe upbringing. Having rejected these ideas as an adult,
Pitcher is able to see the little boy as a victim of circumstances. I think
that his intense reaction to the documentary may have been connected to
the thought of himself as a boy, cut off from compassion because of the
blame that illness always brought with it: in part, he is having compassion for his own childhood self and the lack of care he experienced. The
thesis of Pitcher's book is the Fontane-like thesis that dogs are capable of
an unconditional type of love that humans have difficulty achieving: in
that sense the often errant judgment of fault, with its ability to disrupt
compassion, is very important to his whole analysis.

Pitcher, then, strongly suggests that the judgment of fault is always a
defect, and that animals are better off morally because they lack it. We
should probably not follow him all the way. Dogs' inability to form the
judgment of fault at times leads them to remain loyal despite cruel behavior. Women have frequently experienced a similar problem, and their failure to judge their abusers to be at fault can be a very serious failing. While

not following Pitcher all the way to a fault-free doctrine of unconditional love, however, we can certainly observe that humans often find fault erroneously, hastily, and on the basis of bad social norms—as indeed Pitcher's mother did, blaming his illnesses on his own guilt. To that extent, looking to animals for guidance would seem to be a wise thing to do.

Turning now to the eudaimonistic judgment, we see that, as with seriousness, there is some reasonable analogue in our second and third animal cases. The elephants think that the well-being of their fellow female matters and their behavior betrays their sense of that importance. The dogs, as is usual, ascribe immense importance to their narrow circle of humans, and react to Pitcher's distress in a way that they would never react to the distress of a stranger.

Given that it has recently been shown that elephants can form a conception of the self, passing the mirror test,[36] we should probably conclude that the elephants' ability to form something like the eudaimonistic judgment is more sophisticated than that of the two dogs: having the ability to distinguish self from other, they are able to form a conception of the self as having a distinctive set of goals and ends, to a greater degree, at any rate, than is possible for animals who do not form a conception of the self.

There is something like the eudaimonistic judgment in our two animal cases, then, but there is no reason to suppose that this thought possesses much flexibility. Elephants care about other elephants, and, above all, members of their group. (When they come upon the bones of other elephants, they attend to those bones with great concern, but they do not do this for bones of any other species.) Occasionally this concern is extended, through long experience, to a human who becomes something like a member of the group. Thus when researcher Joyce Poole returned to Kenya after a long absence, bringing her baby daughter, the elephants who knew her greeted her with the ceremony of trumpeting and defecating that typically greets the birth of a new elephant baby.[37] Dogs are much more standardly symbiotic: indeed, far from showing particular concern for dogs as such, they are far more likely to include in the circle of concern whatever creatures they know and live with, including humans, dogs, and, occasionally, even cats or horses. In neither case, however, is the circle of concern very responsive to argument or education. We cannot expect elephants to learn to care for the survival of other African species; we certainly cannot expect predatory animals to learn compassion for the species they kill; and we cannot expect dogs to attach themselves to a person or dog without prolonged experience. In the human case we hope, at least, that there is a good deal more flexibility than this: people can learn to care about the sufferings they inflict on animals by killing them for food; they can learn to care about the sufferings of people they have never met.

What about similar possibilities? Humans learn, fairly early, that there are some forms of vulnerability that human life contains for all: bodily frailty and disease, pain, wounds, death. Indeed, Rousseau believed that the inevitability of this learning was morality's great advantage in the war against hierarchy and domination: whenever a privileged group tries to think of itself as above the common human lot, this fragile self-deceptive stratagem is quickly exposed by life itself. Life is constantly teaching the lesson of human equality, in the form of exposure to a wide range of common human predicaments:

> Human beings are not naturally kings, or lords, or courtiers, or rich people. All are born naked and poor; all are subject to the miseries of life; to sorrows, ills, needs, and pains of every kind. Finally, all are condemned to death. This is what truly belongs to the human being. This is what no mortal is exempt from.[38]

So, to what extent do animals in our second and third cases form such ideas, and in what form? It seems likely that elephants do have some conception of death and of various related bad things, as standard events in elephant life. Their standard and almost ritualized responses to death indicate that they have at least a rudimentary conception of a species form of life and of the events that can disrupt it (or, as in the case of the birth of a child, enrich it). The fact that elephants can form a conception of the self is helpful in forming a conception of the elephant kind: for one can hardly recognize oneself as a member of a kind without recognizing oneself as a unit distinct from others. It seems less clear whether dogs have such ideas, though they certainly can remember experiences of hunger and pain, and, to that extent, conceive of such bad events as future possibilities for themselves.

11.4

Animal compassion is limited, focused on the near-at-hand and relatively rigid. It is, nonetheless, rather predictable, and the natural connection to the pain of another species' member remains relatively constant as a source of emotion in more sophisticated animals, despite variations in circumstance. Human compassion, as my opening cases suggests, is profoundly uneven and unreliable, in ways that make animals look, at times, like morally superior beings. Humans can markedly fail to have compassion for the very acute suffering of other humans, even their own children. They can also take a terrible delight in the infliction or the sight of suffering. Events that are paradigmatic occasions for compassionate response can elicit, instead, sadistic glee.

We can already see one way in which human compassion goes astray: through the judgment of fault. Having the generally valuable capacity to see ourselves as beings who can make choices, pursuing some inclinations and inhibiting others, we also develop the capacity to impute defective choice to others, and we inhibit compassion on that account. This capacity to think about fault and choice is generally valuable, a necessary part of moral life. And yet it can go badly astray. Sometimes it goes wrong because people want to insulate themselves from demands made by others. Thus, it is very convenient to blame the poor for their poverty and to refuse compassion on that account. If we think this way, we don't have to do anything about the situation of the poor.[39] Sometimes, defective social traditions play the deforming role: the idea that a woman who has sex outside marriage is for all time irredeemably stained, unworthy of friendship or love, was a prominent cultural attitude in nineteenth-century Germany, and it is this attitude that blocks the Briests from responding to their daughter's misery. Judgments of fault clearly suffer from a variety of distortions, which cannot be traced to a single source.

For the remainder of this chapter, however, I want to focus on just one central cause of distortion, which affects several of the thoughts intrinsic to compassion. This is what I have called "anthropodenial," the tendency of humans to define themselves as above the animal world and its bodily vulnerabilities. No other animal has this problem: no animal hates being an animal, wishes not to be an animal, tries to convince itself that it is not an animal. Anthropodenial has many aspects; let me, however, focus on its role in the generation of two emotions that are particularly likely to interfere with the formation of appropriate compassion: disgust and primitive shame. (Here I can only briefly state the conclusions of my earlier work on these two emotions, in both *Upheavals of Thought* and *Hiding From Humanity*.[40])

Human infants are extremely needy, physically helpless for far longer than the young of any other animal species. They are also extremely intelligent, able, for example, to recognize the difference between one human individual and another at a far earlier age than had previously been understood—around the age of two weeks, when infants are able to differentiate the smell of their own mother's milk on a breast pad from the smell of another woman's milk. The ability to distinguish reliably between the whole self and another whole self takes a bit longer, but it arrives early too, and between six months and a year a child become aware that it is not part of a symbiotic world of nourishment, but a distinct member of a world whose other members sometimes care for its needs and sometimes do not.

The child's world is painful. It sees what it needs, and it cannot move to get it. It is hungry and thirsty, but sometimes it gets fed right away and at other times not. Always, it suffers—from hunger, excretory distress, sleep disturbances, and all the familiar miseries of infant life, most of them not worrying to the parent, but profoundly agonizing to the infant. Sometimes, as in the womb, everything is perfect and the child is in a state of bliss, hooked up securely to sources of nourishment and pleasure; at other times, it is on its own and helpless. Unable as yet to form a secure conception of the likely return of comfort and security, it experiences (an inchoate form of) desolation and helplessness. Out of the infant's predicament, formed by the *sui generis* combination of helplessness with high cognitive ability, grow numerous emotions: fear that the needed things will never arrive; anger that they are being withheld; joy and even an incipient form of gratitude when needs are met; and, finally, shame.

Shame, in general, is a painful emotion directed at a perceived short-coming or inadequacy in the self. What I call "primitive shame" is a shame that takes as its object the shortcoming of not being omnipotent. In a sense, a baby expects to be omnipotent, because its prenatal experience and many of its postnatal experiences are experiences of a blissful completeness. It cannot yet comprehend the fact that the world has not been made for its needs, nor the fact that other human beings have their own entitlements and cannot minister constantly to the baby's needs. Its state, then, is one of what's often called infantile narcissism, so well captured in Freud's phrase "His Majesty the Baby." The flip side of infantile narcissism is primitive shame. "I'm the monarch, and yet, here I am, wet, cold, and hungry."

Shame, given narcissistic self-focusing, is connected to aggression: "I can't stand being this helpless, but it's your fault, since you are not waiting on me hand and foot." (Rousseau puts this very well in *Emile*, describing the way in which natural human weakness leads to a desire to turn others into one's slaves.) As time goes on, the infant's narcissism may to some extent be mitigated by the development of a capacity for genuine concern for others, and compassion based upon that concern. Learning to get along on one's own also helps: if one can to some extent supply one's own needs, the need for slaves becomes less urgent—the root of the entire program of education in *Emile*. Nonetheless, no human being likes being helpless, and as the inevitability of death dawns on one more and more, we all realize that we are truly helpless in the most important respect of all.

As people struggle to wrest the world to their purposes and to deny the shameful fact of helplessness, it often proves useful to target a group of humans as the ones who are the shameful ones, the weak ones: we are strong and not helpless at all, because we are able to dominate them. Thus, most societies create subordinate groups of stigmatized individuals, whom ideology depicts as brutish, weak, and incapable of transcendence: we fittingly dominate them, because they are shamefully bestial, and we, of course, have managed to rise above our animality.

Disgust aids this strategy. Around the age of two or three, the infant begins to experience a very strong negative emotion directed at its own bodily waste products. Disgust has been the subject of some extremely good experimental work by Paul Rozin and others, and through a wide range of experiments they conclude that the primary objects of disgust are seen as contaminating to the self because they are reminders of our own animality: our own bodily waste products, corpses, and animals who have properties that are linked with our own waste products, animality and mortality (ooziness, bad smell, etc.). I do not accept every detail of Rozin's argument, but in its basic lines it is very successful in explaining the occasions for disgust and its ideational content.

What is particularly interesting for our purposes is that people typically don't stop there. It's not enough to turn away from our own animality in revulsion: people seem to need a group of humans to bound themselves off against, who will come to symbolize the disgusting, the merely animal, thus bounding the dominant group off more securely from its own hated and feared traits. The underlying thought appears to be, "If I can successfully distinguish myself from those animalistic humans, I am that much further away from being merely animal myself." In most societies, women function as such disgust-groups; racial and ethnic minorities may also be stigmatized as dirty, smelly, slimy, and animal-like. (African-Americans and Jews have both been repeatedly stigmatized in this way.)

From this point onward, disgust and primitive shame work in close cooperation. Stigmatized as disgusting, subordinate groups are also branded as shameful: defective, unworthy, sullied, not able to rise to the heights of which transcendent humanity is capable. To the extent that the parties who are strenuously engaged in anthropodenial feel threatened, to that extent their stigmatization of the surrogates for their own animality becomes more aggressive.[41]

11.5

Now we are ready to understand how human compassion is infected by anthropodenial. Once one has targeted a person or group as emblematic of animal decay and animal weakness, this very segmentation of the moral universe will block the formation of an idea of similar possibilities and vulnerabilities. Instead of thinking, in Rousseauesque fashion, "The lot of these unhappy people could at any moment be my own," one will think, instead, "I am above all that. I could never suffer that." The disgusting bodily weakness of others, the shameful condition of mere animal humanity, is seen as foreign: as the way *women's bodies* so often are, or the way *African-American bodies* often have been. One may even become quite incapable of empathetic participation in the plight of these people: for one may see them as so brutish that they could not possibly have insides like one's own, and they are thus to be seen only as objects, the way humans frequently view animals.

This same deformed conception of the species infects the judgment of seriousness. If certain people are mere brutes, they cannot possibly suffer very much: they are just objects, automata, and the appearance of suffering does not reliably indicate a rich inner world, containing suffering similar to one's own.

Finally, shame and disgust infect the eudaimonistic judgment, the judgment of who belongs in one's circle of concern. Compassion is usually underinclusive, favoring the known over the not-known. That in itself poses a great challenge to moral education. In the cases that interest me, however, compassion also segments the known, judging some very familiar human individuals not truly worthy of concern.

Putting my claim this way, however, does not bring out the full riotous-ness of anthropodenial, its hysterical aggressiveness, driven by profound fear. As Rousseau noted, the denial of similar possibilities is a lie, a lie concerning important and obvious matters. And of course the disgust- and shame-driven denial is a version of that lie. You have a body that smells and excretes. I have no such body. You will die. I will not die. You are weak. I am omnipotent. The falsity of these declarations periodically makes itself evident to the declarer—every time he excretes, has sex, gets ill. Then, the denial has to be made in a louder and more aggressive tone of voice, so that it drowns out the voice of truth. Thus a vicious ratcheting process begins, with the voice of anthropodenial more and more aggres-sive—until it demands the utter extinction of the being whose evident kinship to oneself inconveniently exposes the deception.

This vicious process is abetted by, and, to an extent, embodied in, ste-reotypes of masculinity that define the "real man" as one who is sufficient unto himself, in need of nobody, able to rise above the weakness of the mere animal body. In surprisingly many cultures, males, particularly males who have long endured humiliation of some type, tell themselves that a real man must be able to throw off all weakness, like a very efficient machine, displaying his total lack of connection to female receptivity and weakness. One remarkable and extreme form of this view was the widely influential statement of late nineteenth-century German sex-theorist Otto Weininger that women are the body of the man, and that men must repudiate all in themselves that is bodily, ergo female.[42]

Anthropodenial is thus linked with an aggressive and potentially violent misogyny, and it is in relations with women, far more than relations with subordinate ethnic or racial groups, that the anxiety about the unmasking of the lie becomes most prominent. Woman, because of her obvious con-nection with birth and sexual intercourse, comes to emblematize animal nature. The person who is desperate to deny animal nature must not only deny that he is a woman, he must also deny all commonality between him and the woman, imagining himself as sharing none of the inconvenient traits that make woman an object of disgust and shame. But he cannot avoid contact with women, as he may be able to avoid contact with Jews, or blacks, or Muslims. Indeed, he finds himself strongly desiring such con-tact, and repeatedly engaging in very intimate forms of bodily exchange, involving sweat and semen and other signs of his own true nature.[43] So disgust (as so often) follows this descent into the animal, and the only way out of the disgust is to blame it on the woman, to accuse her of luring the otherwise transcendent being into the animal realm. As he repeatedly enters that realm, the denial of his membership must be made in a louder voice, and his conception of himself must be made more metallic, more invulnerable, until the demand for the total extinction of the female, both in the self and in the world, is the logical outcome. The female must be extinguished in the world because she is in the self. She can only cease to be in the self if she ceases to be in the world. And of course compassion, the affirmation of commonality and personal significance, will have been blocked long since.

Let us now return to my three cases, seeing how it happens that humans fall so far below the kindly dogs and elephants, and even below ferocious tigers and lions, who might kill a woman for prey, out of instinct, but not for self-insulation, out of fantasy and denial of their own nature. The case of Tolstoy's murdering husband is a classic case for my thesis. He clearly feels disgust for the female body, and for the sexual act that draws him toward that body. At the same time, he cannot stop feeling himself drawn there, and the very strength of his desire threatens, again and again, to expose his project of rising above the animal. Sexuality and its vulnerabilities are difficult enough for any human being to deal with at any time. All cultures probably contain seeds of violence in connection with sexuality. But a person who has been taught to have a big stake in being above the sexual domain, above the merely animal, cannot bear to be dragged into that domain. And yet, of course, the very denial and repression of the sexual build within a mounting tension. (Tolstoy's diaries describe how the tension mounts and mounts inside him until he has to use his wife, and then he despises her, despises himself, and wants to use force against her to stop the cycle from continuing.) In the end, the husband sees, there is nothing to be done, but to kill the woman. And the husband also suggests that there is no way for women to prevent themselves from being killed by men, unless they stop being animal, sexual bodies, forgoing intercourse. Join the project of anthropodenial, conceal your bodily nature, and you might possibly be saved. While his wife lives, he cannot have compassion for her, because he cannot see her as human: she is an animal, a brute, utterly dissimilar and terrifyingly similar. She is forcibly ejected from his circle of concern by the sheer terror that her presence arouses. Dead, she suddenly looks more like a nonanimal: she no longer has the animal magnetism that repels him, she seems like she might even have been a rational being.

Effi's parents fail to have compassion for her, despite her evident suffering—so moving to Fontane's reader, as to Rollo—because of a deformation in their judgment of fault, we said. But where does that deformation come from? As we soon see, studying the novel further, Effi's is a culture (like so many) that divides women into two types: pure angels, who are not animals, and disgusting whores, who are mere animals. There can be no compassion for the latter, because their base nature brought calamity upon them, and it is just the normal outcome of having a base nature, not really a calamity at all. Thus, the judgment of fault is interwoven with a defective judgment of similarity: much though we thought of her as our child, she must all along have had a disgusting nature, more like the nature of an animal. (That is why Frau von Briest's suggestion that Effi's misdeed resulted not from evil, but, rather, from being married too young, is so threatening to both of them: go down this track, and the whole balance of their human relations would have to be called into question.)

They eject her from their circle of concern through their reasoning about dissimilarity and nature-based fault, and they will not permit truth and reason to threaten the self-protective structure they have built up. Rollo, for his part, thinks nothing of fault and sees only the immensity of Effi's suffering; nor does he segment the world into the pure and the impure. It never occurred to him that there was anything wrong with having a bodily nature.

While depicting the parents' warped judgments of fault, Fontane cultivates in his reader, from the novel's start, a Rollo-like disposition, unjudgmental, focused on actual suffering, and skeptical of social norms about women.[44] Indeed, the reader has for some time understood very well what the von Briests dimly intuit at the end, that Effi, high-spirited and far from evil, was simply too young to get married. Guided by the nonmoral Rollo-like compassion that the reader has formed toward Effi from the very start of the novel, the reader forms judgments of fault, at the end (blaming the parents, the husband, and the surrounding society) that are far more accurate than those formed by Effi's parents.

Now to Gujarat. Lurking beneath any culturally specific scenario lies the general human longing we have described: to escape from a reality that is found to be too dirty, too mortal, too decaying. For a group powerful enough to subordinate another group, escape may possibly be found (in fantasy) through stigmatization of, and aggression against, the group that exemplifies the properties, the dominant group finds shameful and revolting in itself. When this dynamic is enacted toward women, who are at the same time alluring, the combination of desire and revulsion or shame may cause a particularly unstable relationship to develop, with violence always waiting in the wings. Women of a minority group that has already been stigmatized as shameful become targets of reactive shame in a double, and doubly intense, way.[45] The body of the woman, always a convenient vehicle for such displacement, becomes all the more alluring as a target when it is the body of the discredited and feared "other," in this case the hyperfertile and hyperbodily Muslim woman.[46]

In the cultural and historical circumstances of (many) Gujarati Hindu males—to some extent real, to some extent fantasized—conditions are created to heighten anxiety and remove barriers to its expression. Ideology tells such men that they have for centuries been subordinated, first by Muslims and then by the British, and subordinated on account of a Hindu sexuality that is too playful, too sensuous, and too unaggressive. To be as powerful as the Victorian conqueror, the Hindu male must show himself to be both pure and consummately warlike.[47]

At the same time, conditions that would have militated against these tendencies—a public critical culture, a robust development of the sympathetic imagination—were particularly absent in Gujarati schools and civil society. (Here my analysis converges very strongly with Glover's, in identifying a set of factors that might have blocked the turn to violence.) This specific cultural scenario explains why we might expect the members of the Hindu right, and the men to whom they make their political appeal, to exhibit an unusual degree of disgust anxiety, as manifested in a paranoid insistence on the Hindu male's purity and freedom from lust—and, at the same time, his consummate aggressiveness.

The hate literature circulated during the pogrom portrays the Muslim woman as hypersexual, enjoying the penises of many men. That is not by itself unusual; Muslim women have often been portrayed in that denigrating way, as closer to the animal than other women. But it then introduces a new element: the desire that is imputed to these women is to be penetrated by an uncircumcised penis. Thus, the Hindu male creates a pornographic fantasy with himself as its subject. In one way, these images show anxiety about virility, assuaging it by imagining the successful conquest of Muslim women. But of course, like Tolstoy's husband's fantasies, these are not fantasies of intercourse only. The idea of this intercourse is inseparable from ideas of mutilation and violence. Fucking a Muslim woman just means killing her. The fantasy image of the untying of the penises that were "tied until now" is very reminiscent of the explosions of violence in Tolstoy, only the logic has been carried one small step further: instead of murder following sex, because of sex, the murder just *is* the sex. Women are killed precisely by having large metal objects inserted into their vaginas.

In this way, the image is constructed of a sexuality that is so effective, so closely allied with the desire for domination and purity, that its penis just is a pure metal weapon, not a sticky thing of flesh and blood. The Hindu male does not even need to dirty his penis with the contaminating fluids of the Muslim woman. He can fuck her with the clean nonporous metal weapon that kills her, remaining pure himself, and securely above the animal. Sexuality itself carries out the project of annihilating the sexual. Nothing is left to inspire fear.

A useful comparison is the depiction of warlike masculinity in a novel of Ernst Jünger, *Kampf als inneres Erlebnis, Battle as Inner Experience*:

> These are the figures of steel whose eagle eyes dart between whirling propellers to pierce the cloud; who dare the hellish crossing through fields of roaring craters, gripped in the chaos of tank engines...men relentlessly saturated with the spirit of battle, men whose urgent wanting discharges itself in a single concentrated and determined release of energy.
>
> As I watch them noiselessly slicing alleyways into barbed wire, digging steps to storm outward, synchronizing luminous watches, finding the North by the stars, the recognition flashes: this is the new man. The pioneers of storm, the elect of central Europe. A whole new race, intelligent, strong, men of will...supple predators straining with energy. They will be architects building on the ruined foundations of the world.[48]

In this fascinating passage, Jünger combines images of machinery with images of male aggressiveness to express the thought that the new man must be in some sense both predatory and invulnerable. The one thing he must never be is human. His masculinity is characterized not by animal need and receptivity, but by a "concentrated and determined release of energy." He knows no fear, no sadness. Why must the new man have these properties? Because the world's foundations have been ruined. Jünger suggests that the only choices, for males living amid death and destruction, are either to yield to an immense and ineluctable sadness or to throw off the humanity that inconveniently inflicts pain.

Something like this paranoia, this refusal of compromised humanity, infects the rhetoric of the Hindu right, and, indeed, may help explain its original founders' fascination with German fascism, as well as manifesting the influence, over time, of that same ideology. The woman functions as a symbol of the site of animal weakness and vulnerability inside any male, who can be drawn into his own mortality through desire. The Muslim woman functions double as such a symbol. In this way, a fantasy is created that her annihilation will lead to safety and invulnerability—perhaps, to "India Shining," the Jünger-like Hindu-right campaign slogan that betrays a desire for a crystalline sort of domination.[49]

Only this complex logic explains, I believe, why torture and mutilation are preferred as alternatives to abduction and impregnation—or even simple homicide. Only this logic explains why the fantasy of penetrating the sexual body with a large metal object played such a prominent role in the carnage. Only this explains, as well, the repetitious destruction of the woman's body by fire, as though the world cannot be clean until all vestiges of the female body are obliterated from its face.

Human beings are animals, and we inhabit the animal world. We should learn all we can from continuities between the emotions of humans and those of other animals. The diseases of human life, however, are, for the most part, diseases that are utterly foreign to the world of elephants and bonobos, even the more aggressive chimpanzees, because these diseases—many of them, at any rate—spring from a hatred of embodiment and death, of the condition of being an animal—and the human is the only animal that hates its own animality. Jonathan Glover's wonderful inquiry into human depravity refers, in its title, to a problem: "humanity" means the condition of being human, which we are stuck with, but it is also used by Glover to mean sympathy, respect, and kindliness, qualities opposed to "inhumanity," which, as he shows, we humans all too often exhibit. I have argued that "humanity," the condition of being (merely, animally) human, and our painful awareness of that non-transcendent condition, are major sources of "inhumanity," the ability to withhold compassion and respect from other human beings. My argument suggests that a deeper inquiry into the unique problems that humans have in dealing with their mortality, decay, and general animal vulnerability will help us understand inhumanity more fully. Without this further inquiry, indeed, we have little hope of coming up with an adequate account of gendered violence, or of the aspects of violence in general that are implicitly gendered, involving a repudiation of the filth, stickiness, and non-hardness that are the lot of all human beings, but that are all too often imputed to the female body alone.[50]

11.6 POSTSCRIPT

When I think of Jonathan Glover, I immediately think of his compassion. We worked together at the World Institute for Development Economics Research in Helsinki, initially during a time of personal stress for me, and I will always be grateful for the precision of his attention and the pleasure of his company, as well as, of course, the wonderful quality of his philosophical contributions. Later, I lived during two summers in Oxford (while he went back to London for the vacation) in the little college house he used during the term, and I first was drawn to this topic by reading the wonderful books on violence and inhumanity that he had stored there. But I think the stimulus of his own humane and gentle personality was more important by far than the books in generating these thoughts, and I dedicate this chapter to him with deep friendship.

Notes

I am extremely grateful to the editors for their subtle and helpful comments.

1. Not, of course, that they count *as* failures in thinking about nonhuman animals.

2. See Frans de Waal, *Primates and Philosophers: How Morality Evolved* (Princeton, NJ: Princeton University Press, 2006), appendix A, 59–67.

3. Thus "anthropodenial" is a trait that only humans can have: it is the tendency to deny our humanity, or to hide from it. It is conceptually possible for a different sort of animal to have a related flaw, denying that it is the species of animal that it is. In fact, however, this sort of denial appears to be present only in our species.

4. Published in 1894; my own translation from the German.

5. Published 1889; for its close relationship to Tolstoy's diaries concerning his sexual relationship with his wife, see Andrea Dworkin, "Repulsion," in *Intercourse* (New York: The Free Press 1987), pp. 3–20.

6. See Nussbaum, *The Clash Within: Democracy, Religious Violence, and India's Future* (Cambridge, MA: Harvard University Press, 2007), particularly ch. 6, which cites the full text of the pamphlet.

7. *Primates and Philosophers.*

8. See particularly the responses by Christine Korsgaard ("Morality and the Distinctiveness of Human Action") and Philip Kitcher ("Ethics and Evolution: How to Get Here from There") in *Primates and Philosophers*, 98–119, 120–39.

9. Korsgaard, p. 104. See also p. 118: "The distinctiveness of human action is as much a source of our capacity for evil as of our capacity for good."

10. In *Upheavals of Thought: The Intelligence of Emotions* (Cambridge: Cambridge University Press, 2001), ch. 6; see also some elaborations in the response to John Deigh in "Responses," to the book symposium on that book in *Philosophy and Phenomenological Research* 68 (2004) 473–86 and in "Compassion and Terror," *Daedalus* Winter 2003, 10–26.

11. This part of my argument will be closely related to chapters 5 and 15 (on Whitman) of *Upheavals*, and especially *to Hiding From Humanity: Disgust, Shame, and the Law* (Princeton, NJ: Princeton University Press, 2004).

12. Jonathan Glover, *Humanity: A Moral History of the Twentieth Century* (London: Jonathan Cape, 1999).

13. He actually uses, throughout, the term "sympathy," but very much in the way that I use the term "compassion," so I hope I shall be forgiven to sticking to the usage I have already established; on the terms, see *Upheavals*, 301–04. As I note there, Adam Smith uses "compassion" for fellow-feeling with another's pain, "sympathy" for the broader tendency to have fellow feeling with "any passion whatever." This difference is immaterial in the present context, since we are speaking of pain only.

14. Klaus Theweleit, *Male Fantasies*, two volumes, English edition (Minneapolis, MN: University of Minnesota Press, 1987 and 1989). See *Humanity*, p. 343.

15. Ibid.

16. On 343, he writes: "Like many Freudian interpretations, Theweleit's account is suggestive but hard to test." Elsewhere, however, Glover does draw attention to a related matter, the tendency of people to compare subordinate groups to animals: see, for example, p. 339.

17. *Upheavals*, ch. 6, pp. 304–35.

18. Again, see *Upheavals*, pp. 301–14; I avoid the term "pity" because, although used synonymously with "compassion" in translating Greek tragedies and Rousseau's French term *pitié*, in modern English it has acquired connotations of condescension and superiority that it did not have earlier, and I am focusing on an emotion that does not necessarily involve superiority.

19. See *Upheavals*, ch. 6.

20. *Misery and Company: Sympathy in Everyday Life* (Chicago, IL: University of Chicago Press, 1997).

21. See my discussion of her findings in *Upheavals*, pp. 313–14.

22. See *Upheavals*, pp. 315–21.

23. See *Upheavals*, pp. 31–33.

24. Smith, *The Theory of Moral Sentiments*, ed. D.D. Raphael and A.L. Macfie (Indianapolis, IA: Liberty Classics, 1976), p. 136:

> Let us suppose that the great empire of China, with all its myriads of inhabitants, was suddenly swallowed up by an earthquake, and let us consider how a man of humanity in Europe, who had no sort of connexion with that part of the world, would be affected upon receiving intelligence of this dreadful calamity. He would, I imagine, first of all, express very strongly his sorrow for the misfortune of that unhappy people, he would make many melancholy reflections upon the precariousness of human life, and the vanity of all the labours of man, which could thus be annihilated in a moment.... And when all this fine philosophy was over, when all these humane sentiments had been once fairly expressed, he would pursue his business or his pleasure, take his repose or his diversion, with the same ease and tranquillity, as if no such accident had happened. The most frivolous disaster which could befal himself would occasion a more real disturbance. If he was to lose his little finger tomorrow, he would not sleep tonight; but, provided he never saw them, he will snore with the more profound security over the ruin of a hundred millions of his brethren, and the destruction of that immense multitude seems plainly an object less interesting to him, than this paltry misfortune of his own.

25. See *Upheavals*, 327–34.

26. For a similar view, see de Waal, *Primates and Philosophers*, pp. 26–27; Nussbaum, *Upheavals*, pp. 327–28.

27. For a similar argument, see de Waal, *Good Natured: The Origins of Right and Wrong in Humans and Other Animals* (Cambridge, MA: Harvard University Press, 1996), p. 41; Upheavals, p. 329.

28. Important research on this topic has been done by C. Daniel Batson, whose experiments typically involve one group who are asked to imagine vividly the plight of a person whose story is being read to them, and another group who are asked merely to assess the technical qualities of the broadcast. The first group is far more likely to report an experience of compassion, and also more likely (indeed, very likely) to do something to help the person, provided that there is a helpful thing that is ready to hand and does not exact too high a cost. See Batson, *The Altruism Question* (Hillsdale, NJ: Lawrence Erlbaum Associates, 1991).

29. See *Upheavals*, p. 333: Here I discuss Heinz Kohut's remarks about the Nazis, and I consider a variety of different types of psychopaths.

30. Rousseau, *Emile*, trans. Allan Bloom (New York: Basic Books, 1979), p. 224.

31. P. 253. Rousseau puts the introduction of the idea of fault extremely late in the child's development: Emile is already going through puberty before he even experiences compassion (given Rousseau's belief that he will be turned toward others in the first place only by awakening sexual energy), and the thought of fault comes along considerably later than that. I think, by contrast, that children start to ask questions about fault as early as they are able to feel guilt about their own aggression, probably around the age of five or six, and it is only before that that their compassion is consistently of the simple Rollo variety.

32. See de Waal, *Good Natured*, pp. 89–117; Marc Hauser, *Wild Minds: What Animals Really Think* (New York: Henry Holt, 2000), pp. 249–53, argues for a thinner account of animal understanding of rules, denying any rich connection between rule-following and moral agency.

33. Dale J. Langford, Sara E. Crager, Zarrar Shehzad, Shad B. Smith, Susana G. Sotocinal, Jeremy S. Levenstadt, Mona Lisa Chanda, Daniel J. Levitin, and Jeffrey S. Mogil, "Social Modulation of Pain as Evidence for Empathy in Mice," *Science* 312 (2006), 1967–70.

34. Cynthia Moss, *Elephant Memories: Thirteen Years in the Life of an Elephant Family* (Chicago, IL: University of Chicago Press, second edition 2000), p. 73; see also Katy Payne, "Sources of Social Complexity in the Three Elephant Species," in *Animal Social Complexity: Intelligence, Culture, and Individualized Societies*, ed. Frans B. M. de Waal and Peter L. Tyack (Cambridge, MA: Harvard University Press, 2000), pp. 57–86.

35. George Pitcher, *The Dogs Who Came To Stay* (New York: Dutton, 1995), discussed in my *Upheavals*, p. 90 and in "Responses: Response to Deigh."

36. See Joshua Plotnik, Frans de Waal, and Diana Reiss, "Self-Recognition in an Asian Elephant," *Proceedings of the National Academy of Sciences*, published online October 30, 2006.

37. Joyce Poole, *Coming of Age With Elephants* (New York: Hyperion, 1997).

38. *Emile*, p. 222 (with a few revisions to the Bloom translation: "Human beings" is substituted for "Men," "rich people" for "rich men," "the human being" for "man."

39. Clark (see above) finds that this attitude is extremely common in America. Of course, even if we did believe that the poor are poor on account of bad choices, it would not follow that we should have no compassion for their situation: for, as Thomas Paine already observed in *The Rights of Man*, we might conclude that bad choices were themselves an outgrowth of stunting social circumstances, such as lack of adequate education and employment opportunities.

40. I give no references to the psychological literature here, since they are given in great detail in those two books, particularly the latter.

41. Glover draws attention to the many ways in which subordination and violence rely on stigmatization and disgust: see especially pp. 338–9, 340–2, 356.

42. Weininger, *Sex and Character*, anonymous translation from 6th German edition (London and New York: William Heinemann and G.P. Putnam's Sons, no date given—the 1st German edition was published in 1903). This crazy book, by a self-hating Jew and homosexual, had a huge influence, and was considered by Ludwig Wittgenstein to be a work of genius. I discuss some of its wilder claims in *Hiding*.

43. A very good treatment of this question is in William Ian Miller, *The Anatomy of Disgust* (Cambridge, MA: Harvard University Press, 1997)—again, discussed in detail in *Hiding*.

44. See my more general study of Fontane's critique of social norms of gender and purity, in "A Novel in Which Nothing Happens: Fontane's Der Stechlin and Literary Friendship," in Alice Crary, ed., *Wittgenstein and the Moral Life: Essays in Honor of Cora Diamond* (Cambridge, MA: MIT Press, 2007), pp. 327–54.

45. For the stigmatization of minorities as a device to cement a sense of national identity, see *Clash* ch. 6, drawing on George L. Mosse's classic *Nationalism and Sexuality: Middle-Class Morality and Sexual Norms in Modern Europe* (Madison, WI: University of Wisconsin Press, 1985).

46. For the role of a myth of the Muslim woman as hyperfertile—which plays a tremendously prominent role in Gujarati political rhetoric—see *Clash*, ch. 6. Narendra Modi's campaign slogan, on the way to his landslide (postriot) electoral victory in 2002, was "We are two and we have two; they are five and they have twenty-five." In other words, Hindus are monogamous and relatively chaste, only two children per couple; Muslims are polygamous, each man having four wives, and each wife, hyperfertile, has 6.25 children! In reality, the rate of polygamy is identical for Hindus and Muslims, around 5 percent (though it is illegal for Hindus and legal for Muslims), and the growth rates of the two populations are just the same, and not very high.

47. See the cultural and historical material in *Clash*, ch. 6, showing the way in which British contempt for the type of sexuality typical in Hindu mythology contributed to this pervasive climate of shame. A very perceptive example occurs in Rabindranath Tagore's novel *The Home and the World* (1916), concerning the rise of the Hindu nationalist movement. His nationalist antihero finds himself unable to rape the woman he desires, and he is ashamed of that failure. He muses to himself that there are two types of music: the Hindu flute and the British military band. He wishes he could hear in his blood the music of the military band, rather than that disturbingly nonaggressive flute.

48. See discussion in Klaus Theweleit, *Male Fantasies*, vol. 2, 160–2, and in Glover, p. 343 (see above).

49. Interestingly, L.K. Advani, the current leader of the BJP, the political party of the Hindu right, just announced that this slogan was a mistake: they should have said "India Rising." (*Times of India*, December 17, see http://timesofindia.indiatimes.com/articleshow/2629479.cms). Advani, though a hardliner, is extremely perceptive, and he understands, it would seem, that the idea of purity and perfection offended rural voters, whose lives were not particularly shining. Perhaps, too, at a deeper level he understands the importance of not pretending to a manhood that is invulnerable and above others. (As I discuss in *Clash*, ch. 5, Advani's decision to make a respectful visit to the tomb of Mohammed Ali Jinnah, the founder of Pakistan, was greeted with hoots of outraged masculinity by many members of his own group, who accused him of "sucking Jinnah's cock," and other things of this sort.)

50. On filth as a Nazi preoccupation, see Glover, pp. 339, 356.

VI

PERSONAL

12

Jonathan Glover

Alan Ryan

This brief sketch is not intended to do justice to Jonathan Glover's philosophical career, nor yet to the benign influence he has had on the public discussion of topics ranging from population policy to mental illness, and the care (or detention) of individuals with potentially dangerous personality disorders. It is a self-indulgent essay, whose purpose is to conjure up something of the pleasure of working with Jonathan as a colleague, something of the impact he had on his students, and a little of the flavor of the period when I first encountered him. My philosophically intended observations are offered somewhat in passing, since my own aim in what follows is to express my thanks for the most interesting conversations of my life.

First, a little geography; Jonathan went to school at Tonbridge, and read philosophy, physiology, and psychology at Corpus Christi College, Oxford. I went to Christ's Hospital and read Philosophy, Politics, and Economics (PPE) at Balliol. Jonathan and I had encountered each other in passing during our undergraduate years—the very early 1960s; but we met properly only when I was elected to a politics fellowship at New College in 1969. Jonathan had been elected to a fellowship in philosophy three years earlier. By rights he should not have been; New College had set out to find a classical philosopher to succeed David Wiggins, but happily went on to behave as an institution in search of a philosopher should, and took instead the cleverest and most interesting person they could find. At that time, Jonathan was a lecturer at Christ Church, but Tony Quinton contrived the move to New College, where Jonathan remained for more than thirty years.

I was a renegade moral philosopher in the sense that my tastes ran to political theory and the philosophy of the social sciences, taught to social scientists rather than 'pure' philosophers; I spent much time apologizing to Jonathan for the fact that I had already forgotten most of the philosophy I once knew, and was reassured when he replied that I still did what he understood to be philosophy, while unnamed others did what he thought might be a branch of engineering, but did not appear to be philosophy.

This was not luddism; nobody watching Jonathan giving Derek Parfit and Jim Griffin a hard time over rival conceptions of utilitarian ethics could have been in any doubt that rigor came entirely naturally to him. The point, I think, was always that he thought that the method of inquiry should be tailored to the problem in hand, not *vice versa*. It was not that he thought that the "engineering" mode of doing philosophy yielded nothing, but that the distance between the concerns of the engineers and those of moral and political theorists was so great that applying the techniques of the former to the concerns of the latter was unlikely to be fruitful. He was even then unusually attentive to what a theory of ethics implied for practice. What we today take for granted was not so taken in the heyday of R. M. Hare's little book, *The Language of Morals*. The idea that moral philosophy should confine itself to the informal logic of moral discourse never occurred to Jonathan. In justice, it must be said that it was a view abandoned by Hare himself.

Jonathan taught both ethics and the philosophy of mind; in the Oxford system, that meant that he taught many students of whom I saw nothing—students studying philosophy and psychology, for instance. Undergraduates taking PPE were another matter. I do not know what they told Jonathan about working with me, but I know what they told me about working with Jonathan. Indeed, at a New College reunion some months ago, half a dozen of them made a beeline for me to revive their memories of thirty-year-old tutorials with him. They were both awestruck and vastly entertained. The entertainment was partly a matter of Jonathan's fertility in dreaming up counterexamples to the conventional wisdom of the day; the 'Mexican baked bean banditry' example was the best known of these, and became part of the literature on why we ought not to assume too swiftly that marginal changes for the worse don't matter. For those too young to recall, the thought-experiment requires you to test your intuition that stealing a whole plateful of beans from a peasant is very bad for simple utilitarian reasons, while taking one bean from a plate of a hundred beans isn't wrong, by comparing the effect of a hundred bandits taking one plate apiece from a hundred peasants versus the same hundred bandits taking one bean apiece from the same one hundred peasants.

What unnerved the students was the sense that Jonathan had seen right into the depths of their minds and was both amused at the chaos he saw and puzzled that their minds could be in such a disheveled state. This was a pretty accurate assessment of what Jonathan himself thought at the time. Unlike me, he never became exasperated with his students, regarding it as a privilege to be allowed to earn his living exploring the recesses of other people's minds. He was not even particularly pained by the chaos he uncovered, though he was often astonished at it. His pedagogical style was very like that of G. E. Moore in Keynes's famous memoir; there was never the least hint of aggression, and very rarely anything one could call direct contradiction. 'Oh! Do you really think that . . . ?' was quite enough to persuade most students, and certainly myself, that we were talking utter nonsense even if we weren't yet sure how.

Practically, one could hardly have been more chaotic than Jonathan without imperiling one's chances of survival. In the late 1960s, New College was not particularly hard up, but on the whole the then bursar preferred not to maintain a tutor's rooms unless he complained very loudly about their draughty, insanitary, inelegant, or otherwise unsatisfactory condition. And although the college was not hierarchical, there was a general assumption that roughing it was good for young people—and in the mid-1960s we were all appointed to our fellowships absurdly young; most of us felt that thirty marked the beginning of old age. So Jonathan taught in the sitting room of a house that gently fell to pieces around him; students maintained that mice ran across the floor unnoticed by Jonathan, but I never quite believed them. Still, he gained and kept a reputation for spectacular unworldliness in practical affairs.

I experienced this at first hand when he and I shared a house in Camden Town in the 1970s. Jonathan, Vivette, and his two—soon to be three— children lived in a flat above, and my wife and I lived in a flat below. Intellectually speaking, things could not have been better. *Causing Death and Saving Lives* took shape on the front doorstep, while our impatient families suggested more or less loudly that it was perhaps time that their needs were attended to, and that the importance of autonomy to our conception of the human person could wait while for resolution until they had been fed and watered. But Jonathan's capacities as a philosopher were markedly in advance of his plumbing skills, and a good deal of our social interaction revolved around tracing the latest leak that had brought down one or another ceiling in our flat. On one occasion, a contrite Jonathan announced that he was relieved that our two largest rooms were not directly underneath any of his pipe work, only to be reduced to helpless giggles when my wife announced that she found his assurances wholly unconvincing: when gravity failed, the flooding would be all done by mirrors.

Whether Jonathan had worse luck with plumbing than with cars was always a moot point. At this distance in time, it is hard to recall which was the vehicle whose driver's door simply dropped off as Jonathan opened it, and which of them produced a Jacques Tati moment when he tried to open the bonnet, pulled on the little handle that undid the bonnet catch, and found himself the recipient of some five yards of wire—as well as the problem of opening the bonnet now that the wire had come away from the catch. Whether any of this reflected on Jonathan's philosophical tastes is open to argument; I think it was only later that either he or I began to become self-conscious about the extent to which the sheer recalcitrance of the world, human and nonhuman alike, ought to set limits to our theorizing about what outcomes would be desirable if only we could achieve them, and began to think how to build the recalcitrance into the basis of our thinking, rather than to acknowledge it only after constructing an ideal theory.

One occasion when everyday life impinged on our arguments was when Jonathan discovered a nest of mice in a packet of cornflakes; the author of *Causing Death and Saving Lives* turned out to be very squeamish about handling mice. I hope I simply picked up the packet and tipped them into the garden, but I fear that I may have flushed them down the toilet. I, of course, had been trying to argue some kind of 'respect for life as such' case against Jonathan's ingeniously utilitarian approach to these issues, and found I had rather less respect for the lives of small rodents than I had thought, while Jonathan had rather more. But, then he was the sweetest-natured person I had ever encountered.

Jonathan's impracticality was at least partly a pose. I don't think he ever read the little essay in autobiography, that Dewey wrote for his seventieth birthday celebrations in 1929. A piece of advice that Dewey proffered to his younger colleagues was to cultivate a reputation for being a complete disaster on committees. One problem about his doing so at New College was that most of the tutors with whom Jonathan and I worked were quite unfeignedly prone to lose papers, turn up at the wrong time or on the wrong day, and to rearrange teaching schedules entirely off the tops of their heads. Conversely, most of our colleagues who were adept committee men had views on the purpose and organization of the college that might have embarrassed Genghis Khan.

Still, Jonathan gave quite a persuasive impression of being the sort of person you'd not want to have in charge of your expedition to the South Pole—until it mattered. Then, his Colonial Office pedigree would suddenly emerge and we would watch open-mouthed as he skewered opponents of the particular policy he was advocating, and made support for his views seem the only thing open to a person of even modest intellectual attainments and moral integrity. It was a mode that particularly suited the campaign to drag New College into the twentieth century in the matter of coeducation—strictly co-residence, since the sexes were taught together already. The polite incredulity with which he greeted the increasingly desperate arguments of the reactionaries was a technique I admired, but never mastered.

It was a source of deep regret that no sooner had I returned from Princeton to look after New College than Jonathan took off for King's College, London, and the Centre for Medical Law and Ethics. By this time, Jonathan had published widely on the implications of advances in genetics, as he continued to do in well-received little books such as *Choosing Children*, published in 2006. *What Sort of People Should There Be?* in 1984 preceded his work later in that decade for the European Commission on the ethical implications of the new reproductive technologies. It is probably politically impossible to put a man in charge of the United Kingdom Human Fertilisation and Embryology Authority, but it is a pity that Jonathan's humane common sense was never given full scope in some of the controversies in which that body has been embroiled since its institution in 1991.

The subjects Jonathan has tackled have almost invariably been controversial. This was hardly an accident: in an interview with *The Guardian* at the time of the publication of *Humanity* he said "Having been teaching ethics for a very long time...I'm struck by how little reference is ever made to the terrible things that have happened in the 20th Century. Ethics ought to be rooted in some idea of the way in which human nature can go wrong and produce these disasters." The sense that human nature is prone to catastrophic errors, not only of judgment but also of motivation has permeated a good deal of Jonathan's work over the past two decades. It has taken him in very different directions; one is more or less global, as he has from time to time commented on the horrors of civil wars and on the follies of American foreign policy in Iraq and elsewhere; another is much more local, with forays into trying to assist the UK Home Office in its attempts to devise a humane way of controlling predictably dangerous persons who have not yet committed a seriously violent crime, but who are overwhelmingly likely to do so. Behind that lies the concern that animated his Tanner Lecture in 2003, for a better informed and more benign form of psychiatry than any we presently possess.

This is not the place to embark on a long analysis of Jonathan's approach to moral philosophy and to the considerations that should underpin social policy in a liberal state. It is perhaps the place to end by observing that he has steered a very delicate line between the view that a fairly straightforward utilitarianism provides an all-purpose toolkit for the conduct of both private and public life, and the view that just about no tidying-up of our chaotic and conflicting intuitions is possible. He has shown a very deft understanding of the way in which the concern for happiness that pushes us toward a broadly utilitarian approach to the formation of public policy is constantly cut across by affection for and loyalty to the particular other people we spend our lives with, and one way in which his work has always been persuasive is just that it displays these tensions with such clarity, but without abandoning the search for a defensible resolution of them. In 1984, he published *What Sort of People Should There Be?* One answer to that book's question is, 'more philosophers, friends and colleagues like Jonathan Glover.'

VII

RESPONSES

13

Responses: A Summing Up

Jonathan Glover

The contributors to the volume have set me quite a challenge. They have written twelve chapters at a high level on a wide range of topics. Several argue against some central views of mine. All have a lot in them worth responding to. Naturally, it is a bit daunting to embark on the attempt to comment on each of them at something like their level and with the seriousness they deserve.

I mention what for me is a small stylistic problem. As this is a book for readers other than the contributors, I have followed the standard academic practice of mentioning contributors by their surnames. In real life, I do not talk about Davis, Keshen, and McMahan, but about Ann, Richard, and Jeff, and the same with the other contributors, who are colleagues and friends. The formality is a bit uncomfortable. But I follow the convention so that others do not think the book is a private conversation from which they are excluded.

The contributors have set me another problem, though one that is really nice to have to deal with. Some have said astonishingly generous things about my work and about me. The problem is whether my responses will come anywhere near having the intellectual virtues they benevolently say they see in my work. Somehow, I doubt it. We all have a good and a bad side. Of course in a book like this contributors are not likely to dwell on the bad side. But, even making allowances for this bias, I have been pleased and touched by the things said. Other readers will not want the philosophical responses to be repeatedly diverted into thanks to each contributor. So I will leave my thanks to the end.

PART ONE: TORTURE

JAMES GRIFFIN: WHAT SHOULD WE DO ABOUT TORTURE?

James Griffin's chapter is subtle and disturbing. He and I have views that are not very far apart. We both agree that there are conceivable cases where torture might be the lesser evil. And we both agree that in practice the best policy is to maintain the prohibition of torture. Our views are separated by a crack as fine as a hairsbreadth. But I have two reasons for starting with his chapter and spending longer on it than on others. One reason is that the hairsbreadth crack he leaves open is a deep one, through which torture just might seep. I want to close it. The other is the challenge posed by the reasonableness of his defense of being more open than I am (if only by a minuscule amount) to the idea of justifiable torture, and the fact that it is offered by one of the most gentle, civilized, and humane people I know.

Griffin gives an account of what torture is and of why in general it is unjustifiable. But he goes on to challenge reasons often given for an absolute prohibition, claiming that there could be justifiable exceptions to the general prohibition. He then suggests that we do not have (and perhaps never will have) enough information to formulate a policy of "principled torture," where the justifiable exceptions were codified. This argument has the philosophical merit of causing intellectual discomfort to all parties: to those who believe in an absolute prohibition of torture and to those who think justified exceptions are possible.

What is torture? Griffin does not make physical pain as central as many do. The key feature is "an assault on the victim's will," or "the subjection of the will of the victim to the will of the torturers." This can be by physical or mental pain, or by the threat of physical or mental pain, either to the victim or to some other person such as the victim's child. The assault on the will does not have to reduce the victim to a wreck with no autonomy. It just has to be too strong for most of us to resist. Griffin concludes that, while the infliction of great pain is one of the evils of torture, the other central one is its assault on our rational agency. He takes our rational agency to be the best interpretation of "the dignity of the human person," which is said (in the UN Declaration of Human Rights) to be the source of all human rights.

I wonder whether the assault on rational agency is more destructive of the dignity of the person than is being subjected to humiliation. But the emphasis on the subjection of the will of the victim to that of the torturers is an important corrective to accounts of torture purely in terms of pain. Jean Améry was tortured by the Nazis in Belgium. He wrote that the pain could not be described. But, in addition, there is the experience of being totally defenseless: "The first blow brings home to the prisoner that he is *helpless*....They are permitted to punch me in the face, they will do with me what they want."[1]

Griffin's account of torture in terms of compulsion too great to withstand is rather broad. A terrorist is guarding the kidnapped children with a gun. The police announce over the loudhailer that the house is surrounded by marksmen: "Drop your gun or we shoot to kill." With luck, the threat is too great for the terrorist to resist. But it would be harsh to say the police have flouted the ban on torture. Perhaps it is preferable to keep "torture" for the attempt to coerce the victim's will by means of actual physical or mental pain, rather than by threats, even of pain or death. This would allow the police, in the actual German case Griffin cites, to *threaten* violence to rescue the kidnapped child without being guilty of using torture.

Griffin's argument against a theoretically based absolute prohibition of torture takes the form of a challenge. We can say that inflicting extreme pain, or assaulting someone's rational agency, is an evil. But, could even these be sometimes justified as being less than some alternative evil? The challenge is backed up by comparisons. I can *kill* in self-defense, so why can't I defend myself by choking my poisoner to make him tell me the antidote? And, if I can do that, why can't I choke the kidnapper to make him reveal where my child is?

It is indeed hard to maintain that the coercive use of physical or mental pain could not conceivably be a lesser evil than what it prevented. This is the powerful intuitive thought behind the overused thought experiment about torturing a terrorist in the "ticking nuclear bomb" scenario. Suppose torturing a person had yielded information that saved a city with hundreds of thousands of inhabitants from nuclear destruction. After the event, it would be hard to think it would have been better to have let the bomb go off. So, there is the theoretical possibility of a case where torture has a plausible claim to be the lesser evil.

But, as many point out, real-world cases are so complex and involve so many uncertainties (for instance about the reliability of information gained by torture) that the thought experiment may not be a good guide.

Griffin stresses that the issue is a practical as well as a theoretical one. If, at the theoretical level, we cannot justify an absolute ban, ideally we would have "principled torture." This would take into account such things as human motivation and understanding, and the way moral infections spread. We would weigh the various good and bad consequences of torture, including its effects on society, and then have a code of practice that allowed only the cases where the benefits outweighed the harms. But Griffin recognizes that the chances of an agreed assessment of relative benefits and harms are very poor, and so "principled torture" is likely to sink into unprincipled torture. He is highly skeptical about our chances of ever knowing enough to decide on the best policy. So, for him the question becomes one of how to choose a policy in "near-invincible ignorance." He concludes that, in these circumstances, "perhaps we cannot do better" than maintain and strengthen the absolute prohibition of torture. However, he is obviously not overwhelmed by the case for doing so, and thinks that there may, even in practice, be justifiable exceptions: "We could then only hope that anyone who…resorts to torture has correctly identified a particular exception."

I want to defend a more robust rejection of torture in practice. I agree with Griffin that there are conceivable circumstances in which it might be the lesser evil. But, I want it off the policy menu. At one point, he draws a parallel with murder, which is worth following up.

Could murdering someone be the lesser evil? (I mean real murder, not abortion or voluntary euthanasia.) The English doctor Harold Shipman murdered literally hundreds of his patients. Suppose, someone discovers this, but cannot persuade the police or medical colleagues that it is so. (Shipman has destroyed the evidence, and the person who knows about it is discredited by a history of major psychiatric illness including paranoid delusions.) Killing Shipman may save many lives. Of course all this is far-fetched, but perhaps not more so than the ticking nuclear-bomb scenario. Such a thought experiment may show that murder can conceivably be the lesser evil. But, I still want murder to stay off the menu, as it is for most of us. We are safer in a world where in practice, most of us simply do not consider murder as an option. It would not be a better world if people started doing calculations about when murder would be the lesser evil and when not. It is better not to have to hope that anyone who resorts to murder has correctly identified a particular exception.

Torture should stay off the menu for similar reasons. My claim is that there should be an overwhelming presumption against using it, which in practice massively outweighs speculative claims about possible lives lost by rejecting it. (And, even if torture were to prevent a terrorist outrage, there would be the question of whether this is a better means of doing so than alternatives, such as avoiding the kind of military adventures that help terrorist recruitment.) It is true that we do not have scientifically well-supported answers to many factual questions about torture. But that applies to many public-policy decisions. And, in an unscientific way, we do know quite a lot about torture.

We know that while the philosophical and legal arguments about torture focus on extracting information from one of the "ticking bomb" conspirators, the practice hiding behind these justifications is different. The reality is too often the sadistic cruelty seen in Abu Ghraib, or in "Camp Breadbasket," its less-publicized British equivalent. Or, the reality is the horrors inflicted over years on sometimes innocent victims in Guantanamo.

We know that sometimes people will say anything to stop torture. Craig Murray, British ambassador to Uzbekistan until he was removed for speaking out about these things, was at the political trial of an old man: "Two of his children had been tortured in front of him and he signed a confession on the family's links to Bin Laden. Tears were streaming down his face. I have no doubt they had as much connection with Bin Laden as I do."[2]

We know a bit about the effects of torture on victims. (Of course, some transcend our imagination. Take Yaser Esam Hamdi, a prisoner in solitary confinement in a U.S. military brig. For years, he was denied even activities like kicking a ball. For months, he was deprived of natural light. His military guards thought he was being driven near insanity. What must this experience have been like? Who among the rest of us can have an adequate idea of the nightmare that has so far driven one victim of torture in Guantanamo to eight suicide attempts?) But we can learn from what victims say.

Jean Améry said, "I dare to assert that torture is the most horrible event that a human being can retain within himself." He linked the lasting psychological damage to the awareness of being totally defenseless. The victim loses "trust in the world." This includes "the certainty that by reason of written or unwritten social contracts the other person will spare me—more precisely stated, that he will respect my physical, and with it also my metaphysical, being. The boundaries of my body are also the boundaries of myself... At the first blow, however, this trust in the world breaks down."[3] The change is permanent: "Twenty-two years later I am still dangling over the ground by dislocated arms, panting and accusing myself."[4] "The tortured person never ceases to be amazed that...his soul, or his mind, or his consciousness, are destroyed when there is that cracking and splintering in the shoulder joints....Whoever has succumbed to torture can no longer feel at home in the world."[5]

We know a bit about what torture does to those who torture. Some of them fit Améry's account: "They placed torture in their service. But even more fervently they were its servants....In the world of torture man exists only by ruining the other person who stands in front of him."[6]

But others come close to being ruined themselves. Justine Sharrock interviewed some of them, after they had come back to the United States from Iraq. She found "young men hiding their regrets from neighbours who wanted to celebrate them as war heroes. They seemed relieved to talk with me about things no one else wanted to hear—not just about the acts themselves, but also about the guilt, pain, and anger they felt along with the pride and righteousness about their service." One of them, Ben, as an American army prison guard, had kept prisoners in a container. The temperature inside was sometimes 135 or 145 degrees. He kept them blindfolded, hands tied behind backs, sometimes standing in awkward positions for up to forty-eight hours at a time, sometimes blaring loud music or banging on the container so that they would not sleep. Once he made a verbal complaint about abuses, but nothing happened. He tried to mitigate the treatment: "But I could only do so much." After one particularly horrible episode, he hid behind a building and cried: "It was like a loss of humanity." Back in America, he had nightmares and sometimes woke up in the night shouting. He could not remember things. He was diagnosed with post-traumatic stress disorder.[7]

We have also seen a bit of what torture can do to a society that adopts it. We have seen the callousness of those at the top, typified by the cold joke made by Donald Rumsfeld when asked about the indignities and cruelties inflicted in Guantanamo: "It is not meant to be a country club." Then vice president Cheney also liked a cold joke: they were lucky to be "in the tropics." Or there is the Guantanamo phrase for sleep deprivation: "the frequent flyer programme."

There is the shifty evasiveness. Griffin brings out well the verbal twisting by means of which the Bush administration tried to avoid the word "torture." There are the euphemisms ("extraordinary rendition," etc.) that call for an Orwell to do them justice. This is all a part of the smokescreen coming from an embarrassment about being found out. In 2002, Lieutenant Colonel Diane Beaver said at a meeting in Guantanamo, that harsher operations might have to be curbed while the International Committee of the Red Cross was around, in order not to expose them to controversial techniques. The embarrassment is the faint residue of an abandoned moral revulsion against torture.

The smokescreen is maintained, sometimes at great cost to others. Binyam Mohamed faced the death penalty after confessing at Guantanamo to terrorist offences. His defense that his confession was the result of torture is frustrated by official refusal to reveal the contents of relevant documents. In Britain, the High Court said the refusal was "deeply disturbing" and had "no rational basis." Mr. Mohamed's lawyers said that the reason for the refusal was that "torturers do not readily hand over evidence of their conduct." The court said this claim could not be dismissed and required an answer, and that the United States had not explained its refusal, despite "ample time" to do so. ("Court attacks US refusal to disclose torture evidence," *The Guardian*, October 23, 2008.)

We know the way that torture, when admitted for the carefully circumscribed rare cases where it looks like the lesser evil, is not successfully contained. Griffin's phrase about the way moral infections spread is a good one. People imagine that the social machinery of killing or torture, set up to deal with some real or imagined emergency, will be easy to dismantle. Jacobo Timerman, after his own experience of torture in Argentina, saw the illusion of containment as a general pattern. There was

> the great silence, which appears in every civilized country that passively accepts the inevitability of violence.... That silence which can transform any nation into an accomplice. That silence which existed in Germany, when even many well-intentioned individuals assumed that everything would return to normal once Hitler finished with the Communists and Jews. Or when the Russians assumed that everything would return to normal once Stalin eliminated the Trotskyites.[9]

The use of torture also needs people like Diane Beaver, who, this time in her role as Staff Judge Advocate, wrote a letter justifying the legality of various techniques and supporting their approval.[10] These techniques included using a wet towel to make victims think they were suffocating. When public officials make such proposals, society slips a little way down the slope to being brutalized.

Then there are the complicit bystanders, for instance the British ones. Some from British intelligence were present at interrogations in Guantanamo. An official of the Foreign and Commonwealth Office lied to Moazzam Begg's family that he was "fine" and "well treated in Guantanamo." The lawyer for Martin Mubanga's family said the family "has been told he has made allegations of mistreatment, but the Foreign Office refuses to say what they are." In 2005, the then Foreign Secretary, Jack Straw, was asked in Parliament about the use of British airports for American "extraordinary rendition" flights. He said that careful research

by officials had failed to find any request for this by the Bush administration. He refused to say what MI5 and MI6 knew about such flights
because it was a policy not to comment on intelligence matters. In the
same debate, the Armed Forces Minister, Adam Ingram, was asked to say
how many times two specific aircraft suspected of being used for these
flights had landed in Britain. He said the information was not available. It
might seem important to investigate our country's possible involvement
in torture. But, when asked to check the records to find out about these
landings, Mr. Ingram said it would involve "disproportionate cost."[11]

It is important to stress that Griffin and I are on the same side in being
appalled by these things. In attacking the euphemisms, I am building on
his point. I take the phrase "moral infection" from him, and so on. The
difference between us is that I want torture to be totally off the menu,
while he wants it to be *almost* totally off the menu, because he allows that
someone might correctly identify a justifiable exception. The risk with
my policy is that, if something like the ticking-bomb scenario did occur,
a huge avoidable catastrophe might not be avoided through the refusal
to contemplate torture. The risk with Griffin's policy is that allowing the
possibility of justifiable exceptions leaves open the hairsbreadth crack
through which the moral infections which appall us both may seep. Our
difference is over the seriousness and likelihood of these two risks.

I have tried to argue here that experience suggests that the moral infections do seep through the crack. They *have* seeped through. Their symp-
toms are multiple: the cruelty and often permanent devastation heaped
on the victims, the psychological and moral catastrophe of the torturers,
the callousness and the cold jokes of the policymakers, the evasiveness,
and the lies of both policymakers and complicit bystanders.

Are our values really of this kind? Central to the case against torture is
the question of what sort of people we want to be, and what sort of society we want to live in. Henri Alleg, having been tortured by the French
in Algeria, wrote his eloquent book *La Question* against it. He thought
his fellow-citizens should know what was done in their name. About the
campaign of Alleg and others, Jean Améry wrote: "Half the French nation
rose up against the torture in Algeria. One cannot say often and emphati-
cally enough that by this the French did honour to themselves."[12] Saving
people from terrorist attack does matter. But cannot we, like the French
people in the 1950s, opt for means other than these?

PART TWO: WAR

THOMAS HURKA: THE CONSEQUENCES OF WAR

War poses ethical problems, which are among the most important and
most difficult we face. The importance is obvious: it is a horrifying fact

about our species that so much misery and death is caused by groups of people setting out in an officially organized way to kill each other. The easy ethical solution would be pacifism: the view that all this carnage is never justified. The difficulty comes from the implausibility of pacifism, from the familiar point that acts of war may sometimes avert a greater evil. If this is right, ethics has to contemplate the possibility of a justified war. But, if it is allowed, ethics also has to restrict it to the very few cases where it really is the lesser evil, and set limits to the horrible things that may be done in war. The impressive attempt in some of the religious traditions to do this has resulted in Just War theory. An alternative, partly overlapping, attempt has been made in the consequentialist approach to ethics.

The Just War theory is both an ally and an opponent of the consequentialist approach. Thomas Hurka makes a strong case for the view that, where they differ, the Just War approach both is coherent and has intuitive appeal. I will comment briefly on two issues where his claim about the greater intuitive appeal of Just War theory is particularly strong.

The first is Just War theory's absolute ban on the intentional targeting of civilians. I share the intuitive feeling that there is a special moral horror in aiming at civilian areas, where, for instance, old people and children will be in hospitals, or there will be school playgrounds. This is part of the horror of Guernica, of the Nazi bombing of Rotterdam, of the British bombing of Germany in certain stages of World War II, of the American fire-bombing of Japanese towns, of Hiroshima and Nagasaki, and of 9/11 (although 9/11 was only debatably part of a war).

However, there are questions about an absolute ban on intentionally targeting civilians. I do not believe that the bombing of civilian areas of Germany was essential to the allied victory. But, could there have been circumstances in which it was? Suppose Britain and France, in 1939 at the start of the war, had been in possession of a massively strong bomber force. Suppose they had made a strike that obliterated much of Berlin, and had succeeded in ending the Nazi regime and the war? Would that really have been wrong, when compared to the alternative of pursuing the (somewhat) more restrained war that actually took place, leading to the defeat of Nazism only after millions more had died as a result of war and genocide? The wrongness does not seem obvious.

Perhaps that imagined scenario is unrealistic, in a way parallel to the "ticking bomb" thought experiment criticized earlier as inadequate to defend torture. But, in war there have been real cases where respecting the absolute ban on intentionally killing civilians would have entailed huge risks.

One case was the need to thwart a Nazi plan to develop an atomic bomb. For this they needed heavy water, which they planned to move to Germany by rail from the Rjukan plant in Norway. As the allies had not enough time to destroy the plant, the only way to sabotage the plan was to destroy the transport on the way. The train taking the water was also crowded with passengers. Inevitably some would be killed.

Knut Haukelid, leader of the saboteurs, was acutely aware of the moral dilemma:

> It is always hard to take a decision about actions which involve the loss of human lives....In regular warfare it is easier; for then the officer is a small part of an organized apparatus, and his decisions as a rule have consequences only for soldiers, or at most for an enemy population. In this case an act of war was to be carried out which must endanger the lives of a number of our own people—who were not soldiers.[13]

To minimize loss of life, the explosion was detonated at the point where the train was ferried across a lake, with not many people on board. And the plant's transport engineer, who knew of the sabotage, arranged for the crossing to be on a Sunday, the day with fewest passengers. Even so, there were twenty-six dead, including fourteen Norwegian civilians.

Of course, it is always hard to justify intentionally taking civilian lives. But in this case was the blowing up of the ferry justified?

Some would argue that since the precautions taken showed so clearly that the saboteurs did not want the civilian deaths, those deaths were foreseen, but not intended. But this defense has an air of sophistry. When, as in this case, the sabotage and the deaths are so closely linked that it is in practice impossible to opt for one without the other, it is hard to say that the deaths—even though obviously utterly unwanted—were entirely unintended. In such a choice, the boundary between foresight and intention seems too unclear to be a reliable defense. And there is a case for saying that people should be judged on the basis of all the consequences for which they knowingly opt.

The powerful justification for the decision of Haukelid and his team, and of those in London who gave the orders, is that they had good reason to believe that blowing up the ferry was the least morally costly way of impeding the Nazi atomic program. This justification has a seriousness quite lacking in the defense of torture based on the under-described and shadowy "ticking bomb" thought experiment. It needs no emphasis that the scale of the possible catastrophe if Hitler ever commanded atomic weapons would utterly dwarf the losses caused by sinking the ferry. To imagine being faced with this choice should raise serious doubts about the absolute prohibition on taking civilian lives in war.

However, it should be said that even with the heavy water, the Nazi program might well not have succeeded. With hindsight, we know that their research was at least partly on the wrong track, and that some of the scientists involved were unenthusiastic about the program. But perhaps, it still would have succeeded. One of the physicists involved, Kurt Diebner, said later that "it was the elimination of the German heavy water production in Norway that was the main factor in our failure to achieve a self-sustaining atomic reactor before the war ended." To have put the lives of the passengers first would have allowed the Nazis a seriously better chance of an atomic bomb. To me, even with the uncertainty of their success, this terrifying risk seems strongly to outweigh the claim that the prohibition on killing civilians should be absolute.

If targeting civilians would avoid a much larger human catastrophe, some strong reason would have to be given as to why maintaining the ban was more important than avoiding the greater disaster. One possible reason would be that such a case would be so rare that, in the long run, the world will be a better place if targeting civilians is simply excluded from consideration. This is parallel to the exclusion of torture defended earlier. Just as before, I defended exclusion of torture from the policy options by appealing to its actual horrors in practice, so the parallel argument for excluding the intentional killing of civilians could appeal to the undoubted horrors of this aspect of the current practice of war. I respect this argument, while thinking that the heavy-water case gives a powerful reason for leaving a loophole for such extreme emergencies. I think a Just War theorist like Hurka would accept that avoiding a Nazi bomb was very important. But we give different moral weights to the arguments on each side.

How should this weighing be done? There is a case for saying that this weighing should be, at least centrally, consequentialist. How huge is the calamity that will be averted by civilian targeting in the extreme case? How often will the extreme case present itself? How likely, how big, and how frequent are the atrocities that may result from contemplating breaches of the ban?

These consequentialist questions are notoriously hard to answer. The absolute ban may be the right policy. But it is hard to see an adequate basis for it that does not appeal to some view about likely consequences. People have to be very confident in their deontological rules or intuitions for them to override consequences involving so much death and human horror.

The second issue where Hurka's claim about the intuitive plausibility of Just War theory seems particularly strong is about a justified war having to be directed at relevant goods. Two of his examples are very striking. Just War theory does not allow starting a war, where no actual aggression has been committed, in order to remove weapons that constitute a threat. And it does not allow war directed at other benefits, such as ending an economic slump.

The first example will strike a chord with all those of us who were appalled by the use of the "weapons of mass destruction" argument in support of the Iraq war. In that case, grossly distorted interpretations of thin evidence were used to support the "preemptive defense" claim. And the war may well have been motivated by quite different political and economic aims. But suppose things had been different? Suppose Saddam Hussein really had acquired nuclear weapons and was tempted to use them against Israel? Both parts of the hypothesis may be unlikely, but neither seems inconceivable. Is the case against preemptive strikes really so strong? Does it outweigh allowing Jerusalem to be added to the list of towns that starts with Hiroshima and Nagasaki? Perhaps there could be a strong enough case. But it is hard to see a convincing case that is *not* based on avoiding even worse consequences; centrally what *might* be the consequences of future wars in the name of "pre-emption."

. In the other example, intuitively it does indeed seem monstrous to start a war for economic benefit such as ending a slump. But there are many reasons why a consequentialist can agree that the world will be a better place if war is not one of the policies on the menu when we are trying to end a slump. What is special about this economic goal rather than others, such as ensuring a reliable supply of oil? What is special about economic goals rather than others, such as propagating democracy or some religion? And, why not end the slump by economic projects other than mass manufacture of weapons? Why not instead make huge numbers of electric cars, or create vast projects for generating solar power or getting fresh water from the sea?

We live in a world of heavily armed nations and groups, and wars start far too readily. The human costs are normally far beyond the evils that supposedly justify them. They are up there with the human costs of extreme poverty and of environmental disaster. (War is often causally linked with both of these.) It should be a platitude that war is only a last resort, for supreme emergency. Yet, people often resort to war so casually. Take the seriousness with which family members and doctors agonize over a life and death decision about one person in hospital. Compare it with the casual thinking used to support a war in which hundreds of thousands may be killed. Or with the cruel moral and intellectual slackness behind the decision not even to try to count the civilians killed as a result of the Iraq war. In a world where this is the norm, consequentialists have good reason to support keeping war only as a response to supreme emergency, rather than allowing open-ended extensions to the list of justifications.

JEFF McMAHAN: HUMANITARIAN INTERVENTION, CONSENT, AND PROPORTIONALITY

Jeff McMahan gives qualified support to one justification of war that is an extension, in that it is not allowed by the UN Charter. He makes a case for humanitarian intervention: the use of war to stop the persecution, oppression, or massacre of one group by another, where both are inside the same state, in the absence of the persecuting group committing any aggression against another state. He argues against several objections, that humanitarian intervention can be morally permissible. He is uncertain whether it can be morally required. And he discusses the difficult question of how, when intervention is justifiable, the risks and human costs should be shared between the soldiers of the intervening power and the group being rescued. I comment briefly on this last issue, and then turn to the question of whether humanitarian intervention can be justified.

On the sharing of risks and dangers, McMahan aptly cites the case of the Clinton administration's intervention in Kosovars, where bombing was carried out from a great height, a policy that reduced the risks to the aircrews, but increased the risks to the Albanian Kosovars being defended. He calls the policy "unchivalrous" but says it can be defended, because it is reasonable for rescuers to require the beneficiaries to share the risks. With some hesitation, I agree with this conclusion, and accept the argument that it fits our intuitions about individual rescue. If you rescue someone, it may be reasonable to choose a method involving greater injury to them rather than a lesser injury to yourself.

The grounds for hesitation about this come from a general unease about our intuitions about how to balance self-interest (or the interests of those close to us) against the claims of minimizing injury and harm in general. McMahan defends a low baseline for risks we are morally required to accept when intervening to rescue. This conclusion may be right. But I wonder about supporting it by extrapolating from the widespread intuition that we are not obliged to send $500 to famine relief, even when doing so will certainly save twenty lives. This is a widespread intuition, but it may be linked to imaginative failure in ways that cast doubt on its reliability. (As a schoolboy, I saw an Oxfam poster that said, "If you met a starving child you would buy him a meal. Why should it make a difference that he is not in front of you?" This influenced me later to argue that we may have a much stronger obligation to send money for famine relief than is generally supposed. I have not been good at living up to this. But the question on the poster has stayed with me ever since I first saw it.) Perhaps our more comfortable intuitions here should be distrusted?

On the central issue of his chapter, McMahan both makes a good case by saying that in some cases humanitarian intervention is justified, and brings out clearly the clash with the conventional view that aggression can never be justified. Central to his case is the doubt he has about the "domestic analogy" that likens such intervention in another state's affairs to objectionable paternalistic intervention in another person's life. As he suggests, divisions between groups within a state may run so deep that there is "no single collective self" whose right is violated by intervention.

I agree with the case he makes in principle for intervention, and also with his recognition that in practice there will often be justifiable objections to it. He rightly uses the Iraq war to illustrate the risks to the potential beneficiaries, both during a war and in its aftermath. He also rightly raises the issue of consent to an intervention in a country by its inhabitants, which he sees as important for justification.

It is reasonable to presume consent from people being massacred as in Rwanda. But, in less-clear cases, whether or not victims would want outside intervention may have to be largely guesswork. McMahan points out that even the victims may feel it dishonors their country, and that this may be compounded by the past history of relations with the intervening country, as with the United States in Iraq.

These doubts about intervention can be used to strengthen the case for a proper international police force to do the intervening. So does the tension between the moral case for preventing genocide in Rwanda and the fact that military intervention would be ruled out as aggression by the UN Charter. Intervention by a self-appointed country or group of countries runs the risk of being seen as self-interested, aggressive, or colonial, and may feed resentments that lead to a cycle of reciprocal violence between interveners and the people in the country they enter.

We are frequently told we live in a global village. Some villages have the rule of law, with a properly impartial police force backed up by the authority of the courts. Others do not have the rule of law and violence is suppressed by rounding up a posse (a "coalition of the willing"). Our global village is more like the second. The dangers of the posse approach include weakening the taboo on one country invading another and perhaps triggering a mafia-style vendetta. These drawbacks of humanitarian intervention would be much less in the kind of world federation of nation-states Kant suggested, with a world police organization having a monopoly of force, to be used only as authorized by an international court. We all know that police forces have their problems. But a police intervention backed by the authority of law is far less likely to create resentment and a violent backlash.

PART THREE: ETHICS, TRUTH, AND BELIEFS

ANN DAVIS: HUMANITY AND THE PERILS
OF PERNICIOUSLY POLITICIZED SCIENCE

Ann Davis places critical thinking at the heart of a culture of civic virtue needed for a twenty-first century democratic society. We are vulnerable to being manipulated by the rich and powerful into accepting policies that serve mainly their interests. To resist this, we need critical reflection about our own psychology and about society. In particular, we need to understand how social institutions frame our perceptions and our choices.

Davis argues that some of the main obstacles to the awareness we need come from neoliberal ideology, which she characterizes in terms of a particular view of freedom (mainly in terms of lack of government intervention) and a related faith in the market. This goes with hostility to the idea of the public interest: to publicly provided services and to public regulation of commercial activities. One consequence of this ideology is the commercialization of science and of higher education. Another is the growth and dominance of media corporations that put profit before informing the public.

Davis sees these consequences as harmful to the understanding needed in a modern democracy. Some of these harms are immediate and practical. When universities behave like profit-making corporations, there is pressure on their scientists to link up with companies producing medical, agricultural, engineering, or military technology. These links make it harder to find unbiased scientific advice about new technology or genuinely independent regulators of corporate scientific activities. And this may be disastrous. The technologies, through impact on the environment, genetic choices, or nanotechnology, may create more fundamental changes in human life than were possible before.

Davis also points to more subtle harms. What will be the result for people's understanding of the world if the media are dominated by market values? Will analysis at the moral and intellectual level of Fox News drive out analysis at the level of the BBC? And there are the universities that see knowledge mainly as a commodity, primarily useful for the development of marketable technology. Will they gain the whole world but lose their own soul?

If universities assess departments and projects mainly in terms of profitability, this may lead to the undervaluing of teaching. And it may lead to undervaluing of departments, in the humanities and the more humane end of the social sciences, whose main concern is with developing commercially unprofitable kinds of human understanding and imagination. There is not much technical spin-off from literature and philosophy, anthropology, and history. If these fields wither away, the result may be a diminution of our imaginative and moral resources. In a democracy, the sort of people we are affects both our susceptibility to manipulation and the quality of the social decisions we take.

As I am sympathetic to the general thrust of this argument, my comments aim to be constructive rather than challenging. I comment first on neoliberal ideology, and then on one of its implications that Davis notes.

I wonder if Davis is right in characterizing the neoliberal view of freedom in terms of Isaiah Berlin's idea of negative liberty. The contrast between negative and positive liberty, sometimes taken as the contrast between "freedom from" and "freedom to," is not very clear. As others have pointed out, all freedom is freedom *of* a person or group *from* some kind of restriction or interference *to* do something or other. Neoliberalism's departure from traditional liberalism can usefully be seen in terms of *whose* freedoms and *which* freedoms come first. In Britain, the high tide of neoliberal ideology was during the governments led by Margaret Thatcher. The rhetoric of freedom seemed to go with a strange view of which freedoms were most important.

In the traditional liberal accounts of freedom, for instance in John Stuart Mill, *personal* freedom is paramount. It matters to each of us to live our own life in our own way. And society is enriched by people using their freedom to create their own individuality. So, there is a presumption of personal liberty, which should be restricted only to protect others from harm. But, as Mill indicated by his relatively sympathetic attitude to socialism when discussing political economy, there may be social goals that require restricting some of the economic freedom of organizations.

The Thatcher administrations inverted this. Mill liked experiments in living, but these neoliberals did not like the freedom of gays to make such experiments without stigma. (Clause 28 of the Local Government Act banned local councils from producing any literature suggesting that gay couples could be, or could create, a family. They were described in the Act as a "pretended family.") But economic freedom of corporations did better. Public-interest restrictions on multiple media ownership were circumvented or eliminated, with the result that Rupert Murdoch's company added the *Times* and the *Sunday Times* to a British portfolio already bulging with a television station and tabloid newspapers. Corporate freedom from government intervention came before the freedom of the rest of us not to have our access to news and opinion so dominated by a single corporation. A ban on cigarette advertising was opposed on grounds of freedom by Virginia Bottomley. Freedom of tobacco companies to advertise came before freedom of others from pressures to smoke. At the time, Virginia Bottomley was the Minister of Health.

For the effects of commercializing science and the universities it is worth looking at the case of Dr. Nancy Olivieri. (Nathan and Wetherall: Academic Freedom in Clinical Research, *New England Journal of Medicine*, 2002, 347: 1368–71.) Working at the University of Toronto and the Hospital for Sick Children, Dr. Olivieri and a colleague obtained a grant from the pharmaceutical company Apotex to test Deferiprone, a thalassemia drug the company produced. To get the grant, they had to sign a confidentiality agreement. The results looked promising. Dr. Olivieri started a second trial, running Deferiprone against the standard drug. In this study, they found that in a substantial number of patients Deferiprone either brought no improvement or made their condition worse.

Dr. Olivieri thought that it was her duty to her patients and to the public to warn that the drug might be ineffective, and even unsafe. She raised the issue with her institutional review board and at a scientific meeting, and submitted the results for publication. The response of Apotex was legal action for 20 million dollars for her violation of the confidentiality agreement. The University of Toronto was negotiating a large donation from Apotex. The hospital's medical advisory committee referred Dr. Olivieri for research misconduct to the College of Physicians and Surgeons of Ontario. The hospital and the university publicized the referral widely.

Eventually, the College of Physicians and Surgeons found that none of the allegations were justified and completely cleared Dr. Olivieri. But before justice was finally done, a hospital had failed to stand up for a doctor who carried out her ethical duty to warn of possible harm to patients. And a university, with a financial interest at stake, had failed to defend the academic freedom of one of their scientists. Instead, both had joined in the attempt to bully and intimidate Dr. Olivieri. (To flag up a possible bias, I should say that I know and respect Nancy Olivieri. After these events, she came to King's College to do our MA course in Medical Ethics and Law.

I felt like an armchair strategist confronted by a soldier just back from the battlefield. Needless to say, she taught me much more than I taught her.)

The case neatly illustrates several strands of Ann Davis's argument. It brings out the way commercial pressures can conflict with patient safety, medical ethics, and academic freedom. There clearly is a serious problem. As philosophers, we need to think about and criticize the system of beliefs that pushes in this direction. The selective weight given to different freedoms, and particularly the ranking of corporate freedom relative to personal freedom, needs critical examination. And, as a society, we need to devise institutional mechanisms to guard against these abuses, in the way the global medical community responded to the abuses of Nazi medical research.

More generally, in resisting the imperial pretensions of the market, we can perhaps learn from the idea of civil society, as developed by those who resisted the domination of whole societies by communist ideology. In that period, Czechs, Poles, and others used to argue against the monolithic approach to society: for institutions in education, the media and elsewhere that should be independent of government. These institutions should be recognized as having their own goals, and seen to be not just part of the machinery for the development of socialism. Education was about intellectual and human development, not just about producing technologists or believing Marxists. The media were for truthful reporting of the world and for stimulating intelligent thought about it, not for indoctrination and propaganda.

In our society too, the very different dominance of market values could be opposed just on an individual basis: doctors fighting for medical ethics, scientists defending freedom to publish research, media people defending public-service broadcasting, and so on. But there is something more general at stake. The idea of civil society, of professions and institutions with their own values that need to be recognized and protected, is one that can unite us in countering the imperialism of the market. Of course, we should not exaggerate the comparison with communist society. We do not face imprisonment when we speak out. (Though, Nancy Olivieri had to show great courage, as no doubt have others.) But the vision the dissidents had in communist Europe, of a society with a plurality of institutions guided by a plurality of values, is relevant to us. The threat to it is less brutal and more subtle, but the vision is still worth articulating and defending.

ALLEN BUCHANAN: SOCIAL MORAL EPISTEMOLOGY AND THE TASK OF ETHICS

Allen Buchanan says that something lacking in *Humanity* is "a developed conceptual framework that connects belief, institutions, moral–epistemic virtues, and conduct." His project of developing a social moral epistemology to provide this framework, in a pioneering series of articles, is one of the most important current attempts to use philosophy to help make a better world.

His central line of thought seems incontrovertible. Beliefs, both factual and moral, are important determinants of the good and evil things people do. Terrible things have come from beliefs in such things as the inferior humanity of other racial groups, or in there being a catastrophic decline in the gene pool. These false beliefs do not come from nowhere. They are partly shaped by social institutions. They may be distorted by what Buchanan calls our "epistemic dependence" on sometimes unreliable "experts." To be less dependent we need the moral and intellectual virtues that protect us from unfounded beliefs. And, we need to see how different social institutions support or undermine those virtues.

Buchanan points out that a job in government or in the intelligence services may subject someone to pressures that distort judgment about whether a country has weapons of mass destruction. In Britain, there is a possible recent instance. The Attorney General is both a law officer and a member of the government. This position may subject someone to distorting pressures. The Attorney General advises the government on such things as the legality of a preemptive war. Before the Iraq war, the Attorney General advised that it might be illegal. Later, he changed his mind and endorsed its legality, without making public his reasons. Buchanan rightly says that knowledge of these distorting pressures should affect how we judge the moral case for the general permissibility of preemptive defensive attacks.

On the basis of the links between beliefs, virtues, and institutions, Buchanan criticizes the approach I took in *Humanity* for being both conceptually incomplete and normatively inadequate. He also says that my more recent advocacy of "applied epistemology" is somewhat misleading. He sets out to show how the approach of social moral epistemology might make good some of these deficiencies.

The criticism that *Humanity* is conceptually incomplete is correct. There is not just the obvious point that anyone who managed to give a *complete* conceptual map of how the great atrocities happen and how to prevent them would have to be very brilliant or very lucky. Buchanan has identified a specific and major incompleteness. The book indicates that beliefs are important causes of wars, genocide, and other horrors. But it does not attend to the role of social institutions in shaping beliefs, or to the consequence that reflection on this may help us develop institutional defenses against those horrors. The relations between beliefs and institutions are important, but tangled. Ann Davis on how ideology can distort institutions, and Allen Buchanan on how institutions in turn shape and sometimes distort beliefs, are both helping to untangle some knots my book did not try to untie.

It is also highly unlikely that *Humanity* told the whole normative story. But its approach can be defended a bit. Buchanan says that I believe or hope that the conviction that Auschwitz must never be repeated will motivate people to cultivate restraining moral virtues. He thinks this is motivationally inadequate. Citing Turkish denials of the Armenian genocide, he says that it is easy to combine condemning Auschwitz with rationalizations saying that some other case is not really genocide. He says that the approach of *Humanity* does not take rationalization—and the dependence of moral beliefs on factual ones—seriously enough.

I agree that such rationalizations are common. And there is something psychologically implausible in the picture of someone appalled by Auschwitz deciding, "I will cultivate in myself sympathy and respect for other people." The picture I intended to present was slightly different.

Most of us have dispositions that tend to restrain us from doing terrible things. These include sympathy and respect for others, and some conception of the sort of person we hope to be. (We also have other, darker dispositions that push in a different direction.) The claim in *Humanity* was that there are patterns in the ways the restraining dispositions are weakened. Sympathy is deadened by geographical distance or by the "moral distance" created by dehumanizing propaganda. Respect for people is eroded by humiliating them. The sense of moral identity ("I don't want to be a mass murderer") is disabled as a restraint by the fragmentation of responsibility. ("I only put in the gas supply." "I only arrested them." "I only drove the train.")

People with very different views about the ultimate basis of ethical principles often agree on the importance of avoiding atrocities. The intention of the book was to argue that this, combined with awareness of how the psychological restraints are disabled, can motivate us to develop a shared ethical approach despite theoretical disagreements about the basis of morality. If we are alert to the role of cold jokes in past atrocities, alarm bells will ring when people in government start joking about Guantanamo detainees being lucky to be in the tropics or the place not being a country club.

This historically based alertness is relevant to terrorism. Cycles of violence between tribal groups are sustained partly by illusions about all members of a rival group being collectively responsible for past injuries to members of one's own group. These illusions can block the normal restraints on killing. Consider Mohammad Sidique Khan, the British Muslim who took part in terrorist bombing in London in July 2005. In his justificatory videotape, "we" were Muslims and "you" were British. He said, "Your democratically elected governments continuously perpetrate atrocities against my people all over the world. And your support of them makes you directly responsible, just as I am directly responsible for protecting and avenging my Muslim brothers and sisters. Until we feel security, you will be our targets."

What sort of moral education might have led Khan to act differently? It would not have been enough to say to him, "You agree atrocities are horrible, so cultivate sympathy for others." I would want him to have thought about the illusion of collective responsibility as found in the history of Serbia and Croatia, or in vendettas between Sicilian families.

With his bomb at Edgware Road Station, Khan killed six people as well as himself. The relevant ethics teaching would stimulate alertness to the way human responses to people are inhibited by vengeful group stereo-typing. It would aim to stimulate questions about his potential victims. Might some of the six people he was to kill be British *and* Muslim? Is it likely that all six of his victims would be among the minority in Britain who supported the Iraq war? Did the "you" he held "directly responsible" include those who joined London's largest ever demonstration: the one against the war? (Of course, all this is not enough: there are good reasons too for not murdering Tony Blair. But it might have weakened the hold of the categories that made him so morally self-confident about murder.)

Historically informed ethics is less about uplifting injunctions to virtue than about alertness to specific weaknesses, especially in our thinking, that threaten the moral restraints. It is not so far from Buchanan's interest in the rationalizations of those who will not admit the Armenian genocide. The approaches are allies, not rivals. One distinctive feature of his approach, that mine lacked, is brought out in his pertinent call for "a sea change in the way most people think, or fail to think, about how morally relevant beliefs are formed and about their responsibility for the beliefs they hold."

This has links to Buchanan's criticism that it is "somewhat misleading" to commend "applied epistemology" as relevant to tempering ideologi-cal conflicts. He says the need is to recognize about Ethics that, "if it is about right conduct it must be about right belief—and that moral virtues depend on and partly consist of epistemic virtues, both of individuals and of institutions." This point is important and correct. But "applied episte-mology" is relevant to it.

Buchanan's social moral epistemology is about the ways in which beliefs influencing people's actions are themselves shaped by an interplay between social institutions and the presence or absence of certain moral–epistemic virtues. I applaud this approach, but want to defend the relevance of apply-ing to it questions central to more traditional epistemology.

The key question is what counts as an epistemological virtue. Some of the deepest political or religious ideological differences are linked to rival assumptions about this. Is basing belief on faith a virtue, as some reli-gious people think? Or is belief on no evidence a vice? Looking at these assumptions leads into deep epistemological questions. Does science rest on assumptions that cannot themselves be proved?

The scientific world picture does rest on assumptions. These include the reliability of our senses, the legitimacy of extrapolating from observed cases to unobserved ones, and the preference—among explanations that fit the evidence—for simple over complex ones. As Quine and others have argued, these assumptions can be given scientific support. A species whose senses—or whose ways of thinking—systematically gave a false picture of the world, would lose out in the evolutionary struggle to better-equipped species. In this defense of science, the methods and the world picture are in mutual support. Darwinism is defended as based on scientific evidence. And using scientific method has Darwinian support. Is there an objection-able circularity here?

It is hard—perhaps impossible—for a system of beliefs to escape a degree of circularity. When challenged to defend any particular belief, it is hard to see how we could do this without drawing on other beliefs in the system. Rival belief systems may each be internally consistent and, within each system, there may be the "circularity" that the beliefs support each other. Hilary Putnam once wrote that, "madness and sanity can both have a 'circular' aspect....If we have to choose between 'circles,' the circle of reason is to be preferred to any of the many circles of unreason."[14] But how can the preference for one circle over another be defended? Why is *it* the circle of reason? Or, if there is some definitional strategy that makes it so, *why* is "the circle of reason" to be preferred?

Since Socrates, philosophy has been taught by getting people to spell out what they believe and to give their reasons. This is followed by the challenge of counterexamples: "Surely you are not prepared to accept *this* implication of what you say?" Epistemology argues against beliefs by showing their costs. Unwelcome consequences of a belief are an invitation to abandon or modify it. But the fact that the consequences are unwelcome is not itself generated by logic. Logic excludes inconsistent systems, but does not tell us how to choose between consistent ones. We need in addition an intuitive sense of what is plausible.

People with different belief systems often have very different intuitions about plausibility. Often these intuitions are linked to different epistemological approaches. Creationists and Darwinians find each others' worldviews implausible. This is linked to their epistemologies. Creationist epistemology gives weight, perhaps overriding weight, to what they believe to be the word of God, while Darwinians hold that only scientific evidence is relevant. In each case, the worldview and the epistemology are in mutual support. Dialogue between adherents of such rival belief systems, if it is to go beyond the superficial, has to engage with the different underlying epistemologies.

The resources needed for this dialogue will include the way that different belief systems and the presence or absence of cognitive virtues interact, as Buchanan emphasizes, with social factors. But another necessary resource is more philosophical, though it will draw heavily on cognitive science. The applied epistemology needed for dialogue will have to address disagreements about what counts as a cognitive virtue. This requires subjecting cognitive strategies to the same challenge of counterexamples that Socrates applied to beliefs. "Can the way you defend your side's narrative of the Israel–Palestine conflict avoid the charge of confirmation bias?" "Doesn't the way you defend your Marxist theory of history against awkward cases resemble the use of epicycles to defend the Ptolemaic view of the universe?" "How does your response to the evidence for man-made climate change differ from Philip Gosse's way of dismissing the fossil evidence for evolution?" As with the challenge to beliefs, the challenge to cognitive strategies spells out their unwelcome costs.

It is an open question how far this applied epistemology will lead people to converge in their views of acceptable cognitive strategies. There is an optimistic view that humans may be programmed to prefer some cognitive strategies rather than others, and that if we reason together long enough, we will converge on these strategies. But this optimism may be unfounded. Perhaps Jerry Fodor is right that the psychology of human thinking (in science and elsewhere) about how to explain the world is freewheeling in a way that does not allow us to draw up a set of rules for successful cognitive strategies.

Perhaps we will continue to disagree over which costs of a cognitive strategy are great enough to make it unacceptable. There is still the possibility that we will come to agree on the epistemological map. That is, we may agree about how different beliefs and cognitive strategies hang together, and about the different costs of each of those systems of beliefs and strategies. Our disagreements would be about the relative importance of different intellectual costs and benefits. Our situation would be like that of people who agree there is a trade-off, for instance in education, between liberty and equality of opportunity. They may agree on the degree of restriction of liberty needed for a given increase in equality of opportunity, but disagree on whether it is worth it. Even to reach the epistemological equivalent of this will be a long and difficult business. It may or may not be possible.

If we were to reach this agreement on the epistemological map, it would be a gain for dialogue. We would know that we differ over acceptable intellectual costs, and that neither of us has a decisive argument to overthrow the view of the other. (For one of us to reject this is for us not to agree on the epistemological map.) This would show that, while we have differences, we have a shared view of their nature and that we can each see how a reasonable person could adopt the other position.

There are times when it seems that the world may be torn apart by violent conflicts between adherents of different belief systems. Dialogue is better than war. A central concern of philosophy, going back at least as far as Socrates, is whether some beliefs can be shown to be true, or at least more reasonable than others. Yet, in the present world, philosophers hardly ever seem involved in dealing with ideological conflicts. It seems a damning comment on the long history of philosophy if it has nothing to contribute here. But, if there is a contribution, I hope part of it will be to apply epistemology to the most deeply embedded beliefs and cognitive strategies of rival groups.

RICHARD KESHEN: THE STRAINS OF DIALOGUE

Although dialogue is better than war, we cannot assume that it will narrow the gap between the disputants. As Richard Keshen points out in his chapter (an earlier draft of which has greatly influenced my thinking), dialogue may even drive people apart. In the debate he considers between Hyman Bookbinder and James Abourezk about the Israel–Palestine issue, the circumstances were propitious. Each recognized the other as informed, and as reasonable: a quality that includes the ability to think logically, the ability to assess evidence, and the willingness to change view in response to good reasons. They also recognized each other's desire to bridge the gap between them. Yet, the debate did drive them further apart.

Keshen probes this "reasonable but intractable disagreement." He argues that we should find persisting disagreement between reasonable people perplexing. If both participants are reasonable, they will recognize good reasons and be influenced by them. Both will recognize and reject bad reasons. So, surely they should move toward convergence?

This leads to the deep problem that Keshen has identified. Is it possible for Bookbinder and Abourezk to accept the intractable disagreement and still see each other as reasonable? If my opponent does not accept the good reasons for saying my view is better than his (or accepts bad reasons for thinking his view better than mine) mustn't I see him as unreasonable, or at least as less reasonable than me? A rather startling consequence is that we always have to think that persisting intellectual opponents are, at least on the disputed issues, less reasonable than we are. This does not bode well for mutual respect in dialogue.

As Keshen points out, there is a tension between commitment to one's own view and recognizing the equal reasonableness of one's opponent. To recognize equal reasonableness by saying that neither of our views is backed by better reasons than the other is to undermine my commitment to my own view. And to escape the tension by saying that we are equally reasonable, but just operate in a different framework (perhaps, if the dispute is about abortion, Catholic and feminist frameworks) just moves the question back. Are there better reasons for adopting one framework rather than another? At this next level, the same tension emerges between seeing you as equally reasonable and my commitment to my own framework.

The conflict Keshen has seen is real and deep. Nevertheless, there may be an approach that, while not eliminating the tension, weakens both sides of it. This may be enough to make a degree of mutual respect compatible with retaining commitment to our own views. The approach has links to the "applied epistemology" discussed earlier.

Many do think that we should avoid arguing about different frameworks of belief, for instance religious ones. The reasons are not all intellectual. People may be hurt if their deepest personal beliefs are assaulted. In a multicultural society, with its need for mutual tolerance, does debating religion carry too great a danger of fanning anger and hostility? It is important to show respect for the beliefs of others. And so on. These reasons have weight. But they do not exclude debate in a climate where, as in philosophy at its best, people can feel challenged without feeling threatened or attacked.

Another objection is that such a debate will make no progress. This may be linked to the thought that radically different intellectual frameworks may involve not only rival beliefs, but also rival epistemologies. "Applied epistemology" questions this pessimism. Perhaps Socratic counterexamples can successfully challenge epistemological strategies as well as beliefs. They may show that something in our epistemology has to give. We then have to decide what to give up. To the degree that we have a shared a human cognitive programming, the choices we make may move us toward some convergence. The very optimistic version holds out the hope of some convergence of beliefs. The more cautious version settles for the hope of some agreement on the cognitive map. Both hopes may be disappointed. But, if either is right, our position in philosophy is like that of scientists in the middle of an uncompleted research program.

In science, at any time there are both many things accepted as true and many disagreements between supporters of rival conjectures about unsettled issues. People have different hunches about the existence of life on other planets. People have strongly different intuitions about the "many worlds" interpretation of physics, which postulates an endlessly branching multiplicity of universes. Scientists can disagree on these questions while still respecting each other's rationality. Their intuitions are based on ideas of scientific plausibility. But they also know how many advances, such as the use of non-Euclidean geometries in physics, have been at first deeply counterintuitive. A common stance is: "I have good reasons—though not decisive ones—for my hunch, but only scientific progress will show whose reasons are better."

Philosophical disagreements between supporters of rival intellectual frameworks can be modeled on these scientific disagreements. If you are a religious believer and I am an atheist, our frameworks will very likely include rival epistemological principles. In Socratic discussion, we may get each other to spell them out. Each of us may regard the other's approach as counterintuitive. Because the program of searching for the best epistemological principles is unfinished, any adjudication between our different approaches will have to await further philosophical progress. So, if we are rational, each of us will admit that the other's approach may turn out better, while still betting that our own approach will be vindicated.

This does not totally remove the tension Keshen points out. There has been a little giving way on either side of it. I am only betting my approach is right, so my commitment to it is a bit weakened. But it *is* the one I am betting on, so I still think it is a better bet than yours. So I can't think your approach is quite as reasonable as mine. And on your side, the same slight change of position will take place. We each have a slight diminution of our commitment yet still feel that our own approach is at least slightly more reasonable.

The tension remains. But, on this picture of philosophy, it can be reduced enough to allow both a degree of commitment and a degree of mutual respect. This applies to dialogue even about religious and other deep differences. It is part of our humanity to want to respect each other. But it is also part of our humanity, and even part of respecting each other, to want to go deep in exploring our differences. Perhaps, we will not be able to resolve our deepest disagreements. But, other things equal, we should aim to go as deep as possible. We may even make progress as a result.

Keshen raises another deep issue. He talks about how sometimes, in a disagreement between people of strongly opposed beliefs, there can be a breakthrough of mutual empathy. He likens this to cases where, when our sympathy or respect for some other people have been deadened by ideological or tribal hostility, or by propaganda or war, those human responses can suddenly break through again. He gives examples, one from George Orwell's experience in Spain, of soldiers suddenly seeing an "enemy" as a fellow human being.

In the case of the ideological disagreement, he suggests how breakthrough might happen. It could come from the thought that both my opponent's view and mine have been shaped by our different lives, and so I probably have limited insight into his perspective. This, combined with respecting his sincere commitment, could motivate me to try to get a better feel for his life and his outlook. Keshen then points out that this notably does not happen in the dialogue between Bookbinder and Abourezk. He concludes with a pessimistic question. Is it plausible that a human moral identity could ever have enough appeal, or enough psychological richness, to thwart the "malevolent outbursts" of our deeply rooted narrow identities?

It is a deep question, briefly put, which cannot be briefly answered. (Or just "cannot be answered?") It is part of the question of whether it is plausible that the dark side of our nature will ever be contained or overcome by our better side. I wish I knew that the answer is "yes." I wish I knew the answer at all. I am drawn to a Manichean picture of human history as a perpetual struggle inside each of us as individuals, and inside each ideological or tribal group, between the Light and the Dark. It is doubtful if either side will ever have a complete victory. Things are more local, both in place and time. The Light suffers huge, spectacular defeats by the Dark. But the Light also makes almost imperceptibly slow gains over long periods. Although Antonio Gramsci was a Marxist, not a Manichean, "pessimism of the intellect, optimism of the will" comes close to fitting. However, because of the slow gains, "pessimism of the intellect" is—only a bit—too strong. Perhaps here the phrase should be "scepticism of the intellect, optimism of the will."

PART FOUR: BIOMEDICAL ETHICS AND BEYOND

ONORA O'NEILL: HUMANITY AND HYPER-REGULATION: FROM NUREMBERG TO HELSINKI

Onora O'Neill's chapter on the ethics and regulation of medical research characteristically combines hard-headed practicality with acute philosophy to make an impressive challenge to current views. She contrasts the light touch of early approaches to research ethics (symbolized by the *Nuremburg*

Code) with the more cumbersome and bureaucratic "hyper-regulation" of recent times (symbolized by the *Declaration of Helsinki*). The case she makes for preferring Nuremburg to Helsinki is based on comparisons made on two levels: the level of practice and the level of underlying philosophy.

On the practical contrasts, O'Neill makes a convincing case. She brings out the lighter touch of Nuremburg, for instance on the question of the information the participants in research must be given.

The information required by Nuremburg is all centrally relevant: the nature and purpose of the research, its methods, reasonably predictable medical and other drawbacks and risks of participating. Helsinki, pursuing ever more *specific* consent, adds a lot more, including issues of research design, together with various institutional and funding issues. O'Neill rightly says that the additions are often unrealistic. The demand that participants understand all this will exclude from research many suffering from conditions that impair intellectual grasp. And even many generally competent people are unlikely genuinely to have much grasp of some of the scientific and institutional issues.

O'Neill makes a similar case that the Helsinki pursuit of ever more *explicit* consent leads to a proliferation of procedures and protocols, together demands for formal consent in writing, signed and witnessed. She sees the unrealistic specificity as leading to hypocrisy about whether its demands are met, and the demand for the rigmarole of explicitness as leading to both parties "colluding in a charade."

Some other possible costs of the more heavy-handed Helsinki approach are not stressed by O'Neill, but may be worth mentioning. I have no knowledge of social scientific research on the subject. But, anecdotally, in conversations with medical researchers, they have sometimes said that the cumbersome procedures of obtaining consent are a real drain on their time and energy. They suggest that research is sometimes seriously slowed down. Of course, grumbles of people being regulated do not always justify changes, but I have heard this complaint often enough to believe that it is worth investigating. No one wants to go back to unregulated medical research, but looking into this might give further support to the case for Nuremburg over Helsinki.

Another cost is a moral one. I have been dismayed by the attitude toward ethics generated among at least some researchers by the Helsinki cumbersomeness. The process of convincing a research ethics committee to approve a project is often called "getting ethics." And it is often seen as mainly going through a series of pointless and pedantic bureaucratic hoops. Some of this criticism may be unfair. But it is dismaying if "ethics" here is seen, not as a reasoned approach to patient protection, but as creating what O'Neill calls a "tick box" culture. There is a danger that discrediting the word may bring some disregard for the substance of ethics itself.

O'Neill links up the practical drawbacks of the change from Nuremburg to Helsinki with differences of underlying philosophy. Here, I feel some sympathy with her view, but wonder if the philosophical contrast is quite as sharp as she suggests.

O'Neill implies a conceptual mistake in Helsinki when she, rightly, says that fully specific consent is impossible. If supporters of the Helsinki approach demand fully specific consent, their intention may be implicitly limited by an understood context. They may mean something like consent to every detail that is both relevant to the central ethical concerns and above a certain threshold of importance. Telling the whole truth about any episode would be an indefinitely long task, but when a witness in court swears to tell "the truth, the whole truth and nothing but the truth," there is a conventional understanding of what the broad expectations are, and perhaps something like this applies to Helsinki information-giving.

It is a good suggestion that what really matters is the presupposed background of fundamental requirements (not to coerce, injure, etc.), and that consent should be a matter of the participant giving a limited waiver of one of these requirements for a context-specific reason. This is much more elegant than having a set of principles about information and voluntariness unique to the context of medical research. The elegance is an intellectual virtue, but will not necessarily make a great difference in practice. The elaboration of requirements of explicitness may not reflect a difference of theoretical approach. There is the fact, mentioned by O'Neill, that this explicitness can be useful for medical institutions in the event of litigation. There is also the natural impulse of bureaucracies, not only toward defensiveness, but also toward officiousness and elaboration. Perhaps the adoption of the less-elegant theoretical approach by those drawing up ethical guidelines is not needed to explain all the fuss.

O'Neill's practical case for Nuremburg over Helsinki is a valuable piece of resistance to the culture of managerialism and of "box ticking" assessment that has spread so harmfully over so much of our culture. Those who have to endure it include, as well as medical researchers, clinical doctors, nurses, and teachers in schools and universities. This links with the "civil society" issues that are among those raised in Ann Davis' chapter. The idea of civil society goes with sometimes trusting professionals. This may include trusting them to have decent ethics and to have fairly good intuitive judgment about, for instance, what is relevant to consent. The history of medical experimentation warns us that regulation is needed. But awareness of what over-administration is like, and a feel for what people are like, both lend support to O'Neill's case for a light touch.

JOHN HARRIS: TRANSHUMANITY: A MORAL VISION OF THE TWENTY-FIRST CENTURY

Belief in the importance of preserving the genetic barrier between the human and other species is widely held. John Harris has never been drawn to conventional wisdom, and this piece of it appeals to him no more than most. For him "transhumanism," crossing the barrier separating our species from others, is not a dystopian nightmare, but a moral vision. What could be called the "micro" version of transhumanism is the mixing of human and nonhuman genes in ways that do not result in a developed living creature whose species is indeterminate. Transgenic mice used in research may contain human genes, but they are still clearly mice. The "macro" version would be "fully fledged hybrid or chimerical creatures mixing human and animal elements."

Harris defends both micro and macro versions. He uses three strategies. He argues that the barrier around the human species is not so sharp or so deep as we suppose. He makes a moral case for the desirability of crossing the barrier. And he argues against common objections to the macro version of transhumanism.

Harris successfully argues that the boundary is not as sharp as we suppose. We have already blurred it through stem-cell research and, less controversially, in vaccines and in xenotransplants. A defender of the boundary could say that all this has been a mistake and we should go no further. But Harris points out that the blurring includes the ingesting of animal and vegetable genes in our food. His opponent is unlikely to relish the proffered alternative of a purely cannibal diet. Harris also argues that the boundary is less deep than we think: the human genetic constitution is already a mixture including many of the genes of our ape ancestors. This parallels the way facts about ethnic genetic mixing show racial purity to be a myth.

The second strategy is to give positive reasons why crossing the barrier is beneficial. At the micro level, these reasons are the strong intellectual and medical case for such research, especially on stem cells. Transgenic research increases our understanding of basic mechanisms, as in the striking studies of genetic hierarchy, which Harris cites. And it enables the testing of proposed treatments both for effectiveness and safety. The possible benefits are so great that there should be a presumption in favor of this research, only to be overridden by some very serious ethical objection such as some major risk.

The case that Harris makes for crossing the barrier at the macro level seems less strong. Why might we want fully fledged creatures mixing human and nonhuman elements? Of course in the future there may turn out to be strong intellectual or therapeutic reasons for this. If and when these reasons arrive, they will have to be weighed against any disadvantages or risks involved. But are there any likely benefits that should now predispose us in favor of such developments?

The only one mentioned is that "human" traits that improve our lives might do the same for other species. Harris endorses the suggestion that there could be a duty of beneficence to give them these traits too. We can envisage scenarios in which transgenic architects enrich the lives of future members of other species. Chimpanzees might enjoy being able to play chess, or crabs might like to be able to dance to music. But it is hard to see this as a very high priority. Even among policies designed to benefit other species, it would surely come some way below the elimination of battery farming or the liberation of primates from zoos. Some would object to the "colonialism" of one species (ours) deciding to redesign the lives of others. There is a question independent of this. If, in an impersonal way, we are trying to maximize richness of life, and think that some human qualities are very important for this, why not just devote the world's limited resources to supporting more humans and fewer chimpanzees or crabs?

Harris's third strategy is to argue against common objections to transhumanism at the macro level. The idea of keeping the human genome pure sits uncomfortably with the fact that it already contains so much that comes from our ape ancestors. And the thought that, for a mermaid it might be tragic to be neither human or fish, is nicely undermined by the "context is king" response. To support the view that "humanimals" are likely to be more subtle and better functioning than mermaids, there is the beautiful study quoted, showing that the insertion into a mouse of human genetic material for producing an eye will indeed produce an ectopic eye, but a *mouse* eye.

The deepest and most interesting objection Harris considers is the one about blurring fundamental category boundaries. He, like the objectors whose arguments he criticizes, takes the work of Mary Douglas to be central. Like much of the best work in social anthropology that rises above mere description, her account of food taboos is rich, deep, and suggestive, but at the same time it is hard to see what evidence counts for or against it. Her central idea is that we are deeply disturbed by things that pose a threat to the sharpness of our most fundamental category boundaries. Lobsters and other shellfish seem to straddle the boundary between animals and fish, and the disturbance this causes may find expression in seeing them as unclean food.

It is hard to test whether this is a better explanation than the "medical materialist" one about shellfish being a danger to health in hot climates. But the idea that people are deeply disturbed by challenges to fundamental categories has a lot of resonance. Homophobia, including the resistance to gay marriage, may come partly from the challenge gay relationships pose to deep traditional categories about the roles of men and women. Something similar may account for the shock sometimes aroused by transsexuals. The resistance to Darwin may have come not only from the conflict with religious beliefs, but also from the challenge it posed to the deep category gulf between humans and nonhuman animals.

It is this same deep category gulf that would be challenged by macro transhumanism. Harris rightly asks whether such a challenge would really matter at all. One difficulty in answering this is that with category challenges, as with gene expression, context is king. The Great Ape Project, supported by Jane Goodall, Peter Singer, Richard Dawkins, and others, aims to extend to the Great Apes the rights to life, liberty, and not to be tortured. Undoubtedly, it poses a deep challenge to the traditional moral gulf between us and nonhuman species, yet in a way that seems over-whelmingly beneficial. On the other hand, if military research included work on transgenic crocodiles with intellectual capacities enhanced by human genes, this might be more disturbing.

Our entrenched categories stand in the way of both the Great Ape project and the "intelligent crocodiles who can recognize the enemy" pro-gram. The military transgenic crocodile may be far-fetched, perhaps for reasons similar to those that make mermaids unlikely. But the difficulty of assessing the gains and losses resulting from eroding the sharp category boundary comes partly from our lack of knowledge of what will or will not be scientifically possible. It also comes from not knowing the social context in which the technology will be used. The history of commercial and military uses of technology is not entirely reassuring.

On this issue, Harris is right that it should be decided by weighing risks and benefits. But I am more divided than he is about whether the category upheaval of macro transhumanism is *likely* to be beneficial. It is hard to know the likely ratio of humane to harmful transhumanist projects. And, for any one of them, it may be hard to be confident of the overall balance. Even the Great Ape Project has been questioned by Colin Blakemore, on the grounds that, in the event of pandemics affect-ing only humans and the other great apes, the best chance of escape might be medical research on great apes. Context is everything, and at this stage it may be premature to sign up either for or against macro transhumanism.

This is a general problem for all of us who assess policies at least largely in terms of their consequences. Rarely can we do precise calculations. Giving or withholding support depends on rough and fallible estimates. This does not mean we should never support anything new. The reason I find it hard to decide about macro transhumanism is that my attempts to think about consequences are colored by two thoughts, one pulling in each direction.

The negative thought is that macro transhumanism would be a huge social experiment, probably having a deep impact on the contours of human life. The likely benefits do not seem very great. And the history of large social experiments since the Enlightenment, together with the his-tory of militarized science, has its share of discouragements.

The more positive thought comes partly from the history of science and philosophy. We have gained enormously in transcending one inad-equate set of categories after another. The impact of relativity theory or of Darwinism has been wonderfully liberating. And this often applies to social categories too. I cannot summon up the bigotry needed to regret the way gays and lesbians have smashed up and danced all over the nar-row-minded traditional categories. This thought that makes me feel that, on the issue of questioning boundaries, I would much *prefer* to be with

Harris than on the other side. But, in this case, do we really need to *create* the hybrids in order to loosen up our conceptual rigidity?

PART FIVE: SOME SILENCES IN HUMANITY

Sometimes a book is written to convey ideas or a message, already clear in the author's mind. Other books are started in the hope that writing will help the author get clearer about a puzzling topic, one that for the writer is perhaps a bit out of focus. *Humanity*, like all the books I have written, is of the second kind. As a result, its intentions and shape changed a lot during the course of writing.

Since being a teenager, I have wanted answers to some philosophical questions, including ones about morality. And, from the same time, I have been staggered by how easily most of us accept the cruelty and killings that fill the newspapers and the television news bulletins. Always at the back of my mind has been the thought, or hope, that these two concerns might come together. Obviously, this hope may have had an element of wishful thinking or self-deception. Very many academics have a mental intellectual map in which other disciplines occupy small peripheral spaces around the large central area given over to anthropology, physics, medicine, philosophy, history, or whatever their own field is. (F.R. Leavis, writing of a Cambridge era that included Rutherford, Keynes, Russell, and Wittgenstein, wrote of the literary critics who created *Scrutiny* that "we were the essential Cambridge.") My hope may involve a bit of megalomania about my subject.

Humanity started with the vague idea that ethics should not carry on as though none of these horrors in the world were relevant. Should not ethics have something to say about how to avoid them? Should not trying to understand why people did these things shape our thinking about ethics? Then came the thought that, while the abstract philosophical battle between fundamental level ethical theories was like eternally inconclusive trench warfare, there was wide and deep agreement about the moral enormity of the great atrocities. Progress in ethics might be made if we started from this agreement. Understanding more about the psychology of these events might yield a map of some virtues and vices helpful in trying to avoid their repetition. As well as this possible practical contribution, the project might help create a degree of ethical agreement between people with deep disagreements at the level of fundamental theory.

At the start, the book was going to be much less of a history than it turned out to be. There were going to be chapters on the various manifestations of the psychology of violence: war, genocide, and so on. Each would make brief reference to several historical cases. Then two things changed the shape of the book. One was the realization that it was going to be too "bitty." The other was that the brief treatment of the historical cases was going to be absurdly superficial. A coherent account of the psychology of violent atrocities might come from looking at the moral resources we have. What, in everyday life, restrains people from doing horrible things to each other? What happened to these restraints in Nazi Germany, in Mao's China, in the Rwandan genocide, or when the atomic bombs were dropped? And the way to move away, at least a little, from historical superficiality was to treat these episodes at greater length than planned.

So the book evolved into a chain of historical narratives linked by an argument about our central moral resources and how they can be rendered ineffective. In the end, the historical narratives ranged over a variety of twentieth-century historical episodes. A book originally not intended as a history ended up with the title *Humanity, a Moral History of the Twentieth Century*. This was suggested by Will Sulkin, my editor at Jonathan Cape. It was much better than any of the rather lame titles I had come up with, and I continue to be grateful to him. But, of course, the title goes beyond what I managed and this has led to reproaches.

In general, I have no grumbles about the reception of the book. I have been surprised and delighted by the degree of attention and sometimes approval it has been given. But some criticisms are of serious omissions. Different people have said to me that they wish my moral history of the century had not ignored the Armenian genocide, or had given more attention to the evils of British and other colonialism, or touched less briefly on South Africa, India, or the Middle East. Can a serious moral history of the century really not mention Gandhi? Others have let pass these historical lapses, but wished the philosophical issues had been developed more fully. These criticisms have validity. I wish I could have written a book not liable to them. Pulling in the other direction, I wish I could have written a book that was briefer and less dark. If anyone says they have given the book as a present, my heart goes out to the recipient.

One difficult judgment was about how much detail to include of the horrors. I did not want to write a sensational book, appealing to excitement about cruelty. But if too little goes in, it is easy for people to remain complacent about things they too readily accept. Perhaps there is no right balance to strike here. I put in some of the horrors of Hiroshima, but not enough of them to stop one "realist" reviewer from too easily finding it obvious that the bomb should have been used and going on to congratulate himself on his sense of proportion. On the other hand, another reviewer accused the book of being a kind of pornography of the horrors.

However, the book is as it is, and some strong criticisms focus on matters on which it either says too little or is silent.

ROGER CRISP: THE FOUNDATIONS OF HUMANITY

Roger Crisp takes up some of the too brief comments I made about the basis of morality. We have one big disagreement, about the possibility of an "external" moral law. But, as he says at one point, the way many things seem to each of us is quite similar. We both agree that the *Euthyphro* dilemma is fatal to the attempt to ground ethics on religious authority. I have argued this in various public debates with religious believers. It was not discussed in *Humanity*. This was because, despite the existence of a decisive refutation of their view, huge numbers of people in the many centuries since Plato have continued to believe that religious authority provides a basis (even the only possible basis) for morality. The book was written in the belief that (at least in most developed countries) the intellectual and moral authority of religion is in retreat, in a way that heightens the need to rethink both the basis and content of morality. Crisp is right that this assumption can be challenged, that it needs support, and that to provide the support would be a massive empirical task.

Crisp brings out our central disagreement in this sentence: "Glover's view is that, without an external grounding, we are faced by an ethical void to be filled by self-creation (17, 22, 41)." This perhaps oversimplifies the view argued for in *Humanity*. The cited pages of the book give some clue to this. On page 22, projects of self-creation are listed among the "moral resources" we have. Others cited are the "human responses": respect for other people and sympathy for them. The intention was not to suggest that self-creation was the only thing we have to fill the "ethical void."

The limits of self-creation can also be glimpsed on page 17:

> The austere universe left when religious metaphysics is stripped away still allows us to lead rich and satisfying lives. This satisfaction is often linked to the Nietzschean idea of creating ourselves according to our own values. But some of us drawn to these ideas may feel aghast at where they took Nietzsche...
>
> To value self-creation is not necessarily to think that it is the only object of life, which has to over-ride everything else. Nietzsche's self-creation pushes aside people who get in the way, but self-creation can be seen as one value among others. Some who create themselves may also care about other people, and dislike the egoism and ruthlessness admired by Nietzsche. He believed in *unrestrained* self-creation, perhaps thinking that only an external authority could provide a basis for restraint, but this assumption is false. My caring about the sort of person I am motivates the project of self-creation. Why should not my caring about other people set limits to it?

The suggestion that an external authority is not the only possible basis for restraint, but that caring for others can also provide one, could have been formulated using the word "reason" rather than "basis." In this context, I take these two words to be essentially equivalent. This formulation would have made explicit the rejection of what Crisp calls the "strong interpretation" of what *Humanity* says about morality: that the idea of there being any reasons for anything is so outlandish that we should assume there are none. As Crisp rightly points out, no reason for believing that view could consistently be given.

The alternative version of *Humanity*'s account of morality that Crisp offers is the "weak interpretation." On this account, there can be reasons for believing some things ("this is a pen in my hand") or for doing some things (such as engaging in self-creation), but "there are no external or moral reasons to act independently of self creation." The passage quoted earlier from the book indicates acceptance of reasons that are independent of self-creation. Crisp's key disagreement with the book is in the phrase "no external or moral reasons." His account of external reasons is that they are reasons not dependent on the reasons or desires of the agent. He spells this out with an example: "the world—indeed any world—is such that no-one should inflict severe suffering on others for the sake of their own trivial pleasure." I agree—I hope unsurprisingly—that no one should do that. But I am baffled by the claim that "the world is such" that no one should do it. What does this phrase *mean*?

The offered explanation is the analogy with mathematics. This claim about what the world is like resembles mathematical truths in three ways. It is justified independent of experience. It is true in all possible worlds. And it can be justified purely on the basis of grasping the concepts involved. This is obviously a deep and complex issue that is not going to be settled either in Crisp's brief and admirably eponymous chapter or in my even briefer responding note.

But it is worth briefly signaling some skepticism. Are all moral truths conceptual truths? The project of showing that anyone whose moral views on abortion or war you think wrong has made a conceptual mistake is a heroic one: perhaps too much so. Or are only some moral truths conceptual ones? If so, how do we identify them? And what is the status of the others? And even in the case of not frivolously inflicting severe suffering, where agreement is going to be deep and widespread, it is not just obvious how to prove that its denial is a *conceptual* mistake.

If I were trying to persuade someone who thought inflicting severe suffering for trivial reasons was morally acceptable, I should certainly not offer them the reason, "the world is such that you should not do it." (Unless the other person happened to be a philosopher. Then I might offer this reason in the hope of being given an explanation of what I should have meant by it.)

One aim of the book is to suggest that rejecting such external reasons does not entail rejecting moral reasons. One alternative is a constructivist approach to morality. This is briefly indicated on the third page Crisp cites, page 41:

> The prospects for reviving belief in a moral law are dim. Looking for an external validation of morality is less effective than building breakwaters. Morality could be abandoned, or it can be re-created. It may survive in a more defensible form when seen to be a human creation. We can shape it consciously to serve people's needs and interests, and to reflect the things we most care about.

This is one of the places where the book makes a philosophical point in a sketchy and incomplete way. It would have been better if I had gone into detail about the process of re-creating or shaping morality to serve needs and interests, and to reflect the things we most care about. Something like Rawls's method of seeking reflective equilibrium seems the best approach here: the attempt to construct a coherent moral view out of principles that seem intellectually plausible and our often emotionally charged moral intuitions.

Principles and intuitions will often conflict. When they do, the challenge goes both ways. A moral intuition that goes very deep or that seems to reflect a moment of vision will sometimes push us to accommodate it by abandoning or modifying a principle. An overwhelmingly plausible principle will sometimes make us reluctant to endorse intuitions conflicting with it. If we are lucky, out of this interplay we will make progress toward greater coherence. But perhaps, even after a lifetime, *complete* equilibrium will be found only in a *very* lucky few (or a few whose morality has become fossilized with age?).

It is an empirical question how much coherence any one person will attain. It is also an empirical question how much agreement there will be between the relatively coherent systems of different people. The contribution of intuitions and responses, often reflecting different temperaments and experiences of life, makes variation unsurprising. As in epistemology, it may be that some shared human deep structure has emerged from our evolutionary history. But, in morality as elsewhere, there is at least the possibility of continuing deep disagreement. Because, on this constructivist view, the moral system is not expected to track some external truth about how the world is, I am less dismayed than Crisp by the thought that people more philosophically sophisticated or more intellectually able than I am may hold different moral views. The fact that the consensus condition is not satisfied by my views about gay marriage or about torture does not give a reason to weaken my commitment to them even slightly.

But, despite our theoretical disagreement, I very much agree with Crisp about the desirable tone of philosophical ethics. His advocacy of listening to the positions of others, criticizing our own views, and probing the sources of our disagreements is admirable. Neither of our theoretical approaches satisfies his consensus condition. But happily, as often in philosophy, this does not stop a large measure of practical agreement. I recently helped to set up a Global Ethics course at King's College London. This included issues discussed in *Humanity* about avoiding war and genocide. But central to the course are the huge problems of how to avoid environmental disaster and how to stop the continuing catastrophe caused by global poverty. At the heart of the ethics component are precisely the issues Crisp raises, about the effects of our omissions, and about our collective actions. This is because Crisp is quite right that these questions, about which *Humanity* is silent, are—together with those it does discuss—among the great issues of the twenty-first century.

PETER SINGER: BYSTANDERS TO POVERTY

Peter Singer develops further the point Roger Crisp makes about the moral importance of global poverty. Singer is right to argue that the huge numbers of people suffering and dying from poverty-related causes have far stronger moral claims on us than conventional wisdom allows. And he is also right that these moral claims make our position (as citizens of rich countries) disconcertingly close to the position of bystanders to mass killings by the Nazis and others.

Singer makes three central points. One is a criticism of another silence in *Humanity*. He mentions the subtitle *A Moral History of the Twentieth Century*, and rightly says that the preventable deaths from poverty are surely part of that history. His second point is against the conventional view that preventing deaths from massacre or genocide is morally more important than preventing the usually much greater number of poverty-related deaths. He doubts this view is well based. His third point is about what we can and should do in response to poverty. I respond briefly to the comments about the silence in *Humanity*, and then express agreement with his second point, before going on to discuss his views about the appropriate response to the devastation caused by poverty.

Singer says that *Causing Death and Saving Lives* challenged the part of conventional morality that assumes there is a huge moral difference between what we knowingly do and what we knowingly fail to do, for instance between killing someone and knowingly letting someone die. He rightly says that I explicitly accepted the strong conclusion that failure to send money to Oxfam, without being able to justify the alternative, is—disconcertingly—in the same league as murder. He also says that *Humanity* is strongly critical of "free bystanders" who failed to help victims of Nazi atrocities. He rightly thinks that these two views together suggest strong moral failure on the part of bystanders to poverty. He wonders why *Humanity* did not discuss this: "Recognizing the serious nature of our failure to aid those dying from poverty-related causes, by giving the topic at least one chapter in *Humanity*, would have been a good way of making this point, and would not have run the risk of superficiality."

Humanity is an attempt to think about an area of ethics by tracing the moral psychology of violent things people do to each other: of war, massacre, genocide, and torture. Although they differ from each other in some ways, these acts of collective violence have a substantial shared psychology. The psychology of our failure to aid those killed by poverty is very different. This is the reason why it does not figure in the book, rather than a failure to see its importance. The presentation of what was to become the "Acts and Omissions" chapter of *Causing Death and Saving Lives*, that Singer heard at the Parfit–Griffin–Glover class he mentions, was, as far as I know, the first philosophical case made for the ethical importance of this issue. And the parallel with bystanders to atrocities is one I have made in arguing the same case.

Singer rightly says that the seriousness of failure to send aid could have been signaled by giving it at least one chapter of *Humanity*. This is right, but equally the seriousness of our collective contribution to climate change could have been signaled in this way. So could the seriousness of our mistreatment of animals (though on that issue, I am in a much weaker position than Singer to make the point). While the importance of our collective violence led to the writing of the book, including in it sections on important, but different, issues would have undermined its coherence. When planning it, this came before inclusiveness. Nevertheless, as Singer says (and, as the book said too), a more generous interpretation of "a moral history of the twentieth century" would have covered much more, including the devastating consequences of avoidable poverty.

Singer argues that people too readily think the prevention of poverty-related deaths is much less important than the prevention of atrocities of mass killing. He concedes that in the case of genocide, there is the distinctive evil of destroying a whole culture, but says that in a comparison this extra evil of genocide will not outweigh the vastly greater numbers of lives lost to poverty. He also discusses "moral compass" claims that appeal to moral intuitions about genocide being worse. He suggests that our moral intuitions about this, as about different versions of the trolley problem, may be the result of contingent facts about our evolutionary history and so may not be a good moral guide.

Singer is right that moral intuitions should be examined critically rather than treated as infallible, and that their possible evolutionary origins are relevant to this. Kant's marvelous comment about the interrogation of nature in science and philosophy can be adapted here: we should interrogate moral intuitions not like a pupil but like a judge. And the relative weakness of our moral concern about the human devastation caused by poverty is an excellent candidate for some sharply sceptical interrogation.

Despite agreement with Singer's substantive conclusion on this issue, it is worth making a partly dissenting point about intuitions. In some of his writings, Singer has appeared to follow R. M. Hare and others in rejecting any role for moral intuitions in thinking about fundamental-level moral principles.[15] The alternative constructivist approach outlined here is obviously not original in envisaging interplay between principles and intuitions. A morality giving no weight to intuitions runs the risk of being a morality for Martians, one that does not reflect our human values. But these values are not perfectly in order as they are. A major task of philosophy here is critical.

Philosophy should not leave all our values unchanged. But, the method of change should not just start from some Kantian or utilitarian axiom taken to exclude all countervailing intuitions as irrational. The resonance of the resulting morality might be too shallow to engage us. Otto Neurath's much-cited point against Cartesian reconstruction in epistemology may hold here. The boat may need rebuilding. But, since we are at sea in it, at any one time we need to keep enough of it afloat to support us, as we repair the other bits.

Singer's conclusions on the ethics of a practical response to poverty very much adhere to the thoughts we both developed in the 1970s. There is a strong obligation on rich people (that is on nearly all of us who live in the richer economies) to give substantial amounts toward saving people from poverty.

There are major psychological difficulties with this for most of us. (A psychological difficulty is not an ethical refutation.) We find it hard substantially to reduce our own standard of living. And the logic of the argument seems to push us in the direction of saying that we should give to the point where we need the money as much as the people we are helping. If we do anything less, there will be people whose lives we could have saved, but whose deaths we will have accepted rather than make a smaller sacrifice ourselves. I give more than I did before thinking about these issues, but am very far indeed from living up to this demanding standard. I know from Singer's writings that he does far better than I do, giving something like 20 percent of his income. However, even at that level, impressive by comparison with the rest of us, there will be people whose lives would have been saved if 21 percent had been the figure. Wherever we draw the line, this thought is likely to be true.

Our response to this should be twofold. On the one hand we should, as Singer argues, push ourselves to give more. The other response to the way our psychology virtually guarantees huge moral failure here should be to search for alternative strategies. We need to find ways round the roadblocks of our psychology: strategies that will help reduce poverty without the psychological costs that make at least partial failure inevitable. Here, because of the likely readership of this book, I want to suggest that the skills of academics such as philosophy teachers can make two distinctive contributions. One is in the analysis of the sources of our paralysis. There is a need to understand the reasons why (in the message of the Oxfam poster I saw as a teenager) we would give a meal to a starving person in front of us, but less readily to famine relief. The second (related) contribution is to devise effective strategies that work with the grain of our nature.

The paralysis is real. According to one recent estimate, starvation and preventable diseases kill 30,000 children every day. They cause a child's death roughly every three seconds, round the clock every day of the year. Suppose these deaths were not mainly far away, located in many different places. Suppose they all happened in one place and we were there. We would be overwhelmed by the horror and sadness of it all, and overwhelmed by the moral urgency of putting a stop to it. But, not having had that experience, we are not overwhelmed. What in our psychology protects us from the urgency? What are the sources of our moral paralysis?

We are influenced by distance. Paralysis also comes from the vastness of the problem, which can make it seem insoluble. And there is the thought that the disaster is too big for me to make a significant difference. Some of these responses have a grain of reasonableness. But, mainly they rest on cognitive illusions. Here, I touch briefly on the illusions associated with the thoughts that the problem is so big, or is insoluble.

Difficulties of solution come partly from complexity of causes. Poverty and starvation may come from wars. Peasants are driven away by invaders who take their land and crops. Or people are trapped in starvation by cultural beliefs, such as that the claims on food of girls and women should take second place to those of boys and men. Or there is the Hobbesian state of nature, closely approximated to in some of the cultural norms of the vast urban shanty towns of the developing world. (The films *Salaam Bombay* and *City of God* portray the Indian and Brazilian versions of this.)

These complex economic and cultural causes can sap the willingness to help. The paralyzing thought is that tackling poverty means changing the whole social world: eliminating war, redistributing wealth, changing intractable attitudes about men and women, transforming the shanty towns, and undoing the psychological distortions created in those growing up there.

When people's lives are wrecked by some event not entangled in all these complexities, paralysis may not set in. The tsunami and its effects roused sympathy round the world. None of the economic or cultural complications intervened to make action seem useless. The victims needed aid quickly in order to eat, have shelter, and to rebuild their houses. With no seemingly insurmountable preliminaries like stopping a war or changing a culture, sympathy was not paralyzed. The scale of the response from people in richer countries took their political leaders by surprise and embarrassed them into increasing governmental contributions.

Our willingness to contribute after the tsunami does not translate to helping the much slower and more complex project of alleviating long-term poverty, partly because we have the illusion that gradual change is no change at all. Without being able to see the change our aid has made, it is easy to dismiss the effort as futile. And the sense of futility is increased by the lack of transparency of the causal links. An aid agency's irrigation scheme, funded by hundreds of people, may save hundreds of lives. But none of the contributors knows there is a particular person they rescued. Most will not even know that their money went toward an irrigation scheme. This lack of causal transparency makes the help less vivid to the donor. But it is still an illusion that the help was futile.

Similarly, there are size illusions created by large numbers. My contribution may be only a drop in the ocean, but that drop may save several people's lives. If, in a fire, we cannot rescue all ten trapped people, this does not mean we need not bother to rescue the one or two we can. Undistorted thinking would take the same view when those we cannot save run into millions. There are also threshold illusions. The results of one person's contribution may be below the threshold of detectability. But thousands of people making such contributions may create something really substantial.

We are used to correcting for familiar visual illusions. Psychologists have identified some common cognitive illusions and we are starting to correct for them. In morality there are also widespread illusions. Size illusions and threshold illusions help cause paralysis about poverty, a paralysis that kills people. We need to correct for them too. In this way, we need to work against the cognitive psychology that comes naturally to us.

But sometimes it is better to find ways of working with the grain of our nature. This may involve the recognition that *some* of the psychological limits on contributions to humanitarian aid reflect genuine moral claims on us. There are different dimensions of ethics. Support for the needs of family members is not just a selfish diversion from the claims of others more in need.

Another way of working with the grain of our nature is suggested by the thought that sending money—while good in itself—may not always be the best strategy. Contributions not involving great sacrifices sometimes make more difference than those that do. The most effective action may need our intelligence, as we try to match what we like doing and are good at with what will help the problem. Those of us in academic work are often better at thinking and campaigning than we are at raising money. So perhaps we should be thinking creatively about strategies against poverty and campaigning to get them implemented. Here are three possible cases.

In Africa—and elsewhere—wars are a major exacerbation of poverty. Why do the major powers think it right to campaign against the drug trade, but acceptable to profit from the arms trade? The assumptions underlying the justifications for selling arms cry out for the analysis and criticism needed for a campaign to stop the trade.

The lives of many are made shorter and far worse by lack of decent water. The British government plans a rapid reaction military force to intervene in likely future conflicts caused by water shortages. Would it not be better to invest in researching and developing affordable technologies of desalination? Living on a planet mainly sea, it should not be impossible to have enough water.

Then there is the unavailability in many developing countries of affordable medications. Pharmaceutical companies say they cannot afford to sell them at a manageable cost and that generic versions breaching their patents would make research no longer economic. Perhaps this is bluff. If so, could we not use the purchasing power of our own medical systems as leverage to bring about a change of attitude? Perhaps it is not bluff, and research really would be uneconomic if patents were not respected. If so, then we need to explore proposals like that of Thomas Pogge and others to fund companies' research on the basis of their medical benefits rather than on their market profitability.[16] Most of us noneconomists do not know what the best scheme would be. The point is that intelligent thought by competent people about such issues is likely to contribute on a different scale from those same people giving most of their income away.

There are grounds for cautious optimism about how campaigning can change people. The Oxfam poster influenced me. I like to think that my talk at our old class influenced Peter Singer's eloquent and powerful paper on *Famine, Affluence and Morality*. And his paper is so widely read that it must have influenced thousands. This kind of persuasion, together with such things as the immensely influential campaign by the churches in support of debt relief, has contributed a bit to public pressure on the governments of the G8.

Collective action does not remove the moral imperative of individual giving. But it usually dwarfs such giving in scale. The agreement to cancel the debts of the poorest countries has brought results. Zambia has been able to make basic healthcare free. The Tanzanian government bought food for millions hit by drought. Nigeria was able to employ 150,000 more teachers. There are transparent causal links between the campaign, the debt relief, and these benefits.

Part of our paralysis comes from defeatism about what can be done. The defeatism partly comes from the problems getting much more publicity than the progress that sometimes is made. Perhaps here what is needed is optimism of the will and *very* cautious optimism of the intellect.

It is true that money is not enough. There are the dauntingly entrenched cultural constraints, such as attitudes to women in India, China, and some other countries, or the patterns of behavior encouraged by the huge urban shanty towns of the developing world.

But there is room for some cautious optimism of the intellect. Although cultural change is slow, it does happen. Those depressed by the entrenched attitudes to women in India or China should be encouraged by what happened in our society to entrenched attitudes fifty years ago to gay people. Prejudices that stifle people lead to protest. Over time, indefensible prejudices sometimes stop being defended.

Obviously, the culture of the shanty towns will change only gradually. But I take some comfort from this description of the culture of urban poverty:

> The filth and tottering ruin surpass all description. Scarcely a whole window pane can be found, the walls are crumbling, doors of old boards nailed together, or altogether wanting in this thieves' quarter....Heaps of garbage and ashes...the foul liquids emptied before the doors gather in stinking pools. Here live the poorest of the poor, the worst paid workers with thieves and the victims of prostitution. Those who have not yet sunk in the whirlpool of moral ruin which surrounds them, sinking daily deeper, losing daily more of their power to resist the demoralizing influence of want, filth and evil surroundings.

That was Engels describing London in the 1840s. He was reporting on the courts and alleyways near the Strand and Covent Garden. I work in the Strand and it is not like that round here now. One day it will not be like that in Mexico City and Bombay. Cautious optimism of the intellect: we may be able to make the time lag less long.

MARTHA NUSSBAUM: COMPASSION: HUMAN
AND ANIMAL

Martha Nussbaum, in her deep and imaginative chapter, rightly points out two more silences in *Humanity*. Although compassion (and how it can be blocked) is central to the book, there is no discussion of how far it is specific to human psychology or of how close it comes to responses found in other species. And the book is also silent on the human tendency to deny our animal nature and the contribution this may make to male violence against women. While Nussbaum's chapter does a great deal to fill in these gaps in *Humanity*, of course, it considerably transcends this modest aim.

What Nussbaum says about compassion in mice, elephants, and dogs is of great interest. However, this response will concentrate on what her chapter says about human psychology. It will follow her in focusing on male human psychology. Obviously there are also questions about the dark side of female psychology: about women who abuse their children, women leaders who take their countries to war, women in World War I who handed out white feathers to men not in uniform, the *tricoteuses* by the guillotine in the French Revolution, the women guards in the Nazi camps, and so on. But, equally obviously, these women are hugely outnumbered by their male counterparts. And the account of Gujarat is a reminder of the scale, and the horrifying cruelty, of male violence directed specifically against women.

Nussbaum links this violence with the human, and particularly male, desire to transcend our animal nature. Her account of the link rests on three central claims. Men hate the weakness and dependency of their bodily, "animal" nature, and so like to think of themselves as having overcome it. Men evade the falsity of this denial by contrasting themselves with others (whether women or other ethnic groups) on to whom the unwanted "animal" features are projected. And, in turn, this inhibits compassion toward the group on to whom these features are projected. These interesting hypotheses have considerable plausibility. I comment on each of the three main claims, sometimes adding points in support of them, sometimes adding a note of reservation.

Do men hate their "animal" nature? More or less every one of us (men and women) must regret some of our biological limitations and weaknesses: our proneness to illness, our limited energy and powers, and the inevitability of our death. Many also delight in the powers of the body: in sex, in athletic and sporting prowess, and in how they look and move. But the weaknesses and limitations are real. Do men so hate these weaknesses that they like to think they have overcome them? At the conscious level, very few can literally think they have unlimited energy, or that they will never be ill or die. However, being "in denial" is rarely so literal. Unwanted facts can be pushed into the background by countervailing myths and fantasies that, even if only half believed, can still cast an obscuring shadow.

Many men do not live in this shadow. But the fantasies appear in different places, especially where terrible things go on to happen. Nussbaum cites Nazi and proto-Nazi fantasies about male toughness, energy, and hardness, mentioning Theweleit's study and quoting Ernst Junger. It was not only among the Nazis or in pre-Nazi German culture that such images took hold. Dzhugashvili, Rozenfeld, and Skyrabin might still have been leaders under their real names. But, either to fit their own self-image or because they thought others would respond to the fantasy, they chose the names Stalin (man of steel), Kamenev (man of stone), and Molotov (the hammer).

The communist version of the hard male hero who transcends human weakness has done some strange things to Karl Marx. Near the Alexanderplatz in Berlin there is a huge statue of him, together with Engels. Opposite the Bolshoi Theatre in Moscow there is another even more gigantic one of him alone, rising out of a stone base and dwarfing the people passing. This superhuman Marx clearly spent every waking hour grasping the nature of historical development and struggling against capitalism. There is a comic contrast with the more human Karl Marx who lived in London, avoiding bailiffs, or being delighted when his daughter was accepted by the very bourgeois South Hampstead School for Girls.

One evening, Marx, Wilhelm Liebknecht, and Edgar Bauer decided to walk up the Tottenham Court Road, having at least one glass of beer in each of the eighteen pubs between Oxford Street and the Hampstead Road. In the last pub they nearly got into a fight with people offended by Marx's inebriated comments about snobbish, philistine England. After running away, they found a heap of paving stones, which they threw at the gas lanterns, smashing the glass of four or five. Three or four policemen chased after them, but Liebknecht described how "Marx showed an agility I would not have attributed to him," and they escaped down a side street and a back alley. I am not sure if this is our animal nature, but it is certainly a part of human nature not allowed to show in the stone version of the hard intellectual giant.[17]

Nussbaum believes that two emotions, with origins in childhood, are particularly important in people wanting to replace our animal nature by something fantasized in terms of industrial ingredients and tools such as steel, stone, and hammers. One is primitive shame (the shame caused by the fact that we are needy and dependent rather than omnipotent). The other is disgust: Nussbaum makes the point that objects of disgust (corpses and bodily waste products) are reminders of our mortality and animality.

These claims are quite hard to evaluate. How do we know whether the child's discovery that he is not omnipotent leads to shame rather than just anger and frustration? It is true that there is considerable overlap between what disgusts us and what reminds us of our animal nature. But not everything revolting need be like this. (Richard Wollheim, in his autobiographical *Germs*, tells of his own disgust at seeing newsprint.) And not all reminders of our bodily or animal needs arouse disgust. We are not revolted by signs of hunger or tiredness. And there are alternative accounts of disgust. John Harris mentioned Mary Douglas's idea that what we are disgusted by may reflect our aversion to things that straddle our deepest category boundaries. It is hard to see what would count as testing these theories against each other.

Disgust and primitive shame may influence the fantasy of escaping our animal limitations, but questions about interaction with other factors (and about individual differences) seem a field waiting to be explored.

Nussbaum's second claim is about projection. Men who believe (or half believe some fantasy) that they have overcome their animal nature are in the grip of something obviously false. They are not immune to illness, death, or even to some of the gentler emotions. They hide this falsity by contrasting their own steely nature with other groups—whether women, gays, Jews, or African-Americans—on to which they project the "animal" weaknesses. Shame about not being omnipotent becomes the belief that people in these other groups are weak, effete, decadent, or stupid. Disgust is also projected: they smell; they are slimy.

This projection hypothesis seems very plausible, but again as one route among others to these repellent beliefs. (Another might be repressed guilt about, say, African-Americans. If your great-grandfather had African-American slaves, or your grandfather saw a lynching, or your father rode in the White part of a segregated bus, or you have a vastly better-paid job than most of your African-American counterparts, you might find the implications of all this hard to face. Projecting a few weak characteristics could have motives quite independent of any worry about your own animal nature.)

Nussbaum's third claim is that the projection of these "animal" characteristics inhibits compassion. We make "them" so different from "us" that we do not recognize that we too could have experienced their suffering. And, again because they seem so different, we exclude them from the circle of our concern, not seeing their suffering as serious or as having links with what we ourselves think important in life.

Nussbaum's claim that the projection of animal characteristics onto people helps exclude them from our concern is plausible. But, it is perhaps worth remembering that this is only one of the causes of such exclusion.

I have been interviewing people with the diagnosis of "antisocial personality disorder" and who have also committed often terrible crimes, sometimes against women. Their accounts make very different factors causally important, especially the abuse, rejection, humiliation, or lack of love that they experienced in their childhoods. One of them, convicted for rape, answered questions I asked about it:

And the only conclusion I can come to at that time was that the guy was my brother and the woman was my mum. Because on that day I was driving up towards my parents' place because I was going to kill them. And that's where my head was. I was just going to wipe them out altogether. I thought the anger might go away then…
Did you care in those days about hurting people or not really? Oh yeah, I cared, yeah…
So you did care about other people and how they felt? Of course I did, yeah. *But the anger sometimes just overcame that?* It did, it did, it took over. It took over, you know. It was her, she just wouldn't leave me alone.

Your mother? My mother, she just wouldn't leave me alone, one way or another. And I couldn't, like I said, I couldn't talk to people about it. I carried it all the time.

This was sexual abuse? Yeah, sexual abuse. … I might be in a relationship and going through perhaps a difficult patch, which would be nine time out of ten down to my fault. And it would be her, you know.

She'd be in your mind? She'd be in my head. Saying that I was rotten, I should kill myself, and I don't deserve to live and all the rest of it and that sort of stuff…

When you –you don't have to answer any questions if you don't want to but –when you raped a person was that anger, or was it… It was anger.

It was anger. Anger against your mother or anger against…? Yeah, anger against my mother and my brother, in my head that night.

A number of the people I interviewed gave accounts of their violence suggesting roots more of this kind than to do with disgust or primitive shame. Different causal stories may be more often relevant according to whether we are considering violence against people as individuals or as members of particular groups. Rather than being mutually exclusive, Nussbaum's account and mine could each apply in different contexts. As Nussbaum indicates, the horrible male fantasies that appear to have been in the minds of those involved in the cruelties and killing in Gujarat provide a motive for atrocity. And if the effect of projected differences is to block compassion, there will not be much left to restrain people from horrors.

Nussbaum's account seems plausible and important. I wish I had thought of some of this to say in my book. But that is just envy. The serious hope is that Martha Nussbaum's rational warning, that self-aggrandizing fantasies about being hard and tough can erode our moral resources against atrocity, will be heard round the world. I suspect she is not an unqualified fan of Freud. But, as some of her thoughts reflect the influence of the psychoanalytic tradition, perhaps she will not mind my linking her chances of being heard with something Freud wrote:

> We may insist as much as we like that the human intellect is weak in comparison with human instincts, and be right in doing do. But nevertheless there is something peculiar about this weakness. The voice of the intellect is a soft one, but it does not rest until it has gained a hearing. Ultimately, after endlessly repeated rebuffs, it succeeds. This is one of the few points in which one may be optimistic about the future of mankind.

PART SIX: PERSONAL

In my life I have been lucky in many things.

I was lucky in my grandparents, who brought me up. I have been lucky in Vivette, my wife. I have been lucky in my (now grown-up) children Daniel, David, and Ruth, and in Sam, my grandson.

I have been lucky in having jobs enabling me to write about philosophy, and especially to teach it. It is hard to imagine a more privileged working life than to be paid to think and write about what you find most interesting. It is wonderful each year to have a new wave of students willing to discuss these questions, often with an intellectual curiosity I have found inspiring.

And I have been lucky in my colleagues and friends, including all those in this book. One is Alan Ryan, whose friendship and stimulus I have been lucky to have over many years. Anyone who knows his books, or his articles in the *New York Review of Books*, will recognize his combination of a quick critical intelligence with an astonishingly wide range of sympathies. The editors of this book would be unlikely to find anyone else to produce a pen portrait of me of such engaging comedy (I don't remember the mice in the corn flakes packet, but I plead guilty to the rest) and of such generosity. I am grateful to Alan for the portrait, although he understates the tolerance needed to share an old house and its plumbing with me.

I thank this circle of my friends and colleagues, for this lively set of articles, and for the stimulus, as well as the kindness, of their contributions.

I have also been pleased and touched by the generosity of my friends, the three editors, who have created this project and have worked so hard to bring it to fulfillment. They will have found me perhaps their most annoyingly slow and elusive contributor. Despite this contact with one of my bad sides, they have continued to be supportive. I am enormously grateful to Ann, Jeff, and Richard (at this point I am dumping Davis, McMahan, and Keshen in favor of what I think of as their real names) for the whole warm-hearted gesture of this book, which surprised me and which pleased me more than they are likely to imagine.

Notes

1. Jean Améry: *At the Mind's Limits, Contemplations by a Survivor on Auschwitz and its Realities*, translated by Sidney and Stella P. Rosenfeld, New York, 1986, p. 27.

2. Craig Murray, interview with Raymond Whittaker.

3. Améry, page 28.

4. Ibid., p. 36.

5. Ibid., p. 40.

6. Ibid., pp. 31 and 35.

7. Justine Sharrock: *Am I a Torturer?* http://www.motherjones.com/cgi-bin.

8. See http://pubrecord.org/torture/262/cia-may-have-tortured-more-detainees-and-hid-them-from-red-cross/

9. Jacobo Timerman, *Prisoner Without a Name, Cell Without a Number*, translated by Toby Talbot, New York, 1988, p. 51.

10. Diane Beaver, October 11, 2002, Legal Brief on Proposed Counter-Resistance Strategies, in Karen J.Greenberg and Joshua L. Dratel (eds.), *The Torture Papers, The Road to Abu Ghraib*, Cambridge University Press, New York, 2005, p. 235.

11. *The Guardian*, December 13, 2005.

12. Améry, p. 23.

13. Knut Haukelid, *Skis Against the Atom*, Minot, ND, 1989.

14. Hilary Putnam: *Brains and Behavior*, in R.J. Butler (ed.), *Analytical Philosophy*, second series, Oxford, 1965, p. 19.

15. Peter Singer: *Ethics and Intuitions*, The Journal of Ethics, vol. 9, no 3–4, 2005, pp. 331–352.

16. Thomas Pogge: *Incentives for Pharmaceutical Research: Must They Exclude the Poor from Advanced Medicines?*, forthcoming in Roland Pierik (ed.), *Cosmopolitanism in Context: Perspectives from International Law and Political Theory*, Cambridge, 2010.

17. Wilhelm Liebknecht: *Karl Marx: Biographical Memories*, quoted in Francis Wheen: *Karl Marx*, London, 1999, p. 257.

Selected Writings of Jonathan Glover

Books

Responsibility (Routledge and Kegan Paul, 1970)
Causing Death and Saving Lives (Penguin, 1977)
What Sort of People Should There Be? (Penguin, 1984)
I, The Philosophy and Psychology of Personal Identity (Allen Lane, 1988)
Humanity, A Moral History of the Twentieth Century (Jonathan Cape, 1999; Yale University Press, 2000)
Choosing Children: Genes, Disability and Design (The Uehiro Lectures, Oxford, 2004; Oxford University Press, 2006)
(With others): *Fertility and the Family* (A Report to the European Commission, Fourth Estate, 1989), published in the U.S as *Ethical Implications of the New Technologies of Reproduction* (University of Northern Illinois Press, 1989)
(Edited): *Philosophy of Mind* (Oxford University Press, 1976)
(Edited): *Utilitarianism and its Critics* (Macmillan USA, 1990)
(Jointly edited, with Martha Nussbaum): *Women, Culture and Development*, WIDER series in Development *Economics* (Oxford University Press, 1995)

Selected Articles

Freud, Morality and Responsibility, in Jonathan Miller (ed.): *Freud*, 1973.
It Makes No Difference Whether Or Not I Do It, *Proceedings of the Aristotelian Society*, 1976.
The Problem of Abortion, *New York Review of Books*, 1985.
State Terrorism, in R. G. Frey and Christopher W. Morris (eds.): *Violence, Terrorism and Justice*, 1991.
Ethical Relativism, in *Zeit und Warheit, Proceedings of the European Forum* (Alpbach, 1995.)
The Implications for Responsibility of Possible Genetic Factors in the Explanation of Violence, in Genetics of *Criminal and Anti-Social Behaviour*, CIBA.
Foundation Symposium 1994, 1995.
Eugenics: Some Lessons from the Nazi Experience, in John Harris and Soren Holm (eds.): *The Future of Human Reproduction, Choice and Regulation* (Oxford, 1998.)
Eugenics and Human Rights, in Justine Burley (ed.): *The Genetic Revolution and Human Rights* (The Oxford Amnesty Lectures 1988, Oxford, 1999.)

Ethical Lessons from Twentieth Century Atrocities, in Simone Bateman (ed.): *Responsabilite Morale: Situations Extremes et Hommes Ordinaires* (Cahiers du CERCES, Paris, 1999.)

Anna Karenina and Moral Philosophy, in Roger Crisp and Brad Hooker (eds.): *Wellbeing and Morality, Essays presented to James Griffin* (Oxford, 2000.)

Psychiatric Disorder and the Reactive Attitudes, *Public Affairs Quarterly*, Volume 15, No. 4, October 2001.

Are We Justified in Killing the Children of Iraq? *The Guardian*, February, 2003.

Towards Humanism in Psychiatry: Interpretation, Towards Humanism in Psychiatry: Identity, in Grethe B. Peterson (ed.): *The Tanner Lectures on Human Values*, Volume 24, 2004.

Dialogue with Islam is the only way to end the cycle of violence, *The Guardian*, July 2005.

Socrates, Freud and Family Therapy, *Journal of Family Therapy*, Volume 27, No. 4, November 2005.

Should the Child Live? Doctors, Families and Conflict, *Clinical Ethics*, Volume 1, No. 1, March 2006.

Identity, Violence and the Power of Illusion, in Kaushik Basu and Ravi Kanbur: *Arguments for a Better World, Essays in Honor of Amartya Sen, Volume II: Society, Institutions and Development*, Oxford, 2009.

Index